Extreme Programming Perspectives

The XP Series

Kent Beck, Series Advisor

Extreme Programming, familiarly known as XP, is a discipline of business and software development that focuses both parties on common, reachable goals. XP teams produce quality software at a sustainable pace. The practices that make up "book" XP are chosen for their dependence on human creativity and acceptance of human frailty.

Although XP is often presented as a list of practices, XP is not a finish line. You don't get better and better grades at doing XP until you finally receive the coveted gold star. XP is a starting line. It asks the question, "How little can we do and still build great software?"

The beginning of the answer is that, if we want to leave software development uncluttered, we must be prepared to completely embrace the few practices we adopt. Half measures leave problems unsolved to be addressed by further half measures. Eventually you are surrounded by so many half measures that you can no longer see that the heart of the value programmers create comes from programming.

I say, "The beginning of the answer …" because there is no final answer. The authors in the XP Series have been that and done there, and returned to tell their story. The books in this series are the signposts they have planted along the way: "Here lie dragons," "Scenic drive next 15 km," "Slippery when wet."

Excuse me, I gotta go program.

Titles in the Series

Extreme Programming Applied: Playing to Win, Ken Auer and Roy Miller

Extreme Programming Examined, Giancarlo Succi and Michele Marchesi

Extreme Programming Explained: Embrace Change, Kent Beck

Extreme Programming Explored, William C. Wake

Extreme Programming for Web Projects, Doug Wallace, Isobel Raggett, and Joel Aufgang

Extreme Programming in Practice, James W. Newkirk and Robert C. Martin

Extreme Programming Installed, Ron Jeffries, Ann Anderson, and Chet Hendrickson

Extreme Programming Perspectives, Michele Marchesi, Giancarlo Succi, Don Wells, and Laurie Williams

Planning Extreme Programming, Kent Beck and Martin Fowler

Questioning Extreme Programming, Pete McBreen

Testing Extreme Programming, Lisa Crispin and Tip House

For more information, check out the series Web site at http://www.awprofessional.com/series/XP/

Extreme Programming Perspectives

Michele Marchesi
Giancarlo Succi
Don Wells
Laurie Williams

Addison-Wesley

Boston • San Francisco • New York • Toronto • Montreal
London • Munich • Paris • Madrid
Capetown • Sydney • Tokyo • Singapore • Mexico City

The publisher offers discounts on this book when ordered in quantity for special sales. For more information, please contact:

Pearson Education Corporate Sales Division
201 W. 103rd Street
Indianapolis, IN 46290
(800) 428-5331
corpsales@pearsoned.com

Visit Addison-Wesley on the Web at www.awprofessional.com

Library of Congress Cataloging-in-Publication Data
Extreme programming perspectives / Michele Marchesi . . . [et al.].
p. cm.
Includes bibliographical references and index.
ISBN 0-201-77005-9 (alk. paper)
1. Computer software—Development. 2. Extreme programming. I. Marchesi, Michele.

QA76.76.D47 E98 2002
005.I'1—dc21

2002025586

ISBN 0-201-77005-9
Text printed on recycled paper
1 2 3 4 5 6 7 8 9 10—CRS—0605040302
First printing, August 2002

To Uberto, Guglielmo, and Lodovica.
With love

—Michele Marchesi

In memory of my father, Dino Succi, who always
had the right word or the right silence.
With love

—Giancarlo Succi

In memory of my father, James E. Wells, who filled our home
with books, wall to wall, floor to ceiling, two rows deep.
There was always room for just one more.

—Don Wells

To my mom and in memory of my dad.

—Laurie Williams

Contents

Foreword

Why do we need another Agile/XP book? If XP and the Agile Manifesto both value simplicity, then why do we need more books, articles, conference talks, user group discussions, Yahoo! Group e-mails, and coffee break debates? Why? Because simple isn't the same as simplistic. Why? Because an effective set of "simple" principles and practices give rise to complex, intelligent behavior.

The 12 practices of XP, the nine principles of DSDM, the 12 principles of Bob Charette's Lean Development, or the 12 principles articulated in the Agile Manifesto (12 seems to be a very popular number for Agilists) are far from simplistic. Complex problems, those that stretch the limits of technology and human capability, are best approached by internalizing a few rules, practices, and principles whose "application" generates an infinite number of creative ideas that in turn enable us to deliver value to our customers.

This is a key point that many rigorous methodology proponents haven't understood. Many of them believe in inclusive rules, procedures, and processes rather than generative rules. Have a problem? Just turn to process 57, activity 24, task 87, step 4 to find the answer. Unfortunately, or actually fortunately for us, complex problems don't yield to solutions by the numbers. Complex problems, the real problems we each face in the day-to-day, rough-and-tumble world of software product development, yield to creative, innovative thinking guided by a few key principles, grounded in a few key practices. "When the business landscape was simple, companies could afford to have complex strategies," write Kathleen Eisenhardt and Donald Sull in a *Harvard Business Review* article ("Strategy as Simple Rules," January 2001). "But now that business is so complex, they need to simplify."

Simplify doesn't mean simplistic. It means that we need to extract, from the hundreds and hundreds of software development principles and practices, those half-dozen to a dozen that drive us to think clearly and effectively about the problems we face. If simple practices were simplistic, we wouldn't need entire books about single practices: refactoring (Martin Fowler), or pair programming (Laurie Williams and Robert Kessler), or test-first development (Kent Beck).

The diversity of chapters in this book proves my point. Written by both recognized leaders in the Agile/XP field and lesser-known leaders who labor daily to create value for their customers, these chapters reflect the complexity of real-world problems and how they are being solved by helping us understand the incalculable richness of a few key, simple ideas.

Books like this are important. Although not every chapter will be of intense interest to every reader, by skimming some, reading others, and intensely studying still other selections, readers will gain a deeper understanding of how their contemporaries are using Agile/XP practices to solve a multitude of real-world problems. But we must also admit, those of us who participated in the XP2001 conference that generated many of these chapters, that part of the allure of the conference was the Mediterranean beaches of Sardinia.

Jim Highsmith
Salt Lake City, Utah, May 2002

Part I

XAR: Extreme and Agile Review—A Review of XP and AMs

Welcome to yet another book on Extreme Programming (XP)—and agile methodologies (AMs), of course.

Writing a book about new software development methodologies can be both a very easy and a very difficult task. It could be very easy because you could talk about very generic and high-level vaporware without ever entering into the details and by backing your approach with politically correct statements such as "It requires customization," and "No silver bullets."

You could take the completely opposite approach and still have a fairly easy task if you have ever run a project with your methodology. You could enter a detailed description of what you did, distilling a complete approach around your idiosyncrasies. It would be best if you added something esoteric, such as typing on the keyboard with only the right hand and using the left to hold a silk napkin with which you would clean your sweater every other minute.

Software authors are not bad by nature. We should remember that in the early days of studies in electronics, the equation for the resistor was quite complex, with lots of terms that were insignificant. Nowadays, it is a simple algebraic division: $R=V/I$.

However, writing about a new methodology becomes dreadfully difficult if you aim to create something valuable for the reader, combining the limited theoretical understanding with the limited experimental evidence and avoiding terse language.

This book takes that approach. We combine an overview of XP from the hands of the people who proposed it, a description of experiences in specific areas that are as yet unclear and subject to debate, and an empirical evaluation of how XP projects are progressing in software companies.

Part I provides an overview of the methodology. We assume that you have already read the cult books (Kent Beck's, Martin Fowler's, Ron Jeffries', Jim Highsmith's, and so on), so we summarize all the foundations in Chapter 1, by Don Wells.

In Chapter 2, Jim Highsmith presents the essence of "agility." This insightful chapter explores agile methodologies in depth and explains the rationale behind any agile proposal.

The large number of agile methodologies may disorient software managers and engineers. To help overcome this, Michele Marchesi provides guidelines to select which among the several agile methodologies best suits your environment (see Chapter 3).

Most people thinking about XP probably associate it with pair programming. Its detractors say that it is only a fad that wastes the time and money of software companies. Its supporters are convinced that it is the Holy Grail of software development. In Chapter 4, Laurie Williams discusses the principles of pair programming, details when and how to adopt it, and summarizes the expected benefits.

Effective analysis in XP centers on the ability to find a suitable metaphor. This is not an easy task, especially when the project becomes larger and more complex. In Chapter 5, William and Steven Wake focus on the issue of metaphor. In particular, they detail their approach to finding a metaphor, relating the objects of the system to it, and evaluating whether there are "bad metaphors."

XP is not "cowboy coding," nor is it completely uncontrolled development. It is the opposite of these. But how is it possible to couple an agile approach with measurements and process control? They appear to be an antinomy. In Chapter 6, Giancarlo Succi discusses possible avenues for implementing an agile measurement program, taking advantage of data sources naturally available to software engineers and managers.

To what extent is each practice of XP useful? How many of them should we keep in our project for it to be successful? What is a safe level of customization of the practices? In Chapter 7, Ron Jeffries attempts to address these tricky issues that confront managers every day. He analyzes the most relevant practices and concludes with a caveat for agile customizations.

Finally, in Chapter 8 Michele Marchesi explains how you can hit your targets by using XP. He explains how to align business and technical goals, and outlines possible problems that you may face when implementing an XP project as well as how to solve them.

Chapter 1

XP in a Thousand Words

—Don Wells

For some people Extreme Programming (XP) is a new set of rules, for others it is a humanistic set of values, and to some it is a very dangerous oversimplification. XP comes to us at a time when we find computer programming to be a bottleneck. Businesses demand bigger systems faster to gain a competitive edge. The rate at which we can create this software often determines how fast new business opportunities can grow. There have already been many changes in the way software is created over the last few decades, but few have represented such a large change. XP is more than rules or values—it is a reengineering of software development in response to extreme new requirements for our craft.

The most disputed foundation of XP is the idea of doing today only what is needed today. Now before the gentle reader jumps up with fists clenched, we should point out that this doesn't mean there is no designing and no planning. Both of these activities are even more important in XP than in other methods. Actually, the biggest impact of XP is on the cost of the system over time. One of the more important aspects of the business of software is the idea of a life cycle and how cost relates to it. XP proposes new ways to address this life cycle cost and a way to get the most for every dollar we have spent to date for an early delivery or if new development needs to be stopped.

A commonly misunderstood part of XP is the stance on documents. Often it is interpreted that we should write no documentation whatsoever. This is ridiculous. XP isn't about not writing documents—it is about writing more effective documentation. In most cases this results in not writing a document, because a more effective form can be used instead. Much of a project's documentation can be remembered by the team members and communicated to new team members in a conversation. A document cannot be changed nearly as fast as the ideas held in a team's collective mind. A document cannot be accessed as fast as shouting out a question and getting a response. This is not to imply there is a lack of solid documentation. On the contrary, there is a great deal—in the form of automated tests, well-crafted code, and even documents, when appropriate.

This idea of relying on the team and the collective mind is indeed controversial. Not too long ago, one programmer working alone could create software that would become an overnight success. Times have changed. No one person can create an entire system and deliver it to the marketplace in time to be of value to anyone. With the rise of the team comes the need for understanding teamwork. XP stresses ways to enable a team to come together and work as if they were a single entity. The individuals who make up the team may change, but the team itself endures without faltering, making steady, dependable, predictable progress.

Don't do anything without feedback. Many of us take this concept for granted in our daily lives. We see, hear, and feel what is happening around us and use that rich information as a guide. Software development is no different, but we must expend the effort to put appropriate sources of feedback in place. We see, hear, and even feel as we move the mouse and click it to interact with our programs. But we are fooled. Our senses don't provide us with rich information about the code being tested. Programs don't exist in our physical world, so we must extend our senses into the world of software by writing code. We need tools like JUnit to translate the type of feedback we need for software development into the type of feedback our senses can assimilate.

Consider the related idea of not waiting till the end of the project to start testing—in fact, let's completely reverse that and start testing first. We need feedback to monitor our progress and guide us during the project. Knowing what to test and how to test is a valuable skill. Many programmers are not required to do a thorough job of testing their own software. It is often left to a separate quality assurance (QA) group or even the unsuspecting customer to find problems. This must change if we are going to deliver faster. Programmers must learn how to test their software well enough to change their mind-set into one of creating tests even before the code. With or without QA, the team is still responsible for a complete and thorough job of testing.

An XP project is managed with concentric loops of planning and feedback. The "test first, code second" cycle is one example. A test is a plan for what we will code next. We often forget that planning is about predictions and that a prediction not based on historical data is just a guess. The only way to know how long something will take is to make a measurement. We plan only in the presence of a measurement, and we revise our plan whenever we get a new measurement. It is also important to be sure that the right measurement is made. Make the most of the data you have to predict the future. Don't fool yourself into making guesses.

XP is about some new rules, some old forgotten rules, more humane values, and of course teamwork. But there is also more, much more. We have only skimmed the surface here. There are many new ideas about how to do things better and more reliably. We must stop and think about what we are doing and question why we do it. If we take anything away from XP, we should take away the attitude of finding new ways to do more of what helps us produce software and less of anything that holds us back.

About the Author

Don Wells has over two decades of programming experience. He has built financial applications, military applications, expert systems, cockpit simulators, computer-aided engineering (CAE) systems, and Web sites, and even published a video game. Don has been on projects ranging in size from one to 150 people. He has developed software to run on large corporate mainframes, all the way down to shrink-wrapped software for home computers, and everything in between. He has been experimenting with ad hoc software development methods for many years. He was a member of the world's first XP project, called C3, at Chrysler. He applied XP to a second project, called VCAPS, while at Ford. Don created the Web site at http://www.extremeprogramming.org to share his experiences and serve as a first introduction to XP. He was an invited speaker at the XP2001 conference in Italy, and he has been a guest lecturer at universities. He started the XP Universe conferences and continues to serve as co-chair of the program committee. Presently, Don consults on applying Extreme Programming and agile methodologies.

Chapter 2

Agile Software Development—Why It Is Hot!

—Jim Highsmith

In the last year, Agile Software Development has burst upon the development scene, led by the indefatigable XP aficionados. But the Agile pot has been simmering beneath the surface for over ten years. In the past year, articles on Agile development have appeared in ComputerWorld, Software Development, IEEE Computer *and* Software, Cutter IT Journal, CIO, *and even* The Economist. *I think Agile's sudden rise to fame is rooted in two things: Agile Software Development helps companies deliver valuable software in an era of constant change and turbulence; and Agile Software Development helps create a workplace culture that attracts knowledge workers in our Information Age.*

The three key questions in assessing this hotly debated trend in our profession are these: What kinds of problems does agility solve best? What is agility? What are Agile Software Development Ecosystems?

What Kinds of Problems Does Agility Solve Best?

The future of our Information Age economy belongs to the *agile*, those companies that have the capacity to create change, and maybe even a little chaos, for their competitors. If you can innovate better and faster, you create change for your competitors. If you can respond quickly to competitive initiatives, new technology, and customers' requirements, you create change for competitors. If you are slower, less innovative, less responsive, you are doomed to survival strategies in a sea of chaos imposed by others. Is your company going to set the pace of change, or are competitors going to set it? In our Information Age economy, a company's ability to set the pace, to create change, lies in its ability to develop software. In a world of constant change, traditional rigorous software development methods are insufficient for success.

In recent years, software technology has moved from supporting business operations to becoming a critical component of business strategy. It drives new product development, from automobiles with hundreds of chips with embedded software to cellular phones and other wireless devices that are extending the definition of "distributed" systems.

Agile Software Development (ASD) is tuned to innovation and response—to creating new knowledge that delivers value to businesses, and to responding quickly to competitive challenges. Rigorous Software Methodologies (RSMs) are useful, but for a set of problem domains that is shrinking. Many of the techniques from RSMs can be effectively employed by ASD approaches, but the framework and philosophy of the two are different. Agile approaches are best employed to explore new ground and to power teams for which innovation and creativity are paramount.

People have focused on the title, rather than the subtitle, of Kent Beck's groundbreaking book *Extreme Programming Explained: Embrace Change* [Beck2000]. These individuals, especially managers in large organizations, are put off by the word "extreme" and its connotation of daredevils swooping in on their coding snowboards. Or if they manage to force themselves past the word "extreme," they land on the word "programming" and relegate the material to that "mechanical" stuff that the geeky people do. Although the words in Kent's book may talk about programming, and he may even advocate such extreme practices as testing one's own code, the strategic issue surrounding XP, and all other Agile Software Development Ecosystems (ASDEs), concerns embracing change.

Agile organizations create chaos for their competitors, first, by creating change so fast that competitors are left gasping for breath and, second, by responding quickly to competitors' attempts to change the market. Just imagine what it feels like to have a competitor with a new product-development cycle of 12 months to your 18; furthermore, every time you introduce a breakthrough feature, they match it in their next product release. They are attacking; you are always on the defensive. That's the essence of Agile organizations—create change that you can live with and your competition can't. "The source of our competitiveness in this industry is our ability to manage in a chaotic environment," says Silicon Graphics' CEO Ed McCracken. "But it's more proactive than that. We actually help create chaos in the first place—that's what keeps a lot of potential competitors out" [Iansiti1998]. Agile organizations don't just respond to change, they generate it!

What Is Agility?

If turbulence and turmoil define the problem, then agility is key to the solution.

Agility isn't a one-shot deal that can be checked off the organizational initiatives list. Agility is a way of life, a constantly emerging and changing response to business turbulence. Critics may counter, "Agility is merely waiting for bad things to happen, then responding. It is a fancy name for lack of planning and ad hoc–ism." But agile organizations still plan; they just understand the limits of planning. Three characteristics help define agility: creating and responding to change, being nimble and able to improvise, and balancing flexibility and structure.

Agility is the ability to both create and respond to change in order to profit in a turbulent business environment.

Agility is not merely reaction, but also action. First and foremost, agile organizations create change, change that causes intense pressure on competitors. Creating change requires innovation, the ability to create new knowledge that provides business value. Second, agile organizations have an ability to react, to respond quickly and effectively to both anticipated and unanticipated changes in the business environment.

In our volatile economy, companies need to enhance their "exploration" skills at every level of the organization. Good explorers are agile explorers—they know how to juggle and improvise. Indiana Jones was a good explorer, somehow living through every outlandish adventure. Agility means quickness, lightness, and nimbleness—the ability to act rapidly, the ability to do the minimum necessary to get a job done, and the ability to adapt to changing conditions. Agility also requires innovation and creativity—the ability to envision new products and new ways of doing business. In particular, IT organizations have not done an adequate job of balancing the needs of exploration and optimization.

Agile individuals can improvise—they know the rules and boundaries, but they also know when the problem at hand has moved into uncharted areas. They know how to extend their knowledge into unforeseen realms, to experiment, and to learn. When critical things need to get done, call on the great improvisers.

Improvisation makes great jazz bands. From a few key structural rules, jazz bands improvise extensively. Having a solid foundation enables their tremendous flexibility without allowing the music to degenerate into chaos. The proponents of business process reengineering and software engineering methodologies probably blanch at the thought that improvisation, rather than carefully articulated processes, is key to success. Yet in today's turbulent environment, staff members with good balancing, judging, and improvisational skills are truly invaluable.

Being agile means trusting in one's ability to respond more than trusting in one's ability to plan.

What Are Agile Software Development Ecosystems?

I began writing a book about Agile Software Development methodologies, but I kept worrying about the word "methodology" because it didn't fit with the focal points of Agile development—people, relationships, and uncertainty. Furthermore, when the word "methodology" is used, Agile practices are instantly compared with traditional software development methodologies—thereby using the wrong measuring stick for comparison. So I began to use the term "Agile Software Development Ecosystem" to describe a holistic environment that includes three interwoven components—a "chaordic" perspective, collaborative values and principles, and a barely sufficient methodology—and the term "Agilists" to identify those who are proponents of ASDEs.

Some people think that "Agile" means fewer processes, less ceremony, and briefer documents, but it has a much broader perspective, which is the primary reason for using the word "ecosystem" rather than "methodology." Although fewer processes and less formality might lower development costs, they are not enough to produce agility. Focusing on people and their interactions and giving individuals the power to make quick decisions and to self-adapt their own processes are key to Agile ecosystems.

The word "ecosystem" conjures up a vision of living things and their interactions with each other. Within an organizational context, an ecosystem can then be thought of as a dynamic, ever-changing environment in which people and organizations constantly initiate actions and respond to each other's actions. The word "ecosystem" focuses us on the dynamic interactions of individuals and teams rather than on the static lines on organization charts.

Part I

A Chaordic Perspective

To fully understand ASDEs, we need to understand each of the three components and how they relate to each other. First, Agilists share a view that organizations are chaordic—that every organization exhibits properties of both chaos and order that defy management through the use of linear, predictive planning and execution practices. Viewing organizations as chaordic means understanding that the predictability on which traditional project management and development life cycle practices are built is a root cause of dysfunctionality between customer, management, and development organizations. A chaordic perspective impacts both how we respond to change and how we manage project teams and organizations.

In day-to-day project work, a chaordic perspective creates two outcomes that are 180 degrees out of sync with rigorous methodologies.

- Product goals are achievable, but they are not predictable.
- Processes can aid consistency, but they are not repeatable.

Although ASDEs involve careful planning, the fundamental assumption remains that plans, in a turbulent environment, are not predictable, at least at the level of project scope, schedule, and cost. Plans are hypotheses to be tested rather than predictions to be realized. However, the product goals of the business are achievable, in large part because agile people adapt. They can "adapt" to an articulated vision and a schedule, scope, or cost goal through trade-offs in the other two dimensions. Second, although process can aid people in working together, in volatile environments the idea of driving out process variation through measurement and correction—statistical process control—becomes an unworkable hypothesis. Changes that are the result of knowledge gained during the project, knowledge not discernable early in the project, require processes that can respond to change, not ones that attempt to eliminate it.

Peter Senge uses the term "mental model" to identify the perspective—or set of assumptions, stories, and beliefs that each of us carries in our mind—that provides a context for thinking [Senge1990]. In organizations, the collective set of mental models defines an overall cultural context. Companies that are heavily sales oriented differ from those that are heavily engineering oriented. Companies whose driving strategy is customer intimacy differ from those whose driving force is product innovation. Companies whose mental model includes linearity, cause and effect, hierarchy, predictability, and control operate very differently from those whose mental model includes collaborative networks, emergence, decentralization of power, and acceptance of unpredictability. One is Newtonian; the other, chaordic.

Collaborative Values and Principles

The second piece of the interconnected web that defines ASDEs is the statement of collaborative values and principles. Although it is difficult to characterize the Agile Manifesto in one word, "collaborative" seems to be the best single adjective. Values and principles shape the ecosystem. Without a set of stated values and principles, an ecosystem is sterile, reflecting practices but not the people who interact within it.

A collaborative culture includes people and their relationships within a development team and with customers, management, and partnering teams within or external to their own company. Human dynamics, communications, and collaboration may be known as the "soft" sciences, but in practice, they may be the hardest to master. Principles and values help define a culture—the environment in which people want to work.

A Barely Sufficient Methodology

The final component of an ASDE is methodology. The traditional definition of methodology includes things such as roles, activities, processes, techniques, and tools. Alistair Cockburn summarizes these components when he defines methodology as "the conventions we agree to"—the ways in which people work together on a project. In

The Social Life of Information, John Seely Brown and Paul Duguid discuss the major differences between process (as used by the business process reengineering movement) and practice [Brown+2000]. Processes are described in manuals; practices are what happen in reality. Process centrists relegate people to second place; practice centrists place people first. Process centrists focus on explicit (written-down) knowledge, while practice centrists focus on tacit (internal) knowledge. The ASDE model provides a practice-centered, rather than a process-centered, approach to methodology.

There are two reasons to pursue barely sufficient methodologies: value and innovation. Streamlined methodologies concentrate on those activities that create value, and ruthlessly eliminate non-value-adding activities. Programming usually adds value; process management often adds overhead. Bare sufficiency means keeping the former and eliminating the latter. Second, innovation and creativity flourish in chaordic environments, not orderly ones. Barely sufficient methodologies are cauldrons for breeding innovation.

Methodology also relates to organizational model. Agile methodologies contain minimal processes and documentation, and reduced ceremony (formality). Agile methodologies are labeled "barely sufficient" or "a little bit less than just enough" or "minimal." However, this streamlining of methodology isn't just based on reducing work, but, more importantly, it is based on understanding the chaordic world view—one in which emergent (innovative) results are best generated at the "edge of chaos," perched midway between chaos and order.

Practices (or techniques) are the lifeblood of methodology. Whether it's pair programming, Scrum meetings, customer focus groups, or automated testing, the practices of ASDEs, carried out by talented and skilled individuals, produce results.

What Is the Future of Agile Software Development?

So, what about the future? To the extent that the future business environment continues to be turbulent, I think rigorous cultures face a difficult challenge. No amount of process thinning or document pruning will make them agile—agile is an attitude, a sense of how the world works in complex ways. However, to the extent that executives and managers still want the world to be predictable and planable, agile cultures and ASDEs will be difficult to implement. But, in the final analysis, businesses gradually, but inevitably, gravitate to practices that make them successful, and ASDEs will increasingly contribute to successful software projects. Rigorous approaches will remain, but many fewer companies will be using them five years from now.

References

[Beck2000] K. Beck. *Extreme Programming Explained.* Addison-Wesley, 2000.

[Brown+2000] J. Brown, P. Duguid. *The Social Life of Information.* Harvard Business School Press, 2000.

[Iansiti1998] M. Iansiti. *Technology Integration: Making Critical Choices in a Dynamic World.* Harvard Business School Press, 1998.

[Senge1990] P. Senge. *The Fifth Discipline: The Art and Practice of The Learning Organization.* Currency Doubleday, 1990.

About the Author

This chapter is excerpted and adapted from Jim Highsmith's new book, *Agile Software Development Ecosystems* (Addison-Wesley, 2002).

Chapter 3

Which AM Should I Use?

—*Michele Marchesi*

People's attitudes toward communication, user involvement, and frequent releases is more important than the specific process you use. However, if you are a novice in the field, and you want to introduce an agile methodology into your shop, this chapter gives you some advice.

At last you have decided that agile methodologies (AMs) are worth a try, and now you are looking for the right methodology to introduce in a pilot project at your firm. Unfortunately, many AMs happen to be waiting for your decision. Which one should you use?

The first thing to consider is that not all AMs are at the same level. One, Extreme Programming (XP), is quite different from the others because it is a set of very detailed planning, design, and programming practices. The other AMs are much less detailed and typically cover only the planning and project management phases. The programming practices are left to the team's choice. In fact, many XP practices are also recommended by the other AMs, and there are efforts to merge XP with them.

Now let's examine the main AMs, and I'll give some advice on what to choose. (These are, of course, my personal opinions.)

Extreme Programming

XP is the most documented [XPSeries], the most supported, and perhaps the most used AM. It was invented in 1998–99 and started to spread in 2000; it seems that, at the time of writing this chapter, it doesn't yet have many well-known successes.

Because XP is very detailed, it is easy to understand and follow each of its practices. However, it is very difficult to follow them all at once, and to try to follow XP "by the book" is very risky.

XP is the best choice for small development teams (up to ten to 15 people) that agree to follow its practices. Most XP practices are also suited for individual programmers.

Scrum

Scrum is a set of project management practices aimed at coping with continual changes in requirements. It was introduced in the mid-'90s and claims many successes. Scrum is documented in the recent book by Ken Schwaber and Mike Beedle [Schwaber+2001].

Scrum should be easy to adopt because it prescribes a few practices to manage the project but allows the maximum freedom about which programming practices to adopt. So it is suited to teams fervent about their practices and with a management asking for a proven track record of success. Scrum can also be easily merged with XP, as in the xP@Scrum approach, for instance.

Crystal Methodologies

The Crystal family was recently introduced by Alistair Cockburn [Cockburn2001]. It is a set of AMs covering a broad range of needs in terms of the number of developers and project criticality, which may range from C (loss of comfort) to D (loss of discretionary money) and E (loss of essential money). Life-critical projects are not yet covered in these methodologies.

Crystal methodologies are described in terms of mandatory policy standards, which are very synthetic. Implementation details are left entirely to the discretion of the team. A specific methodology for Web development, targeted at 40 to 50 developers and with criticality E, is also presented (Crystal Orange Web).

Crystal methodologies are even less prescriptive than Scrum. They explicitly take into account the project size and criticality, and this could be a plus for project management. At the time of writing this chapter, however, they are less documented than XP and Scrum.

Adaptive Software Development

Jim Highsmith's Adaptive Software Development (ASD) is more a philosophical view on agile development than a definite methodology. Although reading Jim's book [Highsmith2000] is absolutely a must for every "agile" developer, this book does not illustrate in detail a specific software development process.

Recently, Jim and Alistair merged their approaches, resulting in Crystal-Adaptive Methodologies (see http://www.crystalmethodologies.org/).

Lean Software Development

Lean Software Development, or LSD (what a suggestive acronym!), is the application of Lean Thinking to software design, programming, project management, and contracts. Its roots originate from the Lean Manufacturing concept of W. Edwards Demming, who pioneered just-in-time development in the manufacturing industry.

LSD is described in an article written by Mary Poppendieck [Poppendieck2001], and, like ASD, it is presently more a set of good project management practices than a definite process. For this reason, I strongly suggest reading the referenced article on LSD, and I rank LSD on the same level as the Crystal methodologies and ASD as a choice.

Feature Driven Development

Feature Driven Development (FDD) is described in a book by Peter Coad and others [Coad+1999]. It is a structured process to design and code software systems and is designed to scale from small to large teams.

FDD is a model-driven and short-iteration process. The main difference with XP is the development of an up-front object-oriented (OO) model of the system. This model may be changed at each iteration, but it is deemed essential to the process.

The development is driven by the incremental implementation of a list of features describing the system, during one- to four-week iterations. Code ownership is strictly enforced, and code owners are requested to develop the features entailing modification of their code.

FDD is the least "lightweight" of the agile methodologies. It could please teams and managers scared of merging analysis and design with the coding activities of XP, and of other XP characteristics such as collective code ownership. In the end, choose FDD if you fear the fourth value of XP: courage. FDD is agile and well structured, but it prescribes up-front analysis and design, extra documentation besides the code, and personal code ownership. It gives the feeling of being more in control of the project at the expense of part of its agility.

Conclusion

If you want to be agile, the first tenet is "Every project needs a slightly different set of policies and conventions, or methodology." People's attitude toward communication, user involvement, and frequent releases is more important than the specific process you use.

To summarize, if you are a novice in the field, and you really want specific advice, consider these recommendations.

- If you are a lone programmer, use the XP practices that are suitable for you.
- If you are a small team (two to eight people), consider using XP and introducing XP practices in small bunches, each bunch every two to three weeks.
- If you are in charge of a bigger team (eight to 20), consider using Scrum or Crystal as a high-level process "container," together with the XP practices that you deem sensible to use in your project.
- If you don't want to give up what you were taught (and maybe you are doing well) about OO modeling or code ownership, consider FDD, regardless of the size of your team.
- If the team is even bigger than 20 people, again consider Scrum, Crystal, or FDD, depending on your needs and preferences.

In the end, when you become accustomed to agile methodologies, you'll be able to devise and tune your own methodology, one suited for your team and the specific project.

References

[Coad+1999] P. Coad, J. De Luca, E. Lefebvre. *Java Modeling in Color with UML*. Prentice Hall, 1999.

[Cockburn2001] A. Cockburn. *Agile Software Development*. Addison-Wesley, 2001.

[Highsmith2000] J. Highsmith. *Adaptive Software Development*. Dorset House, 2000.

[Poppendieck2001] M. Poppendieck. "Lean Programming." *Software Development*, May and June 2001. http://www.poppendieck.com/programming.htm.

[Schwaber+2001] K. Schwaber, M. Beedle. *Agile Software Development with Scrum*. Prentice Hall, 2001.

[XPSeries] The XP Series. K. Beck, series advisor. Addison-Wesley, 1999–2001.

Part I

Chapter 4

Pair Programming: Why Have Two Do the Work of One?

—Laurie Williams

As a head of the team, I initially thought that we might be wasting human resources by having two engineers do the work of one. Moreover, I thought, they'll be chatting and giggling more than working. "Too many cooks spoil the broth," you know. Though I agreed that there would be fewer syntax errors, I could not comprehend their timesaving effect. To be frank, quite like everyone else in the team, I did not appreciate the idea. And you know how difficult it was initially to get going with it! But as we delved deeper into the project, I realized that it gave us fewer errors, no slippage, and more than everything . . . team strength and companionship.

—Development manager
at a technology corporation in India

Pair programming is a style of programming in which two programmers work side by side at one computer, continually collaborating on the same design, algorithm, code, or test. One of the pair, called the driver, is typing at the computer or writing down a design. The other partner, called the navigator, has many jobs. One is to observe the work of the driver—looking for tactical and strategic defects in the work of the driver. Tactical defects are syntax errors, typos, calling the wrong method, and so on. Strategic defects occur when the driver is headed down the wrong path—what they are implementing just won't accomplish what it needs to accomplish. The navigator is the objective, strategic, longer-range thinker. Any of us can be guilty of straying off the path. A simple "Can you explain what you're doing?" from the navigator can serve to bring us back to earth. The navigator has a much more objective point of view and can think better strategically about the direction of the work. One great thing is that the driver and the navigator can brainstorm on demand at any time. An effective pair programming relationship is very active. The driver and the navigator communicate at least every 45 seconds to a minute. It is also very important to switch roles periodically.

Anecdotal and statistical evidence indicates many benefits of pair programming. These benefits are described in this chapter. However, without a doubt, there is resistance to transitioning to pair programming. One group of people who resist is managers. They often have the knee-jerk reaction "Why in the world would I pay two programmers to do something that one programmer could do?" This is not a surprising reaction. This chapter addresses the concerns of managers who are considering or are resistant to transitioning to pair programming. Specifically, we examine five common motivations of managers that pair programming can address [Williams+2002].

Motivation: Completing Jobs on Time with High Quality

The technique of pair programming has been recently popularized by Extreme Programming—though reports of pair programming pre-date the emergence of the technique. In his 1995 book, *Constantine on Peopleware*, Larry Constantine reported observing Dynamic Duos at Whitesmiths, Ltd., producing code faster and more bug-free than ever before [Constantine1995]. That same year, Jim Coplien published the "Developing in Pairs" Organizational Pattern [Coplien1995].

In 1996, there was a report from Hill Air Force Base [Jensen1996].

> *The two-person team approach places two engineers or two programmers in the same location (office, cubicle, etc.) with one workstation and one problem to solve. The team is not allowed to divide the task but produces the design, code and documentation as if the team was*

a single individual. . . . Final project results were outstanding. Total productivity was 175 lines per person-month (lppm) compared to a documented average individual productivity of only 77 lppm. This result is especially striking when we consider two persons produced each line of source code. The error rate through software-system integration was three orders of magnitude lower than the organization's norm. Was the project a fluke? No. Why were the results so impressive? A brief list of observed phenomena includes focused energy, brainstorming, problem solving, continuous design and code walkthroughs, mentoring and motivation.

In 1998, Temple University Professor Nosek reported on his study of 15 full-time, experienced programmers working for 45 minutes on a challenging problem important to their organization, in their own environment and with their own equipment. Five worked individually, ten worked collaboratively in five pairs. Conditions and materials used were the same for both the experimental (team) and control (individual) groups. This study provided statistically significant results, using a two-sided t-test. "To the surprise of the managers and participants, all the teams outperformed the individual programmers, enjoyed the problem-solving process more, and had greater confidence in their solutions." Combining their time, the pairs spent 60% more minutes on the task. However, because they worked in tandem, they were able to complete the task more quickly and effectively by producing better algorithms and code in less time. Most of the programmers were initially skeptical of the value of collaboration in working on the same problem and thought it would not be an enjoyable process. However, results show that collaboration improved both their performance and their enjoyment of the problem solving process [Nosek1998].

In 1999 at the University of Utah, students in the Senior Software Engineering course participated in a structured experiment. The students were aware of the importance of the experiment, the need to keep accurate information, and that each person (whether in the control or experimental group) was a very important part of the outcome. All students attended the same classes, received the same instruction, and participated in class discussions on the pros and cons of pair programming. When asked on the first day of class, 35 of the 41 students (85%) indicated a preference for pair programming. (Later, many of the 85% admitted that they were initially reluctant, but curious, about pair programming.)

The students were divided into two groups; both groups were deliberately composed of the same mix of high, average, and low performers. Thirteen students formed the control group, in which all the students worked individually on all assignments. Twenty-eight students formed the experimental group, in which all worked in two-person collaborative teams; collaboratively, they completed the same assignments as the individuals. (The collaborative pairs also did additional assignments to keep the overall workload the same between the two groups.) All 28 of the students in the experimental group had expressed an interest in pair programming. Some of the students in the control group had actually wanted to try pair programming. It is important to note that before enrolling in this class, students had significant coding practice. Most students had industry or internship experience and had written small compilers, operating system kernels, and interpreters in other classes. Cycle time, productivity, and quality results were compared between the two groups

As reported [Cockburn+2000; Williams2000; Williams+2000], our experimental class produced quantitative results supporting the pair programming results in industry. The students completed four assignments over six weeks. Thirteen individuals and 14 collaborative pairs completed each assignment. The pairs passed, on average, 15% more of the automated postdevelopment test cases run by an impartial teaching assistant. The difference in quality levels is statistically significant.

The pair results were also more consistent, while the individuals varied more about the mean. Individuals intermittently didn't hand in a program or handed it in late; pairs handed in their assignments on time. This result can be attributed to a positive form of "pair pressure" the programmers put on each other. The programmers admitted to working harder and smarter on programs because they did not want to let their partner down. Individuals did not have this form of pressure and, therefore, did not perform as consistently.

We can also make another statement about the quality of pairs. The pairs not only wrote programs that were of higher externally visible quality, but their programs were consistently more than 20% shorter than their individual counterparts. Implementing functionality in fewer lines of code is commonly viewed as an indication of better design quality and lower projected maintenance costs [Boehm1981]. The individuals were more likely to produce "blob class" [Brown+1998] designs—just to get the job done. The design from the collaborative teams exploited more of the benefits of object-oriented programming. Their classes demonstrated more encapsulation and had more cohesive classes with better class-responsibility alignment. The individuals tended to have fewer classes that had many responsibilities. The collaborative designs would, therefore, be easier to implement, enhance, and maintain.

The other piece of the economic equation is time. If pair programming does double the time, certainly it cannot be justified. Many people's gut reaction is to reject the idea of pair programming because they assume that there will be a 100% programmer-hour increase by putting two programmers on a job that one can do. The University of Utah students recorded how much time they spent on their assignments via a Web-based data recording and information retrieval system. After the initial adjustment period in the first program (the "jelling" assignment, which took approximately ten hours), the pairs spent on average only 15% more than the individuals. Additionally, after the first program, the difference between the times for individuals and for the pairs was no longer statistically significant, because the average was driven up significantly by two of the 13 pairs. The median amount of time spent by the individuals and the pairs was essentially identical. (As a side note, the pairs who spent the most amount of time also spent the most amount of time when they completed pre- and postexperiment programs individually.)

This still invites the obvious question: Why would we invest even an additional 15% on code development by introducing pair programming? The answer is because of the higher quality that is obtained and the resulting cost savings (and increased customer satisfaction) because of this higher quality. Typically, in systems test it takes between one-half [Humphrey1995] and two [Humphrey1997] workdays to correct each defect. Industry data reports that between 33 and 88 hours are spent on each defect found in the field [Humphrey1995]. When each defect saved during code development can save defect detection and correction times of between one-half and 88 hours, pair programming quickly becomes the cost-saving alternative [Williams2000].

We should also note that if time-to-market/cycle time is a prime motivator for you, pair programming can get the job done in about half the time. Could the same thing be done with two programmers working independently? Not likely. Increased communication and integration time would increase their time, as Brooks has told us for over a quarter of a century with his "Brooks's Law" [Brooks1975]. Additionally, the quality would not be as high.

Data with students is a start in convincing you about the improvements offered by pair programming. Descriptions of two industrial case studies follow.

William Wood of NASA Langley reports that a pair of programmers in 2001 reimplemented numerical analysis of wave propagation code that was originally developed in 1997. The individual programmer worked for six weeks to produce 2,144 lines of code. The pair worked for four weeks (eight programmer weeks) to implement the same functionality in 403 lines of code. It is very important to know that during these eight programmer weeks, the pair also wrote 463 lines of testing code, while the individual did not write any testing code, and that the pair was learning a new language, while the individual was very experienced in the language. Combining the pair programming and the extensive testing techniques, they have much higher confidence in the new code.

A technology company in India reports very impressive pair programming results. The prototype of a Voice over IP project was done without pairing. The actual project was done using pair programming. The actual project was much more complex because it had to deal with meeting Quality of Service parameters, scalability, uptime, and so on. The paired project showed significant increases in productivity and quality. The data is summarized in Table 4.1.

TABLE 4.1 Comparison of India Technology Projects

	Project 1: Solo Programmers	**Project 2: Pair Programmers**
Project size (KLOC)	20	520
Team size	4	12
Effort (person months)	4	72
Unit test defects	107 (5.34 defects/KLOC)	183 (0.4 defects/KLOC)
System integration defects	46 (2.3 defects/KLOC)	82 (0.2 defects/KLOC)

Motivation: Reduce the Risk of Losing a Key Person

With pair programming, the risk of losing key programmers is reduced because multiple people are familiar with each part of the system. If a pair works together consistently, two people are familiar with a particular area of the program. If the pairs rotate, many people can be familiar with each part. A common informal metric (invented by Jim Coplien of AT&T Bell Labs) is referred to as the "truck number." "How many or few people would have to be hit by a truck (or quit) before the project is incapacitated?" The worst answer is "one." Having knowledge dispersed across the team increases the truck number and project safety.

As programmers rotate among the group, they get the chance to know many on their team more personally. This familiarity breaks down many communication barriers. Team members find each other much more approachable. They struggle with questions or lack of information for less time before getting out of their chair and going to ask the right person a question—because they know that person quite well. Pair rotation enables person-to-person sharing of tacit knowledge, ideas, and insights that are not documented and are hard to articulate. Through pair programming, sharing of tacit knowledge takes place in the normal course of the programmers' day; no special resources, systems, or repositories need be allocated for this important knowledge sharing. Pair programming provides an organizationally supported vehicle for continual, ongoing conversations between programmers. Through these conversations, knowledge management takes place, along with a corresponding decrease in the risk of losing a key person on the team.

Motivation: Have Happier Employees

Turnover is very costly in both recruiting and training costs. Happier, less frustrated people are more positive about their job and are more eager to help the team meet its objectives.

More than half of programmers resist the transition to pair programming. However, once they try, almost all eventually favor the technique. The incorporation of pair programming has been shown to improve the engineers' job satisfaction and overall confidence while attaining the quality and cycle time results discussed earlier. Pair programmers were surveyed six times on whether they enjoyed their job more when pair programming. First, an anonymous survey of professional pair programmers was conducted on the Internet. Both the summer and fall classes at the University of Utah were surveyed three times. Consistently, over 90% agreed that they enjoyed their job more when pair programming. The groups were also surveyed on whether working collaboratively made them feel more confident about their work. These results are even more positive, with 96% indicating that pair programming made them more confident.

Says Chuck Allison [Williams+2000]:

> *You know what I like about pair programming? First, it's something that has shown to help produce quality products. But, it's also something that you can easily add to your process that people actually want to do. It's a conceptually small thing to add. . . . And, when times get tough, you wouldn't likely forget to do pair programming or decide to drop it "just to get done." I just think the idea of working together is a winner.*

Motivation: Reduce Training Time

In *The Mythical Man-Month*, Brooks states his law: "Adding manpower to a late software project makes it later" [Brooks1975]. He believes that communication costs are the major reason that adding manpower to a late project makes it later. Brooks breaks these communication costs into training and intercommunication. Certainly, reducing training costs is a worthy objective.

Traditionally, people new to an organization are shown different parts of a system by senior staff personnel. This dedicated training time costs the senior personnel valuable hours. During these hours, neither the new person nor the trainer is contributing to the completion of the project. Through pair programming, the trainer teaches by doing (not showing), and direct contributions are made during the training time. Additionally, training seems to go much faster, and the new person learns the system much better.

Motivation: Improve Communication and Teamwork

There are many similar stories of teams who got started with pair programming. Before pair programming, they all walked into work in the morning at different times with a brown bag lunch in their hand. They walked into their office or cubicle and put their lunch down and their headphones on. They tapped on the keyboard all day. At some point, they took their lunch out of the brown bag and ate it. At the end of the day, they took off their headphones and headed home. They communicated with other team members mainly during meetings.

Post–pair programming, these teams were completely revolutionized. Through pairing, the teams got to know each other better in a personal way, through some idle chitchat that goes on while pairing. A programmer might mention that they are going to a ball game or their child's recital that night. Then, the next day, whether they are pairing together or not, one might ask how the recital went or comment on the outcome of the game while they meet at the vending machine. As the team gets to know each other better, they are far more likely to talk with each other about both personal and technical matters. The communication barriers between each other start to crumble. Additionally, they feel better about their jobs because they know their teammates on a personal level.

We contend that communication is made more efficient in another important way. As we said earlier, Brooks considers training and intercommunication costs to be major cost factors. In discussing his law, Brooks asserts, "If each part of the task must be separately coordinated with each other part, the [communication] effort increases as $n(n\text{-}1)/2$" [Brooks1975]. It's easy to think about the items that need to be done to coordinate two interdependent parts—dependencies need to be identified and scheduled accordingly, interfaces need to be specified, technical decisions might need to be jointly made, change management activities need to occur, and so on. Additionally, progress might be slowed if some critical coordination needs to occur when a team member is missing.

Let's think about how pair programming can make this communication more efficient. Consider first if a team does not rotate pairs but assigns larger pieces of functionality to static pairs. Then, instead of being broken into n parts, the project is broken into $(n/2)$ parts and the communication effort increase is reduced from $n(n-1)/2$ to $n(n/2-1)/4$. When pairs work together, they decide on dependencies, technical aspects, and interfaces as they go. No separate coordination activities need to take place, and no dependencies and interfaces need special documentation, thus improving the efficiency of team communication. If pairs do rotate, and programmers partner with the programmer with whom their task is interdependent, we believe this intercommunication cost can be even further reduced.

Conclusion

Pair programming can be a hard sell. Programmers resist transitioning. Managers consider it to be too expensive. This might result in both top-down and bottom-up resistance. However, our research has shown that almost all programmers who bravely transition to the technique ultimately prefer it to working alone. They come to appreciate the camaraderie, the mental stimulation, and the confidence of knowing that someone else agrees with their work.

The results of pair programming research can also allay the fears of managers. Pair programming can significantly benefit an organization. Pair programmers are more likely to produce a higher-quality product. Development time and cost do not increase significantly. The higher quality translates to lower life cycle costs when testing and field support are considered. Additionally, pair programmers are more satisfied in their jobs. The knowledge sharing that happens as a natural consequence of pair programming and pair rotation is an excellent knowledge management strategy. Training time can be reduced and communication and teamwork can increase through the use of pair programming.

References

[Boehm1981] B. Boehm. *Software Engineering Economics.* Prentice Hall, 1981.

[Brooks1975] F. Brooks. *The Mythical Man-Month.* Addison-Wesley, 1975.

[Brown+1998] W. Brown, R. Malveau, H. McCormick, T. Mowgray. *AntiPatterns.* Wiley Computer Publishing, 1998.

[Cockburn+2000] A. Cockburn, L. Williams. "The Costs and Benefits of Pair Programming." *Extreme Programming and Flexible Processes in Software Engineering*. XP2000, Cagliari, Sardinia, Italy, 2000.

[Constantine1995] L. Constantine. *Constantine on Peopleware*. Yourdon Press, 1995.

[Coplien1995] J. Coplien. "A Development Process Generative Pattern Language." In *Pattern Languages of Program Design*. J. Coplien, D. Schmidt, eds. Addison-Wesley, 1995.

[Humphrey1995] W. Humphrey. *A Discipline for Software Engineering*. Addison-Wesley, 1995.

[Humphrey1997] W. Humphrey. *Introduction to the Personal Software Process*. Addison-Wesley, 1997.

[Jensen1996] R. Jensen. "Management Impact on Software Cost and Schedule." *Crosstalk*, July 1996. http://stsc.hill.af.mil/crosstalk/1996/jul/manageme.asp.

[Nosek1998] J. Nosek. "The Case for Collaborative Programming." *Communications of the ACM*, 1998.

[Williams2000] L. Williams. "The Collaborative Software Process." Ph.D. diss. University of Utah. 2000.

[Williams+2000] L. Williams, R. Kessler, W. Cunningham, R. Jeffries. "Strengthening the Case for Pair-Programming." *IEEE Software*, 2000.

[Williams+2002] L. Williams, R. Kessler. *Pair Programming Illuminated*. Addison-Wesley, 2002.

Part I

Chapter 5

The System Metaphor Explored

—*William C. Wake and Steven A. Wake*

The system metaphor can seem like an obscure part of XP, but it can be a powerful tool. We look at what metaphors are, how to find them, their implications, and their limitations.

The system metaphor is one of the areas that seem to give people problems in understanding XP. We say, "Don't get hung up on it." We presented a tutorial that used exercises and games to help people understand the concept of metaphor, and brainstorm and assess metaphors for a variety of hypothetical systems.

What Is a Metaphor?

Webster's Dictionary describes a metaphor as "a figure of speech which makes an *implied* comparison between things which are not *literally* alike." In *Extreme Programming Explained*, Kent Beck says, "The system metaphor is a story that everyone—customers, programmers, and managers—can tell about how the system works" [Beck2000].

The metaphor can provide a "system of names" for your system. In his keynote address at XP Universe 2001, Ward Cunningham described programming with a thesaurus handy, to get just the right shade of meaning that supports subtle expectations about the objects involved. This approach isn't unique to XP, though; terms such as "window," "frame," "pane," or "tree," "hashing," and "queue" demonstrate that metaphors have been part of programming for a long time.

A good metaphor has *generativity*: It helps you ask better questions and understand things you might not have otherwise. For example, consider a call center application that is treated as an assembly line. This metaphor drives us to ask things such as, "What happens when something reaches the end of the line?" or "Where are the bottlenecks?" These questions might not come up if the system were regarded as just nodes and transitions.

Metaphors help with abstraction and modeling of the system: They give you a picture of how it works. We've found it more helpful to use a metaphor as a model of the solution than as a model of the domain; this helps in understanding how changes in the domain affect your system.

How Do You Find a Metaphor?

There are several approaches to creating a metaphor. The simplest metaphor is known as the *naive metaphor*. It says, "Let things be themselves." So an accounting application talks about customers and accounts. The naive metaphor gives you a starting point but doesn't provide much generativity.

In some ways, the *magic metaphor* is the opposite. For example, "A word processor is a magic typewriter." This can give you good ideas, but it doesn't limit you enough. The place you need to understand most gets the least support: "It's magic"—it could be anything.

To come up with metaphors, we typically use two processes: brainstorming and stewing. In brainstorming, you capture a bunch of ideas, which build on each other, and arrive at a workable solution. In stewing, you keep yourself immersed in the problem, and then you get a good idea late one night or in the shower.

One way to evaluate and refine your choice is to consider the implications of your metaphor and the attributes of your problem. For example, consider a system monitor. You might have a number of possible metaphors, each with different strengths and weaknesses, such as the following:

- Alarm—A notification that some attribute is out of bounds
- Report—Detailed information, but not very visual
- EKG—Full graphical history of several variables, but requiring an expert to read
- Graphic equalizer display—Instantaneous readings of several variables

Depending on the system and its goals, any of these might be a good choice.

A metaphor needn't be simplistic. You might use different metaphors for different parts of the system. You might combine metaphors to get a good solution. The goal is to find something effective for the team, not to come up with the "right" answer.

What Are the Objects?

Another way to evaluate metaphors is to look for the "four key objects" they imply. (It might be fewer, but it won't be much more than four objects.) For example, the alarm system might have a current value, limits, and a bell. By looking at the objects behind the metaphor, and especially the interactions between those objects, we can get insights into how our system does work and how it should work.

Can Metaphors Be Bad?

You can have a bad metaphor, one that is misleading or flat-out wrong. You will become especially aware of the limits of your metaphor when you want to change the system, but the metaphor just doesn't give you any guidance on that change.

One type of unhelpful metaphor is one that is unfamiliar; "shouting demons" won't help someone who doesn't know what a demon is. (This metaphor is from Oliver Selfridge's early AI program Pandemonium: "One might think of the various features as being inspected by little demons, all of whom then shout the answers in concert to a decision-making demon" [Selfridge+1963].)

A metaphor can be too weak. A string of characters is not complex enough to explain outline mode in a word processor. Or a metaphor can be too strong. For example, the Web is built around pages; many things are contorted to fit into this overpowering model. Finally, a metaphor can be too magical; it just doesn't tell you anything you can use.

The fact that a bad metaphor can be unhelpful shouldn't paralyze you with fear; you just need to be willing to keep looking and change your metaphor when you get a better idea.

Conclusion

A metaphor can guide system design and give you good intuition about what's easy or hard to do.

Identifying a metaphor is a creative process. The struggle to create a metaphor is part of its value.

Don't let a bad metaphor get in the way; you can always use the naive metaphor until the right insight comes.

A good metaphor is a treasure.

References

[Beck2000] K. Beck. *Extreme Programming Explained*. Addison-Wesley, 2000.

[Selfridge+1963] O. Selfridge, U. Neisser. "Pattern Recognition by Machine." In *Computers and Thought*. E. Feigenbaum, J. Feldman, eds. McGraw-Hill, 1963.

Acknowledgments

We thank the attendees at our tutorial at XP Universe 2001; teaching is a great way to learn, and they were a fun group to learn from.

About the Authors

William C. Wake (William.Wake@acm.org, www.xp123.com) is a programmer, author, and teacher. He's the author of *Extreme Programming Explored* (Addison-Wesley, 2001) and the inventor of the Test-

First Stoplight and the Programmer's Cube. His next two projects are an XP evaluation kit and a refactoring workbook.

Steven A. Wake (SWake@earthlink.net) is a software development manager at a large credit card company. Before that, he worked in the development of configuration management tools and in materials tracking. His professional interest is in how whole teams can best work together to develop software effectively.

Chapter 6

A Lightweight Evaluation of a Lightweight Process

—*Giancarlo Succi*

Chicken Soup and Other Recipes

Each time we think about a lightweight methodology, we somehow have in mind the idea that we do not have to follow any bureaucracy: We can just have fun and tell the boss to get lost.

In XP there is a process to follow, but . . . the common understanding of it is that such a process is more likely to be like the rules for playing soccer—just a way to have more fun in the game. Have you ever tried to play a serious soccer game without rules? I am sure that in the end, there was not much fun.

A big part of the rules for soccer concerns timing and measurement: the duration of the two halves, determining when players are offside, and counting the goals. Similarly, measuring helps improve several aspects of the software development process, including:

- Controlling
- Estimating
- Identifying best practices
- Performing postmortem analysis

Measurement also has managerial value. It helps in understanding how the effort is spent, what products and by-products are generated, and the speed at which the software is being developed. All these are essential parts of XP.

So the point is how we can measure in a lightweight way so that measuring does not become the Trojan horse of our heavyweight friends.

The Quest for Silver Bullets

"No silver bullets!" claims almost any "serious" book on software engineering. This is too easy—people are being cheap.

In almost any discipline there are silver bullets. "Do not smoke!" "Align the digits!" "One concept, one sentence!" Just to cite a few.

So in the following sections, I will be unfashionable and try to determine a few silver bullets for measuring XP and agile development.

Silver Bullet 1: Do Not Be Measure-Obsessed or Measure-Depressed—Just Set Your Goals

There is a kind of syllogism. With measures you get numbers. With numbers you deal with math. In math everything is precise. To get anything sensible from a measurement effort, you need to be 100% precise—*false*.

You will never obtain 100% precision in your measurements, nor do you want it—it is too expensive, and you do not need it. Think of the speedometer—it always shows at least a 10% error. Still, you can use it to drive safely and to avoid tickets.

This is not to advocate sloppiness. It is to prevent a sense of impotence or, worse, the imposition of a measurement mania that ends up either rejecting any measure or artificially creating numbers to please the boss.

The good news is that in most cases, what you have or what you can get with a reasonable effort is enough to quantitatively assess your XP practices.

Moreover, you cannot measure everything, nor would it be useful. Vic Basili has coined a cool acronym to describe how and what to measure: GQM (Goal, Question, Metrics).[1] That is, first determine your

---

1. There are several papers on the GQM. A nice one was written by Yasuhiro Mashiko and Victor R. Basili [Basili+1997].

measurement goal (or goals)—say, to get fit. Then ask yourself questions about how to measure your goal—"What is my weight?" "What size is my waist?" Last, determine the metrics that can answer your questions and how to collect them—pounds are measurable with a scale, and inches are measurable with a rule.

Do not measure more—you would just become confused, and, worse, the power of your statistical inferences may drop. Statisticians call this fact the "principle of parsimony."

Silver Bullet 2: Collect the Information You Already Have and Make the Best Possible Use of It

Measuring an XP project does not require setting up a measurement framework. You may already have sources of information around you. Places to look include the following:

- Accounting department
- Defect database
- Customer service center
- Configuration management system

Accounting Department

Often, the accounting department of your company collects information on projects for billing customers, tracking resources, writing off certain expenses from taxes, and so on. The information available can also be quite detailed, especially if your company uses Activity Based Costing.

In certain cases, you may be surprised to find that your company knows with a fair amount of precision who developed each portion of the code, or who fixed a bug, or how much time was spent developing a file or a class. Using this information, you could try to build models of your development speed, linking time to classes and classes to user stories. Note that this is not contradictory with collective code ownership. The fact that everyone owns the code does not imply that we should not record who (or what pair) worked on a certain day on a certain piece of code. We are dealing with shared responsibility, not with alienated responsibility.

Defect Database

It is a good practice during final testing for the testing group to store the defect information for faulty modules in a defect database. We hope that there will not be too many defects to fix, thanks to the continuous integration effort and the systematic testing in place. Still, there will be a few.

Such a defect database serves two main purposes: (1) It provides precise feedback to the development group about where fixes are required; (2) it tracks the defect discovery rate, thus helping predict the residual defects in the system and when the system will be ready for deployment to the customer.

It is common to find in such a database the operating context for the defects, the possible pieces of code causing the defects, an estimation of the severity and the priority of the defects, the time of finding the defects, and, sometimes, the time and the effort to resolve the defects. Such a database contains a wealth of information useful for measuring the overall XP project.

Customer Service Center

It is quite common for software companies to have a customer service center or department. Usually, such an entity collects information on failures of systems from customers and passes it on to the developer as a "failure record." Typically, the failure record contains the scenarios of the failure, its criticality, a timestamp, and a suggested priority.

This is a wealth of data to be used in measurement. We can easily deduce the mean time to failure, which is required to build reliability growth models, which in turn are useful in debugging and deciding when the system is ready to ship. With minimal additional effort, we can determine the defectiveness of the overall system, which is essential in setting and verifying quality goals. This can also be used in comparing the quality of different teams—say, one using XP and one not using XP.

Often, the developers add to the failure record the files or even the classes that were modified as a result of the failure. If so, advanced statistical models can be built relating internal properties of the code to defects. Best practices on code design could be derived. The need for refactoring could be assessed.

Sometimes, details on the time spent fixing the bugs are also available. In this case more detailed models can be built for both development speed and fixing speed. The cost for nonquality can be precisely assessed, making the case for or against pair programming, test before code, and other supposedly useful XP practices.

Configuration Management System

As soon as development cannot be done by a single person, the problem of tracking the development effort becomes significant. Most development teams use configuration management systems. There are very simple systems and very sophisticated ones.

But even in the simplest ones, important information is tracked: the number of versions of each managed entity, usually the file. It has been empirically verified that the number of revisions usually correlates highly with the number of defects. And here we have a situation similar to the one discussed earlier.

We know that if A is correlated to B with $r^2 = z$ and B is correlated to C with $r^2 = w$, the correlation between A and C may end up having an r^2 as low as the product $z \times w$. But still we have some information that may be useful to build models of quality and so on.

I am sure that if you think carefully, you can find many other places where useful data is stored in your company. You just have to sit down and think.

Silver Bullet 3: Automate Whenever Possible—The Hackystat Model

Murphy's Law states, "If something can go wrong, it will!" We should always keep this in mind. (I think that Kent got his inspiration from Murphy when he created XP. Kent, is this correct?) Being lightweight is a way to minimize what can go wrong.

Now that we know that there are three major sources of information to build statistical models, we should question the integrity of the data we have collected. Data reported from the configuration management system is the least accurate approximation of the defects discovered in the system but is also the most integral. There is no easy way to alter it, and it is very unlikely that someone would alter it accidentally.

Data from accounting and customer service centers or from defect databases may have some problems because it is collected by humans, who may have lots of reasons to alter the data. We know that when we are pressed because, say, a deadline is coming—a week ago—and we are working 24/7 to fix the last thousand defects, the last thing we care about is entering the data on what we are doing. Therefore, it would be advisable to use devices for automatically collecting such data. Of course, if we implement XP, this will never happen, but we are humans after all.

Even though there is no way to monitor the activities with 200% precision, an interesting new generation of tools for process control could be exploited. I find particularly enlightening the approach taken by Phil Johnson in the development of Hackystat [Johnson2001].

He started from the consideration that the Personal Software Process would dramatically increase developers' productivity if people would record their data accurately. As we know, this is not the case. However, for most software development activities, people use tools, and from the analysis of what they are doing in the tool, it is possible to determine with a fair degree of precision the activity they are accomplishing. Hackystat takes advantage of this fact, using plug-ins for extracting from the tools what people are doing.

The good news is that most existing tools are customizable, so the development of such plug-ins is not "mission impossible." Moreover, such customization can be often performed in Java, which is well known inside the XP community. Sometimes, bridges between Java and COM are required.

Silver Bullet 4: There Are Lies, Damned Lies, and Statistics (Disraeli)

Now that we have a lot of data available, we need to process it and try to develop meaningful conclusions.

We know that by trying really hard, we can find some subtle statistics that make the data look like what we would expect. In fact, it is very likely that such statistics could not be correctly applied, because their working hypotheses are far from being satisfied.

Now, even at the risk of losing some significant conclusion, I recommend that nonstatisticians apply simple and general tests, which are robust in data distribution and enable understandable conclusions.

The field of statistics offers us some of these tests, such as the Mann-Whitney U test, the Komogorov Smirnov test, the Spearman Rank test, and many others. The problem is that such tests are often too simple to be explained in university statistical courses, so we may not know about them. To this end, I recommend starting with a good book on statistics for social scientists that usually assumes readers have no university math background. Personally, I like the one by Aron and Aron [Aron+2001]. Then, to move on to some nonparametric reference, you can have a look at the book by Siegel and Castellan [Siegel+1998]. While writing this chapter, I found some interesting and well-formatted information at the URL http://www.cas.lancs.ac.uk/glossary_v1.1/nonparam.html.

Linking Everything Together

Altogether, a lightweight measure is not impossible. It can even be easy to achieve.

The first step is to ask yourself what you want to get from a measurement. Do not consider anything that you do not really need.

Then, determine the data you need to accomplish your measurement goal. Often, enough data is already available for simple models, which are usually the most useful, robust, and likely to be current and not prone to error.

Third, look for such data. There are lost treasures in your company: accounting departments, defect databases, customer service centers, configuration management systems, and others.

Fourth, try to automate the data collection as much as possible. Human-collected data is error prone and unreliable because metrics data collection is not a directly productive activity.

Fifth, collect the artifact measures for your software data. There are a few metrics extraction tools on the market. Some development tools come with metrics capabilities.

Sixth, build the models. I recommend using simple statistics. You can build more advanced models on top of such simple models. However, simple models are the place to start.

Seventh, act on the measures you have collected. The models are there to be used, not to showcase how good you are. If you do not use them to improve, say, the prediction of the development speed of your use cases or the defect rate, you are wasting your time. Soon, your boss, your customer, or even your subordinates will find some more useful way for you to spend your time.

If I managed to reinforce your interest in metrics, I suggest that you read the mythical "Fenton and Pfleeger," a kind of cult book for software metricians [Fenton+1997]. It is a fairly short description of a formal and yet not too difficult process to collect and analyze software measures.

References

[Aron+2001] A. Aron, E. Aron. *Statistics for the Behavioral and Social Sciences.* Prentice Hall, 2001.

[Basili+1997] V. Basili, Y. Mashiko. "Using the GQM Paradigm to Investigate Influential Factors for Software Process Improvement." *The Journal of Systems and Software*, Volume 36, Number 1, January 1997.

[Fenton+1997] N. Fenton, S. Pfleeger. *Software Metrics: A Rigorous and Practical Approach, Second Edition.* PWS, 1997.

[Johnson2001] P. Johnson. "Project Hackystat: Accelerating Adoption of Empirically Guided Software Development through Non-disruptive, Developer-Centric, In-process Data Collection and Analysis." Technical Report, Department of Information and Computer Sciences, University of Hawaii, 2001.

[Siegel+1998] S. Siegel, N. Castellan. *Nonparametric Statistics for the Behavioral Sciences.* McGraw-Hill College Division, 1998.

Chapter 7

Circle of Life, Spiral of Death: Ways to Keep Your XP Project Alive and Ways to Kill It

—*Ron Jeffries*

Extreme Programming (XP) asks teams to use a small set of carefully defined practices. These practices provide enough feedback to keep the project on track. XP projects do in fact go off track. Let's see how to keep yours on the rails.

XP begins with about a dozen practices. As teams become experienced with XP, they develop the wisdom to move beyond the basics—modifying practices, adding them, replacing them. For a team that has done all the practices all the time, this evolution is quite safe and quite natural. Any process, extreme or not, works best when it is customized to the specific team, project, and moment. The process is the beginning, not the end.

Sometimes teams who haven't done all the practices all the time find it necessary to change the process—or they just choose to. Depending on their general wisdom and experience, this can work well or become a disaster. You can tune XP safely based on experience. Or if your judgment is good, you can modify it right out of the box and take your chances. Here, we explore each of the XP practices, with an eye to the issues relating to changing them. The best practice, however, is to start with all the practices all the time, until they become second nature. Then try these ideas.

Whole Team (On-Site Customer)

XP asks that the entire team, including a customer who makes the business decisions, sit together. This practice speeds communication by at least an order of magnitude.

Is the Whole Team Practice Essential?

There are teams who think they are practicing XP without it. In my opinion, they are mistaken. Many of the practices could be done poorly, or even not at all, with the team together. When the team is separated, even all the practices together are less effective than we would like. Without the whole team practice, you'll almost certainly have to increase your paper and electronic documentation. You'll slow down, and your flexibility will be reduced. Don't go there.

Planning Game

The XP planning game enables the team to foresee what features will be available when, using the release planning practice. The iteration planning practice enables the customer to steer the project by defining what to do, and what to defer, in each short iteration.

Part of the planning game is the tracking of velocity. This lets the team know—well—how fast they are going. Observing velocity can give an early warning of problems with testing or refactoring.

Is the Planning Game Essential?

The planning game is very important. The planning game is part of the essential cycle of the XP team's process: It defines what will be done, and it provides key feedback between programmers and customers.

My biggest fear in programming is that the team will do good work and yet not please the customer. The planning game can help you ensure that the programmers and the customers are in sync. Don't drop the planning game—it's key.

Small Releases

XP specifies that the software be built in small releases. This cuts two ways. First, we want to release software as early as possible because it gives us the fastest possible return on investment. Second, we want to give our customers as much vision into the project as possible so that they'll grow in confidence and they'll learn by seeing what they're getting. Small releases reduce risk by making issues visible sooner, and they give the team a sense of accomplishment.

Are Small Releases Essential?

Perhaps not—projects have survived without them. However, if you'll do the math on your return on investment, you'll see that the value of small releases is surprisingly high. Without small releases, you'll be less certain about what you are doing, how well users will like the software, and how well it works. Small releases are quite important because they provide valuable feedback.

Customer (Acceptance) Tests

Customer tests (or, as we also call them, acceptance tests) are defined by the customers. Their purpose is to test every story, to provide the customer with confidence that the story is correctly implemented. Customer tests are supposed to be automated and run regularly to catch regressions as the system evolves.

Are Customer Tests Essential?

In my opinion these tests are quite important, indeed essential. Here's why.

- Customer tests are part of the process of defining requirements. They provide an unambiguous statement of what the program is expected to do. Without them, your risk of defects goes way up.
- Customer tests give the customer confidence. Without them, the customer has to rely too much on trust instead of knowledge.
- Customer tests, when they fail, provide valuable input for how to improve the programmer unit tests.

Running without acceptance tests is running out of control.

Simple Design

XP asks that features be built using the simplest practical design. This practice, combined with design improvement, lets XP teams deliver business value from the beginning, rapidly and safely.

Is Simple Design Essential?

Simple design is essential only if you want to go fast. If you go for a more complex design, you'll not be able to deliver features to the customer as quickly. That would be bad.

The team needs to practice and learn in order to use simple design well—we're not asking for stupid design here. But the practice can make the difference between delivering features in months and delivering them every couple of weeks.

Pair Programming

In XP, all production software is written by two programmers sitting at the same machine. Pair programming provides instant review: Every line of code in the whole system is examined by at least two pairs of eyes. Pair programming results in rapid learning, which in turn increases your schedule flexibility: More programmers are equipped to sign up for more stories.

Is Pair Programming Essential?

You can probably survive without it. However, without pair programming, you'll lose flexibility, you'll need to come up with other ways of communicating the design among the programmers, and you'll see a decline in code quality. You won't die, but your project will suffer.

Programmer Tests

Also called unit tests, programmer tests are written by XP programmers for all classes in the system. Typically written in small increments before the corresponding code, programmer tests are upgraded whenever defects arise, and are run before any release of code. Programmer tests always run at 100% on an XP project.

Are Programmer Tests Essential?

Without programmer tests, your development will slow down. They support evolutionary development and the design improvement that comes from refactoring. They communicate important aspects of the design in support of collective ownership.

In short—yes, programmer tests are essential.

Design Improvement (Refactoring)

XP teams deliver business value from the beginning of the project. For teams to continue delivering value, the design of the system must evolve and improve over the course of the whole project. The process of improving the design of existing code is called refactoring.

Is Refactoring Essential?

Refactoring is essential. If a project is to deliver business value from the beginning, the design must be kept clean. This requires continuous design improvement implemented by refactoring. The only way you can avoid the need for refactoring is to be omniscient and perfect. And so few of us are. . . .

It is possible to do too much refactoring. The best way to avoid that is to refactor very frequently and to focus your refactoring only on code for which you have a story. Spend very little time looking for places to refactor that aren't currently the subject of the customer's attention.

It is also easy to do too little refactoring. When you do too little refactoring, new features become harder and harder to put in. The project slows down. This means that a slowdown in velocity may indicate that you are doing too little refactoring. There are other possible causes for slowdowns, such as insufficient testing, which is often associated with increasing bug lists or rework requests.

Paradoxically, if you can directly measure the amount of time you're spending on refactoring, you are very likely doing too little. Refactoring should be such an intimate and moment-to-moment part of programming that you scarcely notice that it's happening.

Collective Code Ownership

On an XP project, any programming pair who sees an opportunity to add value to any portion of the code can do so at any time. Everyone shares the responsibility for the quality of all the code.

Is Collective Ownership Essential?

Collective ownership is very valuable. It's probably possible to live without it; it's just not a very good idea. Collective ownership improves code quality, provides additional review of all the software without the need for explicit investment of time, and makes pair programming much more flexible and effective.

Continuous Integration

XP pairs integrate their code multiple times every day. Paradoxically, the more frequently you integrate, the easier it becomes. The longer you wait between integrations, the more changes have occurred since the last one. This results in more code conflicts between the working pairs, which makes the integration more difficult and more error prone. To accomplish continuous integration, the team must automate the integration process. That's a good thing.

Is Continuous Integration Essential?

To really accomplish small releases, you need the ability to build the system reliably and frequently. To support collective ownership, you need to avoid code conflicts. The more frequently you integrate, the fewer code conflicts you'll have.

Continuous integration isn't always easy. Once you figure out how to do it, it is always beneficial.

Coding Standard

XP teams all write code in the same style. This makes pairing easier and supports collective ownership. The standard need not be comprehensive, nor need it even be written. You just want everyone writing code that looks the same way. (Note that coding standard interacts with metaphor, which follows.)

Is a Coding Standard Essential?

You can probably live without a formal written standard. With good will, you can even let the team evolve to a common style. But I do mean good will: If everyone goes off in their own direction, or if people are inflexible about their favorite indenting style, your code will look chaotic and will be harder to understand. It's easy to pick a coding standard, and I recommend that you do so.

Metaphor

The metaphor practice asks that the design use a simple common system of names and that—if possible—the design should have a simple, easily explained pattern of design, enabling you to say, "The program is like an assembly line" or "The program is like bees bringing pollen back to the hive." A clear metaphor and naming convention reduces the need for documentation, reduces the need for up-front design, and makes pairing and collective ownership easier.

Is Metaphor Essential?

The stronger the imagery you have in your design, the faster you'll go. The better chosen your names, the faster you'll go. You can survive with a naive metaphor and thrive with an expressive one. Avoid completely chaotic naming, strive for consistency, and you'll be OK.

Sustainable Pace

This practice used to be called "40-hour week." It has evolved this far to reflect a more general need, which is to keep the team healthy. The practice means to work hard and to rest when you need it.

I believe that the sustainable pace practice needs enhancement, to cover reflection, retrospectives, and other life-sustaining practices. But for now, about all we can say is to stay healthy.

Is Sustainable Pace Essential?

When you put it that way, the answer is obvious: yes. A death-march project cannot possibly produce software of good quality over an extended period of time.

Conclusion

XP's practices come from many years of experience of some of the industry's best programmers and teams. They are designed to be as light as possible, to provide very high feedback and very intense communication among the members of the team. When you begin your project by doing all the practices all the time, you'll get enough feedback to be equipped to modify the practices to fit your project even better.

Chapter 8

Hitting the Target with XP

—*Michele Marchesi*

Following the Extreme Programming (XP) practice of using a metaphor to help in understanding and naming concepts, this chapter presents the metaphor of hitting a target, to explain the difference between traditional predictive software development processes and XP, a new adaptive agile methodology. The traditional waterfall process is viewed as the attempt to hit the target on the first shot, which works only if the aim is very accurate and the target is fixed. The spiral process can be viewed as firing at the target a series of shots, each more precise than the preceding. Agile methodologies are like firing a guided missile, which is able to track and hit a moving target, provided its sensors and control system are effective.

Modern software systems are perhaps the most sophisticated and complex systems ever designed and built by man. This huge complexity should be managed by following detailed methodologies for software development and maintenance.

This is the field of software engineering, which strives to apply to software development the sound practices of traditional engineering, a method that has proved effective in developing very complex systems.

The development is done through the phases of requirements elicitation, analysis, design, coding, testing, and deployment. The activities preceding coding may take more than 50% of the total cost and time of the project. They must be accurate enough to enable the system to be coded and released based only on analysis and design documents. These documents usually include many diagrams in the Unified Modeling Language (UML).

In big systems, the analysis and design phases may last for years, which is too long, even if requirements are stable. This is called *analysis paralysis.* To avoid this, a strict waterfall approach to software development is seldom applied. More likely, a spiral approach [Boehm1988] is followed, in which the various phases are iterated several times, each time evaluating risks and performing the needed corrective actions.

Even with the spiral model, however, each iteration may last several months, often more than a year. If system requirements are stable—as in the big space and military projects of the '60s, when software engineering was born—the traditional approach enables controlling the development process and obtaining systems that are well structured and documented.

Nowadays, however, we live in the Internet Age. The technology and the market are changing at a speed unthinkable even a few years ago. Consequently, the requirements of software systems are very unstable.

Traditional software engineering simply cannot release software systems on time and keep up with the continual requirement changes of the Internet Age.

Hitting a Target

To better explain the concepts of software system development, I will use a metaphor: Software development is like hitting a target.

The target is the customer's expectations about the software being developed. These expectations consist of having satisfied functional requirements, having the system developed on time, and having sufficient quality and maintainability. If the software system developed meets the expectations, the target is hit.

The target remains fixed if both functional and technical requirements do not change during development. If they do change, we have to deal with a moving target.

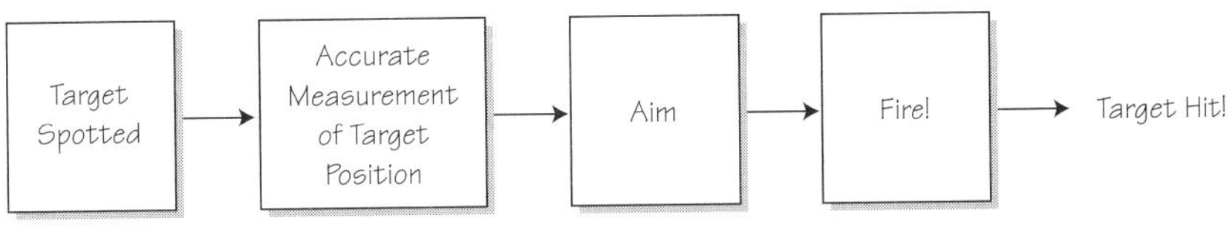

FIGURE 8.1 Hitting a fixed target

Artillery—The Waterfall Model and the Spiral Model

Artillery is suited for a fixed target. An effective way to hit the target is to spend a long time computing its exact position, the wind speed, and other factors and then to shoot a single shell with a heavy gun. With this technique, the target is hopefully destroyed on the first shot (see Figure 8.1).

This is the waterfall approach of traditional software engineering: Spend a long time performing analysis and design, and do the system right the first time (see Figure 8.2).

An alternative technique for hitting the target is to fire a sequence of shells toward it. An observer spots the explosion of each shell, and its position is compared with the target position, enabling correcting the aim and firing a subsequent shell, which is more precise than the preceding, until the target is destroyed. This is a typical artillery technique and may work even if the target is slowly moving.

In software development, this technique is the spiral methodology. Each shot corresponds to an iteration of the spiral process. Each iteration performs risk evaluation, then analysis and design (the aim phase of each shot), and eventually the coding of a portion of the system. The prototype resulting from each iteration does not satisfy all customer re-

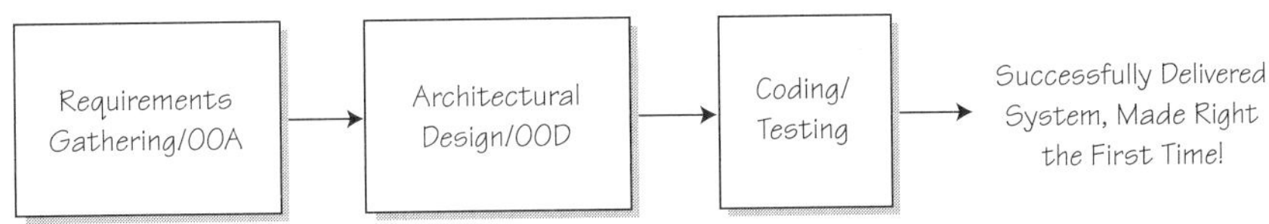

FIGURE 8.2 Traditional cascaded software development

quirements, but each iteration gets closer to the goal. The final system results from the last iteration, corresponding to the last shot, which hits the target.

Artillery works well if the target is fixed. But what about moving targets?

Missiles and Agile Methodologies

Nowadays, in a world moving at Internet speed, the goals and requirements of software systems are continually reviewed and changed, and programmers must be able to hit a moving target. In this case, artillery does not work. We need a guided missile able to follow the target by using efficient sensors, and a feedback control system able to dynamically minimize the distance between the missile and the target (see Figure 8.3). The lighter the missile, the smaller its inertia and the easier to follow the movements of the target, eventually hitting it.

Our goal is to develop software in the presence of changing requirements. At first sight, we could deem that software, being immaterial, should have little inertia. In fact, it is very easy to modify a program: We only have to change the code and recompile the system. Unfortunately, this is not the case. Software systems can be extremely complex and difficult to modify. Moreover, if the development process is heavyweight, as in traditional software engineering, it is not possible to hit a moving target; in our metaphor, the missile feedback control system

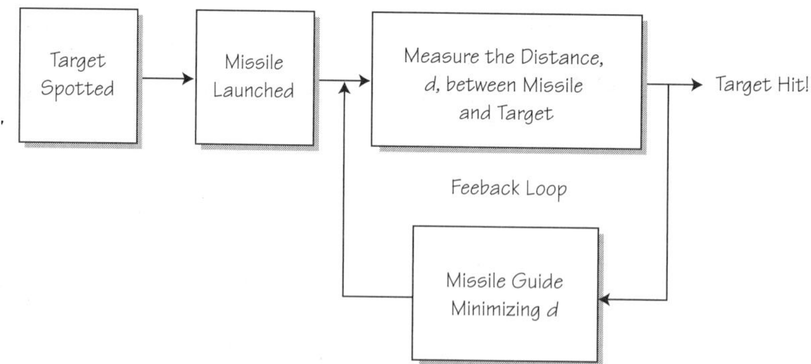

FIGURE 8.3 Hitting a moving target with a missile

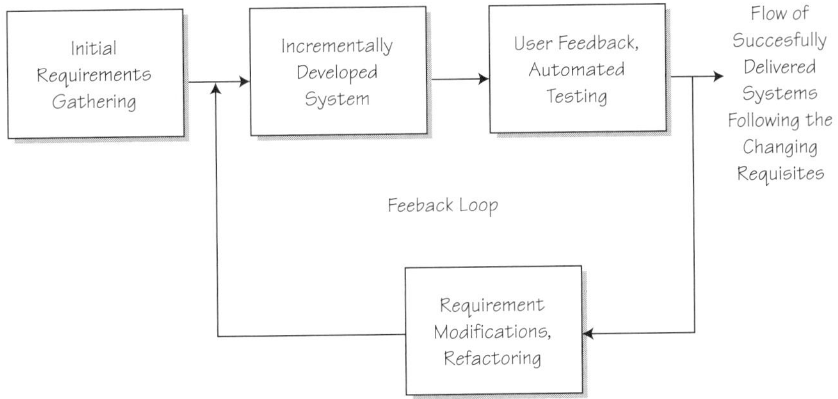

FIGURE 8.4 Developing a software system with changing requirements

(the development process) is so heavy and slow that the target cannot be tracked.

Actually, our goal is not to destroy the target. In software development, hitting the target means developing on time a working system that satisfies requirements. However, because requirements are continually changing, we must be able to hit the target many times.

Agile methodologies are software development processes recently introduced and studied as an effective answer to changing requirements. The key principles behind agile methodologies are reported in the Agile Manifesto [Agile2001].

Among agile methodologies, the most popular is Kent Beck's *Extreme Programming* [Beck2000].

In the rest of this chapter, I examine XP by using the metaphor of the missile. My aim is to help in understanding why XP practices enable us to hit the "moving target" of software development (see Figure 8.4).

How Extreme Programming Enables Our Missile to Hit the Target

The features enabling a missile to track and hit a moving target are powerful thrust, low inertia, good sensors, and an effective feedback control system, able to both minimize the distance between the missile and the target and avoid instabilities.

XP is based on four values and 12 practices. These are the four values, viewed from the perspective of our metaphor.

- Simplicity—A way to keep the missile's inertia low.
- Communication—With the customer, it enables accurately defining the customer's requirements. Among developers, it enables spreading information about the development status, issues, risk, and problems. Communication is at the heart of the sensors and control system of our missile.
- Feedback—The mechanism to manage requirement changes and keep the missile on track.
- Courage—A consequence of the other values. We may consider it the ability to proceed at maximum speed, trusting that our missile will not deviate from its trajectory and will not explode on its course.

The 12 practices of XP are planning game (with user stories and engineering tasks), short cycles, metaphor, simplicity, refactoring, continuous testing, pair programming, collective code ownership, continuous integration, 40-hour week, on-site customer, and coding standards.

Also "The documentation is the code" and "Split business and technical" are key XP practices, even though not explicitly mentioned among the 12.

Let's now examine these practices from the perspective of the missile metaphor.

Powerful Thrust

Our missile can hit the target only if its speed is high enough. From the metaphor, this means that software must be developed efficiently. This is, or should be, a characteristic of every software process and is based not only on the process, but also on the skills of the development team and on the productivity of the software development environment. The practices helping efficiency, without compromising quality, are these.

- *Pair programming.* In XP, all code is developed by pairs of programmers. Pairs are not constant; they continually change. This is an efficient way to review the code while it is being written, to spread knowledge of the system among developers, to protect against people leaving the team, and to keep programmers more focused while they are working. There is empiric evidence that pair programming increases the overall efficiency of the team and the software quality [Williams+2000].

- *Continuous integration*. The work done by the various developers must be integrated daily into the system. In this way, all integration problems are discovered and solved while they are small, and there is no big-bang integration at the end of the project. The technology used must allow daily integration.
- *Forty-hour week*. If developers are tired, their work will be inaccurate and inefficient. For this reason, XP dictates that developers must not work more than 40 hours a week. If overtime is needed to follow the schedule, it is a symptom of other problems, which must be discovered and solved. Working in an XP team, performing pair programming, and following other practices demand attention and concentration throughout the workday. Eight hours of this way of working is enough for everybody and gives a lot of thrust to the development team. This XP practice, together with others, focuses on human factors, which are of paramount importance in all agile methodologies.
- *Collective code ownership*. In an XP team, everyone is allowed to modify any part of the system, even if written by other programmers. Possible errors are detected by automated tests. In this way, when a modification is needed, it can be made immediately, and the development can proceed at high speed.
- *Coding standards*. The code must be written in a uniform style by every member of the team. In this way, every member can more easily understand the code written by other members, and the development is eased.

Low Inertia

Because software is immaterial, it should have zero weight. But this isn't true. In software there is no space constraint as with material goods, so software complexity and module interdependencies are unlimited and can be extremely high. Thus, systems can be very difficult to change and consequently very heavy. XP strives to keep the system inertia (complexity) as low as possible. The practices related to this feature are these.

- *Simplicity.* The system must be kept as simple as possible. Only the features that are actually needed must be implemented, with no provision for possible future reuse. When a new feature is needed, it can be implemented easily because the system is simple and well understood by its developers. Traditional software engineering, on the contrary, strives for reuse, and it is customary among programmers to develop features that could be useful in the future. XP prohibits doing so. This is the main rule for having a system with low inertia.
- *Refactoring.* The system must be continually improved and made clearer, simpler, and less redundant. This process is called refactoring and must be applied whenever the developers realize that it is possible. Automated testing ensures that nothing will be broken by these modifications. Refactoring, too, enables having systems with low inertia.
- *The documentation is the code.* Avoiding big up-front analysis and design and avoiding having many design documents that must be kept aligned with the code are popular among programmers and reduce the complexity of the overall system (documentation plus code). To be effective, however, the code must be simple and continually refactored, and must reveal the programmer's intention.

Good Sensors

To hit the target, we need to spot it and efficiently measure its distance from the missile. From the metaphor, XP provides practices to continually get the requirements from the customer and assess how many features of the system are implemented and to what extent. The practices related to this feature are these.

- *Metaphor.* This is one of the most controversial and least understood practices of XP. It enables better communication between the customer and the developers when they talk about the system. Therefore, it is a way to improve gathering the requirements (spotting the target).

- *Continuous testing.* XP prescribes writing automatic unit tests even before coding. These tests are run very often and are invaluable for detecting whether something has been broken somewhere when the system is modified. Therefore, unit tests are very important sensors for keeping the missile aligned with the target. The acceptance tests, on the other hand, are dictated by the customer and are used to verify whether the system complies with its requirements. They, too, are a feedback sensor, able to track the number of features implemented so far and whether they meet the requirements.
- *On-site customer.* Having a customer on-site who cooperates in developing the system helps clarify the requirements, makes it possible to have instantaneous feedback on the system features as soon as they are implemented, and minimizes the time needed to communicate to the development team the requisite changes. It is a powerful feedback sensor.
- *User stories.* These are short descriptions of the functional features of the system. They resemble use cases, but in general they are more concise. All system development is based on user stories, and each iteration strives to implement a number of them. They are a tool for gathering requirements and tracking the system implementation.

Feedback and Efficient Guide

The control system changes the missile's course, continually reducing the distance between the missile and the target measured by the sensors. An efficient guide should give orders to the missile actuators very quickly. In software development, this is the task of the development process. In XP, the practices related to feedback and the process are these.

- *Planning game.* This activity enables controlling the whole development. Development occurs in iterations, through implementing user stories. The customer chooses which stories must be implemented in each iteration. The time needed by the various pairs to implement the system features they choose is recorded and used to estimate project velocity. Overall, it is a light and efficient way to plan software development.

- *Short iterations.* These are the essence of the feedback. Systems are implemented in iterations, each providing a system with features of business value for the customer. Iterations (or feedback loops) must be kept as short as possible. In XP, an iteration typically lasts from one to three weeks. Only in this way it is possible to efficiently track a target moving at high speed.
- *Split business and technical.* As mentioned earlier, the customer chooses which user stories must be implemented in each iteration. The developers, however, are responsible for estimating the time needed to implement the various stories. The customer and management cannot impose on developers schedules that they cannot follow. On the other hand, only customers can assign business value to the various features. In this way, the system implementation can produce the highest value for the customer, following a realistic time schedule and not pushing our missile off-track.
- *Task-based development.* The user stories chosen by the customer and to be implemented at each iteration are decomposed into engineering tasks. Each developer commits to implementing certain tasks. The task is thus the basic unit of system development and control.

This classification of practices must not be viewed as exclusive. Many practices could be assigned to more than one feature that a missile must have to be able to hit the target. For instance, the metaphor is also a way to improve productivity and thus enhance thrust; the on-site customer is also a feedback mechanism; and so on.

Conclusion

The metaphor is one of the most important and least understood XP practices. It helps in understanding and naming concepts, and improves communication among developers and with the customer.

In this chapter, I followed this XP practice to explain the difference between traditional predictive software development processes and the new adaptive agile methodologies.

The metaphor was hitting a target, an actual problem in military science and a metaphor for many human activities, including software development.

I described how the more traditional approaches of waterfall and spiral development and the new agile methodologies can be viewed from the perspective of the metaphor, and I examined more deeply the practices of XP from the same perspective.

I hope that I helped the reader better understand the values and practices of this popular new methodology for effectively developing quality software.

References

[Agile2001] *Manifesto for Agile Software Development.* http://agilemanifesto.org. 2001.

[Beck2000] K. Beck. *Extreme Programming Explained.* Addison-Wesley, 2000.

[Boehm1988] B. Boehm. "A Spiral Model of Software Development and Enhancement." *IEEE Computer*, Volume 21, Number 5, May 1998.

[Williams+2000] L. Williams, et al. "Strengthening the Case for Pair-Programming." *IEEE Software*, Volume 17, Number 2, July/August 2000.

Part II

XD: Extreme Development—Analysis of XP Development Practices

Extreme Programming (XP) is defined in terms of values and practices. In Part II we explore the practices half of the XP equation. We first explore testing, one of the most fundamental practices, in great depth. We then explore some proposed new practices and extensions to current practices. We begin with an overview of testing by Don Wells in Chapter 9.

Chapters 10 and 11 are written from a quality assurance (QA) point of view. There are many advantages to including the QA department as an integral part of an XP team. The XP requirement of acceptance tests directly reinforces it. First, Lisa Crispen asks the question, "Is quality negotiable?" She answers this and other questions that arise when customer requirements do not include standards of quality. There is a difference between internal quality, which is controlled by the developers, and external quality, which should be driven by customer needs. Quality from a customer's perspective is what happens when your user does something unexpected. Quality is about filling in all the unknowns in the product specification. Quality is about the compromise between new features and well-defined behavior. Lisa Crispen describes why and how to negotiate external quality with customers in Chapter 10.

The collaboration between developers and QA members of the XP team is explored by Michael Silverstein and Mark Foulkrod. The primary job of QA on an XP project has always been to write acceptance tests. Chapter 11 explores the idea that QA may be involved in additional support activities. Increasing the robustness of unit test suites is one such activity. But for QA to become more involved, some compromises must be made. Testers do not always have coding abilities sufficient for using bare-bones unit testing frameworks like JUnit. Suggestions for collaboration between QA and developers are explored, and the requirements for a framework that would allow both developers and testers to contribute to unit testing are outlined.

Shaun Smith and Gerard Meszaros further explore unit testing in Chapter 12. Unit testing with databases and enterprise information sources poses some unique problems. One problem that XP teams often must deal with is the requirement of running tests very often. These tests must run quickly. Some ideas for speeding the execution of unit tests are explored.

In a test-first environment, how do we choose which test to implement next? Allen Parrish, Joel Jones, and Brandon Dixon explore a simple algorithm for ordering a set of tests to maximize the impact of each test on the evolution of the code as it matures. A detailed example of how this works is given in Chapter 13. The authors make a good case for not ordering tests in an ad hoc way.

Once your tests have been created, they need to be maintained. Arie van Deursen, Leon Moonen, Alex van den Bergh, and Gerard Kok present many refactorings targeted specifically for unit test code. "Code smells" are specific things to look for as a symptom of something that needs refactoring. The first half of Chapter 14 introduces many code smells specific to unit test code. Each code smell is also associated with a general refactoring or a test-specific refactoring introduced in the second half of the chapter. Together, the two sections form a broad basis for efficiently refactoring unit test code.

Testing is just one form of feedback. XP thrives on feedback, and that means measurements. Christian Wege and Martin Lippert explore the application of metrics to measure the effects of aggressive unit testing and refactoring in Chapter 15. They use historical data from an actual project to demonstrate how their metric can be applied and to validate their hypothesis. As you will see, they apply this metric to look for potential improvements in the project's process.

In Chapter 16 Julian Higman, Tim Mackinnon, Ivan Moore, and Duncan Pierce address the intensity of working on an XP project. After two years they found that complete immersion in this environment could lead to a decline in personal satisfaction. Everything is by the team, for the team. They became focused on sustaining their project velocity. They seemed to be losing a personal sense of accomplishment. Another problem results from a tight focus on customer goals. Without time to explore, they lost touch with current technologies that could be incorporated into the project. And third, they found that doing spike solutions to get better story estimates often delayed the start of an iteration. The "Gold Card system" was introduced at Connextra to address these issues on XP projects.

Part II

The concept of Design by Contract was originally explored by Bertrand Meyer. At first glance it may seem incompatible with an agile methodology such as XP, but Hasko Heinecke and Christian Noack explain why it could be beneficial to combine them. The controversial idea of scaling XP up to a large team could justify the use of Design by Contract. And although Design by Contract does not contradict XP, there may very well be a more positive statement to make about the synergy of contracts and unit tests. Chapter 17 is a convincing argument in favor of combining XP with Design by Contract.

A "cost of change" curve that rises slowly over time, as proposed for XP, has been a very controversial idea. Does this also mean a change in the cost of fixing bugs? Under what conditions would the "cost of change" curve be difficult to keep low? Pascal Van Cauwenberghe addresses this question in Chapter 18.

Incremental change is different from refactoring. Refactoring is intended to make no computationally noticeable change. Incremental changes add new functionality or change the program in recognizable ways. Václav Rajlich explores a methodology for incrementally changing a program's functionality. The problem is how to propagate those changes throughout the program while avoiding the introduction of subtle errors. Chapter 19 explores such a methodology and includes a case study of a small Java application to illustrate the problem.

Maintaining legacy code is not considered by most as exciting as new development. Programmers in such a situation tend to have low morale and motivation. But does it have to be that way? Charles Poole and Jan Willem Huisman explore the application of XP techniques to exactly this circumstance in Chapter 20. A short history of the Orbix Generation 3 project and how they were able to introduce XP is reported. Their findings are backed up with some metrics taken from the project.

Chapter 9

An Introduction to Testing, XP-Style

—*Don Wells*

Extreme Programming (XP) is based on four humanistic values. These values are communication, feedback, simplicity, and courage. Testing is one incarnation of the feedback value. Testing also indirectly supports communication by providing a practical and precise way to communicate about bugs and specifications. Testing indirectly supports simplicity by enabling merciless refactoring. Testing also supports courage by removing the doubts that are often associated with changes and postponing decisions. This makes testing a very important aspect of any XP project.

Four Types of Testing

There are four basic types of tests on an XP project: acceptance tests, unit tests, performance or load tests, and hand testing or visual inspection. These last two types are not usually mentioned, but they are required on most projects. One distinction that XP projects have is well-defined ownership of the different test types. Acceptance tests and visual inspection tests belong to the customer, while unit tests and load tests belong to the developer. Ron Jeffries likes to highlight this ownership by renaming acceptance tests and unit tests as customer tests and programmer tests, respectively (see Chapter 7). We should note, however, that developers often support the customer's acceptance tests. Each type of test has a specific goal to achieve, but the ultimate goal of testing is confidence that things are going well and courage to make changes when necessary.

Acceptance Tests

The goal of acceptance tests is to check the functionality of the entire system as specified by the project's customer. At the system level, acceptance tests should not include specific knowledge about the internals of the system and are said to be "black box" tests. These tests touch the system only at predefined APIs or GUIs. To be effective, system-level tests often require large amounts of domain-specific data. The customer's involvement in creating this data and specifying system behavior is critical.

On an XP project, the customer is said to "own" the acceptance tests. This serves to highlight the idea that the customers must take time to ensure the acceptance tests are correct. Customers must specify valid and complete tests for the system that they want. Ron Jeffries has proposed the name "customer tests" as being more descriptive of the way acceptance tests need to be created and maintained. Of course, it is the entire team that is responsible for these tests. To create the acceptance tests, the customers require technical support from the quality assurance (QA) people, who may in turn require support from the developers.

Peculiar to an XP project is the idea that acceptance tests are created before the end of each iteration to test functionality that is created during that iteration. Acceptance testing of the software is never put off till just before production launch; it is an ongoing process. Each user story that is implemented will have one or more acceptance tests associated with it. These tests are used to determine when a user story has been successfully implemented at each step of the project. If the acceptance tests do not pass, the user story is considered unimplemented.

The customer is the final arbitrator and judge if the acceptance tests run at less than 100%. This can occur because acceptance tests are often highly biased toward unusual examples. That is, acceptance tests may contain a single typical case for every ten cases that test things that occur only occasionally. The customer is allowed to review the failed test cases and either declare success and release the product or hold the product back until specific cases are repaired. During planning, the customer also sets the relative priority of fixing acceptance tests versus developing new functionality.

Keyboard-capture-and-replay test utilities are often employed to automatically press buttons on the GUI and compare the results. This is a quick and easy solution but is not usually the optimal solution. It is best to implement a strict Model-View-Controller (MVC) architecture to minimize the amount of button pressing required. GUIs that are kept simple require little testing. Make GUIs trivially simple by pushing functionality into the control layer, where it can be tested directly. Testing the system by interfacing directly with the control layer makes the acceptance tests more robust in the long term.

Overall, the acceptance tests inform us when the customer's functionality is working, regression test functionality that has already been finished, and enable the release to production. That is, acceptance tests document and verify system requirements, guard against bugs creeping into the system, and give us confidence to put our system into production on a regular basis. Without acceptance tests, fixing one bug can often cause another bug, and releasing to production is often postponed or attempted only irregularly. On an XP project, the current system is always in a state that is ready to move from development to production.

Unit Tests

The goal of unit testing is to ensure that a particular module does exactly what the programmer intended it to do. Unit tests are "white box" tests. That is, a unit test can be created with knowledge of the unit's implementation. Unit tests are also allowed to call methods not in the public API. One might even go so far as to make a method public just to allow its use in a test. Isolating small units of functionality for validation is what unit testing is all about.

What is a unit, anyway? Most often, a unit is identified as a class or an object. But this tells us nothing when we are not using an object-oriented language, and is not entirely accurate. A unit is essentially one idea, one focal point. Most classes have a reason for existence; the basic idea for the class to exist is then implemented by supporting methods. This is a unit. This one-idea rule also applies to nonobject languages. A unit is a specific idea and all the code that supports it. "Function" is intentionally avoided because that can be misunderstood. Several functions might implement a single idea.

On an XP project, the developer creates the unit tests. Ron Jeffries has proposed that these tests be called programmer tests to reflect this philosophy and responsibility. Many organizations provide separate testers or QA experts to do the unit testing in a "throw it over the wall" style. This works, but within the XP methodology, unit testing is an integral part of the development process and so must be the responsibility of the developers.

Unit tests should always run and score 100% passed. If all the tests always run, then whenever a test fails, it indicates that a problem has just been introduced by the development pair. Unit tests guard functionality in the environment of collective ownership. One of the biggest fears encountered while contemplating collective ownership is that code will be changed by someone who introduces a bug. This doesn't happen if the unit tests have proper coverage. Unit tests also ensure quick and accurate integration. We can always assume that if a unit test fails during integration, the cause of that failure is some incompatibility of code. We can also assume that fixing that test indicates that the integration is now correct. Fixing a test is everyone's responsibility, and whoever breaks a test fixes it. The implications of this simple rule are enormous.

Unit tests enable refactoring boldly and mercilessly. Without unit tests, refactoring must be carried out in a robotic style, with transformations being applied and, hopefully, no mistakes introduced. In the presence of good unit test coverage, refactoring can be carried out with confidence. Large refactorings can be tried out to see just how extensive they are. That is, you can try changing something and reviewing the unit test failures to decide whether you wish to continue and complete the refactoring. If you see from the tests that too much will need to be changed, you can back out the change before too much effort has been invested. This enables exploring very bold refactorings without risk and waste.

In the context of XP, unit tests and code are created together in a symbiotic relationship not seen elsewhere. In fact, the preferred method is to create one unit test at a time and then create code to make that one test pass. There is a rhythm to this method. Test fails, test passes, test fails, test passes . . . When unit testing is done this way, it becomes natural to create the test first, and it ensures that all code will have tests. One of the biggest impacts, though, is that all code created is readily testable. In many ways, the tests are more valuable than the system code. Take extra care when changing test code because a failure has occurred, and never change both test code and system code at the same time. Take small steps during development, allow the tests and code to grow slowly together, and never leave any tests broken.

Unit tests are created to run in a simple framework such as JUnit. One thing to be very suspicious of is unit-testing tools that automatically create the unit tests. Generally, such tools are useless in an environment where the unit tests are created before the code. And more specifically, these tools do not create the harder tests. The 80-20 rule applies here. Automatic creation of unit tests will create the tests that take only 20% of your time. The tests that require 80% of your time will still need to be created with handcrafted code.

If done well, unit tests can keep you out of the debugger, which is a huge time-saver. Unit tests should be formulated to be independent of each other. Each test should set up the state of the system to be exactly what is required for the test to be valid and should not depend on some side effect from a test run before the current test. This is important for debugging because independent tests point to specific areas of failure, while dependent tests can cause a cascade of failures, thus masking the real problem. By creating tests so that it is obvious where the problem lies, it becomes possible to review test failures quickly to gain insight into a problem and fix that problem without the overhead of single stepping into the code. With good coverage and independent unit tests, it becomes much easier to locate and repair problems.

Although unit tests are very important, they are not more important than acceptance tests. It is easy for developers to get carried away with creating the unit tests and ignore the customer's acceptance tests. Both sets of automated tests are of equal importance, and both sets of tests require their own specialized framework. The symmetry of Ron Jeffries' new names, customer tests and programmer tests, should not be overlooked.

Performance Tests

The goal of performance testing is to help quantify the performance and capabilities of the software system. Performance tests may also be called load tests, depending on context and the measurements being made. Developers or the QA department may create these tests to verify specific speed or load requirements of the system. Performance tests are a direct incarnation of the feedback value in that they measure the system directly and give qualitative results about performance.

Performance tests are required to determine whether something needs to be optimized. Trying to optimize without feedback is not a reliable way to optimize. It is easy to optimize in a penny-wise, pound-foolish way. People who claim that something must be coded one and only one way for performance sake are often shown to be wrong when a measurement is made. Having feedback to quantify improvement is critical to quickly zero in on what needs to be optimized.

By-Hand Testing

The goal of "by hand" tests is generally to test GUIs. Usually, such tests are expressed as scripts to be executed by a person clicking on the system's GUI. These tests are created and maintained by the QA department or the customer. By-hand tests are, of course, black-box tests. Because these types of tests are time-consuming to run, by-hand testing must be limited to things that are not likely to break and do not need to be tested often. In other words, by-hand tests should be kept to an absolute minimum.

Visual inspection should be used only where appropriate. Your eyes and brain are highly specialized for pattern recognition. You must consider this specialization when deciding what can be tested by hand and what cannot. Determining whether a GUI is laid out correctly is the domain of the human eye and not the computer. On the other hand, comparing long columns of numbers is the domain of the computer and should not be taken on by hand. Comparing a spreadsheet full of expected results with actual run numbers is not an adequate form of testing. You should automate these types of tests and use by-hand (or more correctly, "by eye") testing only when appropriate.

Testing as Part of Development

Planning and feedback are an essential part of XP, and tests are an essential part of planning and feedback. Acceptance tests define the functionality to be implemented during an iteration. A unit test is just a plan for what code you will write next. Tests give feedback by defining exactly when a task is done. Tests give feedback by announcing when a requirement has been violated. Tests watch over all integration activities and give feedback on integration problems. Altogether, tests form a concrete and decisive form of planning and give enormous amounts of feedback well beyond that which ordinary documents can give.

Create the Test First

One of the biggest changes in testing on an XP project is *when* the testing occurs. You create the test first, not last. This is a difficult concept to grasp at first. We make no apologies for it, because it is worth the effort to learn how to do this well. When a test has been created first, development is driven to completion with greater focus. Less time is spent postulating problems that might not require a solution. Less time is spent generalizing interfaces that may never be used. Unit tests are equivalent to creating a very detailed specification of the code you are about to write. Acceptance tests are equivalent to very detailed requirements documents. The difference is that tests enforce their requirements concisely and unambiguously.

The way to get started coding tests first is to just write a test by assuming a simple interface to some code that does exactly what you need. Do a little bit of thinking first to have a direction in mind when you start. Think about what you could implement simply. If you always implement the simplest thing next, you will always work as simply as you can. Then get into the habit of writing code after the test is run and has failed. The paradox of test-first coding is that tests are easier to write if you write them before the code, but only if you are experienced at writing tests. Just get started and stick with it until it becomes natural to work this way.

Test-first coding does not allow you to be sloppy. To do things test-first, you must decide what it is you want to accomplish and know exactly what it means to be done with it. You plan in advance what functionality is added next. You then design the interface to your code before the code is written. This creates a focused design that is easy to test.

Testable code is inherently more reliable than untestable code, assuming we take the time to test it. If the tests take only a couple of minutes or less to run, we will run them often. An entire unit test suite should take around ten minutes to run. Any more, and we begin to see less frequent integration, which leads to even less frequent integration. To keep the team working in the context of the latest versions of the code, the tests must execute in a reasonable amount of time. Optimize, prune, and combine tests that are taking too long. Subsets of tests are a viable alternative for running often during development but cannot be used for integration and are not as good as running all the tests all the time.

How Much Do We Test?

This is a very important question with a very unsatisfying answer: just enough and no more. Unfortunately, every project is different, and what might be enough for one project may not be enough for another. You must ask yourself and the team members whether your goals are being met at the current level of testing. If they are not, do more or do less until you find the sweet spot, where the cost of adding more tests would be greater than the cost of fixing the bugs that will escape to the user. How many tests are enough is obviously different for each project because the cost of a bug getting to a user is highly variable.

How much we test is variable and highly subjective. Some guidelines are available, though. On an XP project, tests are used to communicate requirements; thus anything specified by the customer should have a test. Remember the saying "If it doesn't have a test, it doesn't exist." Tests are also used as reminders to ourselves about things we had a hard time coding. We should create a test for anything we want to remember about our code. And when we have all those in place, we can look around for anything that looks interesting and create a test for that. We should also create tests as a form of documentation. Anything we want someone else to be able to use can have a test showing how it is used. Ask yourself whether you have enough tests to guard your code from bugs during refactoring, integration, and future development.

It is important to consider not only how much to test but also how much to *not* test. A general rule is to average about as much test code as there is system code. Some code will take many times more to test; other code may not need to be tested at all. We want to test everything that might break, not trivial things that can't break. You don't need to test with invalid data unless it really is possible to receive it. By mercilessly refactoring, we can break our code into independent pieces and test separately with a few tests instead of all the combinations of all the inputs. The idea is to test just enough so that we can behave as if we had complete coverage even when we don't.

Ultimately, test coverage is about courage. We need to release to production, refactor mercilessly, and integrate often. If we are unsure and begin to doubt our ability to do these things without introducing bugs, we cannot apply XP as intended.

Testing Frameworks

It is recommended that an automated acceptance test framework be custom crafted for every project. Acceptance tests generally contain large amounts of data that must be maintained. Being able to input data in a form that relates directly to the customer's domain will easily pay for itself in the reduced cost of acceptance test creation. It is also a requirement that the data be manipulated in ways that make sense from a domain-specific point of view. A framework that encapsulates domain concepts usually requires the team to create it specifically for the project.

Being able to specify input data, a script of actions, and output data for comparison will encourage customers to manage the tests themselves. If the customers can use the tool to create acceptance tests and maintain them, they can begin to truly "own" the tests that verify their user stories. This means that a general tool will not be as helpful as you think it will be. These types of frameworks evolve during the lifetime of the project, and the sooner the team starts to create this framework, the better off the project will be in the long run. You should never try to maintain acceptance test data with a bare-bones language-level framework intended for unit testing.

The Web site at http://www.xprogramming.com has a very good selection of unit test frameworks for most programming languages. Using an available framework as a shortcut can pay off, but only if you take the time to learn it well, inside and out. Not too long ago, everyone wrote their own unit test framework from scratch, but these days frameworks such as JUnit [Gamma+2001] are becoming the standard in testing tools. JUnit comes with instructions on how to integrate it into many different Integrated Development Environments (IDEs).

If you choose not to write your own, at the very least you must get your hands on your unit testing framework's source code and refactor it to the point of feeling ownership of it. Only when your team owns its own test framework can they feel confident and not hesitate to extend it or simplify it as needed. Consider the saying "Your unit test framework is not a testing tool, it is a development tool." Because unit testing is now a large part of development, even a small change to the framework can translate into a big boost in productivity.

Conclusion

Getting started with testing to such an extreme degree is difficult. The key is to just get started. A comprehensive suite of tests is collected over time, not created in the last few weeks of a project. Start collecting them today instead of tomorrow. You don't need to know what you are doing—you can learn as you go. Skipping the tests always takes longer, even if it needs to be done by tomorrow. When you create the tests first, it seems as if you are not making much progress during the first 30 minutes. You will make up for it during the hours that follow when things are still progressing steadily and under control.

It can be a particularly daunting task to have to start writing tests when a large body of code already exists without tests. Don't become overwhelmed. Add tests when you need to fix a bug. Add tests when you need to change something. Add some black-box-like unit tests to quickly cover stable portions of the system. What you will soon find is that areas of code being changed often quickly acquire more than adequate test coverage.

Software that was delivered on time but has so many bugs that it is rendered useless should not be considered delivered on time at all. So often, we see projects in which time is scheduled at the end of the project for final testing. This time is always overrun by development because testing was not performed as part of the development process. The only way to ensure that software remains usable in the future is to test it today.

References

[Gamma+2001] E. Gamma, K. Beck. *JUnit.* http://www.junit.org. 2001.

Acknowledgments

The author wishes to acknowledge the tireless efforts of Michele Marchesi, Giancarlo Succi, Angelique Thouvenin-Martin, and Laurie Williams in preparing for the XP2001 and XP Universe conferences. Without these conferences, this chapter and many other papers would never have been written.

About the Author

Don Wells has over two decades of programming experience. He has built financial applications, military applications, expert systems, cockpit simulators, computer-aided engineering (CAE) systems, and Web sites, and even published a video game. Don has been on projects ranging in size from one to 150 people. He has developed software to run on large corporate mainframes, all the way down to shrink-wrapped software for home computers, and everything in between. He has been experimenting with ad hoc software development methods for many years. He was a member of the world's first XP project, called C3, at Chrysler. He applied XP to a second project, called VCAPS, while at Ford. Don created the Web site at http://www.extremeprogramming.org to share his experiences and serve as a first introduction to XP. He was an invited speaker at the XP2001 conference in Italy, and he has been a guest lecturer at universities. He started the XP Universe conferences and continues to serve as co-chair of the program committee. Presently, Don consults on applying Extreme Programming and agile methodologies.

Chapter 10

Is Quality Negotiable?

—*Lisa Crispin*

Part II

The morning I sat down to start writing this chapter, my contractor called (we're in the middle of building an addition to our house). He told me the painter would apply one coat of paint to the primed siding. If I wanted a second coat of paint, it would cost $275 extra. Higher quality often costs extra. It struck me how often we make decisions and compromises about quality in our daily lives. Shall I buy a Yugo or a Volvo? Eat at McDonald's or go home and cook? It all depends on what I need most—money, safety, time, nutrition.

In *Extreme Programming Explained*, Kent Beck describes the four variables of software development: cost, time, quality, and scope [Beck2000]. As he says, "Quality is a strange variable." If you try to save time or money, or increase scope, by sacrificing quality, you will pay a price in human, business, and technical costs. XP teams have the right to do their best work.

On the other hand, customers have the right to specify and pay for only the quality they need. How does one reconcile two potentially conflicting points of view? Is quality negotiable? If so, how do we go about negotiating it?

This chapter explores these questions.

- ✧ Is quality negotiable?
- ✧ How can we negotiate quality?
- ✧ What are internal and external quality, and are either or both negotiable?
- ✧ What is the XP tester's quality assurance role?
- ✧ How far should testers go in helping the customer define acceptance criteria?

Introduction

When my husband and I decided to put an addition on our house, we chose to include a basement. We signed a detailed contract with our contractor that specified many little details. We thought that we read this carefully. When the basement was built and a hole cut for the door, the contractor pointed out that he had neglected to include the door itself in the contract. We had access to the new basement—it was functional—just no way to close it off if we wanted. Because the door was not included, we would either have to do without it or pay extra.

Naturally, we had *assumed* there would be a door to the basement room that we could open and shut. But because we had not specified this, the contractor hadn't included the price of the door or the labor to install it in his price. We couldn't expect the contractor to just give us a free door. How nice it would have been if someone else had looked at the contract with me and asked, "There isn't a door specified here; don't you want one?" Then I could have decided whether or not to spend the money—it wouldn't have been a surprise later.

I've participated in XP projects where I've seen this type of thing happen. (OK, it happens in all software projects, no matter what practices are used.) For example, the customer has a story for an add screen and just assumes that the developers know he also wants the ability to update, read, and delete. Or maybe there's a story for a login screen with authentication, but nothing about what should happen if the same user logs in twice. At the end of the iteration, an exception thrown by having the same user log in twice looks like a defect.

As a tester and quality assurance engineer of long experience, I'm something of a tyrant about quality. I have my own standards that, naturally, I think everyone should follow. When I started working on XP projects, I realized it wasn't about *my* quality standards—it was the customers'.

Here's an example. Say we have a start-up company as our customer. For now, they just need their system up and running to show to potential investors. They just need a system that's available one or two hours a day for demos. They aren't looking for a bulletproof 24/7 production server. In fact, they can't afford to *pay* for a bulletproof system right now. They'd rather have more features to show off, even if they might not handle a high level of throughput. It would probably take significantly more time and resources to produce a system with guaranteed stability. If the customer isn't willing to pay the price, they can't expect to get it for free.

In XP, the customer's role is to make business decisions, not to be a quality expert. Face it: Some people are always on the "happy path"—just as my husband and I were when we signed a contract with our builder for our home addition.

As the tester, I feel it's my responsibility to help the customer make conscious decisions about quality during the planning process. If the customer is clear about their acceptance criteria, and these are reflected accurately in the acceptance tests, we're much more likely to achieve the level of quality the customer wants, without giving our time away for free.

Part II

Internal and External Quality

In *Extreme Programming Explained*, Kent Beck writes:

> *There is a strange relationship between internal and external quality. External quality is quality as measured by the customer. Internal quality is quality as measured by the programmers.*

He goes on to explain the human effect on quality:

> *If you deliberately downgrade quality, your team might go faster at first, but soon the demoralization of producing crap will overwhelm any gains you temporarily made from not testing, or not reviewing, or not sticking to standards.*

In this light, it looks as if we should always strive for the highest standard of quality. This would, of course, make me very happy. But is the customer willing to pay for it?

I think the important concept here is the difference between internal and external quality. Whenever I meet someone who works in an XP environment, they always tell me that one of the reasons they love coming to work each morning is that they know they'll be allowed to do their best work. If you take that away, XP won't work. It's good to have 100% successful unit tests. In the long run, it speeds up development time. Internal quality should be a given.

External quality can be defined as a set of features. For example:

- Whenever the user makes a mistake, a user-friendly error screen appears.
- It's impossible to crash the server via the user interface.
- The system can handle a hundred concurrent logins.
- The system will stay up 99.995% of the time.

Negotiating with the customer on external quality doesn't mean skimping on acceptance tests or deliberately producing unstable code. It means that the customer asks for a certain standard of quality and pays for it. If they want a system to handle all exceptions, that should be in the story—or multiple stories. Story 1 says to implement this functionality; story 2 says to make the functionality work with *n* concurrent users hammering it.

The XP Tester as Quality Assurance Engineer

The XP books say that the customer writes the test. In *Extreme Programming Explained*, Kent Beck says that customers need to ask themselves, "What would have to be checked before I would be confident this story was done?" This very question implies tests that check for intended functionality, or what my boss calls "happy path" testing.

Beck goes on to say that XP teams should have a dedicated tester who "uses the customer-inspired tests as the starting point for variations that are likely to break the software." This implies that the tester *should* guide the customer in defining tests that will really stress the application. He also mentions "stress" and "monkey" tests designed to zero in on unpredictable results.

In practice, when I neglected to negotiate quality with a customer, acceptance testing became as treacherous as the mud pit that currently surrounds the new wing of my house. I wrote and performed acceptance tests according to my own standard of quality. Naturally, the tests, particularly the load tests and "monkey" tests, uncovered issues. To the XP-naive customer, these just look like bugs, and they're upsetting. The customer starts to worry that their stories aren't really being completed.

The XP way to deal with any kind of issue or defect is to turn them into stories, estimate them, and let the customer choose them for subsequent iterations. We know that some defects and unexpected issues will always crop up. However, to minimize the pain of dealing with these, it's best to set the criteria for quality at the start of each iteration.

Set the Quality Criteria

As the XP tester, ask lots of probing questions during the planning game. If the customer says, "I want a security model so that members of different groups have access to different feature sets," ask, "Do you want error handling? Can the same user be logged in multiple times? How many concurrent logins should the system support?" This may lead to multiple stories, which will make estimation much easier.

Our customers have rarely thought of things like throughput capacity and stability up front—instead, they assume that their intentions are obvious: "Well, of *course* I want to have more than one user log in at a time." The tester should turn assumptions into questions and answers. This way, you don't end up with doorless rooms.

Write acceptance tests that prove not only the intended functionality, but also the desired level of quality. Discuss issues such as these with the customer.

- What happens if the end user tries a totally bizarre path through the system?
- What are ways someone might try to hack past the security?
- What are the load and performance criteria?

As a result of these discussions, you may need to get the team back together to see whether stories need to be split up or new stories written, and reestimate stories to reflect the quality standards the customer has set in the acceptance tests. The customer will have to drop a story or change the mix, but they will be happier with the end result. Higher external quality means more time and more cost! Both a VW Beetle and a Hummer will get you to the grocery store, but if you need to cross the Kuwaiti desert, you're going to have to pay for the vehicle that's designed for the job.

Participate in developers' task assignment and estimation sessions. Testers often have more experience in dealing with customers and a better understanding of what the customer meant to request. If the story is for a screen to add a record to the database, it's likely that the customer also meant they wanted to be able to read, update, and delete records. Get everyone back together if there have been assumptions or a disconnect in understanding. Testers are in a unique position to facilitate this process.

I work in the same room as the developers, pair with them when needed, and participate in the stand-up meetings. At the same time, I try to have as much contact with the customer as possible: We discuss the tests, get together to run them, and look at the results. Testers are part of the development team—much more so than in a traditional software process. But as a tester, you need a level of detachment; you have to be able to be an advocate for the customer and at the same time a guardian of the developers. This can be a lonely and difficult role at times. The beauty of XP is that you're never alone. With the help of your team, you can enhance the customer's satisfaction.

Running Acceptance Tests

The fast pace of XP iterations makes it difficult for acceptance testing to keep pace with development. It's much better to do the acceptance testing in the same iteration with the corresponding stories. If you've ever done "downstream" testing, where you don't get the code until development is "finished," you know that developers are looking ahead to the next set of tasks. It's painful to have to stop the fun new stuff you're doing and go back to fix something you've already put out of your mind.

In our projects, writing, automating, and running acceptance tests are part of each story's task, and estimates for finding and fixing bugs are included in the story estimates. The developers try to organize tasks so that we can start acceptance testing components early in the iteration. This way, we can find defects and they can fix them *before* the end of the iteration. I think it makes everyone happier. Most likely, some defects or issues will still be left over that have to become stories for future iterations, but it's possible to minimize these, and we should try.

As iterations roll along, regression testing of acceptance tests from previous iterations also has to be performed. In an e-mail to the Yahoo-Group extremeprogramming, Ron Jeffries says that once an acceptance test passes, it should pass forever after, so any regression defects for previously working tests must be addressed [Jeffries2001]. Regression testing is when you'll really see the value of automating those tests!

How do you do acceptance testing that fast? That's another topic in itself, but here are some tips.

Part II

- Make acceptance tests granular enough to show the project's true progress. Fifty tests of ten steps each is better than ten tests of 50 steps each.
- Separate test data from actions in the test cases. Spreadsheet formats work well; we've experimented successfully with XML formats too. It's easy to produce scripts to go from one format to another; a script that turns your spreadsheet test data into a form your test tool can use is invaluable.
- Identify areas of high business value and critical functionality. Automate tests for basic user scenarios that cover these areas. Add to them as time allows—don't forget to budget time to maintain and refactor automated tests.
- Modularize automated tests; avoid duplicate code and create reusable modules. For example, if you are testing a Web application, have a main script that calls modules to do the work of verifying the various interfaces, such as logging in, running queries, and adding records. Split functions such as verifying that a given set of links is present in the HTTP response into separate modules that can be reused from test to test and project to project.
- Make automated tests self-verifying. Both manual and automated tests should produce visual reports that indicate "pass" or "fail" at a glance. One way to do this is to write test results in XML format and have your team write a tool that reads the XML and produces an HTML page with graphic representation of tests passed, failed, and not run.

- Verify the minimum success criteria. As they say in the Air Force, if the minimum wasn't good enough, it wouldn't be the minimum.
- Apply XP practices to test automation. Do the simplest thing that works, continually refactor, pair test, and verify critical functionality with a bare-bones "smoke" test.

Conclusion: Delivering Quality

In the abstract, I asked some questions that I've discussed in this chapter. Here's a summary of what I have concluded. Disclaimer: Despite almost a year of doing XP, I have almost as many questions as I have answers. Practice XP and come up with your own conclusions!

Is quality negotiable? If negotiation means a dialog between the tester and the customer to make sure that the customer has clearly defined their quality criteria and that the acceptance tests are written to reflect these, then quality is negotiable. Because you, as the tester, and the customer talk about all aspects of quality, the customer can be specific about what they wanted and perhaps even define stories that address criteria such as stability and performance under load. The developers can accurately estimate stories, and the customer can get the quality they're paying for.

How can we negotiate quality? By asking lots of questions of both customers and developers and making sure that nobody makes assumptions. By making sure the customer understands how XP works and what their role is in the planning game, and knows what to expect in each iteration. By putting a price on quality in the form of story estimates and letting the customer decide what is most important for their business.

What are internal and external quality, and are either or both negotiable? Internal quality is quality as measured by the programmers. XP works best when all members of the team are allowed to do their best work. Internal quality may actually save money. External quality is quality as measured by the customer. The customer has to pay whatever it costs, so the customer should set the standard. The XP team helps the customer do this by telling them how much the criteria for quality will cost, in the form of story estimates.

What is the XP tester's quality assurance role? Help the customer set quality criteria and write tests that verify them. Provide a reality check for the developers. Mentor the developers in testing and quality assurance practices. Developing and testing share a lot of skills but are distinctly different professions.

How far should testers go in helping the customer define acceptance criteria? As far as possible in the given timeframe. Ask all the questions you can think of.

The XP books state that acceptance tests don't have to pass 100%. The closer you come to clearly and completely defining the stories and the criteria for proving the stories work, the closer to 100% success you will have.

Negotiating quality makes the end of each iteration much more constructive and comfortable. The customer is satisfied that the stories were completed. They knew what to expect, and their criteria for quality were met. The developers are satisfied that they did their best work and produced functioning code that is up to the customer's standards. The tester is satisfied that the customer got what they paid for, without the developers having to give away the store for free.

The acceptance test results may prompt the customer to change their mind about what their quality standards are. That's OK, this is XP. The customer is allowed to reduce scope in return for increased quality. We'll negotiate about that in the next iteration.

Part II

References

[Beck2000] K. Beck. *Extreme Programming Explained*. Addison-Wesley, 2000.

[Jeffries2001] R. Jeffries. "New file uploaded," e-mail on extremeprogramming YahooGroup. March 12, 2001.

About the Author

Lisa Crispin has more than ten years' experience in testing and quality assurance and is currently quality assurance manager for KBkids.com LLC (http://www.kbtoys.com and http://www.etoys.com). She has been working on Extreme Programming teams since July 2000. Her article "Extreme Rules of the Road: How an XP Tester Can Steer a Project Toward Success" appeared in the July 2000 issue of *STQE Magazine*. Her presentation "The Need for Speed: Automating Acceptance

Tests in an Extreme Programming Environment" won Best Presentation at Quality Week Europe in 2000. She is cowriting a book, *Testing for Extreme Programming*, which will be published by Addison-Wesley in October 2002. Her presentations and seminars in 2001 included XP Days in Zurich, Switzerland; XP Universe in Raleigh, North Carolina; and STAR West. Lisa can be contacted at lisa.crispin@att.net.

Chapter 11

A Collaborative Model for Developers and Testers Using the Extreme Programming Methodology

—Michael Silverstein and Mark Foulkrod

One of the central tenets of Extreme Programming (XP) is relentless testing throughout the development cycle. In the XP methodology, QA personnel, or "testers," are responsible for interacting with the users to create acceptance tests, while developers are responsible for unit testing of classes, subsystems, and frameworks (components). This chapter discusses a model for collaboration between developers and testers in which testers augment the developers' unit testing activities without additional process overhead.

Introduction

There is no question that a large body of unit tests adds to overall code quality and developer confidence. In XP, the "burden" of creating unit tests has been placed squarely on the shoulders of developers because of the perception that only a developer can create unit tests. The advantage of this arrangement is that it forces developers to think about how their components are supposed to function, often leading to better code. The disadvantage is that developers may cast a less than critical eye on their code and miss writing robust tests. Writing unit tests, regardless of the ultimate benefit of having them, is a parallel development activity that detracts from the overall amount of time available for developers to write code.

In XP, the role of testers is to collaborate with users to derive and execute acceptance tests. Although a very necessary task, testers are often used less than 100% during the early part of the development cycle while they wait for an end-user interface or a special test-specific user interface to become available. This is often exacerbated by XP's Model First rule, which suggests that developers defer working on the graphical user interface (GUI) as long as possible.

Our goal is to bring testers into the process earlier rather than later, making them an integral part of end-to-end development. Doing so implies moving the responsibility for creating unit and integration-level tests for some parts of the code from developers to testers. Enabling testers to participate in early unit testing tasks accomplishes the following.

- Decreases the amount of time required to develop the full body of test cases that serve as the gateways for new product features.
- Increases the amount of time available for developers to create new functionality and refactor code.
- Makes better use of the QA team earlier in the development cycle.
- Engages testers in validating the implementation, as well as the user interface.
- Brings to bear an impartial set of eyes, experienced in the practice of testing and more critical than the code owners.
- Increases the overall efficiency of the team, leading to greater likelihood of project success.

Involving testers in unit testing does *not* accomplish the following.

- Alleviates developers of all unit testing responsibilities. It simply adds another set of helping hands.
- Alleviates testers of their acceptance testing responsibility.
- Requires that the testers become developers, although it does provide introductory exposure to code. We have seen several instances of testers whose involvement with unit testing has led them down the development career path.

Inhibitors to Collaboration between Developers and QA Members

Skills

Testers who perform late-cycle testing typically operate on systems using a graphical user interface, an activity that does not normally require programming skills. As evidence of this, testers usually tend to automate tests by recording user interface interactions, with the addition of lightweight scripting. If we assume that testers do not possess strong programming skills, this raises the question of how we can expect them to create tests that interact directly with code.

Testers need the following skills or abilities to participate in early testing of components.

- Testers must understand the nature of components as service providers. That is, they must understand that components provide services via calls to methods in objects that may or may not require parameters and may or may not return values. This implies the need to understand the mechanics of passing parameters in the form of objects and, in the case of languages like Java, to understand concepts such as primitive types and operator overloading.
- Testers must understand the notion of object instantiation and the mechanics of creating object instances and holding them within a fixture.
- Testers must understand how to perform validation on:
  - Simple and recursive object state. That is, testers should be able to describe a strategy of extracting an object's field (or fields), including those of any referenced objects, as required.
  - Returned values, ranging from primitive to complex objects.
  - Exceptions that are expected to be thrown as a result of calling methods under certain circumstances.
- Testers must understand how to test objects that are distributed on application servers, if that deployment scheme is used. In Java, objects that have been deployed on application servers, such as Enterprise JavaBeans (EJBs), require extra effort to test because the test case is a remote client of the bean and needs to interact with middleware to access it.

One possible answer is to train testers to have the minimal programming skills required to develop tests in the required programming language. For testing Java components, implementing a reasonable set of unit tests would require understanding all or most of type casting, primitive/reference type conversions, exception handling, file access, and other Java syntax and language specifics. Unfortunately, training, especially to the level required to write unit tests, incurs a very high cost.

Rapid Design Evolution

XP is low on up-front design and high on rapid evolution through incremental functionality, refactoring, and feedback through testing. Because code is constantly in flux, it follows that tests need to change rapidly as well. Given this, one might conclude that communication and synchronization overhead between developers and testers as code evolves might add an undue burden on the team.

Test First

An ideal practice would be for testers to develop unit tests and then pass them to developers, who would then create code that satisfies those tests. This is certainly a clean separation of labor but ignores the practicalities of evolutionary design—that is, that the entire set of interfaces for each component would need to be known beforehand, which is not always the way things work out. It also ignores the benefit of the incremental "create test and write code for test" cycle. An alternative approach would be for developers to follow standard XP practices to create a minimal set of tests that validate basic functionality, with testers following up to add a set of tests that validate interesting variations and boundary conditions.

Poorly Factored Code

Poorly factored code helps no one, least of all test developers. Cumbersome component interfaces, side effects, private implementations, large numbers of dependencies, and high object coupling all contribute to overly complex and convoluted component user stories, which make writing tests for those components that much more difficult. Fortunately, applying the test-first approach as a process imperative helps identify design deficiencies, which then contributes to their elimination.

Note: Within the context of unit testing, a "user story" is a story that describes the interactions necessary to validate some aspect of a component's functionality. In this case the "user" is a consumer of the component's services, such as another component or, in this context, a unit test case. A user story may or may not be as detailed as a use case scenario. The level of detail depends on the test developer's familiarity with the component.

Enablers to Collaboration between Developers and QA Members

Test First

Despite the previous reference to "Test First" as an inhibitor, it is also an enabler. XP's prescription to create tests first substantiates the practice of involving testers as early as possible, provided that component interfaces and the tests for them are *designed* before code implementation. By design, we mean creating a reasonably representative set of component user stories from which to implement tests, in much the same way that the code is created to satisfy those same stories. Given the same set of user stories for a component whose interface is clearly defined, it is conceivable that testers could create tests for components before their development, or at least in parallel.

Well-Factored Code

If developers have followed good design principles, the interfaces to their components will be as simple as possible and easy to describe in terms of user stories. It follows that if the user stories are simple, the tests that reify them will be simple to implement.

Tools

Tools such as JUnit provide a framework for developers to create and execute unit tests [Beck+1999]. JUnit requires programming skills and thus is geared more for developers than testers, according to the definition of testers used here. To accommodate the tester skill set, we would require some mediating technology that makes it possible for testers to create unit tests, without the need to acquire deep programming skills, while still supporting the preference by developers to create tests in the language of the component under test.

Requirements for a Unit Testing Tool That Enables QA and Development Collaboration

Because we are augmenting the XP process, our view is that we should not significantly change the way developers perform testing, but extend XP to include testers where appropriate. Any test tool should reflect the same viewpoint.

To promote developer and tester collaboration, a test tool should do the following.

- ✧ Make it possible for testers to describe the services to be tested and what to validate, without having programming skills. In addition, the testing tool should provide a lightweight test definition representation that is rich enough to represent aspects of testing such as stimuli on objects under test, preconditions, postconditions, invariants, expected exceptions, and input data sources, without the need to write test code.
- ✧ Allow developers to continue to develop simply. The testing tool should appeal to developers' preference for lightweight tools and for being able to quickly create test cases as code, preferably in the same programming language that is used for the project. If developers are faced with learning a new scripting language or creating test cases as anything other than code, it reduces their willingness to participate in continuous testing.
- ✧ Have built-in test behavior that testers can leverage to create better tests faster. This is important because we do not want to require testers to become bogged down in implementing test-specific infrastructure.
- ✧ Enable developers and testers to share their automated test assets so that each group can reference, use, and expand on the other's work. These automated test assets become the common currency of exchange between the two groups. There will be cases where testers create tests to be used by developers and where testers need to integrate more code-intensive tests as provided by developers. A tool should promote back-and-forth sharing and reuse.
- ✧ Facilitate brief and concise problem reports so that any problem can be expressed by referencing one or more automated test cases. Now that developers and tests can share a common set of test cases, it is possible to specify problem reports in terms of an automated test case. For example, "If you run *x* test, it will fail with *y* results."

Example Unit Testing Tool

We have created a unit testing tool called *Test Mentor* that embodies many, if not all, of the previous requirements. Although it is a commercial tool, the principles outlined as follows are general enough to be applicable anywhere.

Test Representation

We chose to provide a dual representation for tests. For developers, code is the representation of choice. For testers, we developed a representation that enables them to describe test cases without writing code.

Developer Test Representation

At the highest level, tests are composed of *suites*, which in turn are composed of test assets. Suites are physically represented as classes within a test hierarchy. Test assets are represented by methods.

Integration with JUnit

To support developers who are already comfortable with developing tests with JUnit, we chose to integrate the JUnit and Test Mentor frameworks rather than substantially changing the way developers work.

Changing the superclass of `junit.framework.TestCase` to inherit from Test Mentor's hierarchy makes all JUnit tests visible to Test Mentor without the need to change the tests themselves. Test Mentor also provides a means to register JUnit tests as Test Mentor assets available for reuse by testers.

Test Representation for Testers

The representation of a test for a tester takes one of two forms:

- An XML description of the complete test.
- A visual representation that testers edit through a specialized GUI. The visual representation is saved as Java code, although this is transparent to the user.

These representations are robust enough to represent instantiation, interaction, and validation, as described earlier.

The representation for testers adds the notion of a *test step*. A test step is the unit of greatest granularity and is modeled after the notion of intelligent test artifacts [Silverstein2000]. Test Mentor provides a number of step types, each providing its own specific behavior, such as the following.

- Calling methods and constructors
- Setting/getting fields
- Iterating over test data
- Referencing test assets (asset reuse)
- Sequencing other test steps
- Running a piece of Java code (script)
- Recursively extracting object state
- Validation (assertion-like behavior)
- Accessing distributed objects such as EJBs or through distribution schemes such as RMI or CORBA

Testers use the editing tools provided by Test Mentor to organize steps in a particular order and configure steps to operate on target objects.

Test steps are configured through common properties such as the following.

- Name and description (documentation)
- Expected exception (class of exception expected to be thrown by executing the step)
- Iterations (number of times to execute the step)
- Performance criterion (maximum time the step should take to execute)
- Precondition (step to execute as a precondition; similar to the setup method in JUnit)
- Postcondition (step to execute as a postcondition; similar to the teardown method in JUnit)
- Failure (step to execute if the owning step fails for any reason)
- Invariant (step to execute, which performs an assertion on some state that is assumed to be true under all circumstances)
- Maximum execution time

All of these common properties except for "name" are optional, which reduces the overhead of step configuration. Individual step types have their own configuration properties.

For example, a *method step* is a type of step that calls a method. A method step is configured by the method name, the receiver (usually the object under test, known as a *test subject*), and any parameters. In this case the tool GUI provides lists of available methods in the class or provides a way for the tester to specify a method that does not yet exist in a class that may or may not yet exist. Figure 11.1 shows the part of the tool user interface for configuring a method step.

The execution framework takes care of the underlying details of assembling parameters and handling returned values.

To instantiate an object, Test Mentor provides a step similar to the previous called a *constructor step*. Users configure constructor steps by selecting a constructor from a list and specifying the required parameters. When a constructor step is executed, it returns an instance of the object in question.

In the case of remote objects, such as EJBs, access is provided by special steps called *EJB steps* that encapsulate the mechanics of remotely accessing an EJB on an application server. All the tester needs to know to test an EJB is the name that the bean has been registered under and its type (interface) as well as certain deployment-specific properties such as application server address and port. From the perspective of a tester, an EJB step performs exactly the same way as a constructor step (it returns an object) and can be used interchangeably. The tool hides the fact that what is actually returned is a stub for a remote object.

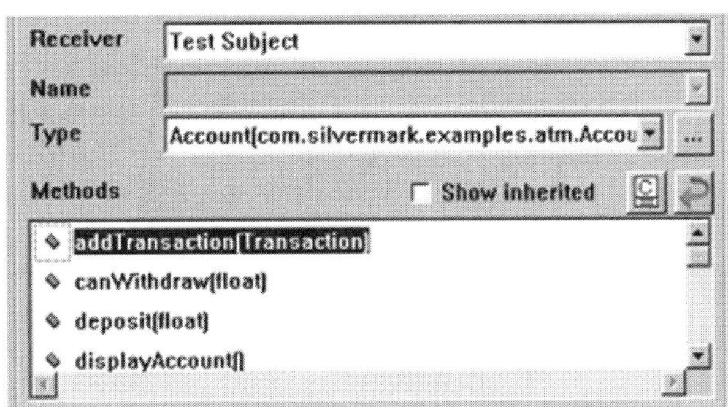

FIGURE 11.1 Configuring a step to call a method

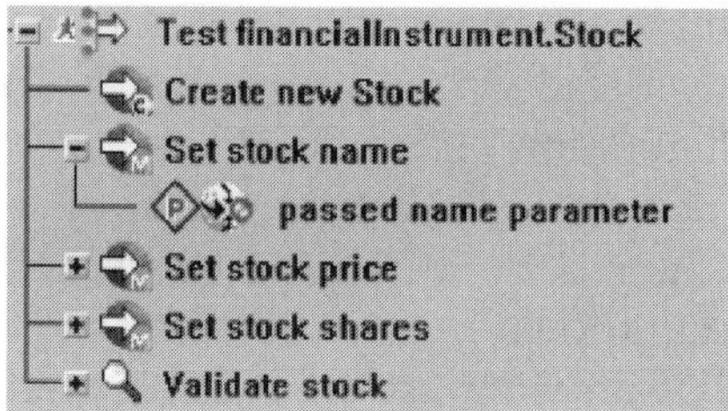

FIGURE 11.2 A sequence of steps

Sequences of steps are organized as tests to create, apply stimuli to, and validate the component under test. Figure 11.2 shows a simple test asset (named "Test `financialInstrument.Stock`") that creates an instance of a `financialInstrument.Stock` class, calls several methods, and then validates the state of the object.

Finally, test assets can be reused through a type of step called a *shortcut step*. These steps are configured by specifying the name of a target suite and an asset within it. Because assets can be parameterized, and steps can be passed as parameters, there are few limits on the way tests can be composed and reused.

Universal User Interface

One of the side benefits of the availability of a visual test composition facility is that it provides a universal user interface for interacting with arbitrary objects, as shown in Figure 11.3.

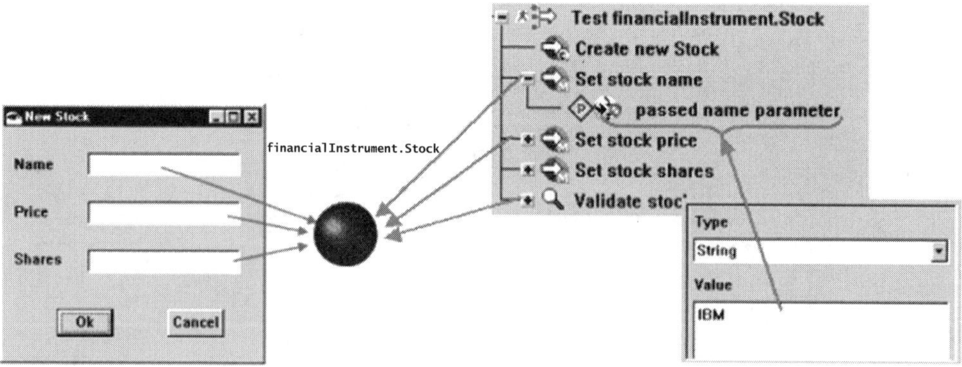

FIGURE 11.3 End-user interface and visual test steps operating on an object under test

The visually composed test steps stand as a surrogate for a user interface. A user interface might be the final end-user interface or one created solely for the benefit of testing.

More detail about Test Mentor is beyond the scope of this chapter. To summarize, Test Mentor is an example of a tool that enables developers to create unit tests as they always have—as code—and a visual representation that enables testers to define unit tests without requiring programming skills, the end goal being collaboration and sharing between the two groups during early testing.

Collaboration Relationship between Developers and QA Members

With skills removed as an inhibitor to early tester involvement, we can then concentrate on the working relationship between developers and testers according to the following guidelines.

- Attach a tester to one or more working pairs of developers to collaborate on creating user stories for the components. The testers then use those user stories as input to creating unit tests.
- In creating user stories, the dialog between developers and testers maintains the benefit to developers of forcing them to think about how to test their components just as current XP practices suggest, but under the critical guidance of a tester. This helps developers think like testers and helps testers understand component implementation and risks.
- Given a component user story, the tester is responsible for the mechanics of creating and validating the test, except for cases in which a test might require elaborate scripting beyond the abilities of a tester or their tool's test representation scheme.
- Regardless of who creates a unit test, it is always the responsibility of developers to ensure that their code passes all available tests before release into a new build. That is, test execution remains the responsibility of the developers.

Practicalities

We would not be foolish enough to suggest that testers should, or even could, create the full body of unit tests to validate a nontrivial application.

Tester involvement stands the greatest likelihood of success in areas of the system under development where interfaces are clearly defined ahead of time. Subsystems and frameworks that are provided for the benefit of other subsystems typically fall under this umbrella. They provide a well-defined set of services that can be described by user stories that are not likely to change a great deal from moment to moment. The key is to be able to describe the services provided by the components under test beforehand so that developers and testers can create their assets relatively independently.

Tester involvement is less applicable where code interfaces are highly volatile, such as in private or helper classes. These classes tend to spring into existence and evolve rapidly as code is written or refactored, and thus possess interfaces that are difficult to anticipate. Developers will want the flexibility to create and alter code as needed without the communication overhead of notifying testers of changes and additions.

Some tests or parts of tests will not be practical for testers to write because they require more expressiveness than the tester or the test representation's capabilities can provide. In such cases it is reasonable to expect testers to pass these tests back to the developer. Sometimes it is sufficient for a developer to provide one or more code-based utilities for testers to use. This is a truly collaborative relationship that benefits both parties.

Project Scale

Developer and tester collaboration tends to become more practical as project scope and scale increase. Smaller projects tend to be more inwardly focused, in terms of both component interfaces and developer perspective. Larger projects tend to be composed of groups of smaller teams that provide subsystems for consumption by other teams on the project. These subsystems' interfaces are perfect candidates for tester involvement.

Case Study

Consider a particular implementation of the described XP process augmentation.

A company, "C," moved from a traditional development process toward XP. After successful early product iterations, time pressures and perhaps a reluctance to spend time creating tests bore down on the developers, and they began to do less unit testing. The QA team, recognizing lower quality levels in the code they were receiving, decided to step in to provide testing. The team adopted the following guidelines.

- The team standardized on the use of both JUnit and Test Mentor for unit testing. They took advantage of Test Mentor's integration with JUnit and the ability to enable testers to create unit tests simply.
- Each day the development and QA team conducts a stand-up meeting in which testers and developers coordinate which tests are going to be needed to validate components. If it turns out that a tester is too loaded with work to be able to supply a test to a developer within the required time, the developer takes on that test development task.
- Once a component is identified and its interface is defined, the developers involved sit down with a tester and define a set of component user stories. At this time they perform light design of the tests to identify which tests should be developed by the tester and which ones by developers. Often, this dialog identifies design decisions that hamper testability, which may then result in redesign or refactoring of the component in question.
- Developers create unit tests for lower-level and implementation-dependent component functionality. This functionality typically is not part of the component's public interface.
- For distributed components such as EJBs, developers are responsible for deploying the components on an application server and notifying the testers of how to access them.
- As the end-user interface becomes available, testers transition into a more traditional role of validating at that level.

Observed Results

The quality of unit tests, as shown by Test Mentor's code coverage profiling, has improved because of the dialog between testers and developers in designing those tests, and as a consequence, the quality of the code under test has also improved.

Despite their general reluctance to create tests, the developers are perfectly happy to run tests created by testers, as a gateway to code release. An unanticipated but beneficial side effect is that developers tend to be more inclined to build on existing tests created by testers than to create and organize tests completely from scratch.

Testers have a higher rate of use (they are more consistently occupied) throughout the development process.

Conclusion

Testers can augment developer unit testing activities by acquiring either programming skills or tools that present a simple test representation.

Tester participation in early testing is most practical where component interfaces are well defined before coding.

Allowing testers to wait until a user interface is available to test with may not be as efficient as possible. When testers help developers create unit tests, they speed product delivery, deepen the collaborative atmosphere between developers and testers, and increase the quality of the tests themselves.

References

[Beck+1999] K. Beck, E. Gamma. *Test Infected: Programmers Love Writing Tests.* http://junit.sourceforge.net/doc/testinfected/testing.htm. 1999.

[Beck2000] K. Beck. *Extreme Programming Explained.* Addison-Wesley, 2000.

[Binder2000] R. Binder. *Testing Object-Oriented Systems.* Addison-Wesley, 2000.

[Jeffries2000] R. Jeffries. *Model First.* http://c2.com/cgi/wiki?ModelFirst. 2000.

[Silverstein2000] M. Silverstein. Automated Testing of Object Oriented-Components Using Intelligent Test Artifacts. Proceedings of the Thirteenth International Software & Internet Quality Week. May 30–June 2, 2000.

Acknowledgments

The authors would like to thank the colleagues who provided comments on this chapter and especially the clients who provided encouragement and experiences.

About the Authors

Michael Silverstein is lead architect and a cofounder of SilverMark, Inc. (http://www.silvermark.com), a leading provider of automated testing tools for object-oriented systems. He has been developing software since 1980, in the last ten years using object-oriented techniques, specializing in Java and Smalltalk automated testing tools. Before founding SilverMark, Michael developed a wide variety of applications at IBM and was a member of the VisualAge development team. Michael has published and presented on a number of automated testing and tools topics. Michael can be reached at msilverstein@silvermark.com.

Mark Foulkrod is product manager and a cofounder of SilverMark, Inc. He has been developing software since the early 1990s, using object-oriented techniques, specializing in Java and Smalltalk automated testing tools. Before founding SilverMark, he developed applications at IBM, and formed and led the first automated testing team for IBM's VisualAge product line. Mark has published and presented on a number of automated testing and tools topics. Mark can be reached at mark@silvermark.com.

Chapter 12

Increasing the Effectiveness of Automated Testing

—Shaun Smith and Gerard Meszaros

This chapter describes techniques that can be used to reduce the execution time and maintenance cost of the automated regression test suites that are used to drive development in Extreme Programming (XP). They are important because developers are more likely to write and run tests, thus getting valuable feedback, if testing is as painless as possible. Test execution time can be reduced by using an in-memory database to eliminate the latency introduced by accessing a disk-based database or file system. This chapter also describes how the effort of test development can be reduced by using a framework that simplifies setup and teardown of text fixtures.

Introduction

Automated testing is a useful practice in the toolkit of every developer, whether they are doing XP or more "traditional" forms of software development. The main drawing card is the ability to rerun tests whenever you want reassurance that things are working as required. However, for tests to provide a developer with this valuable feedback, they have to run relatively quickly. On a series of Java projects building business systems, we have found that running large numbers of JUnit tests against a relational database is normally too slow to provide the kind of rapid feedback developers need. As a result we have developed a collection of techniques, practices, and technologies that together enable us to obtain the rapid feedback developers need even when a relational database underlies the system under construction.

Developer Testing Issues

XP is heavily reliant on testing. Tests tell us whether we have completed the implementation of some required functionality and whether we have broken anything as a result. On an XP project without extensive design documentation, the tests, along with the code, become a major means of communication. It is not just a case of letting "the code speak to you." The tests must speak to you as well. And they should be listened to over and over again.

Slow Test Execution

Because we rely so heavily on tests to guide development and report on progress, we want to be able to run tests frequently for feedback. We have found that it is essential for tests to execute very quickly; our target is under 30 seconds for the typical test run.

A purely economic argument is compelling enough by itself. Assuming a developer runs the test suite every ten minutes while developing, they will have run the suite 24 times in a single four-hour programming session. A one-minute increase in test execution time increases development time by 10% (24 minutes)! But the result of slow tests is even more insidious than the economic argument insinuates.

If test execution is too slow, developers are more likely to put off testing, and that delays the feedback. Our preferred model of development is making a series of small changes, each time running the appropriate test suite to assess the impact of the change. If tests run slowly, developers will likely make a number of small changes and then take a "test timeout" to run the tests. The impact of this delayed use of tests is twofold. First, debugging becomes more difficult because if tests fail after a series of changes, identifying the guilty change is difficult. Developers may even forget they made some changes. Murphy's Law says that this forgotten change will most likely be the source of the failing tests.

Second, if tests take so long to run that a developer leaves their desk while a test suite runs, their train of thought will likely be broken. This routine of starting a test suite and then getting up for a stretch and a chat was observed regularly on one project. The lengthy test suite execution time was due to the large number of tests and the relational database access required by each test. This combination became a recurring pattern on a number of projects.

Expensive Test Development

Given the test-first approach taken by XP, the cost of writing and maintaining tests becomes a critical issue. Unit tests can usually be kept fairly simple, but functional tests often require large amounts of fixture setup to do even limited testing. On several projects, we found that the functional tests were taking large amounts of time to write and needed considerable rework every time we added new functionality. The complex tests were hard to understand in part because they contained too much necessary setup. We tried sharing previously set-up objects across tests, but we also found it difficult to write tests that did not have unintended interactions with each other.

Possible Solutions

Business systems need access to enterprise data. In traditional business systems, queries are made against databases for such data. In testing such systems, we have experienced slow test execution because of the latency of queries and updates caused by disk I/O. The time to execute a single query or update may be only a fraction of a second, but we have often had to do several such queries and updates in each test as text fixtures are set up, tests are performed, and test fixtures are torn down.

Running Fewer Tests

One way to reduce the time required to obtain useful feedback is to limit the number of tests that are run. The JUnit Cookbook describes how to organize your tests so that subsets can be run. Unfortunately, this strategy suffers from the need for developers to choose an appropriate subset of the tests to use. If they choose poorly, they may be in for a nasty surprise when they run the full test suite just before integration.

Nevertheless, there is value in these techniques. The key challenge is to know which tests to run at a particular time.

Faster Execution Environment

Another approach is to increase test execution speed by using faster hardware, dedicated IP subnets, more or better indexes for the database, and so on. However, these techniques tend to yield percentage increases, while we need guaranteed improvements measured in orders of magnitude.

In-memory Testing

Because the problem preventing running many tests is the time required to query or update a database, the ideal solution is to somehow avoid having to do this whenever possible. Another approach is to continue to perform queries but to replace the database with something faster. We have replaced a relational database with a simple in-memory "object database." To obtain rapid feedback from test suites, developers run against the in-memory database while coding. The development process focuses on the use of in-memory testing during development and then switches to database testing before a task is integrated and considered complete.

Although our experiences are with relational databases, this approach could also be used to speed up testing with object databases or simple file-based persistence.

In-memory Testing Issues

The challenges for running tests faster by running them in memory are these.

- How do you eliminate the database access from the business logic? This requires *separation of persistence from business logic*, including *object queries.*
- How do you know which tests can run in memory? And how do you know which tests can only be run against a real database? We use standard JUnit test packaging conventions, and aggregate tests capable of being run in memory in a separate test suite from those that require a database.

- How do you specify whether they should be run in memory on a particular test run? This requires *dynamic test adaptation*.
- How do you deal with configuration-specific behavior? This requires *environment plug-ins*.

Separation of Persistence from Business Logic

Switching back and forth between testing in memory and against a database is possible only if application code and tests are unaware of the source of objects.

We have been building business systems using a "Business Object Framework" for about five years in both Smalltalk and Java. The objective of this framework is to move all the "computer science" out of the business logic and into the infrastructure. We have moved most of the "plumbing" into service provider objects and abstract classes from which business objects can inherit all the technical behavior. The technical infrastructure incorporates the Toplink Object/Relational (O/R) mapping framework. Toplink is primarily responsible for converting database data into objects and vice versa. It eliminates the code needed to implement these data/object conversions (which means no SQL in application code), and it does automatic "faulting" into memory of objects reached by traversing relationships between objects. This eliminates the need for having explicit "reads" in the business logic.

In essence, Toplink makes a JDBC-compliant data source (such as a relational database) look like an object database. Our infrastructure makes persistence automatic, which leaves developers to focus on the business objects in an application and not on the persistent storage of those objects. By removing all knowledge of persistence from application code, it also makes in-memory testing possible.

This approach is described in more detail in [Meszaros+1998].

Querying (Finding Objects by Their Attributes)

If applications access relational databases, querying by using table and column names, then replacing a relational database with an in-memory object database becomes problematic because an in-memory database contains objects, not tables. How do you hide the different sources of objects from the application, especially when you need to search for specific objects based on the values of their attributes?

Solution: Object Queries

All queries are performed against the objects and their attributes, not against the underlying database tables and columns. Toplink's query facility constructs the corresponding SQL table/column query for queries specified using objects and attributes. Application code is unaware of where and how objects are stored—which provides for swapping the "where and how" between an in-memory and a relational database.

Our initial approach to querying was to move all database queries into "finder" methods on `Home` (class or factory) objects. But to support both in-memory and database querying, we had to provide two implementations of these finder methods: one that used Toplink's query facility against a relational database and another that used the API of the in-memory database to perform the query.

We quickly tired of having to implement queries twice and have now implemented support for the evaluation of Toplink's object/attribute queries against our in-memory database. With this technology, the same query can be used to find objects in our in-memory object database or can be translated into SQL to be sent to a relational database.[1]

Configuration-Specific Behavior

When testing in memory, how do you handle functional features of databases, such as stored procedures, triggers, and sequences?

Solution: Environment Plug-ins

The functional features of databases can be implemented in memory by environment plug-ins (*Strategy* [Gamma+1995]). Each function provided by the database has a pair of plug-ins. When you test with a database, the database version of a plug-in simply passes the request to the database for fulfillment. The in-memory version of the plug-in emulates the behavior (side effects) of the database plug-in.

In a relational database, a sequence table may be used to generate unique primary key values. The in-memory version of the plug-in keeps a counter that is incremented each time another unique key is requested.

---

1. Since this technology was developed, Toplink has incorporated limited support for queries that run against its in-memory cache. This is a step in the right direction but does not yet address all our testing needs.

Stored procedures can be particularly problematic when you build an interface to an existing (legacy) database. On one project, we had to create an account whose state was initialized by a stored procedure. During in-memory testing, the state was not initialized, so business rules based on the account's state failed. We could have added code to set the state during the account object initialization, but we did not want to have any code specific to testing in the production system. We were able to avoid this using an `InMemoryAccountInitializationStrategy` that performed the required initialization during in-memory testing and a *Null Object* [Woolf1997] that did nothing when the database's stored procedure initialized the state.

Because an in-memory plug-in may behave differently than the database functionality it replaces, it is still necessary to run the tests against the database at some point. In practice, we require a full database test before changes are permitted to be integrated.

Environment Configuration

How and when do you set up the test environment with the appropriate configuration-specific behavior? How do you decide which environment to use for this test run?

Solution: Dynamic Test Adaptation

We use test decorators to specify whether the test environment should be in-memory or database. Using this technique, we can choose to run a test in memory for maximum speed, or we can run the test against the database for full accuracy. One hitch is the fact that you can choose to run all the tests, just the tests for a package, just the tests for a class, or just a single test method. To ensure that the tests run in the right environment regardless of how they are invoked, we have added methods to our `TestCase` base class that push the decorators down to the individual test instance level.

On a recent project, we created two Java packages: one containing tests that could only be run in memory (because the O/R mappings were not yet complete) and one for multimodal tests (tests that could be run either in memory or against a database.) As the project progressed, tests were moved from the in-memory test package to the multimodal test package. Combining this organizational scheme with dynamic test adaptation, we were able to run the multimodal tests against either the in-memory or the relational database.

Optimizing Test Development

The JUnit test life cycle specifies setting up a test fixture before a test and tearing it down afterward. But we found that many of our functional tests depended on a large number of other objects. A test can fail if it depends on a previous test's side effects, and those effects can vary, depending on a test's success or failure. We divided the objects used by a test into three groups.

- Objects referenced but never modified. These *shared objects* can be set up once for all tests.
- Objects created or modified specifically for a test. These *temporary objects* must be created as part of each test's setup.
- Objects created, modified, or deleted during the test.

We made it a hard-and-fast rule that tests could not modify any shared objects, because to do so makes tests interdependent, which in turn makes tests much harder to maintain.

Shared Test Objects

In database testing, these shared objects would be the initial contents of the database before any testing started. How do you ensure that the shared objects are available in both in-memory and database testing modes?

Solution: In-memory Database Initializer

For in-memory testing, we define an `Initializer` object, whose responsibility is to create all the objects necessary to replicate the expected static database contents. The test infrastructure delegates to it to ensure that these objects are created before any tests need them.

If there is an existing legacy database, testing can be performed before the database O/R mappings are in place by manufacturing objects in memory that correspond to legacy data and placing them in the in-memory database.

When we are building applications that require a new database, an in-memory database can be populated with objects created by the `Initializer`. When the database schema is finally defined, the `Initializer` can be run with persistence enabled. The objects created by the `Initializer` are automatically written to the database to create the initial database content.

Temporary Object Creation

At any one time, several developers may be running the same tests. We need to ensure that the tests don't interact either with themselves or with other tests. How can we ensure that newly created objects have unique keys and contain all data required to make them valid? How can we ensure that several instances of the same test being run from several workstations aren't using the same values for keys, thus causing transient test failures?

Part II

Solution: Anonymous Object Creation

We created a `TestScenarioManager`, which is the hub of all test object creation. Whenever a new kind of object is needed for a test, a `createAnonymousXxxx()` method is added (with any arguments required for customization). These methods create a fully formed object that may be used in tests without worrying about details like unique-key constraints and unintended test interactions—generated identifiers that are guaranteed to be unique.

Temporary Object Cleanup

Tests may create many new objects. Depending on where a test failed, the objects to be cleaned up could vary significantly. How can you ensure that all the temporary objects are cleaned up properly without having to write complex teardown logic?

Solution: Automatic Fixture Cleanup

To simplify teardown, each `createAnonymousXxxx()` method registers the newly created object as a transient object that needs to be deleted. Each test inherits a teardown method from our `TestCase` base class that automatically deletes all the registered test objects. This eliminates the need to write any test-specific teardown code. The test need only ensure that any objects it creates as part of the testing logic (as opposed to fixture setup) are also registered for automatic removal.

Results

Reduced Test Execution Time

We have been able to run test suites of up to 260 tests in under a minute when running against an in-memory database. Those same tests run orders of magnitude slower when running against a relational database. On a project we are currently involved with, 53 tests are executing in memory in a time of around ten seconds, while the same 53 tests running against an Oracle database have an execution time of about ten minutes. This is not surprising given the relative cost of memory access (measured in nanoseconds), compared with the cost of disk access (milliseconds.)

Reduced Testing Code

By continually improving our testing infrastructure, we have reduced the average size of our tests by 60%. We estimate that this translates into an effort reduction of 70%. We also suspect that the quality of testing has improved, but this is hard to measure directly.

Conclusions

The effectiveness of a test-first development process is inversely proportional to the execution time of the tests. The execution time of each test can be reduced by orders of magnitude by removing the latency introduced by disk-based I/O. This can be achieved by replacing the disk-based database with an in-memory database. This is most easily done if the application logic works exclusively with objects rather than interacting with the database via SQL. Test development and maintenance effort can be reduced significantly by improving the testing framework. There are a number of issues, but each is surmountable.

References

[Beck+1999] K. Beck, E. Gamma. *Test Infected: Programmers Love Writing Tests.* http://junit.sourceforge.net/doc/testinfected/testing.htm. 1999.

[Dustin+1999] E. Dustin, J. Rashka, J. Paul. *Automated Software Testing.* Addison-Wesley, 1999.

[Gamma+1995] E. Gamma, et al. *Design Patterns: Elements of Reusable Object-Oriented Software.* Addison-Wesley, 1995.

[Meszaros+1998] G. Meszaros, T. O'Connor, S. Smith. Business Object Framework. OOPSLA'98 Addendum. http://www.clrstream.com/papers.html. 1999.

[Woolf1997] B. Woolf. "Null Object." In *Pattern Languages of Program Design 3.* Addison-Wesley, 1997.

Acknowledgments

The authors would like to thank Denis Clelland at ClearStream for supporting their XP efforts in recent years. Thanks also go to the colleagues who provided comments on this chapter and especially the clients who provided the opportunities for these experiences.

About the Authors

Shaun Smith was an early adopter during the object-oriented software development process formulation era, survived the process wars era, and helped companies adapt during the process alliance era. Presently, he's enjoying the agile era enormously, assisting companies in adopting agile methods and building frameworks to accelerate test-first development. He has been with ClearStream Consulting for eight years and is chief technical architect there. He has presented at OOPSLA, Smalltalk Solutions, XP2001, and XP2002.

Gerard Meszaros is chief scientist at ClearStream Consulting, where he leads teams applying advanced software development techniques (such as Extreme Programming) to help ClearStream's clients achieve faster and higher-quality systems solutions. He helps clients apply object and component technology to a variety of problem domains, including telecommunication, e-commerce, and gas transportation. Previously, he served as chief architect of several major projects at Nortel Networks' R&D subsidiary, Bell Northern Research. He has had patterns published in each of the first three PLOPD books, and has been invited to serve on panels, conduct workshops, and present papers and tutorials at several OOPSLA and other conferences. Gerard uses patterns actively in designing software and in mentoring software developers in good software design practices.

Chapter 13

Extreme Unit Testing: Ordering Test Cases to Maximize Early Testing

—*Allen Parrish, Joel Jones, and Brandon Dixon*

Part II

Extreme Programming (XP) is one of several lightweight software development methodologies. It involves extremely short incremental release cycles, early and frequent testing, heavy use of design refactoring, and pair programming. In this chapter, we propose a lightweight approach to ordering test cases to maximize the amount of testing that can be conducted early in the development process. We argue that our approach is efficient and easy to apply with tool support, and does not differ significantly from typical XP testing process models.

Introduction

XP is one of several lightweight software development methodologies. It involves extremely short incremental release cycles, early and frequent testing, heavy use of refactoring, and pair programming [Beck2000]. XP has had early success on its first project [C3Team1998].

Testing is a particularly important part of XP. In particular, XP requires unit testing, with a strong emphasis on early and frequent testing during the development process. XP also requires that test cases be written before coding and (typically) that test cases be written in a form in which they can be automated. A popular testing tool is the JUnit suite for Java [Beck+1998]. This tool eases the execution of unit tests. Its focus is to automate the process and to reduce the amount of manual output checking (that is, GuruChecksOutput, where an expert reads the output of every test run [Farrell2000]).

In previous work [Parrish+1996], we proposed the notion of *micro-incremental testing* to refer to testing in multiple iterations during the development of a single class. The goal of micro-incremental testing is to reveal defects in the context of the simplest possible collection of methods by testing small numbers of methods first. Micro-incremental testing is consistent with the goals of XP and should be practiced as part of an overall XP methodology.

In this chapter, we present two separate process models for conducting micro-incremental testing. One such model involves developing test cases one at a time in an ad hoc order. As each test case is developed, the methods needed to execute that test case are written, enabling the test case to be executed. This process model is effectively the prevalent testing model in XP and is consistent in its details with the approach proposed in [Beck+1998].

The other micro-incremental testing model involves developing larger sets of test cases and then using a simple, greedy strategy to determine a desirable order in which to develop the methods in those test cases. This strategy attempts to maximize the amount of testing that can occur after each method is developed. Although such a strategy requires some overhead that may not appear to be consistent with the goals of XP, we claim that it is paradigmatically similar enough to the commonly employed ad hoc model that, with tool support, it can be regarded as a legitimate XP testing process model. Although the applicability of this strategy-based approach may be limited in the context of new development, it appears to be particularly useful in the context of refactoring.

We present both of these process models as ways of doing testing that are consistent with the goals of XP. Both have relative advantages and disadvantages, which we also discuss. To make our discussion concrete, our discussion takes place in the context of developing and testing an example ordered list class.

The remainder of the chapter is organized as follows. In the next section, we present our ordered list class along with some test cases that are appropriate for that class. We also define some basic testing terminology needed for the remainder of the chapter. We then present the two testing models, followed by a discussion of their relative applicability to XP.

Example and Background

Our discussion in this chapter centers on an ordered list class, in which the elements of the list are integers, and the list is maintained in ascending order. Listing 13.1 contains the method signatures for this class (written in Java).

This simple class contains several categories of relatively standard methods, as follows:

- A constructor (`OrderedList`) that returns an empty list
- Methods to insert a new item at the appropriate location and maintain ascending order (`add`) and to delete an item by value (`delete`)
- Methods to return the integer head of the list (`head`) and the list with the head removed (`tail`)
- Methods to return the length of the list (`length`) and to examine the list to determine the presence or absence of a particular item (`member`)
- A method to compare two lists for equality (`equals`)

LISTING 13.1 Method signatures for the ordered list class

```
public class OrderedList {
  public OrderedList() {}
  public boolean member(int v) {…}
  public OrderedList add(int v) {…}
  public int head() {…}
  public int length() {…}
  public boolean equals(OrderedList list) {…}
  public OrderedList tail() {…}
  public OrderedList delete(int v) {…}
}
```

It is possible to identify a large number of test cases for this class. We design test cases as assertions on the relationship between objects produced by the various list methods. This is a relatively common XP practice because it supports test automation [Beck2000; Beck+1998]. Table 13.1 contains a set of test cases for this class written as Java assertions, sometimes preceded with additional Java code. We do not claim that these test cases constitute adequate testing for this class; our interest here is simply to define a large enough set to be interesting for a discussion of the micro-incremental testing process. (Note that Table 13.1 uses the notation "<1,2>" to denote a list consisting of 1 as the first element and 2 as the second element. Also, `Create` is a method external to `OrderedList` that invokes the `OrderedList` constructor to generate a new, empty list object.) This method is used for the expository purpose of brevity.

TABLE 13.1 List Test Cases

	Assertion	Explanation
1.	`assert(Create().add(1).head()== 1);`	Adding 1 to <> and taking the head should return 1.
2.	`assert(Create().member(1)== false);`	1 is not a member of <>.
3.	`assert(Create().add(1).tail.` `equals(Create());`	Adding 1 to <> produces <1>. Taking the tail of <1> should produce <>.

4.	`OrderedList L = new OrderedList();`
	`L = L.add(1);`
	`assert(L.add(2).head() ==`
	`L.head());`
		L = <1> (after the add on the second line). After adding a 2, returning the head of the list <1,2> should be equal to returning the head of L itself.

5.	`OrderedList L = new OrderedList();`
	`L = L.add(2);`
	`assert(L.add(1).head() == 1);`
		L = <2> (after the add on the second line). After adding a 1, returning the head of the list should be equal to 1 (the item just added).

6.	`OrderedList L = new OrderedList();`
	`L = L.add(2);`
	`assert(L.add(1).tail().equals(L));`
		L = <2> (after the add on the second line). After adding a 1, the list is <1,2>; returning the tail is <2>, which is equal to the original list L.

TABLE 13.1 *Continued*

	Assertion	Explanation

7.	`OrderedList L = new OrderedList();`
	`L = L.add(0);`
	`assert(L.add(1).tail().equals`
	`(L.tail.add(1));`
		L = <0> (after the add on the second line). After adding a 1, the list is <0,1>; returning the tail yields <1>. This is asserted to be equal to `L.tail` (<>), followed by adding 1 (which yields <1>).

8.	`assert(Create().add(1).member(1)` `== true);`	Adding 1 to <> and then doing a `member` test on 1 should return `true`.
9.	`assert(Create().add(1).member(2)` `== Create().member(2));`	Performing a `member` test for the existence of 2 in list <1> should be equal to performing a `member` test for the existence of 2 in <>.
10.	`assert(Create().add(1).length() ==` `Create().length + 1);`	Performing a `length` test on <1> should be 1 greater than a `length` test on <>.
11.	`assert(Create().delete(1).` `equals(Create()));`	Based on the spec (not provided here), deleting 1 from <> should be a no-op and simply produce <>.
12.	`assert(Create().add(1).delete(1).` `equals(Create()));`	Deleting 1 from <1> should equal <>.
13.	`assert(Create().add(1).delete(2).` `equals(Create().delete(2).add(1)));`	Deleting 2 from <1> should result in <1>. Deleting 2 from <> and subsequently adding 1 should also result in <1>.

In the rest of the chapter, we use this example (both the ordered list class and associated test cases) to explore our two process models for conducting micro-incremental testing. The next section contains a relatively ad hoc model, while the model of the following section involves more extensive test planning before coding.

To clarify the subsequent discussion, we define some basic testing terminology that is consistent with the development cycle discussed previously. We say that a *test run* is the actual execution of a test case. Test runs are said to be *expected-positive* whenever it is expected that they will run properly (that is, after the methods have been implemented). Test runs are said to be *expected-negative* whenever it is expected that they will not run properly (that is, in the second phase, before the methods have been implemented). A test run is said to be *successful* if its goal is met. That is, an expected-positive test run is successful if it *does not* reveal a defect; an expected-negative test run is successful if it *does* reveal a defect. A test run is *feasible* if it is possible to achieve success when executed, and *infeasible* if it is impossible to achieve success. For example, if one or more methods referenced by a test case have not been written yet, an expected-positive test run of that test case is infeasible.

Testing Model 1: Ad Hoc Method Ordering

With this model, test cases are written one at a time, without regard to a specific overall ordering of test cases. Then once a particular test case is tested in an expected-negative test run, the methods referred to in the test case are implemented, and the test case is once again executed (this time in an expected-positive test run). Once this test run is successful, the next test case is written, and an expected-negative test run is conducted with that test case. If any of the methods in this test case are not written yet, they are written now, and an expected-positive test run is conducted. In subsequent iterations after the first, it may not be necessary to implement all the methods referred to in that iteration's test case, because some of those methods may have been implemented in a previous iteration.

Assume that n test cases and k methods are in the class under development. We note that the entire set of n test cases may not be known *a priori* but may very well be developed individually as each is tested. Still, we assume that the total number is finite (n). We can state this model as a relatively straightforward procedure.

For each test case $1 \ldots n$:

1. Write the test case (which references methods $m_i \ldots m_j$).
2. Conduct an expected-negative test run of this test case. Debug the class and repeat this test run until it is successful.

3. For any method *m* in $m_i \ldots m_j$ that has not previously been written, write method *m*.
4. Conduct an expected-positive test run of this test case. Debug the class and repeat this test run until it is successful.

We now apply this testing model in the context of our `OrderedList` class, for which we identified 13 test cases in Table 13.1. As earlier, we do not assume that all these test cases are known *a priori*. Because our process does not dictate a specific ordering of test case runs in the absence of specific business values, we arbitrarily assume the same ordering as in Table 13.1. We then have the following:

1. Develop and run test case 1 (`assert(Create().add(1).head()== 1);`).
   - Write test case 1, which references `OrderedList` (through `Create`), `add`, and `head`.
   - Conduct an expected-negative test run of this test case. Debug the class and repeat this test run until it is successful.
   - Write these three methods (`OrderedList`, `add`, `head`).
   - Conduct an expected-positive test run of this test case. Debug the class and repeat this test run until it is successful.

2. Develop and run test case 2 (`assert(Create().member(1)== false);`).
   - Write test case 2, which references `OrderedList` (through `Create`) and `member`.
   - Conduct an expected-negative test run of this test case. Debug the class and repeat this test run until it is successful.
   - Write the `member` method. The `OrderedList` method was already written as part of the testing process for test case 1.
   - Conduct an expected-positive test run of this test case. Debug the class and repeat this test run until it is successful.

3. Develop and run test case 3 (`assert(Create().add(1).tail.equals (Create());`).
   - Write test case 3, which references `OrderedList` (through `Create`), `add`, `tail`, and `equals`.
   - Conduct an expected-negative test run of this test case. Debug the class and repeat this test run until it is successful.

- ✧ Write the `tail` and `equals` methods. The `OrderedList` and `add` methods were already written as part of the testing process for test cases 1 and 2.
- ✧ Conduct an expected-positive test run of this test case. Debug the class and repeat this test run until it is successful.

4. Continue this pattern for test cases 4 through 13.

Given the order of test cases presented in Table 13.1, we can determine the number of methods that must be implemented on a particular iteration before an expected-positive run for each test case. The number varies depending on how many methods have been implemented on a previous iteration. For example, if test case 1 is tested first, three methods are referred to by the test case, and all three must be implemented before an expected-positive run of that test case. However, if test case 2 is tested next (as earlier), two methods are referred to by the test case, but only one must be implemented in this iteration (because the constructor was already developed in the previous iteration). Table 13.2 lists the methods referenced by each test case and the methods that must be developed as each test case is run, assuming this particular ordering of test runs.

Ideally, it would be nice to minimize the number of methods that are developed at each iteration. The smaller the number of methods that are introduced anew as each test case is run, the easier it will be to pinpoint errors. In this particular example, only two test cases could be completed after the first four methods were developed. Two additional methods had to be written before test case 3 could be completed, at which point test cases 4 through 9 could also be completed. Of course, the number of methods that must be developed at each iteration depends heavily on the order in which the test cases are run. However, other than business value, nothing in this particular process model dictates this order.

A second issue is that test cases should ideally be run as early in the development process as possible. In this example, test cases 8 and 9 could be run immediately after test case 2, immediately after `member` was written. If we ran these test cases earlier, defects in the methods they refer to (such as `add`, which is heavily referred to by almost all the remaining test cases) could be exposed in the context of a smaller number of methods. Again, this simpler context could make it easier to pinpoint errors.

TABLE 13.2 Methods Developed before Each Test Run (Ad Hoc Ordering)

Test Case	Methods Referenced	Methods Developed
1. `assert(Create().add(1).head()== 1);`	`OrderedList,add,head`	`OrderedList,add,head`
2. `assert(Create().member(1)== false);`	`OrderedList,member`	`member`
3. `assert(Create().add(1).tail.equals(Create());`	`OrderedList,add,tail,equals`	`tail,equals`
4. `OrderedList L = new OrderedList();L = L.add(1); assert(L.add(2).head()== L.head());`	`OrderedList,add,head`	
5. `OrderedList L = new OrderedList();L = L.add(2); assert(L.add(1).head() == 1);`	`OrderedList,add,head`	
6. `OrderedList L = new OrderedList();L = L.add(2); assert(L.add(1).tail().equals(L));`	`OrderedList,add,tail,equals`	
7. `OrderedList L = new OrderedList();L = L.add(0); assert(L.add(1).tail().equals(L.tail.add(1));`	`OrderedList,add,tail,equals`	
8. `assert(Create().add(1).member(1) == true);`	`OrderedList,add,member`	
9. `assert(Create().add(1).member(2) == Create().member(2));`	`OrderedList,add,member`	
10. `assert(Create().add(1).length() == Create().length + 1);`	`OrderedList,add,length`	`length`
11. `assert(Create().delete(1).equals(Create()));`	`OrderedList,delete,equals`	`delete`
12. `assert(Create().add(1).delete(1). equals(Create()));`	`OrderedList,add,delete,equals`	
13. `assert(Create().add(1).delete(2). equals(Create.delete(2).add(1)));`	`OrderedList,add,delete,equals`	

In the next section, we consider an alternative testing model that specifies the ordering of test case runs and (correspondingly) method development.

Testing Model 2: Optimized Method Ordering

Here we consider a second testing model. The basic idea is that a set (of size greater than one) of test cases is initially identified. Frequently, this might be the entire set of all test cases for the class, although not necessarily. Once a set of test cases is identified, an attempt is made to order the test case runs in a way that maximizes early testing. This means that defects are potentially revealed in the context of as few methods as possible, making those defects easier to localize.

To understand this approach, we first consider a procedure that produces an ordering in which methods should be developed (called a *development ordering*), based on the test cases in which those methods appear. Our procedure attempts to maximize the number of opportunities to test as methods are developed. These opportunities are called *test points*. More specifically, a development ordering is just an ordered sequence of methods; a test point is a position following a method, *m*, within a development ordering, where an expected-positive test run of a particular test case is feasible following *m*, but not following any method in the ordering before *m*. At each test point, we also attempt to maximize the number of test runs that can be conducted. In this way, we attempt to maximize the amount of meaningful testing that can be done early in the development process.

One algorithm to produce optimal development orderings is to generate all possible orderings (all permutations of methods) and then count the number of test points for each ordering as well as the number of test cases for which expected-positive test runs are feasible at each test point. Because this algorithm is NP-complete, we propose a greedy heuristic. Specifically, to choose the next method in a development ordering, we first identify all methods that, if chosen next, would enable at least one expected-positive test run to be feasible. Of these methods, we select the method with the highest *impact score*. The impact score attempts to quantify which method provides the most "progress" toward making test runs feasible for additional test cases. If no method will result in a test point, we choose the method with the highest impact score among all methods that have not been previously chosen.

We compute the impact score based on the number of test cases by which the method is referenced, weighted for each test case. The weight for a given test case is based on the inverse of the number of methods that appear in that test case. For example, suppose a method, *M*, appears in two test cases, *A* and *B*. Moreover, three methods are referenced by test case *A* and two methods referenced by test case *B*. The impact score for method *M* is 1/3 + 1/2 (0.33 + 0.50), which equals 0.83. (Note that multiple references to a method within the single test case are ignored in computing weights.)

Our `OrderedList` example will clarify the use of this heuristic. Our objective in this example is to define a development ordering among all methods in the ordered list class of Listing 13.1, based on the test cases that appear in Table 13.1. Our first step is to determine, for each method, whether the selection of that method will result in a test point. There is no method that we can choose initially that will make an expected-positive test run feasible (for any test case). Thus, we must look at the impact scores for all methods. Table 13.3 contains the impact scores for all methods in the ordered list class. Recall that `Create` is a method that invokes the `OrderedList` constructor, so we compute the impact score for `OrderedList` based on the appearance of `Create` as well as direct references to `OrderedList` in the various test cases.

Part II

TABLE 13.3 Initial Impact Scores

Method	Impact Score
`OrderedList`	4.08
`add`	3.25
`head`	1.00
`member`	1.16
`tail`	0.75
`equals`	1.58
`length`	0.33
`delete`	0.83

The constructor method (OrderedList) has the highest impact score, so it is chosen as the first method in the development ordering. This is also the intuitive choice because it is clear that no expected-positive test runs are feasible until this method is written.

To find the next method, we first determine whether the selection of any particular method results in a test point. Because of test case 2 (assert(Create().member(1)== false)), selecting member next will result in a test point (enabling a feasible expected-positive run for test case 2). The member method is the only method that will result in a test point and is thus chosen next. Similarly, because of test cases 8 and 9 (for example, assert(Create().add(1).member(1) == true)), selecting add next will result in a test point and is again the only such method. Thus, our development ordering so far is OrderedList → member → add.

Now we have two possible methods that will result in test points if chosen next: head and length. We therefore choose the method with the higher impact score. Because our previously computed impact scores from Table 13.3 were influenced by methods that have already been chosen (and are therefore now irrelevant), we recompute the impact scores with OrderedList, member, and add removed from consideration. The head method appears in three test cases and is by itself in those test cases (other than the already chosen methods). Thus, its impact score is 3. On the other hand, length appears in only one test case (also by itself except for already chosen methods); thus, its impact score is 1. As such, head is chosen next.

Once head is chosen, no additional methods besides length will result in a test point. So length is chosen next. Thus, our development ordering so far is OrderedList → member → add → head → length.

At this point, tail, equals, and delete remain to be chosen. None of these methods, if chosen next, will result in a test point. Once again, we must recompute the impact scores for these three methods, with methods already in the development ordering removed from consideration. The recomputed impact scores are given in Table 13.4.

The equals method has the highest impact score and is chosen next. Choosing equals enables either tail or delete to result in a test point if chosen next. Because both appear in the same number of test cases (three), the choice for the next method is arbitrary. We choose delete next, followed by tail. Thus, our final development ordering is OrderedList → member → add → head → length → equals → delete → tail.

TABLE 13.4 Recomputed Impact Scores

Method	Impact Score
`tail`	1.5
`equals`	3.0
`delete`	1.5

Part II

Once the optimal development ordering for the methods is known, it is straightforward to get an analogous optimal ordering for test cases. In particular, it is straightforward to determine which test cases have feasible expected-positive test runs after each method in the development ordering. Table 13.5 for this model is the analog of Table 13.2 for the ad hoc model; it contains the 13 test cases from Table 13.1 in an order consistent with the development ordering for the methods. Each test case is accompanied by the methods referenced in that test case, along with those methods that must be developed to make an expected-positive test run of that test case feasible. If no methods are listed beside a particular test case, an expected-positive run of the test case is immediately feasible after the previous test case is run. Our heuristic attempts to minimize the number of methods that must be developed for each test case. As Table 13.5 shows, no more than two methods at a time have to be written before conducting some testing. For most test cases, an expected-positive test run is feasible after writing at most one method.

Our example assumes that the development orderings for both methods and test cases are computed once for the entire class. In fact, such orderings may be computed on subsets of methods and test cases. For example, given the "on demand" nature of XP, it may be undesirable to focus on an entire class in this fashion. Instead, the XP design process will naturally identify the appropriate set of test cases for the current story under development.

Also, we have developed a tool that implements this heuristic [Parrish+1996]. Thus, application of this approach does not require large amounts of manual effort. With small numbers of methods and test cases, the proper selection of the next method to be developed or the next test case to be executed may be obvious without a tool. Our tool has been applied to a number of different data structures–based classes,

TABLE 13.5 Methods Developed before Each Test Run (Optimized Ordering)

Test Case	Methods Referenced	Methods Developed
2. assert(Create().member(1)== false);	OrderedList,member	OrderedList,member
8. assert(Create().add(1).member(1) == true);	OrderedList,add,member	add
9. assert(Create().add(1).member(2) == Create().member(2));	OrderedList,add,member	
1. assert(Create().add(1).head()== 1);	OrderedList,add,head	head
4. OrderedList L = new OrderedList();L = L.add(1); assert(L.add(2).head() == L.head());	OrderedList,add,head	
5. OrderedList L = new OrderedList();L = L.add(2); assert(L.add(1).head() == 1);	OrderedList,add,head	
10. assert(Create().add(1).length() == Create().length + 1);	OrderedList,add,length	length
11. assert(Create().delete(1).equals(Create()));	OrderedList,delete,equals	equals,delete
12. assert(Create().add(1).delete(1). equals(Create()));	OrderedList,add,delete,equals	
13. assert(Create().add(1).delete(2). equals(Create.delete(2).add(1)));	OrderedList,add,delete,equals	
3. assert(Create().add(1).tail.equals(Create());	OrderedList,add,tail,equals	tail
6. OrderedList L = new OrderedList();L = L.add(2); assert(L.add(1).tail().equals(L));	OrderedList,add,tail,equals	
7. OrderedList L = new OrderedList();L = L.add(0); assert(L.add(1).tail().equals (L.tail.add(1));	OrderedList,add,tail, equals	

including a text editor class and classes implementing various kinds of lists, stacks, queues, complex numbers, and arrays.

Discussion

In considering the suitability of these two models for XP development, we note that the ad hoc model requires no *a priori* test planning beyond the current test cases. Test cases can be identified and tested one at a time on demand. This approach is consistent with common XP testing practice. Although with XP the order in which test cases are developed is based somewhat on business value, the factors considered by our optimized ordering method are not explicitly considered. So the amount of testing early in the development process is not *guaranteed* with XP to be maximized, and it may be necessary to develop a number of methods before any expected-positive test runs can be executed. On the other hand, because the development ordering in XP is driven by the order in which functionality is needed, the optimized ordering method may have limited utility in new development situations, although empirical work is needed to validate this one way or the other.

Regardless of its applicability to new development situations, however, the optimized ordering method appears to be promising in the context of refactoring, particularly with respect to certain refactorings [Fowler2000]. In particular, consider the Extract Class refactoring [Fowler2000]. This refactoring provides transformation rules to extract one class from another. We note that in such a case, the test cases for the class being extracted *already exist* before the refactoring is initiated. Our optimized development ordering model provides an easy-to-determine (with tool support) ordering for extracting methods, attributes, and their associated test cases. In [Fowler2000], the only constraint placed on such an ordering is to ensure that methods are extracted in an order that considers calling interdependencies among methods (for example, called methods are extracted before caller methods). Our development ordering tool also considers such interdependencies in generating its development orderings.

We are currently initiating experimental work to evaluate the utility of generating optimized development orderings in the context of various refactorings. A list of refactorings that we are considering from [Fowler2000] follows. In each of these refactorings, a new class is generated in which all methods, attributes, and test cases for the new class existed before initiating the refactoring.

- Extract Class
- Extract Hierarchy
- Extract Subclass
- Extract Superclass
- Inline Class
- Introduce Null Object
- Introduce Parameter Object
- Replace Array with Object
- Replace Data Value with Object
- Replace Delegation with Inheritance
- Replace Inheritance with Delegation
- Separate Domain from Presentation
- Tease Apart Inheritance

Conclusion

In this chapter, we have identified two process models for conducting micro-incremental testing (that is, incremental testing with short iteration cycles). The first model does not dictate an ordering for constructing methods or for developing and running test cases but is specific about the structure of test cases and the steps required at each iteration. This model could be viewed as a formalization of the process described in [Beck+1998].

The second model requires the identification of multiple test cases at each iteration of the development cycle and then provides guidance as to the order in which those test cases are tested and their methods implemented. With this model, seven test cases could be run as the first five methods are developed; in contrast, only two test cases could be run as the first five methods are developed with the ordering that we chose under the ad hoc model. Our heuristic simply and efficiently gives an ordering over the set of possible methods that is consistent with the XP practice "Do the simplest thing that could possibly work." Our heuristic seems to hold particular promise in the context of certain refactorings in which the extracted methods, attributes, and test cases are known before the refactoring is initiated. Future work will consider the impact of discovered tests (where the need for a test becomes apparent while code is being developed), testing partially completed methods, and application of this technique to testing during refactoring.

References

[Beck2000] K. Beck. *Extreme Programming Explained.* Addison-Wesley, 2000.

[Beck+1998] K. Beck, E. Gamma. "Test Infected: Programmers Love Writing Tests." *Java Report*, Volume 3, Number 7, 1998.

[C3Team1998] C3 Team. "Chrysler Goes to 'Extreme.'" *Distributed Computing*, October 1998.

[Farrell2000] J. Farrell. *Tactical Testing.* http://c2.com/cgi/wiki?GuruChecksOutput. 2000.

[Fowler2000] M. Fowler. *Refactoring: Improving the Design of Existing Code.* Addison-Wesley, 2000.

[Parrish+1996] A. Parrish, D. Cordes, D. Brown. "An Environment to Support Micro-Incremental Class Development." *Annals of Software Engineering*, Volume 2, 1996.

About the Authors

Allen Parrish is an associate professor in the Department of Computer Science at the University of Alabama. He received a Ph.D. in computer and information science from Ohio State University in 1990. His research interests are in software testing, software deployment, data analysis and visualization, and highway safety information systems. His sponsors have included the National Science Foundation, the Federal Aviation Administration, the Alabama Department of Economic and Community Affairs, the Alabama Department of Transportation, and a variety of other highway safety–related state agencies. He is one of the leaders of the CARE research project, which is a major funded effort in the area of highway safety data analysis.

Joel Jones is an assistant professor in the Department of Computer Science at the University of Alabama. He is currently finishing his

Ph.D. in computer science from the University of Illinois. His research interests are in compiler optimizations, software design patterns, and agile development methodologies. He has a wide variety of industrial experience, including research work at Apple Computer and Hewlett-Packard Laboratories.

Brandon Dixon is an associate professor in the Department of Computer Science at the University of Alabama. He received a Ph.D. in computer science in 1993 from Princeton University. His interests are in computer science theory, algorithm design and software engineering. His current research sponsors include the National Science Foundation, NASA, the Federal Aviation Administration, and the Alabama Department of Transportation.

Chapter 14

Refactoring Test Code

—*Arie van Deursen, Leon Moonen, Alex van den Bergh, and Gerard Kok*

Part II

Two key aspects of Extreme Programming (XP) are unit testing and merciless refactoring. Given the fact that the ideal test code/production code ratio approaches 1:1, it is not surprising that unit tests are being refactored. We found that refactoring test code is different from refactoring production code in two ways: (1) A distinct set of bad smells is involved, and (2) improving test code involves additional test-specific refactorings. To share our experiences with other XP practitioners, we describe a set of bad smells that indicates trouble in test code, and a collection of test refactorings to remove these smells.

Introduction

"If there is a technique at the heart of *extreme programming* (XP), it is unit testing" [Beck1999]. As part of their programming activity, XP developers continually write and maintain (white-box) unit tests. These tests are automated, written in the same programming language as the production code, considered an explicit part of the code, and put under revision control.

The XP process encourages writing a test class for every class in the system. Methods in these test classes are used to verify complicated functionality and unusual circumstances. Moreover, they are used to document code by explicitly indicating what the expected results of a method should be for typical cases. Last but not least, tests are added upon receiving a bug report to check for the bug and to check the bug fix [Beck2000].

A typical test for a particular method includes four components: (1) code to set up the fixture (the data used for testing), (2) the call of the method, (3) a comparison of the actual results with the expected values, and (4) code to tear down the fixture. Writing tests is usually supported by frameworks such as JUnit [Beck+1998].

The test code/production code ratio may vary from project to project but is ideally considered to approach a ratio of 1:1. In our project we currently have a 2:3 ratio, although others have reported a lower ratio.[1] One of the cornerstones of XP is that having many tests available helps the developers overcome their fear of change: The tests will provide immediate feedback if the system gets broken at a critical place. The downside of having many tests, however, is that changes in functionality typically involve changes in the test code as well. The more test code we get, the more important it becomes that this test code is as easily modifiable as the production code.

The key XP practice to keep code flexible is "refactor mercilessly": transforming the code to bring it in the simplest possible state. To support this, a catalog of "code smells" and a wide range of refactorings are available, varying from simple modifications up to ways to introduce design patterns systematically in existing code [Fowler1999].

When trying to apply refactorings to the test code of our project, we discovered that refactoring test code is different from refactoring production code. Test code has a distinct set of smells, dealing with the ways in which test cases are organized, how they are implemented, and how they interact with each other. Moreover, improving test code in-

1. This project started a year ago and involves the development of a product called DocGen [Deursen+2001]. Development is done by a small team of five people using XP techniques. Code is written in Java, and we use the JUnit framework for unit testing.

volves a mixture of refactorings from [Fowler1999] specialized to test code improvements, as well as a set of additional refactorings, involving the modification of test classes, ways of grouping test cases, and so on.

The goal of this chapter is to share our experience in improving our test code with other XP practitioners. To that end, we describe a set of *test smells* indicating trouble in test code, and a collection of *test refactorings* explaining how to overcome some of these problems through a simple program modification. This assumes some familiarity with the xUnit framework [Beck+1998] and refactorings as described in [Fowler1999]. We refer to refactorings described in Fowler's book using the format *Name (F:page#)* and to our test-specific refactorings described in the Refactorings section of this chapter using the format *Name* (#).

Test Code Smells

This section gives an overview of bad code smells that are specific for test code.

Smell 1: Mystery Guest

When a test uses external resources, such as a file containing test data, the test is no longer self-contained. Consequently, there is not enough information to understand the tested functionality, making it hard to use that test as documentation.

Moreover, using external resources introduces hidden dependencies: If some force changes or deletes such a resource, tests start failing. Chances for this increase when more tests use the same resource. The use of external resources can be eliminated using the refactoring *Inline Resource* (1). If external resources are needed, you can apply *Setup External Resource* (2) to remove hidden dependencies.

Smell 2: Resource Optimism

Test code that makes optimistic assumptions about the existence (or absence) and state of external resources (such as particular directories or database tables) can cause nondeterministic behavior in test outcomes. The situation in which tests run fine at one time and fail miserably another time is not a situation you want to find yourself in. Use *Setup External Resource* (2) to allocate and/or initialize all resources that are used.

Smell 3: Test Run War

Such wars arise when the tests run fine as long as you are the only one testing but fail when more programmers run them. This is most likely caused by resource interference: Some tests in your suite allocate resources, such as temporary files, that are also used by others. Apply *Make Resource Unique* (3) to overcome interference.

Smell 4: General Fixture

In the JUnit framework, a programmer can write a setUp method that will be executed before each test method to create a fixture for the tests to run in.

Things start to smell when the setUp fixture is too general and different tests access only part of the fixture. Such setUp methods are harder to read and understand. Moreover, they may make tests run more slowly (because they do unnecessary work). The danger of having tests that take too much time to complete is that testing starts interfering with the rest of the programming process, and programmers eventually may not run the tests at all.

The solution is to use setUp only for that part of the fixture that is shared by all tests using Fowler's *Extract Method (F:110)* and put the rest of the fixture in the method that uses it using *Inline Method (F:117)*. If, for example, two different groups of tests require different fixtures, consider setting these up in separate methods that are explicitly invoked for each test, or spin off two separate test classes using *Extract Class (F:149)*.

Smell 5: Eager Test

When a test method checks several methods of the object to be tested, it is hard to read and understand, and therefore more difficult to use as documentation. Moreover, it makes tests more dependent on each other and harder to maintain.

The solution is simple: Separate the test code into test methods that test only one method using Fowler's *Extract Method (F:110)*, using a meaningful name highlighting the purpose of the test. Note that splitting into smaller methods can slow down the tests because of increased setup/teardown overhead.

Smell 6: Lazy Test

This occurs when several test methods check the same method *using the same fixture* (but, for example, check the values of different instance variables). Such tests often have meaning only when we consider them together, so they are easier to use when joined using *Inline Method (F:117)*.

Smell 7: Assertion Roulette

"Guess what's wrong?" This smell comes from having a number of assertions in a test method that have no explanation. If one of the assertions fails, you do not know which one it is. Use *Add Assertion Explanation* (5) to remove this smell.

Smell 8: Indirect Testing

A test class is supposed to test its counterpart in the production code. It starts to smell when a test class contains methods that actually perform tests on other objects (for example, because there are references to them in the class that is to be tested). Such indirection can be moved to the appropriate test class by applying *Extract Method (F:110)* followed by *Move Method (F:142)* on that part of the test. The fact that this smell arises also indicates that there might be problems with data hiding in the production code.

Note that opinions differ on indirect testing. Some people do not consider it a smell but a way to guard tests against changes in the "lower" classes. We feel that there are more losses than gains to this approach: It is much harder to test anything that can break in an object from a higher level. Moreover, understanding and debugging indirect tests is much harder.

Smell 9: For Testers Only

When a production class contains methods that are used only by test methods, these methods either are not needed and can be removed or are needed only to set up a fixture for testing. Depending on the functionality of those methods, you may not want them in production code where others can use them. If this is the case, apply *Extract Subclass*

(F:330) to move these methods from the class to a (new) subclass in the test code, and use that subclass to perform the tests on. You will often find that these methods have names or comments stressing that they should be used only for testing.

Fear of this smell may lead to another undesirable situation: a class without a corresponding test class. This happens when a developer does not know how to test the class without adding methods that are specifically needed for the test and does not want to pollute the production class with test code. Creating a separate subclass helps to deal with this problem.

Smell 10: Sensitive Equality

It is fast and easy to write equality checks using the `toString` method. A typical way is to compute an actual result and map it to a string, which is then compared to a string literal representing the expected value. Such tests, however, may depend on many irrelevant details, such as commas, quotes, and spaces. Whenever the `toString` method for an object is changed, tests start failing. The solution is to replace `toString` equality checks by real equality checks using *Introduce Equality Method* (6).

Smell 11: Test Code Duplication

Test code may contain undesirable duplication. In particular, the parts that set up test fixtures are susceptible to this problem. Solutions are similar to those for normal code duplication, as described in [Fowler1999, p. 76]. The most common case for test code is duplication of code in the same test class. This can be removed using *Extract Method (F:110)*. For duplication across test classes, it may be helpful to mirror the class hierarchy of the production code into the test class hierarchy. A word of caution, however: Moving duplicated code from two separate classes to a common class can introduce (unwanted) dependencies between tests.

A special case of code duplication is *test implication*: Tests A and B cover the same production code, and A fails if and only if B fails. A typical example occurs when the production code gets refactored: Before this refactoring, A and B covered different code, but afterward they deal with the same code, and it is not necessary anymore to maintain both tests.

Refactorings

Bad smells seem to arise more often in production code than in test code. The main reason for this is that production code is adapted and refactored more frequently, allowing these smells to escape.

One should not, however, underestimate the importance of having fresh test code. Especially when new programmers are added to the team or when complex refactorings need to be performed, clear test code is invaluable. To maintain this freshness, test code also needs to be refactored. We define *test refactorings* as changes (transformations) of test code that do not add or remove test cases, and make test code more understandable, readable, and maintainable.

The production code can be used as a (simple) test case for the refactoring: If a test for a piece of code succeeds before the test refactoring, it should also succeed after the refactoring (and no, replacing all test code by `assert(true)` is not considered a valid refactoring). This obviously also means that you should not modify production code while refactoring test code (similar to not changing tests when refactoring production code).

While working on our test code, we encountered the following refactorings.

Refactoring 1: Inline Resource

To remove the dependency between a test method and some external resource, we incorporate that resource into the test code. This is done by setting up a fixture in the test code that holds the same contents as the resource. This fixture is then used instead of the resource to run the test. A simple example of this refactoring is putting the contents of a file that is used into some string in the test code.

If the contents of the resource are large, chances are high that you are also suffering from the *Eager Test* (5) smell. Consider conducting *Extract Method (F:110)* or *Reduce Data* (4) refactorings.

Refactoring 2: Setup External Resource

If it is necessary for a test to rely on external resources, such as directories, databases, or files, make sure the test that uses them explicitly creates or allocates these resources before testing and releases them when done (take precautions to ensure the resource is also released when tests fail).

Refactoring 3: Make Resource Unique

A lot of problems originate from the use of overlapping resource names, either between different test runs done by the same user or between simultaneous test runs done by different users. Such problems can easily be prevented (or repaired) by using unique identifiers for all resources that are allocated—for example, by including a timestamp. When you also include the name of the test responsible for allocating the resource in this identifier, you will have fewer problems finding tests that do not properly release their resources.

Refactoring 4: Reduce Data

Minimize the data that is set up in fixtures to the bare essentials. This offers two advantages: (1) It makes them more suitable as documentation, and (2) your tests will be less sensitive to changes.

Refactoring 5: Add Assertion Explanation

Assertions in the JUnit framework have an optional first argument to give an explanatory message to the user when the assertion fails. Testing becomes much easier when you use this message to distinguish between different assertions that occur in the same test. Maybe this argument should not have been optional.

Refactoring 6: Introduce Equality Method

If an object structure needs to be checked for equality in tests, add an implementation for the `equals` method for the object's class. You then can rewrite the tests that use string equality to use this method. If an expected test value is represented only as a string, explicitly construct an object containing the expected value, and use the new `equals` method to compare it to the actually computed object.

Related Work

Fowler presents a large set of bad smells and the refactorings that can be used to remove them [Fowler1999]. The difference between his work and ours is that we focus on smells and refactorings that are typical for test code, whereas his book focuses more on production code. The role of unit tests in [Fowler1999] is also geared more toward proving that a refactoring didn't break anything than to being used as documentation of the production code.

Instead of focusing on cleaning test code that already has bad smells, Schneider describes how to prevent these smells right from the start by discussing a number of best practices for writing tests with JUnit [Schneider2000].

The introduction of *Mock Objects* [Mackinnon+2001] is another possibility for refactoring more complex tests. With this technique, one replaces parts of the production code with dummy implementations that both emulate real functionality and enforce assertions about the behavior of the code. This enables the tester to focus on the concrete code that has to be tested without having to deal with all surrounding code and the side effects that it may cause.

The C2 Wiki contains some discussion on the decay of unit test quality and practice as time proceeds and on the maintenançe of broken unit tests.[2] Opinions vary between repairing broken unit tests, deleting them completely, and moving them to another class to make them less exposed to changes (which may lead to our *Indirect Testing* (8) smell).

Conclusions

In this chapter, we have looked at test code from the perspective of refactoring. While working on our XP project, we observed that the quality of the test code was not as high as the production code. Test code was not refactored as mercilessly as our production code, following Fowler's advice that it is OK to copy and edit test code, trusting our ability to refactor out truly common items later [Fowler1999, p. 102]. When at a later stage we started to refactor test code more intensively, we discovered that test code has its own set of problems (which we translated into smells) and its own repertoire of solutions (which we formulated as test refactorings).

2. See http://c2.com/cgi/wiki?TwoYearItch and http://c2.com/cgi/wiki?RefactorBrokenUnitTests.

The contributions of this chapter are the following.

- We have collected a series of test smells that help developers identify weak spots in their test code.
- We have composed a set of specific test refactorings that enable developers to make improvements to their test code in a systematic way.
- For each smell, we have given a solution, using either a potentially specialized variant of an existing refactoring from [Fowler1999] or one of the dedicated test refactorings.

The purpose of this chapter is to share our experience in refactoring test code of our ongoing XP project with other XP practitioners. We believe that the resulting smells and refactorings provide a valuable starting point for a larger collection based on a broader set of projects. Therefore, we invite readers interested in further discussion on this topic to the C2 Wiki.[3]

An open question is how test code refactoring interacts with the other XP practices. For example, the presence of test code smells may indicate that your production code has some bad smells. So trying to refactor test code may indirectly lead to improvements in production code. Furthermore, refactoring test code may reveal missing test cases. Adding those to your framework will lead to more complete test coverage of the production code. Another question is at what moments in the XP process test refactorings should be applied. In short, the precise interplay between test refactorings and the XP practices is a subject of further research.

References

[Beck1999] K. Beck. "Embracing Change with Extreme Programming." *IEEE Computer*, Volume 32, Number 10, October 1999.

[Beck2000] K. Beck. *Extreme Programming Explained*. Addison-Wesley, 2000.

3. See http://c2.com/cgi/wiki?RefactoringTestCode.

[Beck+1998] K. Beck, E. Gamma. "Test Infected: Programmers Love Writing Tests." *Java Report*, Volume 3, Number 7, 1998.

[Deursen+2001] A. van Deursen, T. Kuipers, L. Moonen. "Legacy to the Extreme." In *Extreme Programming Examined*. Addison-Wesley, 2001.

[Fowler1999] M. Fowler. *Refactoring: Improving the Design of Existing Code*. Addison-Wesley, 1999.

[Mackinnon+2001] T. Mackinnon, S. Freeman, P. Craig. "Endo-Testing: Unit Testing with Mock Objects." In *Extreme Programming Examined*. Addison-Wesley, 2001.

[Schneider2000] A. Schneider. "JUnit Best Practices." *Java World*, December 2000. http://www.javaworld.com/javaworld/jw-12-2000/jw-1221-junit.html.

Part II

About the Authors

Arie van Deursen and Leon Moonen are cofounders of the Software Improvement Group (SIG), an Amsterdam-based company that specializes in helping customers solve their legacy problems. Arie van Deursen and Leon Moonen work for CWI, the National Research Institute for Mathematics and Computer Science in the Netherlands. They can be reached via e-mail at arie@cwi.nl and leon@cwi.nl, and they maintain Web pages at http://www.cwi.nl/~arie/ and http://www.cwi.nl/~leon/.

Alex van den Bergh and Gerard Kok are employed by the Software Improvement Group. They are part of the development team of the DocGen documentation generator, one of SIG's main products. They can be reached via e-mail at alex@software-improvers.com and gerard@software-improvers.com, and they maintain a Web presence at http://www.software-improvers.com/.

Chapter 15

Diagnosing Evolution in Test-Infected Code

—Christian Wege and Martin Lippert

Part II

In this study, based on historical information, we trace the effects of applying the techniques of refactoring and aggressive unit testing in source code. We show how their impact on the evolution of the architecture can be proved. The study consists of the analysis of many individual integration versions of a large framework. The method described here can help development teams find weaknesses in their application of the two traced techniques.

Introduction

In a world of constantly changing requirements, systems development must ensure that it can quickly respond to changed user requirements or technology updates. One major promise of Extreme Programming (XP) [Beck2000] is to enable the construction of an evolvable system. Instead of planning all possible future enhancements from the beginning, Extreme Programmers rely on their ability to incorporate changes to the system and its architecture at an arbitrary point in the future.

In this study, we investigated the artifacts (the source code and other historical information) of a project that used aggressive unit testing and refactoring techniques extensively for development. We traced the effects of applying these two techniques in the developed source code. Our system under investigation is JWAM, a framework for constructing large-scale interactive software systems.[1]

In their well-known article, Beck and Gamma introduce the testing style "test infection" [Beck+1998]. For every class in the system, you write a unit test. New requirements are implemented in the system by refactoring the unit tests first and then the system classes [Fowler1999]. So when those two techniques are applied strictly, we talk about test-infected code. Given this definition, JWAM is test-infected. Its test suite was created with the Java testing framework provided by Beck and Gamma.[2]

The JWAM development relies on an integration server that ensures that for every update of the source code, all tests still run [Lippert+2001]. The study is based on 254 individual integration versions of the framework that stem from this continuous integration process. In addition to the source code, we used the integration log, which contains a small description for every update of the source tree.

Lippert et al. state, "With Pair Programming we have improved framework quality, with test cases we maintain it. Without the test cases a lot of the refactoring we did in the past would have been less smooth"[Lippert+2000]. With the help of our analysis, we validated this rather intuitive statement by observing the history of specific system properties in the produced artifacts. Also, with the help of our analysis, we can point out some areas for potential improvement of framework development.

This study concentrates on tracing the effects of aggressive unit testing and refactoring directly in the code and in historical information. It doesn't investigate the correlation between requirements changes and defect rates, which would be of high interest as well.

The Case Study

The Method

The method used in our study is an adaptation of the approach proposed by Mattsson and Bosch for observing software evolution in ob-

1. See http://www.jwam.org.

2. See http://www.junit.org.

ject-oriented frameworks [Mattsson+1999]. Based on historical information about the subsystems, modules, and classes, they investigated the size, change rate, and growth rate of the system. The work of Mattsson and Bosch is based on a method proposed in [Gall+1997] that focused on observing macro-level software evolution using the version numbering of a system. Mattsson and Bosch adapted this approach for investigating object-oriented frameworks. The system was divided into a number of subsystems, which were themselves divided into several modules. In the adapted approach, each module consisted of several classes (instead of programs, as in the original approach).

Size is calculated by the number of classes in each module or subsystem. The calculations of change and growth rate are made in terms of changed classes as units. Class change is measured in terms of the change in the number of public methods for each class. The focus on public methods stems from the fact that a change in the public methods reflects a better understanding of the boundary of the system. Changes in private methods, however, mainly reflect refinements of implementation details and thus are of minor interest.

These are the steps of the method in the original approach.[3]

1. Calculate, for all releases, the change and growth rate for the whole system.
2. Calculate, for all releases, the change and growth rate for each subsystem.
3. For those subsystems that exhibit high growth and change rates, calculate, for all releases, the change and growth rates for the modules.
4. Identify those modules that exhibit high change and growth rates as likely candidates for restructuring [Mattsson+1999].

For our study, *we based our calculations for the system, subsystems, and modules on the package/subpackage structure of Java*. The packaging feature of Java is a natural structuring mechanism provided by the language. In JWAM this mechanism is used to distinguish between the core and several noncore parts of the whole system, and inside the core to distinguish between the framework layers. We will discuss this in more detail later. Java interfaces are treated exactly the same way as Java classes.

---

3. See the Diagnosing Evolution and Test Infection section for our modifications.

The second important adaptation is that *we changed the top-down approach to a bottom-up approach.* Instead of starting with the top-level system, we calculate the values for every class and subsystem and go up to the top. We try to trace the development method in the code; therefore, we are interested in all developed artifacts. To be able to give advice on possible restructuring candidates (as in the approach by Mattsson and Bosch), we first have to widen the empirical base.

The third and most important adaptation is the *introduction of the test coverage rate.* If aggressive unit testing is one central part of test-infected programming, the results should depend on the number of system classes covered by unit tests.

The Investigated System

JWAM is a Java framework supporting the development of large-scale interactive software systems according to the tools-and-materials approach [Züllighoven1998]. The foundation of the JWAM framework was laid in 1997 by research assistants and students of the Software Engineering Group at the University of Hamburg [Lippert+2000]. In 1998 the commercialization of the framework began. In 1999 the team started to use XP techniques. Our study covers 254 individual integration versions of the whole system from April 2000 to December 2000, with roughly one version per day.

The top-level package structure of JWAM 1.5 differentiates between the framework core and several collections of other components, which are the following:

- de.jwam—The framework core, which contains the interfaces and classes necessary to create a simple application according to the tools-and-materials approach
- de.jwamx—JWAM components that provide technical or domain-oriented services
- de.jwamy—Third-party components that provide technical or domain-oriented services
- de.jwamdev—Tools used for working with the framework
- de.jwamalpha—New JWAM components and new JWAM tools[4]

4. Adapted from the program documentation of JWAM 1.5

The framework core in de.jwam is divided into several layers to separate different concerns. This is the most fundamental part for building new applications on top of JWAM and is the groundwork for the architecture of applications based on JWAM.

Diagnosing Evolution and Test Infection

Based on the structural observations derived from the 254 integration versions, we can make statements about the system's evolution and the influence on this evolution of the techniques used during development. We have extracted information about the following subset of system properties, which is an adaptation of the descriptions found in [Mattsson+1999].

- The *size* of each package and subpackage is the number of classes it contains. Only top-level classes (no inner or nested classes) are used because they reflect the behavior of the system to the outside world.
- The *change rate* is the percentage of classes in a particular package that changed from one version to the next. To compute the change rate, two versions of a class are needed. The relative number of the changed classes represents the change rate.
- The *growth rate* is defined as the percentage of classes in a particular package that have been added (or deleted) from one version to the next. To compute the growth rate, two versions are compared, and the numbers of the added and deleted classes are computed. The relative number of the new classes (that is, the difference between added and removed classes) represents the growth rate.
- The *test coverage rate* is the percentage of classes that are covered by test classes. Given the convention to name a test class with the suffix "Test," we can count the number of test classes for a given package. The test coverage rate is the number of test classes divided by the number of system classes in the package subtree (that is, the number of classes without the test classes).

One important detail for calculating the system properties is the way we deal with package restructurings. Given a class in version *n* of the system, we first look for that class in version *n–1* with exactly the same package qualifier. If this class is not found, we look for the class in version *n–1* without the package qualifier. Because of the nature of the development method of making small iterations and increments, we are likely to find those classes that are only moved to another package but not renamed. Now we can identify the predecessor of a given package in version *n–1* by looking for the packages from which the classes in the package of version *n* originate.

System Observations

Figure 15.1 shows the historical development of the size of JWAM for the 254 observed integration versions. Around version 19, you see an irregularity of shrinking framework size. Here, a library that had once been part of the framework was deleted completely. At integration version 33, another outdated library was deleted. The other exceptionally high change in the system size is at integration version 219, where a large number of old test cases and old examples were integrated at once. Except for those singularities, a more or less linear growth of the framework's size can be seen over the observed period.

Mattsson and Bosch see a linearly growing size as a sign of the maturity of a framework. The change rate and growth rate of such a system should fall more or less linearly. They explain any nonlinear behavior in

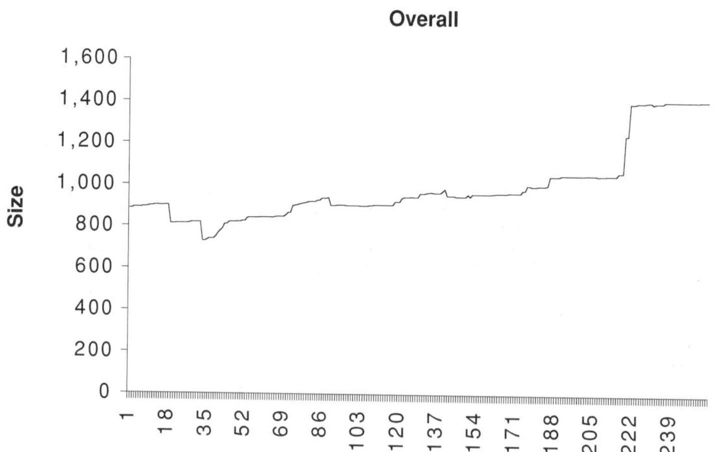

FIGURE 15.1 Overall size

the change rate of the overall system as a major architectural change (that is, the introduction of online capabilities into a batch-oriented system). In JWAM, the nonlinear change rate and growth rate curves stem from the fact that we observed every integration version of the system—not only the released versions. Thus, in the context of investigating test-infected code, we are more interested in the frequency of the change and growth rate peaks than in their absolute height.

Part II

Figure 15.2 shows the change and growth rate history for the whole system. Compared with the size history, this diagram shows the individual development steps (the dynamics of the development process). A change rate average of 0.005 indicates the iterative development in small steps.[5] A growth rate average of 0.002[6] indicates the incremental[7] development in small steps. A general observation is that a change oc-

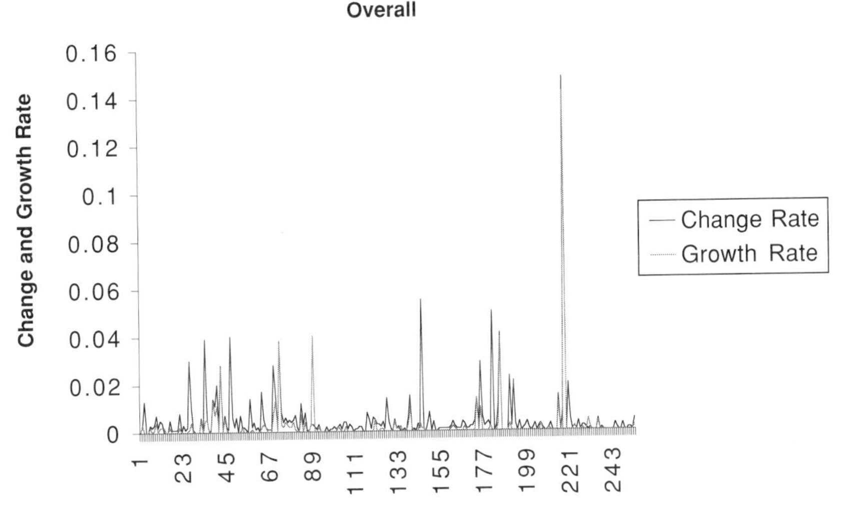

FIGURE 15.2 Overall change and growth rate

5. A change rate of 0.005 means that five classes are changed, given an average overall system size of 1,000 classes.
6. A growth rate of 0.002 means that two out of 1,000 methods are added or deleted.
7. Cockburn distinguishes between incremental and iterative development. "Incremental development is a staging strategy in which portions of the system are developed at different times or rates, and integrated as they are ready. . . . Iterative development is a rework scheduling strategy in which time is set aside to revise and improve parts of a system" [Cockburn1998].

curs more often than growth in the system. This indicates that after or before the addition or deletion of new methods or new classes, some refactoring steps are performed. This matches perfectly the test-infected development style.

In this study, we introduced the system property *test coverage rate*. This can be seen in Figure 15.3 for the overall system. Except for the singularities explained in the discussion of the size history for the overall system, the test coverage rate history exhibits more or less constant growth. For example, starting with a test coverage rate of less than 0.2, it reaches more than 0.5 at the end of the observed period.[8] This is an indication of the growing maturity of the application of the techniques for framework development.

A test coverage rate of about 0.5 doesn't seem to be very sophisticated for a development process that claims to be a form of XP, because to be successful, XP requires a very high test coverage rate. As shown in Figure 15.4, we have to differentiate between the different top-level packages to make a more qualified diagnosis. This figure shows the test coverage rate for the individual top-level packages.

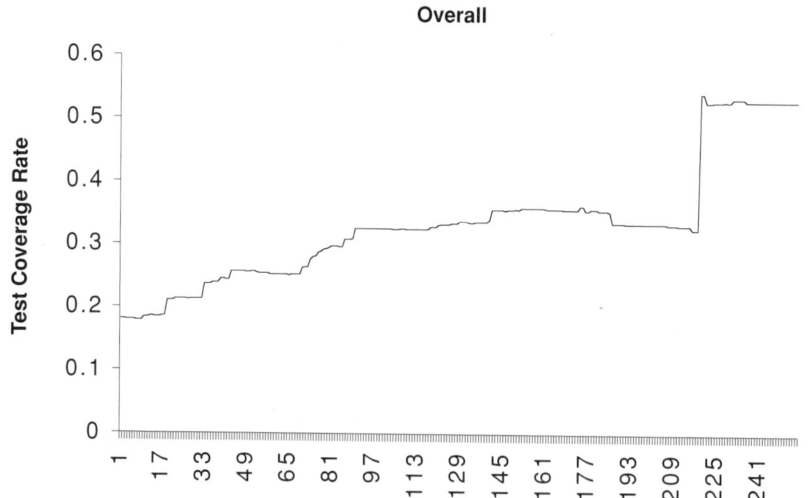

FIGURE 15.3 Overall test coverage rate

8. A test coverage rate of 0.2 means that only two out of ten system classes are covered by a test class.

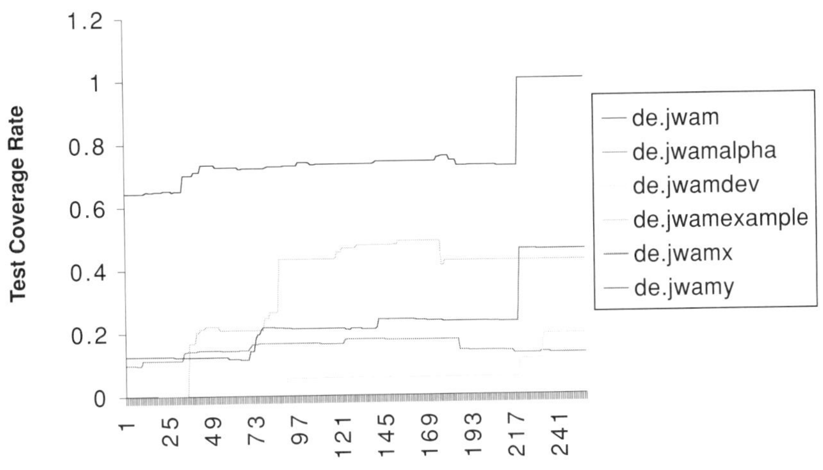

FIGURE 15.4 Test coverage rate of top-level packages

The framework core in de.jwam exhibits more or less healthy growth in the test coverage rate, from below 0.7 to 1. This fits with the nearly ideal size history for the framework core shown in Figure 15.5. For the de.jwamexample package, the development team seems to have realized the importance of test cases for the examples during framework development.

Starting from a test coverage rate of 0, it ends at 0.4. At the same time, the package de.jwamexample is the only other top-level package that reveals nearly linear growth, as shown in Figure 15.5. The development team seems to have understood the value of a suite of examples and the importance of ensuring their high quality. Application developers could base their development on the examples provided along with their associated test cases.

The developers seem to have realized the importance of a test suite for the de.jwamx package (containing additional components on top of the framework core), which exhibits a growing number of test cases. But the number of test cases still didn't reach a level that could ensure healthy behavior in the size history curve for this package, as can be seen in Figure 15.4. The packages de.jwamalpha and de.jwamdev have by far the worst test coverage rate history. The developers obviously didn't see the need to put the same amount of effort into the evolution

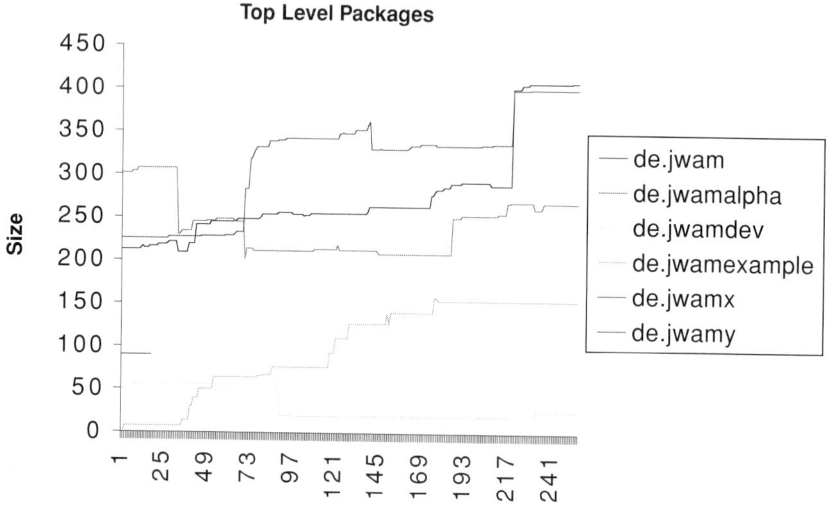

FIGURE 15.5 Size of top-level packages

of their development tools as they did for the rest of the framework. The de.jwamalpha package is planned to be a test area for new ideas. In XP terms, these new ideas are spike solutions that do not have to be developed with the same care as the rest of the system. Development of a proper test suite for the new ideas is deferred until those ideas are incorporated into the base system. This is completely valid for XP and does not exhibit a fallacy in the development process. Figure 15.5 confirms this behavior for the size history of the two packages.

The differences between the top-level packages can also be traced in the change rate history shown in Figure 15.6. For the framework core, the development seems to be very close to the ideal: Many small peaks with a high frequency indicate many iterative steps. In the other top-level packages, the change rate peaks are less regular. Here, the development is performed in fewer and bigger steps.

Diagnosis and Recommendations

Generally, the development team seems to be on the right track for applying the two techniques. The analysis of the code shows the positive effects of building and maintaining a good test suite on the evolution

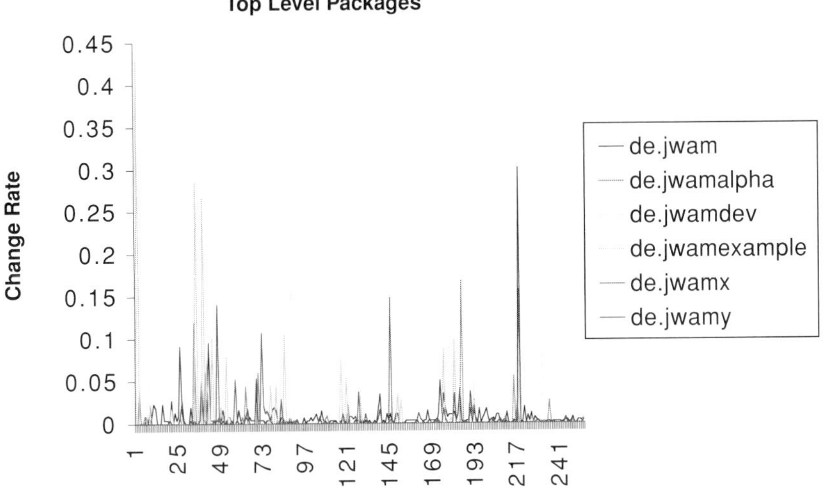

FIGURE 15.6 Change rate of top-level packages

Part II

of the system. The iterative and incremental development steps are most clearly seen in the most mature parts of the system. The distribution of effort in the development resources seems to be effective in the sense that a complete test suite is maintained only for those parts that have to be of high quality (that is, the framework core). The experimental parts of the framework (that is, the alpha package) have a poor test coverage rate, a nonlinear size history, and a few big change and growth rate peaks (as opposed to many, equally distributed small peaks for the framework core).

It is a good idea to provide framework users with a set of examples that come with a whole suite of tests specific to those examples. These examples could show the users how to write tests for typical uses of the framework and could help improve overall quality.

However, the analysis also exhibits some possible weaknesses in the system development. The size history of the overall system shows some nonlinearity. This seems to indicate large steps and big changes in the development. That would lead us to conclude that these steps did not happen in an XP-like style. But the current system in use demonstrates that the method used in this chapter also has its weaknesses. The changes mentioned affected a lot of classes, but they were not "big" changes in the sense of XP. The changes were made in a few minutes, maybe one hour, and did not affect many other parts of the system. So we would say they were not big or complicated changes. This "quality of the change" is not measured by the measurement method used here.

Related and Future Work

The work of Mattsson and Bosch is the basis for our approach to identifying the software evolution through examining historical information. We extended their approach in some ways to fit the specific needs of our research question. Mattsson and Bosch extended the original approach of Gall et al. in the sense of smaller granularity of the entities examined [Gall+1997]. Our method extends the approach of Mattsson and Bosch in the sense that we examine the software evolution over smaller periods of time to better fit the incremental and iterative development in small steps.

An empirical study by Lindvall and Sandahl shows that software developers are not so good at predicting, based on the requirements specification, how many and which classes will be changed [Lindvall+1998]. In the context of XP, the idea of a requirements document is omitted completely in favor of user stories, which contain only the next most important requirement for the evolution of the system [Beck2000].

Simon and Steinbrückner have analyzed JWAM 1.5 with their high-quality metrics tool. They are working on an analysis of a more recent version of JWAM to study the effects of their first recommendations on the quality of the framework in that version [Simon+2001].

Our analysis concentrated on public methods given by the method we base our work on. Experience shows, however, that refactoring is applied to private methods in many cases. On the other hand, our analysis didn't take into account the correlation between requirements changes and defect rates, which could reveal other insights into the development process.

Conclusion

In this study, we presented an approach for tracing the effects of techniques for refactoring and aggressive unit testing in code. We examined 254 integration versions of a large Java framework. The integration versions stem from a continuous integration process that enables XP-like development of the framework.

We showed the usefulness of our approach and discussed how the effects of "test-infected development" can be seen in the history of specific system properties. In addition, we were able to highlight some areas for potential improvement in the development process.

Part II

References

[Beck2000] K. Beck. *Extreme Programming Explained*. Addison-Wesley, 2000.

[Beck+1998] K. Beck, E. Gamma. "Test-Infected: Programmers Love Writing Tests." *Java Report*, Volume 3, Number 7, 1998.

[Cockburn1998] A. Cockburn. *Surviving Object-Oriented Projects: A Manager's Guide*. Addison-Wesley, 1998.

[Fowler1999] M. Fowler. *Refactoring: Improving the Design of Existing Code*. Addison-Wesley, 1999.

[Gall+1997] H. Gall, M. Jazayeri, R. Klösch, G. Trausmuth. Software Evolution Observations Based on Product Release History. Proceedings of the Conference on Software Maintenance. 1997.

[Lindvall+1998] M. Lindvall, K. Sandahl. "How Well Do Experienced Software Developers Predict Software Change?" *Journal of Systems and Software*, Volume 43, Number 1, 1998.

[Lippert+2000] M. Lippert, S. Roock, H. Wolf, H. Züllighoven. JWAM and XP: Using XP for Framework Development. Proceedings of the XP2000 conference. Cagliari, Sardinia, Italy. 2000.

[Lippert+2001] M. Lippert, S. Roock, R. Tunkel, H. Wolf. Stabilizing the XP Process Using Specialized Tools. Proceedings of the XP2001 conference. Cagliari, Sardinia, Italy. 2001.

[Mattsson+1999] M. Mattsson, J. Bosch. Observations on the Evolution of an Industrial OO Framework. Proceedings of the ICSM'99, International Conference on Software Maintenance. Oxford, United Kingdom. 1999.

[Simon+2001] F. Simon, F. Steinbrückner. *Analysis of JWAM 1.5 with the Metrics Tool Crocodile.* http://www.jwam.de/home/quality_assessment_jwam15.pdf. 2001.

[Züllighoven1998] H. Züllighoven. *Das Objektorientierte Konstruktionshandbuch.* dpunkt Verlag, 1998.

Acknowledgments

We would like to thank the JWAM team for providing the daily builds.

About the Authors

Christian Wege is an enterprise application architect at DaimlerChrysler, where he is doing development and consulting, especially in the area of enterprise portals. Before joining DaimlerChrysler, he worked for IBM and HP in OO and client-server development. He is vice president of the Java User Group Stuttgart, Germany. He holds a diploma of computer science from the University of Tuebingen, Germany. Christian was a speaker at JavaOne '99, OOP 2000, XP2000, XP2001, WebSphere 2001, and other conferences and serves as a program committee member of XP2002 and XP Universe 2002. Christian can be reached at wege@acm.org.

Martin Lippert is a research assistant at the University of Hamburg and a professional software architect and consultant at IT Workplace Solutions. Among his current research interests are framework design and implementation, tool support for framework specialization, refactoring, Java, and Extreme Programming. He is senior architect of the JWAM framework and has gathered experience with Extreme Programming techniques over the past three years. He is project coach for Extreme Programming and software architectures and has given a number of talks, tutorials, and demonstrations on various topics of software engineering at international conferences, including ICSE, ECOOP, Extreme Programming, OOPSLA, HICSS, ICSTest, and OOP. He cowrote the upcoming book *Extreme Programming in Action.* Martin can be reached at lippert@acm.org.

Chapter 16

Innovation and Sustainability with Gold Cards

"I am not a load factor—I am a free man."

—*Julian Higman, Tim Mackinnon, Ivan Moore, and Duncan Pierce*

Part II

An XP team delivers what the customer asks for and is collectively responsible for successful delivery. This can lead to two problems. The first is technical: There can be a lack of innovation because the customer does not necessarily explore options that are technically possible but not currently required. Consequently, cutting-edge knowledge may be slowly lost from the team. The second is personal: Team members may not feel that they have individual recognition, and managers may find it difficult to assign credit for individual contributions because of collective responsibility.

Perversely, both of these problems are more noticeable as the team becomes more experienced at executing the XP process. At Connextra, we have experienced this effect over the last two years and have successfully implemented a new practice called "Gold Cards" that addresses these issues. XP takes away the blame culture; Gold Cards promote a praise culture. Gold Cards allow developers time to explore technical possibilities in a controlled and focused way that leads to innovative stories that give team members a chance to be individually recognized. This has resulted in a noticeable increase in innovation and improved job satisfaction among developers.

Introduction

Connextra is a two-and-a-half-year-old company with 35 employees, working with Internet technologies. When the company was started, the founders were interested in using XP to create their first product. To this end, the company (right down to the design of the office) was based on XP principles.

The Physical Environment

One of the key XP principles is to program in pairs, and from the second week of development, convex desks were installed to facilitate side-by-side paired programming. There are no individual desks or computers, so for access to e-mail, there are some "Web café"–style machines, where any developer can log in as required. There are also several screened booths that are equipped with phones, where personal calls can be made, or individual work can be performed. Furthermore, each developer has a locker, where they can keep personal items.

Twenty Iterations and Counting

We have been working in this environment for 20 iterations, each lasting three weeks. Every morning we gather around a planning board and hold a stand-up meeting, where we discuss the progress on yesterday's tasks, select new partners, and focus on completing the remaining tasks in the iteration. We have found that we have become very good at this mode of work and have rarely missed a delivery target. We have really seen the benefits of applying the XP process to customer requirements.

Story Processing Machines

As a team, we have a real sense of accomplishment and are always striving to improve our velocity and deliver greater value to our customers. To this end, we are constantly looking at our storyboard and trying to check off as many stories as possible. We have become a software factory in the true sense. Worryingly, we began to observe that we were missing something.

Religious Guilt

In conversations with colleagues in other companies, we noticed that we were missing the ability to sit alone at a desk and try out ideas, untroubled by the work of the rest of the team. These colleagues were able to "waste time" on nondeliverables without suffering from the "religious guilt" that such time was not contributing to the project velocity.

In our working environment there were only two legitimate places to be for any length of time: (1) at a development machine, pairing, or (2) at a Web café machine, checking and replying to e-mail. If you weren't in either place, you felt that you were wasting time. There was no place to be where you could think of new things without feeling guilty. However, any development effort needs to look continually for innovations in technology and process, which often come from the lateral thinking of individuals rather than a collective focus on task completion.

Spikes Were a Delay

Once the team had finished the iteration and were preparing for the next planning game, we found that we weren't always able to accurately estimate items being introduced in new user stories. In those cases, we took several days to spike potential solutions and play (to a limited extent) with new technologies. Although this helped us give accurate estimates, unfortunately the users viewed it as an activity that was getting in the way of starting the next iteration. We also noticed that this time rarely allowed us to experiment with blue-sky possibilities, because our mind-set was constrained by the existing expectations of both customers and developers. Customers didn't know what possibilities existed, while developers didn't know whether they were feasible (if requested).

Positive Recognition

As we have been working together, we have formed a real sense of team. We pair with each other, share knowledge, and have a collective responsibility to make sure that the best job gets done. In a "no blame" culture, there also needs to be room for positive contributions that don't detract from the sense of team. Many team members had some great ideas but found that there was no way to explore them without feeling that they were letting the rest of the team down. It is a perfectly human impulse to want to impress your peers with new ideas, but not at the expense of leaving other team members to bear the burden of finishing the committed work.

The Dreaded Review

As the company grew, more formal personnel procedures were introduced, including a regular review process. This was viewed as a healthy addition to our working practice. However, in a team-based process like XP, it was difficult to point to specific achievements that would enable individuals to be recognized and rewarded. We tried agreeing on action points that would be reviewed in the next period; however, in our software machine, there was never a good way to make sure that these points were addressed adequately. Again, the religious guilt was kicking in.

Velocity Was High, Morale Wasn't

At about the fifteenth iteration, we began to notice that although everyone was making sure that they contributed to the velocity, there was a certain sense of dissatisfaction with our success. We are all aware that every day new tools, new APIs, and new products are likely to have an impact on our business, and we all want to stay ahead of the curve. It's good for developing an individual's skills to be able to practice new techniques, and good for morale to sort out aspects of the development environment that are annoying. Some of us tried to work on this stuff after working hours; however, a full day of guilt-free paired programming is extremely tiring. An XP practice is the 40-hour week, and we were devoting this to task completion, leaving no room for individual achievements.

Remembering the Old Days

When you pair-program with people every day, you often reminisce about how it was in the "good old days." Some of us tried working alone on pet projects after hours and reported back to the others that it was a useful reminder that paired programming is actually a more efficient way of working—you just need a reminder from time to time. Sometimes, however, it is nice to work alone for a short duration and have the time to cover new material, unhindered by a partner's questions. Furthermore, some days people just feel unsociable and want to work by themselves for a change.

Everything Goes Gold?

To address these issues, we introduced a new practice that we call "Gold Cards." Because we are used to planning and working using index cards, we decided that a special kind of card would be a suitable way to integrate a new approach to innovation and sustainability.

The Gold Card System

A Gold Card is an index card with a gold star on the top left-hand corner, and a developer's name and the month of validity written on it. Each developer is allocated two Gold Cards at the beginning of each calendar month, which makes managing and issuing the cards very easy. This allocation amounts to about one-tenth of a developer's time and is treated as a fixed overhead. Gold Cards can be used at any time during a month but cannot be carried over into the next month. If a developer has any holidays booked in the allotted time period for the card, we use an honor system, where people prorate their Gold Card allowance, rounding to the nearest half day.

Each card grants the developer who has it one day of work on a topic of their choice. An explicit aim of the scheme is for developers to try to convert their Gold Card work into stories. Ideally, topics should have some potential for business value, such as the following:

- Creating new business opportunities by exploiting new technologies. These could become customer stories.
- Reducing cost by improving the efficiency of the team—for example, by developing new tools.
- Reducing risk by exploring new and alternative technologies.

Unlike development code that requires a pair, Gold Cards can be worked on alone or in a pair, the latter requiring both developers to use a Gold Card.

Recalculating the Velocity

Having proposed the scheme to management, we agreed on an allowance of two Gold Card days a month. To introduce Gold Cards, we needed to recalculate our velocity for the first iteration that included them (the seventeenth iteration). We calculated that two Gold Card days a month is approximately 10% of the working time available, if each month is considered as having approximately 20 working days. Thus, our new velocity was calculated as 90% of our previous velocity (meaning that our load factor has risen to take account of this extra overhead). We used this figure for the velocity in the next iteration, and it worked out fine. In subsequent iterations, we have simply used our velocity from previous iterations (that include Gold Cards) without any further adjustments.

Although there is no relationship with iteration length and Gold Card expiration times, we have found that the stability of our velocity has not been adversely affected, and the simplicity of monthly allocations means that there is little overhead in running the scheme.

How to Take a Card

At the morning stand-up meeting, a developer can express their intention to take a Gold Card that day. It is usual to explain what they are going to investigate so that other people know what they will be doing and can make suggestions. Doing this helps make the system self-managing in that people take Gold Cards only when it will not adversely affect the iteration. In practice, most Gold Cards are taken without difficulties. On the rare occasion that a large number of people have been inspired to step forward to use a Gold Card, some team members have simply opted to use their card on an alternate day. Whole days of work are preferred to avoid fragmented working, but card allocation is reduced pro rata with holidays taken in the month, so half days can occur.

Before people start work on a Gold Card, we encourage them to write on the card what they intend to achieve. At the end of a Gold Card day, the developer summarizes the results of their work on the company intranet (we use a Wiki based on Ward Cunningham's original Perl script),[1] and this forms a learning repository for other developers to refer to or to contribute related ideas [Kerievsky2001]. The developer keeps the card to produce at their next review.

Finally, at the next stand-up meeting, a developer who has worked on a Gold Card briefly summarizes what they did and what future work or possibilities that Gold Card has created. Sometimes this summary may be a warning that the idea is one that should not be considered any further.

Although a developer chooses the topic for a Gold Card, they do not necessarily have to think of a topic themselves—a number of topics

1. See http://c2.com/cgi/wiki?WikiWikiWeb.

proposed by other developers, or even customers, are available. These are organized on sticky notes on poster boards to stimulate discussion and establish relationships among various ideas. We have four poster boards, each covering a different topic area: New Technology, Tools, Cool Sidewize Services, and XP Process. Each poster has an owner, who encourages work in that area, maintains an overview of progress to date, ensures that work is not repeated, and offers advice on any of the topics. The poster owner also offers a point of contact with the rest of the business to ensure that potential business value is not missed.

Developers who are unsure of how to spend a Gold Card can look at these posters for inspiration and can discuss ideas at the stand-up meeting. We have noticed that many people begin to consider and discuss the work they will do a few days in advance. We also try to encourage each other to try out varied topics.

A Little History

The Gold Card system was partly inspired by the book *The Natural Advantage: Renewing Yourself* [Heeks2000]. This book gave rise to the idea of how to enable developers to renew themselves but still give business benefit. In discussions between the authors, we imagined a scheme akin to undergraduate professors posting ideas on their office doors to encourage students to choose interesting thesis topics. In our office the use of cards is pervasive, even in other parts of the business, so it seemed natural to use cards as a way of introducing this idea in an XP way.

With a basic proposal in place, we approached the chief technical officer (CTO) and described the aims and benefits of the scheme. These discussions were particularly helpful because we hadn't clearly defined the potential business benefits of the cards, so it initially proved difficult to get his support. Once we adjusted the proposal to clearly state the rules for providing business value, we obtained his backing, and the idea was then easy to sell to our users. We also conferred with the other developers on our team to make sure that the idea was addressing the issues that we had observed. We launched the scheme with much fanfare, gold star badges, and a presentation of the posters.

Observed Results

Having run the scheme for a few iterations, we have observed many examples of Gold Cards that have satisfied the aims of the scheme.

A Gold Card That Created New Business Opportunities

One of our current products, Sidewize, delivers contextually relevant information in a separate window from the user's Web browser.[2] A Gold Card was undertaken that investigated a new style of user interface for content delivery, where relevant information is shown directly in the browsed Web page instead of a separate window. This work spanned two days of Gold Card time, and the end product of the investigation was a working prototype of a new interface. This demonstrated that the technique was viable, formed a useful basis for demonstrations, and gave us enough knowledge to estimate subsequent stories.

A Gold Card That Increased Efficiency

Our development environment is VisualAge for Java, with a single code base for all developers. After completing some code, a pair releases it on the release machine. One time-consuming aspect of this was the need to load in all the classes that have changed in an open edition of a package, one by one before integrating and releasing them. VisualAge offers no built-in mechanism to support this integration activity; however, it does provide a tool API through which operations can be automated. A Gold Card was completed that enabled a list of versioned classes to be loaded from a file. The resulting tool has increased the speed and accuracy of the release process.

A Gold Card That Reduced Risk

For historical reasons, our software has a dependency on the Microsoft Java Virtual Machine (JVM). Microsoft doesn't support Java after version 1.1, but Java development has moved on considerably since then. This represents a significant business risk. To reduce this risk, a Gold Card demonstrated the feasibility of replacing the Microsoft-specific Java code with native code, enabling us to use any JVM. This work has generated several new stories, which have been incorporated into our normal development effort.

We have been pleased that the results from many of the Gold Cards undertaken have inspired our users to propose stories that are related to Gold Card ideas. Furthermore, some of these stories have been

2. See http://www.sidewize.com.

given high priorities, so they have been scheduled into our development iterations.

Although we can only refer to three iterations' worth of measured velocity data, our early indications are that we have not observed any additional decrease in project velocity. Although we feel that the Gold Cards have been beneficial, we have not measured an increase in velocity. This is because the results of the Gold Cards have enabled us to estimate stories that were too risky to consider before, accept stories that previously we were unable to consider, or more optimistically estimate stories related to Gold Card topics. Unfortunately, these improvements are not reflected in our project velocity.

Although we have not yet had any employee reviews that have been able to use Gold Cards as a discussion point, our feeling is that we have observed individual contributions that warrant recognition.

Finally, we have also noticed that the more junior programmers on our team have benefited from the scheme in a slightly unexpected way. The time alone gives them an opportunity to make mistakes, and learn from those mistakes, while alone without feeling embarrassed or restricted. These valuable lessons are then used when they return to work with a partner the following day. This effect has been a pleasant surprise to us.

Warnings

Although the scheme has generally been a success, we have had a few "teething" problems.

A few times a Gold Card was not converted into a real story soon enough. This is noticeable when a single developer works on the same topic continually, and it results in a form of code ownership that is undesirable on an XP team. Fortunately, this type of problem is quite easy to spot and deal with because developers have only two cards a month that they can use. In these cases we have made sure that everyone is aware of the danger of using a Gold Card in this way and have ensured that if the idea merits further work, a proper story card is written up, and the knowledge is spread through the team.

We have also had to make sure that our users are clear on the meaning of Gold Cards. In a few circumstances, users have tried to request features by suggesting them as Gold Cards. Although we are not averse to users contributing additional ideas, we have had to make sure that they understand that Gold Cards may never necessarily be completed.

If something is so important that it must be done, it should be written as a proper story and prioritized with other stories in a planning game. Once this distinction has been made clear, and some of the results from previous Gold Cards have been observed, this has not been a problem.

We have also found it important to monitor the use of Gold Cards to ensure that they are exercised evenly throughout the month by the team as a whole. We have had some situations where people have been unable to take their full allowance of Gold Cards because too many of them were left until the end of the month. Circumstances have sometimes meant that the team couldn't afford to have everyone exercise their unused Gold Cards in the space of a few days. With a team of ten developers, we need an average of one Gold Card to be exercised per day to spread the allocation evenly throughout a month. Fortunately, because the Gold Cards are pinned to the planning board along with user stories, it is easy to notice that they aren't being checked off at the correct rate.

Comparison with Other Approaches

There are approaches similar to Gold Cards, which we considered when devising the scheme.

The fact that a developer generally works alone on a Gold Card naturally prompts comparison with a developer acting as a "Lone Ranger." The term Lone Ranger was coined to describe the role of a developer who has no partner in an odd-numbered team. The Lone Ranger carries out tasks that are usually administrative and that the team has identified as needing doing but not requiring a partner—for example, tasks such as checking for development tool and API updates or answering support questions. In contrast, Gold Card work is chosen by a developer.

Study groups are an excellent way of spreading knowledge in a team [Kerievsky2001]. In study groups, developers optionally meet to discuss important technical topics. Gold Cards and study groups are not mutually exclusive; however, study groups do not address the issues of innovation and individual recognition that motivated the introduction of Gold Cards. Although study groups are ideal for a team starting out with XP, we would introduce Gold Cards as a practice when indications of religious guilt are encountered.

Some teams do experimental and administrative tasks in the morning and pair program in the afternoon [Deursen2001]. Gold Cards do not allow as much time for such activities but do allow a developer to work for a whole day of their choice. This means that on a day when a developer really wants to explore something in detail, they have enough uninterrupted time to tackle a significant task. In our opinion Gold Cards are a much easier practice to sell to management. Furthermore, they do not impose a time slot that could correspond to the most productive time of day. We also envisage that the half-day approach would need much more careful monitoring to prevent the adverse effects of code ownership.

At a company that two of the authors worked for (OTI),[3] developers were allowed to work on self-directed tasks on Friday afternoons. Although this is a simple scheme, there was no explicit mechanism for feedback from the results of the work undertaken, which reduced its benefits. In practice, Friday afternoons were not always available for self-directed tasks because of pressures to finish work before the end of a week, or simply because the inspiration for an idea had been lost by the time Friday arrived. Feedback from our team has indicated that the ability to pursue an idea when it is hot is important and very satisfying.

Conclusion

Our experience has shown that Gold Cards have increased innovation, improved efficiency, and provided greater recognition and motivation for developers.

By setting aside time for legitimate investigations, Gold Cards have addressed the problem of developers feeling constrained to think only about current tasks. They have allowed for blue-sky experiments that have led to genuine business opportunities and new ideas that have inspired developers and users alike. These investigations have also enabled us to estimate new development tasks more accurately.

Furthermore, tools created in Gold Card time have improved the efficiency of the development process and addressed those issues that were most annoying to developers.

Finally, developers have enjoyed the time they've spent working on things that they have chosen, without feeling as if they were cheating on the team or detracting from the completion of the customer's stories.

3. See http://www.oti.com.

References

[Deursen2001] A. van Deursen. Personal communication. May 2001.

[Heeks2000] A. Heeks. *The Natural Advantage: Renewing Yourself.* Nicholas Brealey Publishing, 2000.

[Kerievsky2001] J. Kerievsky. Continuous Learning. XP2001 Conference proceedings. 2001.

Acknowledgments

We gratefully acknowledge the contributions of John Nolan and the Connextra development team. This chapter also benefited from feedback from the attendees of the XP2001 Experience Exchange workshop.

About the Authors

Julian Higman has gray hair and plays ice hockey. Julian can be reached at julian@connextra.com.

Tim Mackinnon has 1980s hair and is a Mock Canadian. Tim can be reached at tim@connextra.com.

Ivan Moore has limited hair and drinks tea. Ivan can be reached at ivan@connextra.com.

Duncan Pierce has normal hair and climbs. Duncan can be reached at duncan@dunkworks.com.

In total, they have been programming professionally for over 40 years. They all worked together for more than a year, doing XP at Connextra.

Chapter 17

Integrating Extreme Programming and Contracts

—Hasko Heinecke and Christian Noack

Part II

Extreme Programming[1] *(XP) is a lightweight software engineering methodology, conceived by Kent Beck, with a strong focus on business value. Design by Contract is a software design technique defined by Bertrand Meyer that stresses stability and maintainability of large systems. The two are regarded as incompatible by many of their respective followers.*

In this chapter, the authors describe why contracts can nonetheless offer benefits to XP and how they can be used in an XP environment. Contracts are particularly helpful in large systems development, an area that has not yet been well investigated by the XP community. The authors describe how applying Design by Contract in an XP project can work and what benefits can be expected.

Extreme Programming

This chapter assumes a working knowledge of standard Extreme Programming concepts. We therefore do not explain the various aspects

---

1. XP advocates usually prefer the fancier spelling "eXtreme Programming." The authors, despite their affection for orthographic idiosyncrasies and their fondness for XP, have decided to stick with the more conventional way.

of XP. Good references can be found in [Beck2000; Jeffries+2001; Beck+2001].

XP is designed to address the specific needs of software development conducted by small teams. It is less well understood how it applies to large systems development. The ideas described in this chapter are an attempt to integrate one well-known technique for this with XP.

Design by Contract

A full tutorial on Design by Contract is beyond the scope of this chapter. The following section gives a brief introduction to the basic concepts and the purpose of contracts. Readers who are familiar with those concepts may want to skip them.

Pre- and Postconditions

The basic components of Design by Contract are preconditions and postconditions. Both are sets of logical (Boolean) expressions, with no side effects, that are attached to individual methods.[2] They describe semantic properties that are required to hold when the respective method is executed.

Preconditions describe the required conditions for the method to return a reasonable result. They are checked before the actual method is executed. Postconditions describe to some extent the expected result of the method, provided the preconditions were kept. Postconditions are checked after method execution but before returning to the calling context.

Invariants

Class invariants are contracts attached to a *class* that are to be checked as both preconditions and postconditions and that are checked for *every* public method of a class. Therefore, most of what is said about either of the other two kinds of contracts is also valid for class invariants.

2. As a recent discussion in some newsgroups showed, the concept of side effect freeness is somewhat hard to define. We do not discuss it in this chapter but only give an intuitive definition: Pre- and postconditions must not alter the state of the system they describe.

The rest of the chapter therefore in most cases addresses only preconditions and postconditions. Class invariants are discussed only where they differ from the other two.

Inheritance

Contracts are, by definition, inheritance-aware: The methods of a subclass must obey the rules given by its superclass [Meyer1997; Liskov1998]. When method `m` of class `A` is overwritten in subclass `B`, the contracts for `A.m` must also automatically be checked for `B.m`.

Furthermore, subclasses must require no more than their superclass—that is, they can only *weaken* preconditions. Conversely, they must promise at least what their superclass does. So they can only *strengthen* postconditions. This is usually implemented by combining all preconditions for a method in an inheritance chain with a logical `or` and all postconditions with a logical `and`.

Implementing Contracts

A detailed discussion of different implementations is beyond the scope of this chapter. Instead, we point the reader to existing products such as iContract for Java or the Eiffel language.[3]

An implementation of Design by Contract should provide some tools for formulating contracts, either in a repository or inlined in the method and class code. It should enable switching on and off contract checking for performance. It should offer additional constructs beyond the standard logical operators, such as the following.

- `old` in postconditions provides access to the state of a variable at the time of the method call—that is, when the precondition was checked. This is necessary to compare the old versus the new state of the variable.
- `forall` in pre- and postconditions checks a condition against all elements of a collection.
- `exists` in pre- and postconditions checks whether at least one element of a collection satisfies a condition.

3. See http://www.reliable-systems.com and http://www.eiffel.com.

Why Contracts?

In their article [Jézéquel+1999], Jean-Marc Jézéquel and Bertrand Meyer comment on the Ariane 5 disaster, in which a $500 million rocket exploded about 40 seconds after takeoff because of a software failure. They cite the official analysis of that incident, stating that a piece of software reused from the predecessor Ariane 4 was called in a situation that violated its implicit preconditions, crashing the system. They claim that having the routine's contract stated *explicitly* would have made finding this violation much easier and would probably have prevented the system crash.

Although not all software defects cause such spectacular crashes, contracts do provide a means to tell a developer about the constraints and promises of a piece of code. Particularly when reusing existing code that has been around for a while or that was developed by third parties, this can give quality assurance teams a hint of what to look out for. Sometimes, contracts may even help discover defects nobody was expecting, simply because they are enforced automatically.

Contracts Versus Assertions

The logical expressions that constitute pre- and postconditions are frequently referred to as assertions. For this reason, they are sometimes mistaken as the assertions known in C and similar programming languages. However, they are both more and less powerful than those. They are more powerful in that they are aware of inheritance and polymorphism. They are also less powerful because they can only be attached to method invocations and returns, while assertions can be interspersed in a method's code. We have therefore mostly avoided the term "assertion" in this chapter.

Contracts can be implemented using assertions, but it takes additional effort besides writing down the plain assertions themselves. The additional operators have to be provided, and—more important—their behavior with respect to inheritance has to be simulated.

Simplicity Versus Contracts

The central coding practice of Design by Contract is the addition of contracts—expressed through preconditions, postconditions, and invariants—to classes and methods. On the other hand, two of the most important coding practices in XP are "Do the simplest thing" and "You ain't gonna need it." The crucial question when discussing Design by Contract from an XP perspective is, "*Why would you want to add the complexity of contracts to your system?*"

In XP, only user stories can justify raising the complexity of a system. So the question can be restated as, "What user stories require the addition of contracts to a system?" In many software projects, two such stories could be the following.

- *User story 1:* We have several teams working on different subsystems, and we want to protect their interfaces against mistakes and misinterpretations. Also, our corporate quality assurance strategy requires such protection.
- *User story 2:* We want to automatically generate some documentation on the semantics of the interfaces of each subsystem—for example, for use by other teams and projects.

A brief explanation of why the two are reasonable and how they connect XP and Design by Contract is given in the following section.

Subsystems in XP

XP is usually viewed as applicable only in small teams of up to ten or 12 developers. Although this is not a definitive upper limit, most people regard it as a practical rule of thumb for the team size. A team of 20 developers is regarded as too large for effectively applying XP. In his well-known work *The Mythical Man-Month*, Fred Brooks says, "Adding more men . . . lengthens, not shortens, the schedule" [Brooks1995]. This is viewed as justification for XP's call for small teams. But in the same book, Brooks also mentions, "This then is the problem with the small, sharp team concept: *It is too slow for really big systems.*" Quite often, systems are just too big to be developed in time by a single XP team.

One possible solution is to partition a large set of requirements into subsystems that interact only through well-understood interfaces. This may seem hard to do, but in practice a lot of business domains do have such interfaces. They are either company or industry standards, required by existing architectures, or they are imposed by third-party software, such as SAP. The interface between payroll and financial accounting is an example, as are industry standards such as SWIFT for interbank messaging, or separate front-office and back-office systems. Whenever such interfaces exist, they can be used to partition a system into subsystems.

In environments like that, the stories like user story 1 (described earlier) can be satisfied by introducing Design by Contract. According to our understanding, contracts are most beneficial to XP projects when used for interfaces between subsystems. Through preconditions and class invariants, they force calling subsystems to provide the required environment to use an interface. At the same time, the calling subsystem can rely on the interface semantics that are enforced by the callee's postconditions (and class invariants).

System Documentation

Besides runtime enforcing contracts and error notification, contracts also serve well as semantic subsystem interface documentation. They explicitly state the expected context in which an interface can do useful work. Additionally, they even specify the results that can be expected, to a certain extent.

Documentation like that when done manually is notoriously incomplete and outdated. Besides, qualified team members usually are needed to produce it, and as part of the workforce, they are often indispensable. In contrast, contracts can be picked up by using suitable tools, and up-to-date documentation can be created anytime it is needed—for example, to satisfy corporate quality assurance policies (see user story 2).

Thus, contracts make code even more self-documenting, a goal that is clearly expressed in the XP core practice "The source code is the design." Meyer also mentions this aspect of contracts, for example, in [Meyer1997].

XP Values

Besides simplicity, Design by Contract also affects the three other values of XP: communication, feedback, and courage. Communication is increased by the documentation effect of contracts, as explained earlier. Feedback is increased by providing developers with early notice of interface misuse, when contract checking is switched on during test runs.

Concerning courage, developers often hesitate to change or refactor their own code when it is using or providing external interfaces, because they fear breaking them. Contracts are a safeguard against breaking interfaces and therefore encourage programmers to make the necessary changes.

Contracts and Unit Tests

One might think that contracts are not needed when unit tests are written to the extent demanded by XP. However, we believe that contracts and unit tests supplement each other.

Unit tests set up a context, then perform a task and check the result. The context has to satisfy the task's preconditions for the test to work, but it never explicitly mentions those preconditions. A person browsing through some unit tests can derive the preconditions from the contexts that are set up. This is feasible for relatively simple test units. For subsystem interfaces, the unit test is complicated. In this case, implicit preconditions are hard to derive from the unit tests alone.

There is a partial solution to this problem: It is possible and frequent practice to write specialized unit tests that check whether interfaces fail gracefully when their implicit preconditions are *not* satisfied. However, it is hard to distinguish these unit tests from those testing for real user stories, and it is not much easier to derive the actual preconditions from them. Furthermore, multiple preconditions result in a combinatorial explosion of the number of unit tests. Therefore, unit tests cannot substitute explicitly formulated preconditions.

The relationship between unit tests and postconditions is somewhat less obvious. Both unit tests and postconditions give evidence of the expected result (or resulting context) of an action. Unit tests create an example situation and check an operation's result. Postconditions, though, describe the expected result in a more general manner, even though less detailed. As logical functions, they can describe an infinite set of possible results, *and* they can even exclude impossible ones.

Furthermore, contracts fit well into the "once and only once" principle of XP. They represent the *universal* (desired) semantics of a method, whereas unit tests represent only its semantics under a given assumption. Therefore, associating the contracts with their methods instead of their multitude of tests follows that principle. Besides, contracts for a set of classes that have a common superclass can be expressed in the superclass itself instead of repeating them in the unit tests of each subclass. This is also useful when the superclass is abstract and cannot be instantiated for testing.

As has been illustrated, unit tests and contracts address different, if somewhat overlapping, issues. Unit tests are a core practice of XP. Their presence is required throughout the life cycle of every XP project. Contracts are not crucial for XP to work. However, in a large system development effort that is partitioned into several loosely coupled subsystems, they can help ease communication difficulties that arise at their interfaces.

Contracts as an Implementation Pattern

The inventor of Design by Contract himself, Bertrand Meyer, notes that the contracts look formal and "shocking to most" who first encounter the concept [Meyer1997]. He adds that they are the foundation of code stability and other quality goals. The authors agree in that contracts are indeed a means to achieve those goals, where it would be hard with unit tests alone.

However, contracts are not as strange to developers as they might appear at first glance. In fact, they are an implementation pattern commonly found in existing code.

Assertions Again

Contracts are a particular form of assertions, as explained earlier. Assertions themselves are not unknown to most developers, and they are frequently used by those more careful in large systems projects. Plain assertions are sometimes considered unnecessary in the presence of unit test suites, but they are hardly a strange and new concept.

Preconditions

In many methods, preconditions are disguised as Guard Clauses.[4] Using preconditions instead makes them easier to locate and enforces sensible rules for methods overwritten by subclasses.

---

4. A Guard Clause, as described in [Beck1997], is a condition that is checked at the beginning of a method and that raises some kind of exception when it fails.

Postconditions

Postconditions are often simulated by methods checking a message's result. This is commonly used when the message sent belongs to another module or is supposed to call a different application.

Code like this expresses a healthy mistrust in the developers who wrote the called code. However, it should be the other code's responsibility to enforce the promises made, if only to have it in one place instead of dispersing it throughout the client code. This only works when those promises are documented, which postconditions do better than API documentation.

Class Invariants

Class invariants are not frequently encountered in existing code. However, they are sometimes present without being explicitly formulated. Then, they are an annoying source of what is often called "beginners' faults." An example of this is the `equals/hashCode` relationship in Java.[5]

When you overwrite `equals()` in a class, you have to make sure that equal objects still return the same hash code. However, this is enforced nowhere, and it's stated only in the class library documentation and therefore easily missed by beginners.[6] Of course, veteran developers will always remember it, unless they are in a hurry.

Again, having explicitly stated invariants will help locate and enforce them. Developers *encountering* class invariants (as opposed to those *writing* them) will probably not find them strange and burdensome but will welcome them as an additional aid.

Conclusion

Design by Contract is certainly not a core practice of XP, but neither does it contradict the XP values. It has been shown that Design by Contract does offer benefits in an XP environment, if wisely applied. In

5. The same relationship exists in Smalltalk.

6. Interestingly, this is considered a class invariant of the class `Object` by both the Java and Smalltalk documentation. It should instead be an invariant of an interface that specifies hashing (for example, `Hashable`). However, there is no such interface in Java and of course none in Smalltalk.

particular, large systems efforts can use contracts to specify and document their subsystems' semantics to a certain degree.

The authors are currently applying the approach described here in their projects. An empirical analysis of its success will show to what extent the described effects will benefit large XP projects.

References

[Beck1997] K. Beck. *Smalltalk Best Practice Patterns.* Prentice Hall, 1997.

[Beck2000] K. Beck. *Extreme Programming Explained.* Addison-Wesley, 2000.

[Beck+2001] K. Beck, M. Fowler. *Planning Extreme Programming.* Addison-Wesley, 2001.

[Brooks1995] F. Brooks. *The Mythical Man-Month, Anniversary Edition.* Addison-Wesley, 1995.

[Jeffries+2001] R. Jeffries, A. Anderson. *Extreme Programming Installed.* Addison-Wesley, 2001.

[Jézéquel+1999] J. Jézéquel, B. Meyer. "Design by Contract: The Lessons of Ariane." *Computer*, Volume 30, January 1999.

[Liskov1998] B. Liskov. "Data Abstraction and Hierarchy." *SIGPLAN Notices*, Volume 23, May 1998.

[Meyer1997] B. Meyer. *Object-Oriented Software Construction, Second Edition.* Prentice Hall, 1997.

Acknowledgments

We thank Bertrand Meyer for giving interesting and entertaining talks that introduced us to the concept of contracts; our employer, the Daedalos group, for providing the resources and patience while we were researching the topic presented here; and our partners and families for bearing with us while we were immersed in it.

About the Authors

Hasko Heinecke and Christian Noack both work for Daedalos International AG in Switzerland and Germany, respectively. They have a strong background in OO technology and the Smalltalk programming language, complemented by several years of experience in Java. Not being advocates of any one programming language, they are more interested in the inner workings of object-orientation itself and its implications on project management. They can be reached at hasko.heinecke@daedalos.com and christian.noack@daedalos.com.

Part II

Chapter 18

Refactoring or Up-Front Design?

—*Pascal Van Cauwenberghe*

Among supporters and detractors of XP, the debate rages whether up-front design or incremental design combined with refactoring is the optimal method of implementing systems. This chapter argues that neither method is clearly better in every circumstance. Instead, the experienced software engineer uses a combination of both methods. This chapter also argues that the "cost of change" curve presented in Extreme Programming Explained *[Beck2000] does not replace the classic "cost of fixing errors" curve presented by Barry Boehm in [Boehm1981]. Instead, XP is a method of attacking the costs described by this curve.*

XP, as an incremental method of software engineering, is only applicable in circumstances where the cost of implementing functionalities does not grow rapidly as development progresses. Some heuristics and examples for deciding when to use each technique are presented.

Introduction

In *Software Engineering Economics*, Boehm presented the classic cost curve shown in Figure 18.1. As we progress from analysis to design, coding, testing, and production, the cost of fixing a problem rises.

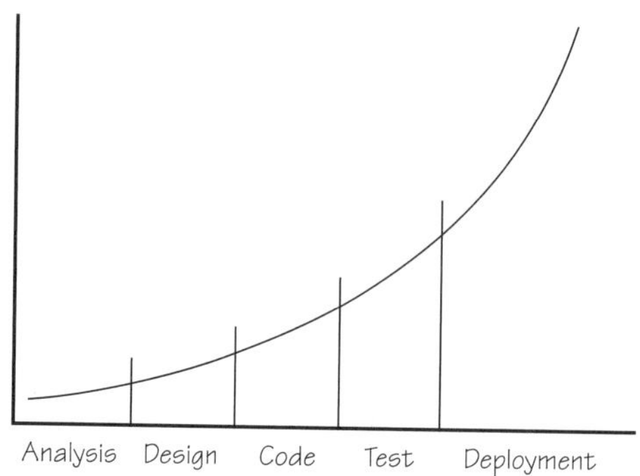

FIGURE 18.1 The "cost of fixing errors" curve

Note that the sharpest rise occurs when the system is released and distributed to its customers.

In *Extreme Programming Explained*, Kent Beck argues that this curve no longer represents the current state of software engineering. Instead, this curve is said to be flat. Two remarks can be made.

- Originally, this curve represented the cost of *fixing errors* introduced in earlier phases of a project. Kent Beck presents the curve as the "cost of *change*" curve.
- In his online article "Reexamining the Cost of Change Curve," Alistair Cockburn demonstrates that the cost of *fixing errors* still rises rapidly as the project progresses [Cockburn2000].

Does the "Cost of Fixing Errors" Curve Invalidate XP?

If this curve is still valid, does this mean XP is invalid? I argue that it is not. Several of the XP practices specifically ensure that the costs associated with this curve are kept minimal.

- *Unit testing* and *test-first design* ensure that bugs are found quickly when they are cheap to fix.
- *On-site customer* and *functional testing* ensure that the analysis and specification of the system are precise and up to date with business requirements.

- *Pair programming* finds bugs quickly and spreads knowledge.
- *Refactoring* and *"once and only once"* ensure that the system remains well designed and easy to change.
- *Regular releases* gives regular customer feedback and forces the team to make the "release to production" and maintenance phases (where the cost of fixing errors rises dramatically) as cheap as possible.

Thus, XP attacks the roots of the high cost of fixing errors (with good specifications, good design, good implementation, and fast feedback). Furthermore, by using very short cycle times, the cost is never allowed to rise very high.

Part II

Not-So-Extreme Programming

Note that, with the exception of the very short cycle times and pair programming (which in XP replaces the inspections, design sessions, and training that are accepted in most methodologies), these practices are neither very original nor extreme.

Although errors are most costly to fix when found in later phases, each later phase is more likely to find errors in previous phases. This is because each phase produces a more concrete, more tangible, more testable output. Therefore, we need an iterative process that incorporates feedback to improve earlier work.

Iterative Versus Incremental

The well-known "waterfall" method is rarely used, even by those who claim (or are forced) to use it. Most development methods are *incremental* and *iterative*. What do those words mean?

- Iterative—Repeating the same task to improve its output
- Incremental—Dividing a task into small tasks, which are completed one by one (sequentially or in parallel)

Now let's see how different types of methods use iterations and increments.

Waterfall

Analyze, design, code, integrate, test—done! No iterations, no increments, no feedback; everything works the first time.

Classic RUP-Like Process

Analyze until 70–80% done. Start the design phase, but keep updating the analysis with any feedback you receive. Design until 70–80% done. Start the coding phase, but keep improving with feedback. And so on for the other phases.

This is an iterative process—feedback is used to improve the work done. The process is not incremental, except in the coding and integration phases, where some parts of the application may be delivered incrementally.

Incremental Architecture-Driven Process

Analyze the application until 70–80% done. Design the application so that the architecture and high-risk elements are relatively complete. Define functional groups. Refine the analysis and design as the project progresses.

For each functional group, a detailed analysis, a detailed design, coding, integration, and testing are done. Each increment is handled like a small RUP-like project, with iterations to improve the output. When the functional group is finished, it is delivered as an increment to the customer.

We have an iterative first step, which looks at the whole application. The application is then delivered incrementally, with each increment developed using an iterative process.

Extreme Programming

Gather an initial set of stories from the customers (high-level analysis). Define a metaphor (high-level analysis and design).

For each release, perform the planning game to allocate stories. For each story, define acceptance tests (analyze), write unit tests (design), code, refactor, integrate, test, and repeat frequently (iterate) until done.

The basic process is incremental on the level of releases and stories. Within those increments, the process iterates rapidly, based on feedback from acceptance and unit tests.

From Shack to Skyscraper

So what is extreme in XP? It is the assumption that analysis and design can be done incrementally; the assumption that *a complex system can be grown incrementally with hardly any up-front work*. XP detractors liken it to "building a skyscraper out of a shack."

This assumption is in no way trivial or obvious. Where this assumption does not hold, we will not be able to apply XP successfully.

Which XP practices depend on the incremental assumption?

- *The planning game* grows specifications story by story, expecting each story to deliver business value.
- *Simple design* solves today's problems, assuming that we will be able to solve tomorrow's problems when they arise.
- *Small releases* assumes that we can deliver regular, *useful* increments of the system to the customers.
- *Customer in team* assumes that we can refine the specification of the system gradually, when we need to.

Working incrementally delivers some benefits.

- We learn all the time from the customer, from the system being developed. If we can make decisions later, they will likely be better.
- We keep the system as simple as possible, making it easier to understand, easier to change, less likely to contain errors.
- The customer quickly gets useful output. The system can be used to generate value and to guide further specification, planning, and development.

Preconditions for Incremental Methods to Work

Under what conditions do incremental methods work? Let's examine how the cost of implementing one feature (which includes analysis, design, coding, integration, and testing) changes throughout the duration of a whole software system.

As shown in Figure 18.2, one feature quickly becomes more expensive to implement, while the other feature's price rises slowly.

In the first case, we would be wise to spend effort as soon as possible while the cost is low. We want to analyze and design this feature as

Part II

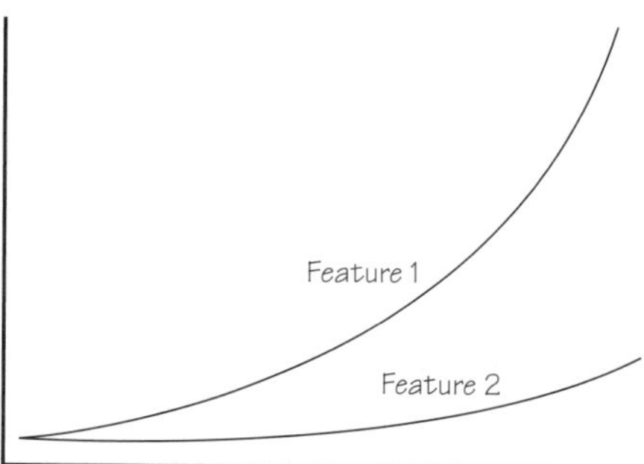

FIGURE 18.2 The cost of implementation

completely as we can; we want to address not only our current needs but also our future needs. If we don't do it today, we will pay dearly for it later. A common cause for rising implementation costs is the breakdown of the design under the stress of new functions when the design is not kept up to date by refactoring.

In the second case, we can safely delay addressing the feature until we really need to. It might be somewhat more costly to design and implement later. For example, the system will have more functions and thus will probably be more complex. But we can invest the unspent effort in other, more profitable features.

It's in this situation that the planning game brings a large benefit to customers: They can select stories to implement based on their business value, without having to be concerned about technical dependencies and future costs.

Surprising Cost Curve

One of the surprising and pleasant effects that the incremental method can have is that the cost of some functionalities decreases over time. The following factors can cause this.

- Well-designed (refactored), simple code in which no duplication is allowed often presents the developer with opportunities to reuse significant parts of the code, which makes new features easier to implement.

- Over time we learn to better understand the problem domain, the design, and the software. We see new abstractions, simpler ways to solve problems, and better ways to apply our designs.

So, we find another heuristic for selecting the incremental method: Use the incremental method when you expect to learn more so that you can make better decisions later. This applies especially to situations where requirements are unclear or changing.

Analogy with Investment

If you want to invest in a company, you can buy shares. You make the decision based on your knowledge of the market, the company, the risk you run, and speculation about the future. Your money is tied up. If it turns out as you predicted, you can gain a lot. If it doesn't, you lose money. That's the risk you take.

Sometimes you can buy options. These enable you to buy or sell stock in the future at a price that is agreed to now. You invest very little, but you buy the right to wait to make your decision. If the value of the stocks rises, you buy and make a profit. If the value of the stocks decreases, you don't buy and lose only the price of the option.

Likewise, investing in keeping your software malleable is a small investment that pays off by giving you more options. See Chapter 43, which is based on the papers presented by John Favaro (at XP2001) and Hakan Erdogmus (at XP Universe 2001), for a complete treatment of this analogy.

Analogy with House Building

Often, software development is compared with more mature engineering disciplines. An analogy with building construction is sometimes used to demonstrate the value of good architectural design, detailed planning (as if construction projects always deliver on spec, on time), and a solid mathematical and scientific basis. Let's see how one would approach a house-building project under both cost-of-implementation assumptions.

Imagine that an architect discusses the specifications for a house to be built for a couple. An important factor is the number of bedrooms to be built. The couple must decide *now* how many bedrooms they will need in the foreseeable future. How many children will they have? Hard to predict. But they must decide now, because it will be very costly to add more rooms to the house later. They must invest now—their money is tied up in those rooms they may never need. If they underestimate the number of rooms needed, they will be faced with costly modifications or will have to build a new house. If they overestimate, they waste money.

If, on the other hand, adding a room later costs not much more than building it now, the couple would be wise to postpone the decision until they really need extra rooms. In the meantime, they can invest their money elsewhere. They don't face the risk of over- or underestimating the need for rooms and thus wasting money. They have lowered their financial risk considerably.

Maybe software and houses aren't the same [Jeffries2000].

Typical Examples of Rapidly Rising Cost Features

In some situations, we are faced with features whose cost rises sharply. We should take this into account and expect to perform more work up front. We should also try to minimize the cost so that we can gain the benefits of the incremental method. Here are some examples.

- Externally used, published APIs. Once the APIs are in use, customers will demand backward compatibility or a simple upgrade path. Effort should be spent on keeping the APIs flexible, minimal, and useful.
- Development teams that aren't colocated. Up-front effort should be spent on partitioning the system to be developed.
- Databases used by multiple, independent applications. Common abstractions should be used to encapsulate persistence. When applications are released independently, the persistence and model layer should support some level of multiple version support.
- Software in which release to customers or distribution is expensive. Frequent releases can train the development and production team to perform these tasks as efficiently as possible.

- Aspects of the application that have an overall effect on all of its parts. Examples are internationalization, scalability, error handling, and so on. Having to make changes that affect all of the software makes refactoring very expensive.

Interfaces between different teams, global properties of the system, and software that is distributed to remote customers have a high cost of change. Some areas that are commonly thought to have a high cost may have a surprisingly low cost of change.

- Except for hard, time-critical software, well-factored code can be changed to meet performance criteria. A few simple and general design techniques can be used up front. Most of the performance-related work can be done only after measurements have been made on the integrated system. A process that integrates and delivers often, combined with performance measurements, is the most effective way of developing well-performing software.
- Database schema changes for software that is owned by one team. A team can get very good very quickly at dealing with schema or interface changes if all of the software is owned by the team. Version detection, upgrade programs, and encapsulation of version-dependent modules enabled my team to make fundamental changes to the database structure, without any customer noticing it.

Conclusion

The choice between up-front work and refactoring should be made case by case. There is always some up-front work and some refactoring. It is up to the software engineer to make the right trade-off, based on the following heuristics.

- If you can postpone decisions, you will be able to make better decisions at a later time.
- Invest in more up-front work if the implementation cost of the functionality is likely to rise rapidly in the future.
- Investing is dangerous unless you know the domain well and can make informed projections.

The choice comes down to selecting the method that implies the least risk. Good, experienced software engineers are able to make this choice. Instead of using the disparaging term "big design up front" (BDUF) we should be investigating how best to determine what is "just enough design for increments" (JEDI). This will enable us to make better-informed decisions.

Maybe software engineering should look not only to other engineering disciplines for analogies and techniques, but also to the way risk and return on investment are analyzed in the financial world.

References

[Beck2000] K. Beck. *Extreme Programming Explained*. Addison-Wesley, 2000.

[Boehm1981] B. Boehm. *Software Engineering Economics*. Prentice Hall, 1981.

[Cockburn2000] A. Cockburn. *Reexamining the Cost of Change Curve*. http://www.xprogramming.com/xpmag/cost_of_change.htm. 2000.

[Jeffries2000] R. Jeffries. *House Analogy*. http://www.xprogramming.com/xpmag/houseAnalogy.htm. 2000.

Acknowledgments

I would like to thank Vera Peeters and Martine Verluyten for reviewing and discussing this chapter.

About the Author

Pascal Van Cauwenberghe is the CTO of Lesire Software Engineering, where he leads the software development teams. He has been designing and building object-oriented systems for more than ten years.

Chapter 19

A Methodology for Incremental Changes

—*Václav Rajlich*

Part II

Incremental changes add new functionality and new properties to the software. This chapter presents a methodology for incremental changes, where domain concepts play a key role. A case study of a small application written in Java is also presented.

Introduction

Software evolution is a phase in the software life cycle in which major changes are made. It is based on iterative enhancements to the software [Rajlich+2000], called "small releases" in [Beck2000]. Each small release adds new functionality previously not available and results in a working program. The strategy of small releases is to provide valuable feedback to programmers, managers, and customers and give them the opportunity to adjust future direction, goals, schedule, and budget [Beck2000].

Software methodologies have been used for a long time in initial development, which starts from scratch and ends with the first working version of software. There are a great variety of methodologies for initial development, supporting diverse software engineering processes and resulting in diverse software architectures.

In software evolution, the type of change that has been extensively studied and supported by methodologies and tools is software refactoring [Fowler1999; Fanta+1999]. Refactoring is a special kind of change that modifies the software's structure but does not affect the software's functionality. It is an important ingredient of software evolution because it enables programmers to restructure software and keep it understandable and evolvable. However, it is obvious that software evolution cannot consist of refactoring only; the thrust and purpose of evolution is to change software functionality and properties.

The change that modifies software functionality and other software properties is incremental change. It is the basic building block of software evolution, far surpassing in importance all other kinds of change. However, at this time, there are no integrated methodologies for incremental change. Instead, incremental change is largely a self-taught art that programmers learn by trial and error, sometimes at great cost. This chapter is a step toward a methodology and presents an outline of a methodology and a case study. It emphasizes the role of domain concepts in incremental change.

Role of Domain Concepts

The methodology presented in this chapter is based on the observation that requests for iterative change are formulated in terms of domain concepts, and these new concepts are already latently present in the code. For example, a Point Of Sale application needs to deal with several forms of payment, so there is an incremental change request to introduce "credit cards," "checks," and so on. However, even before this request, the concept "payment" was already in the program, represented as just one variable, allowing only cash. The incremental change expands this latent concept and adds new functionality to it.

To make the change, the programmer locates the latent concepts and then reifies them, or implements them explicitly and fully. Based on this observation, we can formulate the steps of a methodology for incremental changes.

1. Formulate the change request.
2. Locate the latent concepts in the code.
3. Implement the concept explicitly and fully in new classes (concept reification).

4. Replace the latent concept in the old code with program dependencies (function calls, data flows, instance definitions) between the old and the new classes.
5. Propagate changes through the old code.

Let us look at these steps in more detail, using the previously mentioned change request to implement payments by credit card.

First, in the current program, the concept "payment" must be located. It can be a class, or it can be part of one or several classes. It can be implemented explicitly like a variable, or it can be a subset of values of a type, or it can be an implicit assumption that guided an implementation of an algorithm or data structure. Once the concept has been located, it becomes clear how hard or easy it will be to incorporate the requested change into the existing program. The changes in concepts that are localized—that is, implemented in one or a few classes—are easy to incorporate. On the other hand, the changes in concepts that are delocalized are hard. In the case of credit card payments, the concept is implemented explicitly as the variable `payment` inside the class `sale`.

After the old concept has been located, the next step is to implement the concept fully with new functionality. In our case, the new implementation consists of a hierarchy of classes consisting of the base class `payment` and derived classes for cash and authorized payments, with further derived classes for credit cards and checks. This new hierarchy is then plugged into the old program and replaces the old implementation of the concept. This means that in the program, all references to the old concept must be replaced with references to this new hierarchy. Thus, the old variable `payment` is replaced with an instance of the new class `payment`. All references to the old variable must be replaced with calls of the methods of this new class.

After that, the old relationship of the class `sale` with its neighbors may be broken because of the changes in the class. Thus, the programmer must check all its neighbors to see whether the relationship with the class `sale` has been affected. If not, there is no need to make any changes. However, if the relationship has been affected, it requires secondary changes in the neighbors. After these changes, the neighbors of the newly changed classes must also be checked, and so forth. This iterative process is called *change propagation* and continues until all real or potential inconsistencies have been removed.

Concept location has been extensively studied; for example, see [Bohner+1996] and [Chen+2000]. Change propagation has also been studied; for example, see [Rajlich2000]. The following case study contains examples of the methodology.

Case Study

The case study deals with a Point Of Sale application for small stores. The application keeps an inventory, receives deliveries, supports sales of items to customers, and supports cashiers and cash registers. It is implemented in Java through several incremental changes.

Initial Development

The initial development implemented a greatly simplified version of the Point Of Sale application, in which all payments are in cash, prices are constant, taxes are uniform, and there are one register and one cashier in the store. The initial development introduced five classes: `register`, `store`, `item`, `sale`, and `saleLineItem`.

Support for Payment

Support for various forms of payment, including credit cards and checks, was implemented in the next iteration. Following the methodology, we first located the latent concept "payment" in the class `sale`, where it was implemented as a local variable of type integer. The member functions `setPayment()` and `payForSale()` deal with this variable and support cash payments. We reified the concept "payment" in a new class hierarchy consisting of the base class `payment` and its subclasses for cash and authorized payments, with further subclasses for checks and credit cards. This class hierarchy was integrated into the original program by replacing the old variable with an instance of the class `payment`. Other changes in the class `sale` involved changes in the member functions `setPayment()` and `payForSale()`. A secondary change propagated to the class `register`.

Price Fluctuations

This incremental change introduced price fluctuations. Products can have different prices at different times. In the old program, price was implemented as a single variable in the class `item`. We implemented the new classes `price` and `promoPrice` and replaced the variable in the old class `item` with an instance of the class `price`. After additional changes to the class `item`, the change propagated through the old classes `store`, `saleLineItem`, and `sale`. Figure 19.1 shows a Uniform Modeling Language (UML) diagram [Booch+1998] of the program at this stage.

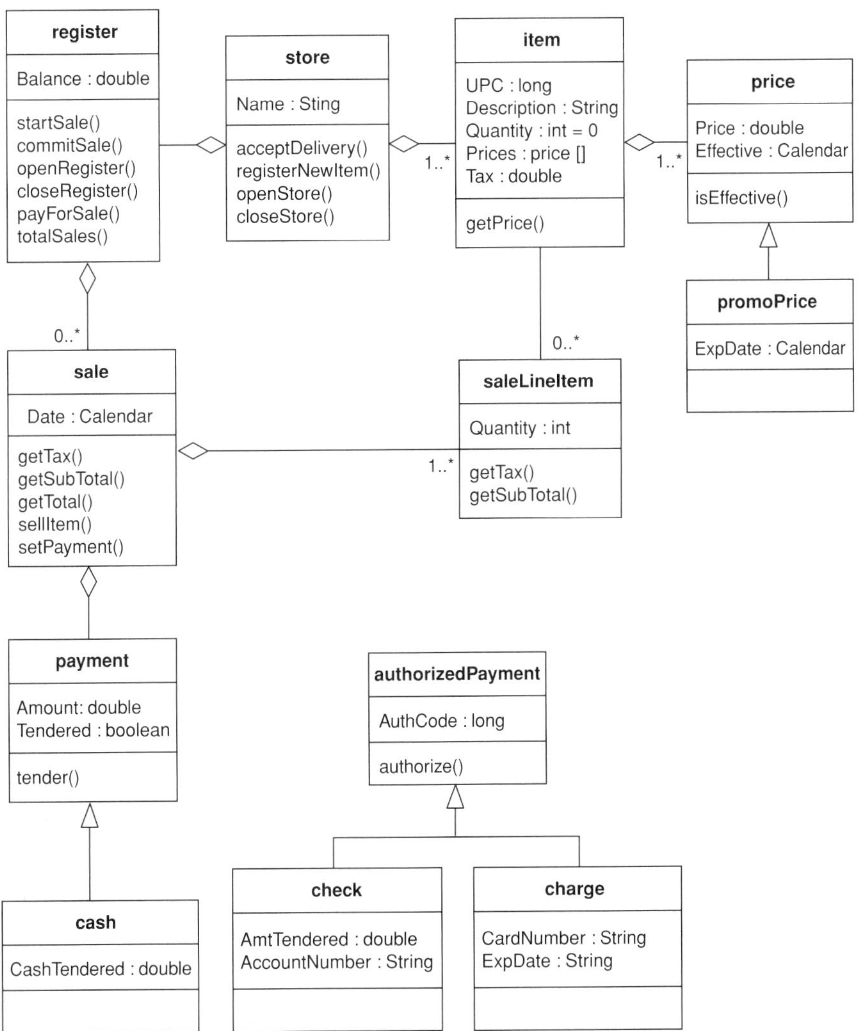

FIGURE 19.1 UML diagram of the Point Of Sale application

Sales Taxes

This incremental change introduced the complexities of sales taxes. We describe this change in more detail with the help of the UML-like class diagrams shown in Figures 19.2 through 19.6. The boxes stand for classes, and the lines represent all associations. The arrows indicate the inconsistencies in the program and point to the classes that have to be changed. See [Rajlich2000] for further details.

Different products may have a different sales tax, depending on state law. The old program contained a single tax rate as an integer within the class `item`. We implemented a new class, `taxCategory`, and then replaced the integer in the class `item` with an instance of `taxCategory`. The current state of the program is represented in Figure 19.2. In it, the arrow points to the class `item`, where several additional changes must be made.

To remove the inconsistency, we examined the class `item` and made all necessary changes. The class `item` interacts with the classes `store`, `saleLineItem`, and `price`. Thus, they have to be checked and changed if necessary, as shown in Figure 19.3. The check of the class `price` revealed that it does not need any changes and that it does not propagate the change further. We then examined the class `store` and modified it.

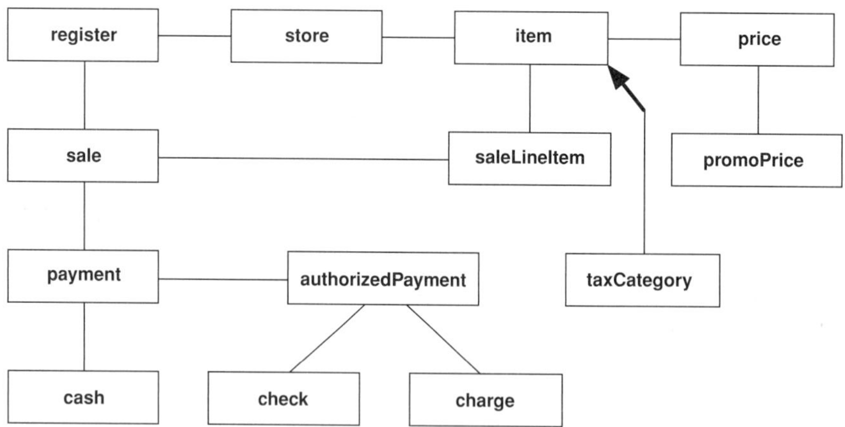

FIGURE 19.2 Point Of Sale application after implementing the class `taxCategory`

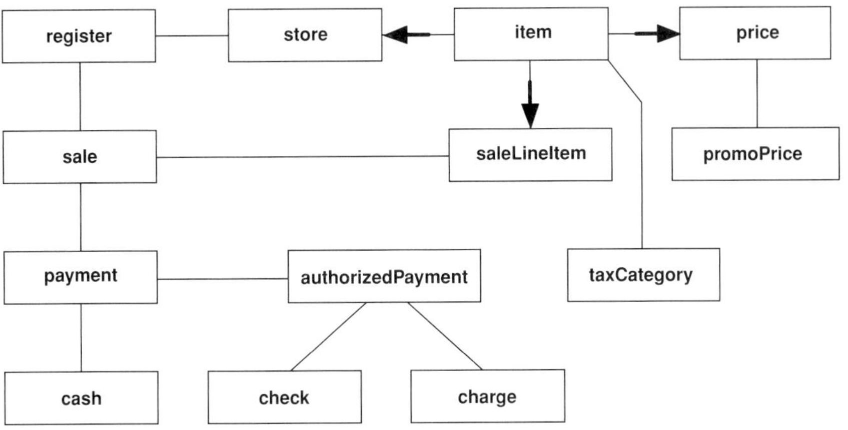

FIGURE 19.3 Examining classes that interact with the class `item`

The next class, `register`, was checked but did not need any modification, and the change did not propagate in that direction. The resulting diagram is shown in Figure 19.4.

The next class we checked was `saleLineItem`. After the changes were performed, the neighboring class `sale` could be influenced by the changes. Thus, the class `sale` is marked, as shown in Figure 19.5.

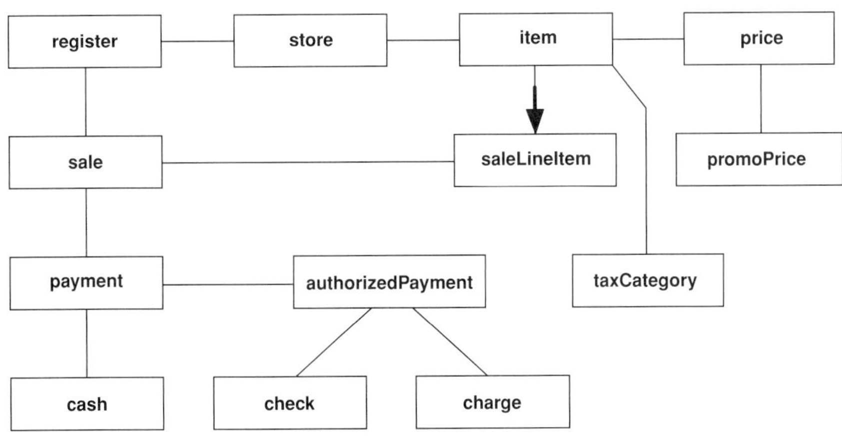

FIGURE 19.4 Examining the class `saleLineItem`

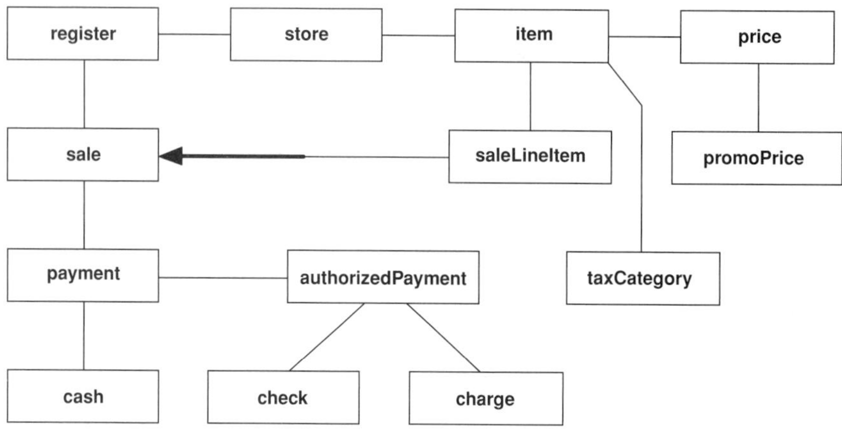

FIGURE 19.5 Marking the class `sale` for examination

The class `sale` required only one small change. Still, it interacts with two other neighboring classes, as shown in Figure 19.6, and they may also need a change.

The class `payment` did not have to be changed, and the change did not propagate further. The class `register` did not use the tax information contained in the class `sale` and relied on prices supplied by the

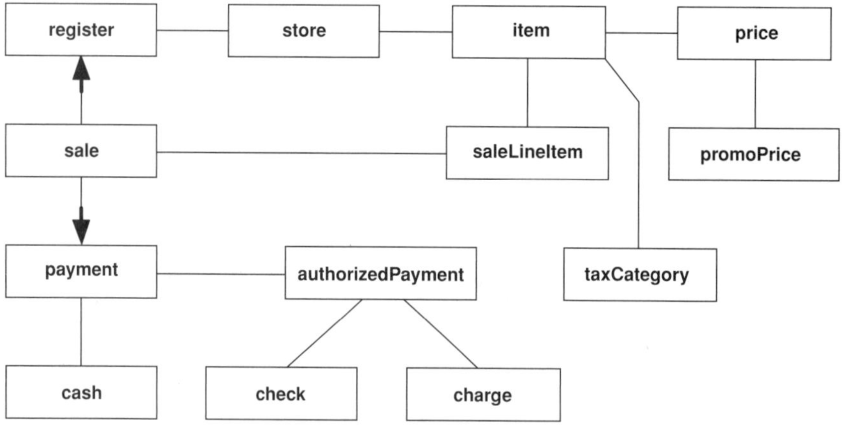

FIGURE 19.6 Examining classes that interact with the class `sale`

class sale. Therefore, no change was needed, so we unmarked it, without propagating the change further. That completed this incremental change.

Several Cashiers

Stores often have several cashiers who take shifts at registers. This incremental change introduces multiple registers, cashiers, and their sales. The old version of the application assumes one cashier and one register, and this assumption is implicit in the implementation of the classes store, register, and sale.

New classes cashier and session reify information about the start and the end of the cashier's sessions, about sales realized within each session, and about the specific register used by the cashier during the session. They are interconnected with the old program by using the classes sale, register, and store, as shown in Figure 19.7.

Then we examined and modified the old class register, adding support for several sessions on the register and the cashiers' PIN numbers. After the changes, the class register no longer directly references the class sale but references the class session instead. A check of the class

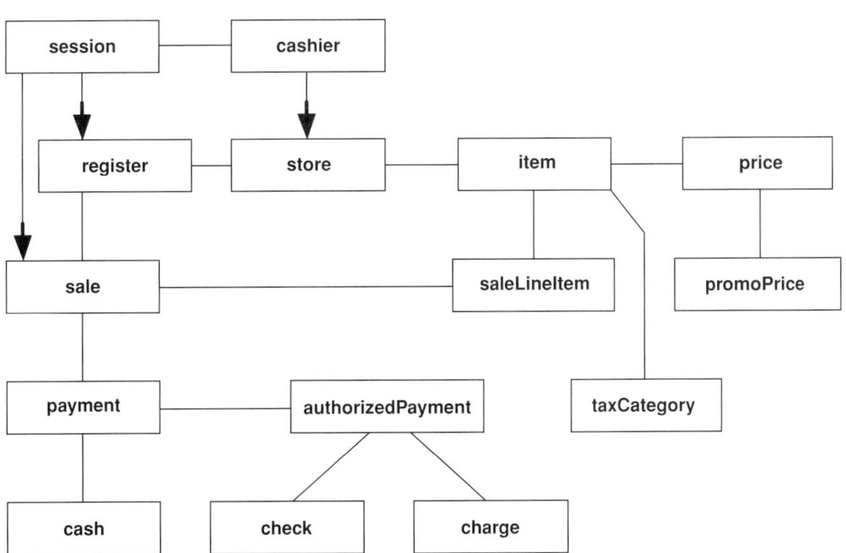

FIGURE 19.7 Interconnecting the new classes to the old program

Part II

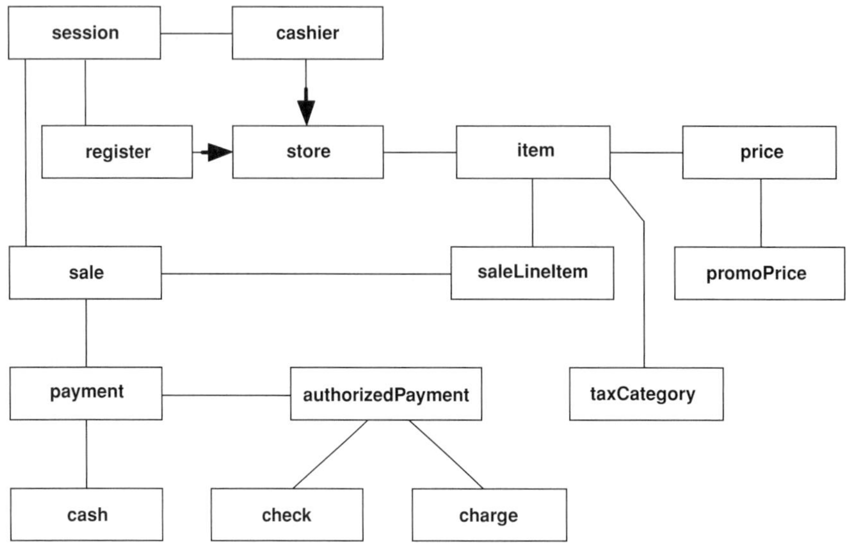

FIGURE 19.8 Examining the class `store`

`sale` and its neighbors showed that the change does not propagate any further, as shown in Figure 19.8.

The last remaining class to examine is `store`. During the check, we propagated changes from both the class `cashier` and the class `register`. The changes include adding new data members for a list of cashiers and a new method, `registerCashier`, as well as modifying the methods `openStore` and `closeStore` to allow the store to open only when some cashiers are available. The check of the neighboring class `item` showed that there is no need to propagate the change further.

Observations

In the case study, we observed that both concept location and change propagation are an overhead of the change, and the overhead is the same whether the change is large or small. For example, if we introduced just credit card payments in an incremental change without also dealing with payments by check, the same concept location and change propagation would have to be done to implement that smaller change.

Small changes lead to the repetition of the overhead tasks and result in decreased efficiency and increased likelihood of errors.

On the other hand, changes that are too big and deal with too many issues at once may overload the cognitive capabilities of the programmers and again lead to increasing the likelihood of error. Thus, there is an optimal size of the incremental change. In this case study, all the incremental changes introduced one to five new classes into the program, examined three to seven old classes, and modified up to four of them.

As we stated earlier, change propagation is a process that requires a check of all the neighbors of a changed class. To miss a change propagation means to introduce a subtle error into the code that will be hard to find later [Yu+2001]. Therefore, in our case study, we chose to be cautious and inspect more classes than absolutely necessary. However, there is a practical limit to how far to carry out change propagation; otherwise, every class of the program would be checked for every incremental change. In our case study, we used the following criterion: We inspected all classes that are direct neighbors of changed classes. Also, we inspected all classes that participate in a data flow with a changed class and checked whether the meaning of the data changed. If so, we made the appropriate changes. If not, we no longer propagated the change. This criterion worked well in all instances in our case study.

Conclusions and Future Work

In this chapter, we presented an outline of a methodology and a case study of incremental change. We observed that domain concepts play an important role in incremental changes.

An interesting question is the optimal sequence of incremental changes that minimizes the changes' impact and any rework needed. Certain concepts depend on others, such as the concept "tax" depending on "item." In that case, the concept "item" must be introduced first, because without it, the concept "tax" is meaningless.

Another interesting question is the relationship between refactoring and change propagation. One of the purposes of refactoring is to minimize the propagation by localizing concepts in one or a few classes. However, it is not clear whether it is always possible to shorten change propagation by refactoring. There may be certain changes that are always delocalized and are "refactoring resistant." Additional case studies are needed to answer this question.

A hope is that the methodology of incremental change will improve the current situation, in which the incremental change is largely a self-taught art. This will enable the accumulation of knowledge in this important field.

References

[Beck2000] K. Beck. *Extreme Programming Explained*. Addison-Wesley, 2000.

[Bohner+1996] S. Bohner, R. Arnold. *Software Change Impact Analysis*. IEEE Computer Society Press, 1996.

[Booch+1998] G. Booch, J. Rumbaugh, I. Jacobson. *The Unified Modeling Language User Guide*. Addison-Wesley, 1998.

[Chen+2000] K. Chen, V. Rajlich. "Case Study of Feature Location Using Dependency Graph." *Proceedings of Eighth International Workshop on Program Comprehension*. IEEE Computer Society Press, 2000.

[Fanta+1999] R. Fanta, V. Rajlich. "Removing Clones from the Code." *Journal of Software Maintenance*, 1999.

[Fowler1999] M. Fowler. *Refactoring: Improving the Design of Existing Code*. Addison-Wesley, 1999.

[Rajlich2000] V. Rajlich. "Modeling Software Evolution by Evolving Interoperation Graphs." *Annals of Software Engineering*, Volume 9, 2000.

[Rajlich+2000] V. Rajlich, K. Bennett. "The Staged Model of the Software Lifecycle." *IEEE Computer*, July 2000.

[Yu+2001] Z. Yu, V. Rajlich. "Hidden Dependencies in Program Comprehension and Change Propagation." *Proceedings of Ninth International Workshop on Program Comprehension*. IEEE Computer Society Press, 2001.

About the Author

Václav Rajlich is a full professor and former chair in the Department of Computer Science at Wayne State University. He has published extensively in the areas of software evolution, maintenance, change, and comprehension. He received a Ph.D. in mathematics from Case Western Reserve University. Contact him at vtr@cs.wayne.edu.

Chapter 20

Extreme Maintenance

—Charles Poole and Jan Willem Huisman

Part II

This chapter examines some of the problems experienced by IONA Technology's Orbix Generation 3 maintenance and enhancement team and how the adoption of Extreme Programming (XP) has further improved the team's ability to deliver quality support and enhancements to the products they work on. The issues identified and discussed are common issues for companies moving from the start-up pressures of time-to-market to those related to supporting large numbers of customers with bug fixes and enhancements to existing applications in existing deployment scenarios.

The chapter briefly reviews the history of the team's development and maintenance practices before implementing the XP practices. It then focuses on how XP was implemented and used to resolve some of the identified problems. Results are detailed as both a qualitative view on the XP project and the impacts on morale, along with some of the quantitative analysis related to productivity and customer satisfaction. This experience has shown that XP is a viable and very successful model for teams involved in pure maintenance and enhancement of a legacy code base.

Introduction

IONA Technology's flagship product during the 1990s was a CORBA middleware product called Orbix. There are currently two versions of the product. This chapter deals with the development and, in particular, the maintenance of the older version, which represents the early evolution of the CORBA specification, and, correspondingly, the inherent problems of code entropy because of specification instability and time-to-market pressures. In such an environment and with the rapid growth in the engineering team, the tendency to ignore good engineering processes and practices was quite prevalent. As a result, the overall health of the code base had degenerated over time and was salvaged only through two very successful refactoring efforts and a series of infrastructure projects designed to improve overall engineering practices. The Orbix Generation 3 team is currently doing this maintenance and enhancement activity.

The Problems

We focus on four areas in looking at the problems that were identified. Again, these problems are all related to how IONA moved from a start-up to a market-leading provider of middleware products.

Processes and Practices

In early 1999, you could have asked two different engineers from the same Orbix team how they did their job, and they both would have given you a different answer—a reflection of the lack of process documentation and visibility as well as a lack of emphasis on making process part of an engineer's personal software practices. Also, there was no focus on process improvement, because the junior engineers assigned to work on maintenance and enhancement had no experience with good engineering practices and had only a rudimentary understanding of process. To compound the problems, the maintenance and enhancement team used disparate source control elements across two globally distributed development sites, and a well-defined and tested interface between configuration units was nonexistent. Dependency management was a nightmare.

Testing

In general, quality for the Orbix product was never one of its high points. Test coverage was not well documented, so good metrics were not available. Test suites were cumbersome, difficult to run, and impossible to report on accurately. Product releases were difficult to system test because the test suite used to provide interoperability testing with other IONA products and product components, or against other CORBA middleware products, was not automated across the platform set that we delivered our product to. Responsibility for quality, instead of lying with the development and maintenance teams, was focused in a quality team that sat outside the engineering effort and monitored quality through quality checklists and forms.

Part II

Code Entropy

By the end of 1997, the Orbix code had already been patched and re-patched hundreds of times to address large numbers of customer issues as well as the changing CORBA specification. The patching reflected many instances of Band-Aid approaches to resolving problems or adding functionality and was a major factor in the rapid entropy of the code. Many of these unreviewed changes were made to a code base that was never designed to withstand the punishment meted out by many of IONA's larger customer deployment environments. Customers were screaming for fixes and faster resolution times. The degradation of the code was further accelerated by the fact that more and more of the senior development staff were moved off the maintenance team to focus on new products development. Finally, there was limited acceptance of the well-documented style guides that were specified by IONA's chief architect for all code development, making it very difficult to read the code. Poor structuring of the source code's directory space also made it difficult to quickly become familiar with the overall code structure.

Team Morale

The morale of the people working on the maintenance and enhancement team was very low. Several review comments indicated that people didn't feel that there was cohesiveness in the team. Many reported that visibility of all the efforts that people were working on was poor. In general, they felt underappreciated and overworked.

So, these were the major problems facing the team as it started 1999. An initial refactoring project that had run from 1997 to 1999 was finishing up, and although it focused a tremendous amount of resources on refactoring, improving testing, and making necessary changes to the code base to comply with the latest version of the CORBA specification, it still had failed to address most of the issues identified earlier in this chapter. Essentially, it skimmed the surface of what needed to be done.

Initial History of Change

In 1999, before the release of Kent Beck's book on Extreme Programming, several projects were undertaken to try to address the problems. They are relevant because it is in the context of these projects that Extreme Programming was introduced and began to take hold. In this context we saw that many of the things we were already doing were elements of Extreme Programming.

Refactoring

A second refactoring effort was started late in 1999. This project focused on implementing continuous change and is ongoing today. The initial focus was around resolving problems reported by many customers that related to poorly implemented modules. Bug clusters highlighted in our defect tracking system clearly identified these problem areas.

This refactoring project continues as part of our Extreme Programming effort, as part of every engineer's response to problem resolution. An additional outcome was to reduce the complexity of the code by stripping out unused code and implementing several patterns that have made it easier to maintain, test, and understand the code. Code size has been reduced by over 40%.

Improving Engineering Practices

The refactoring project was led by one of IONA's distinguished engineers, who, in addition to providing strong technical insight into the problems in the code, was also instrumental in helping promote stronger engineering practices. He initiated several practices to encourage growth in the engineering team, including such things as weekly presentations to give not only himself but others in the engineering group an opportunity to present technical topics of relevance or interest, such as merge strategies, patterns, and estimation. He drove code reviews, advocated adherence to source code management guidelines, and focused people on ownership and responsibility for code style. He made engineers think of how they could constantly improve the quality of their work in areas such as test coverage, and in general established a more proactive approach to problem solving. His practices continue to strongly influence the team.

Automating Everything

A project was established to clearly understand all the build and test dependencies across all the elements of the older product set and to fully automate the entire build and test process. This project is ongoing but has resulted in the ability to build and unit test the complete product set nightly. Efforts continue to improve the automation of the interoperability and system tests that still need some manual intervention.

Team Consolidation

We should make a final comment on the team and the state of affairs just before our initial experiments with Extreme Programming. Before starting the projects described earlier, over 70 engineers maintained and enhanced the Orbix products. By the time we completed the major portion of those projects, we had been able to reduce the team to around 40. We continued to see the same trends in the number of issues coming into the Generation 3 team that we had always seen, but we were servicing three times the number of customers. Besides consolidating personnel, the team managed a single mainline of code using a well-defined set of common rules of the road, which govern the merging of fixes and enhancements into the consolidated mainline.

This was a remarkable transformation. We had started down the road toward a consistent, automated build, test, and release infrastructure that would enable complete product build and test every night. The refactoring efforts were eliminating much of the code complexity and stagnant code and had resulted in a clean, well-structured code base that conformed to IONA code standards.

So if we were seeing all this improvement, why look at Extreme Programming? It's all about constant improvement. We hadn't resolved the issues around testing, visibility, morale, and fundamentally personal work practices. We wanted to continue to do better. From a management standpoint, we wanted to be able to do more with less. Higher productivity, coupled with increased quality, leads to decreased team size with improving customer satisfaction. The engineers wanted more time to do good work, as opposed to always feeling under pressure to deliver fix after fix.

Even with the projects we had put in place, we still weren't where we felt we should be. This came from both management and the team. Many engineers and managers had started to look at Extreme Programming, and guess what? Many of the elements of Extreme Programming come naturally to teams working the maintenance game. We didn't know it, but we were already doing a lot of Extreme things. Extreme Programming validated some of the ideas that had initiated the previously described projects—refactoring, testing, and test automation in particular. It also suggested some approaches that could help us resolve the issues that were still outstanding: increased productivity, visibility, team morale, and improved testing. Extreme Programming started to make some sense.

Extreme Maintenance

The Orbix Generation 3 Engineering and Management team realized that XP represented a model for maintenance and enhancement that fit very well in the context of the process improvements that we were initiating at the time. Kent Beck himself notes that "maintenance is really the normal state of an XP project" [Beck2000]. Both managers and engineers felt that this statement was correct.

In our earlier projects, we had created a set of maintenance processes that described how a bug was created, prioritized, analyzed, fixed, and delivered to the customer. The Generation 3 team also had a set of processes that described how incremental enhancements were requested, described, prioritized, implemented, and delivered to customers. It was clear in looking at these processes that they already incorporated important elements of XP. The synergy was so great that we started to use the term "Extreme Programming" to describe the set of processes and practices used by the Generation 3 element and product teams. We started the XP experiment in earnest by looking at the continuing problems mentioned earlier to see how some of the XP approaches might help us improve.

The Stories

When customers report a bug, they provide a description of the bug in the form of a short "story" that describes what they are trying to do and how the problem manifests itself. This story is stored as a note in our defect tracking system and is available to everyone working with the customer, including the customer.

When we get an enhancement request or a functional requirement, we currently provide it as a requirement specification on our requirements Web page. Because of the need for global visibility and the ability to update globally by customer services and engineering, these requirements are not in the form of index cards. They also do not read as stories (yet), but they do contain essentially the same information.

For the purposes of our XP experiment, we left the enhancement requests until a later improvement phase and instead focused on ensuring that the bug-fixing stories were being tracked in a well-structured Web-based queuing system that was visible to the internal customer (customer services) as well as to engineers and engineering managers.

Task Cards and Storyboards

We liked the idea of using index cards to track tasks and decided to implement a storyboard for each of the element teams that made up our consolidated Generation 3 team, to try to fix the problem of poor visibility of each engineer's work effort. Each task, regardless of whether it is a customer issue or an internal project task, is written on a color-coded card (see Figure 20.1), which is placed on a storyboard. The Generation 3 operations lead sits down with our customer (customer services representative), and the customer prioritizes all the customer tasks. The customer also has visibility of internal tasks and may at their prerogative ask to have customer tasks escalated above internal tasks. Currently, only the customer issues are rigidly prioritized, but we intend to integrate internal tasks into that prioritization process as well.

An engineer provides an estimate for completion on the card once they have had 24 hours to do some initial analysis. When the task is completed, the actual date of completion is recorded. If there were delays in completing the work, the engineer simply notes on the back of

Task:			
Area: Customer: Engineer:	Details:		
Date queue	Date active	Expect finish	Date closed

FIGURE 20.1 Task card

the task card the facts about the delays, their observations concerning the delays, and some lessons learned. Cards for all closed tasks are removed from the board, data is extracted from the cards and put in a spreadsheet, and the task cards are stored in a task log.

Stand-up Meetings

One aspect of XP that was also incorporated into the team was the daily stand-up meeting (see Figure 20.2). Each team in the group takes 15 to 30 minutes to review their progress. Each person takes a couple of minutes to talk about what they did the previous day and a little about what they are doing today. Again, the focus was on improving visibility but also on encouraging communications between team members who may not necessarily (it's not part of the culture yet) talk to each other regularly.

The qualitative results were immediate. Some of the engineers found it difficult to explain to peers why they were spending so much time on issues or why they were looking at things that weren't high priorities on the team's list of tasks.

Testing

One of the first initiatives we undertook in 1999 was to automate our test suites and speed them up. We completed an extension of that effort in 2000, enabling developers to build and test the entire product set on any platform combination we support by clicking a single button from a Web-based interface or using the workstation command line. These initiatives enabled us to start testing the entire product set against the CORBA specification, against the Orbix API, and against customer-

FIGURE 20.2 Stand-up meeting at the storyboard

supplied test cases, nightly or at the engineer's discretion, on all 17 platforms that we support.

Both the stories describing the functionality supported by the software and the stories describing the bugs that the customers encountered have tests associated with them. Engineering requires that each customer provide a test case for each reported bug before doing any work on the issue. This test case is automatically included in the nightly runs of the test suite. Again, in hindsight, the processes that we decided to follow map very well to the ideas about testing, which are the foundation of the XP model: Test before you implement, and test everything often.

Pairing

First Experience

Our pair programming experiment came about accidentally late in 2000. The Generation 3 team worked on a particularly difficult set of customer issues. We had a customer engineer working on-site with us.

(Having customers on-site is another principle of XP, although normally we treat our on-site product managers and customer service representatives as our customers.) At different times, the customer teamed with various members of the Generation 3 team to do some pair programming. Likewise, members of the team gravitated toward a pair programming approach as they progressed with the issues they were working on for this particular customer.

The Results

In the end, the qualitative feedback from the team was very positive. They felt that they worked much more effectively and that there was a much higher level of communication when they worked in this way as opposed to working independently on individual issues. The senior staff also noted that they enjoyed some of the mentoring that naturally occurred as they interacted with the junior members of the group.

The overall productivity during this period was also high. Figure 20.3 shows that for the weeks from November 16, 2000 to December 7, 2000, on average, approximately 67% more issues were fixed than in previous periods. This higher productivity registers as a bump on the eight-week running average. Granted, not a lot of data is there to back it up, but when combined with all the positive feedback, it was definitely felt to be significant.

The bottom line is that morale improved. Engineers got a lot of positive reinforcement from each other. Engineering practices and quality improved as we actively noted coaching interactions between engineers. We also got no patch rejections for the work these engineers did.

Team Environment

This pair programming could not have happened without the changes that were made to the engineers' workspace. Before initiating our XP project, IONA's engineering workspace consisted of the typical floor plan with multiple bays of six shoulder-height cubicles in each bay (see Figure 20.4).

The engineers and engineering managers initiated a project to restructure the space they worked in to enhance team communication. A large central area was created by eliminating 20% of the individual cubicles and establishing nondelineated group workspaces. The group workspaces consist of either a round or rectangular meeting

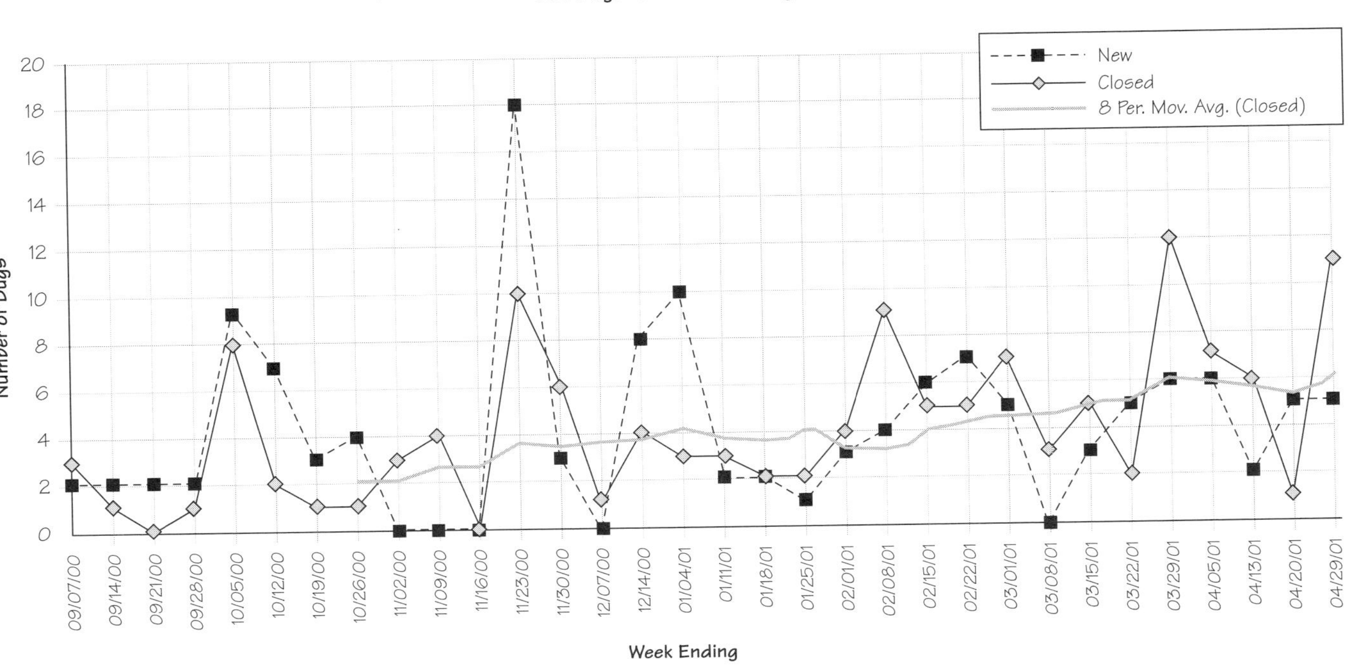

FIGURE 20.3 Team bug-fixing productivity

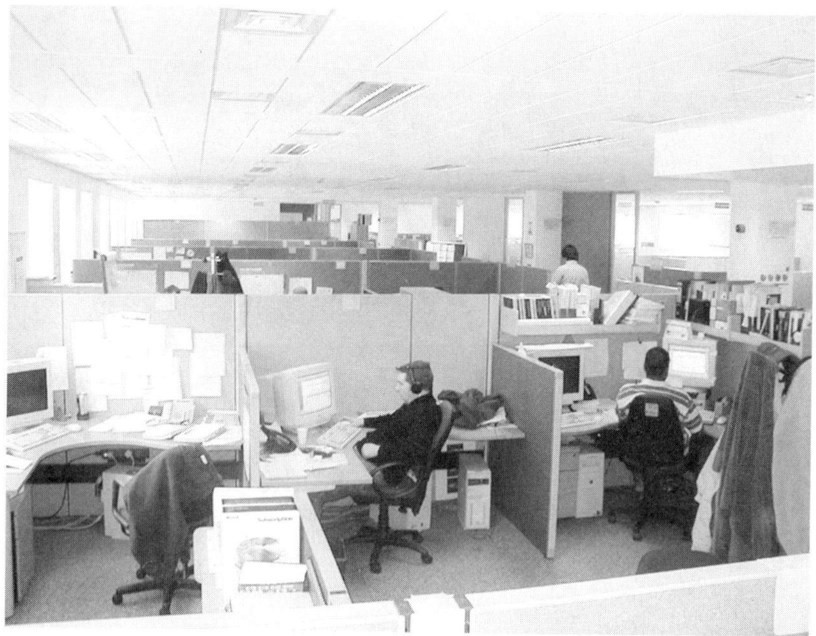

FIGURE 20.4 Orbix Generation 3 cubicles

table or workstation area. In addition, whiteboards and flipcharts on tripods were made available in each work area. A couch was purchased, and catering services bring in snack food (fruit and so on) weekly (see Figure 20.5).

The results are very noticeable. Code reviews are happening in the group area; pair programming is happening at the workstations. People are discussing their ideas on the whiteboards and large flipcharts. There is a measurable increase in the visibility of what everyone on the team is doing and in the number of conversations and collaborations that are occurring. These changes to the environment were instrumental to our success in improving overall team morale. We also have had a visible increase in the number of team interactions on code reviews and have seen many more discussions in the group areas about ongoing tasks. It is felt that these changes have also improved visibility on tasks.

FIGURE 20.5 Orbix Generation 3 new team area

Part II

Feedback and Refactoring

Rapid Feedback

As well as describing functionality, XP focuses on increments of functionality that can be merged into the mainline rapidly. Bug fixes are naturally merged in quite rapidly, and with the improved nightly build and test and the one-button test, systems can be made available as a temporary or permanent patch within one day. We also can see how healthy the mainline is daily across all platforms. Because we have just started collecting metrics on mainline breakage, we don't have any statistics to show what is currently a qualitative analysis of the improvement.

Refactoring Improves Maintainability

Because we were working with a legacy code base, we did not have much to say about how it was put together. However, we needed to make it maintainable and add functionality if required. As mentioned earlier, one of the improvement efforts we undertook was a major refactoring of elements of the Orbix product. This refactoring effort incorporated stories or functionality implementation that typically lasted three to four weeks. By keeping these increments relatively short, we could more effectively manage the delivery schedule of our last minor point release by modifying the scope of the project because we were almost always at a point where we could deliver a functional product. We achieved this without knowing Beck's approach, and in hindsight we recognized that what we achieved was in fact an implementation of XP principles.

We continue to monitor problem modules using our defect tracking system, and using our code reviews, we have started to see refactoring become part of the engineers' toolkit when they approach a problem. The benefit to all this is that we are seeing far fewer problems reported against our new releases. In addition, the code entropy has decreased significantly as measured by the comments from code reviewers.

Starting Extreme

So, what is Extreme Maintenance? It is following the XP model while a product is in the mainstream of its product life cycle [Moore1999]. If we look at what the Orbix Generation 3 experience has shown us about Extreme Maintenance, we can highlight the following key elements.

The Stories

Solving the visibility problem was key to moving beyond the gains in productivity realized by the projects detailed in the section Initial History of Change. The stories and the tasks that were identified or created needed to be visible to everyone. The storyboard with the cards is an important element of the approach we have taken.

Discussing the stories and tasks is important, but the real value in the stand-up meeting is that it coaxes people to talk about what they are doing and about some of the approaches they are taking. It's an essential lead-in to a future conversation.

In general, bug-fixing tasks for teams should be completed as two-week pieces of effort. If, after analyzing an issue, an engineer gives an estimate of more than two weeks, they need to split the story into several tasks. Anything more is a refactoring project and should be structured more along the lines of an enhancement, with clear incremental delivery of functionality based on tasks extracted from the original customer stories.

Prioritization of the fixing and enhancement is managed from a highly visible queue from which everyone can take their next task. The customer should manage the work of prioritizing. In most maintenance situations, this is the customer services organization.

We use an online queue that is available globally across our development and customer services sites. Kent Beck has suggested having a Web-accessible digital camera positioned so that people can regularly look at and zoom in on the storyboards. We are thinking about that one.

Testing

Automation is essential. Any engineer must be able to build the entire product or system and run the test suite to get immediate feedback on changes made. Nightly builds are a reasonable intermediate step to this test-on-demand requirement.

A reproducible test case must be available before detailed analysis begins and a fix implementation is provided. Testing before you fix ensures that whatever you do, you have solved the problem.

Pairing

Pair programming in XP is critical to improving collaboration and greatly facilitates mentoring and improvements in engineering practice. However, it is also one of the hardest things to get engineers to agree that it is useful and that they should sign up to make it part of their work practices. We are currently trying to get that buy-in. Until we do, we have asked each engineer to take on one or two tasks each quarter, in which they pair with another team member. We'll note which ones they paired on and then show them the data at the end of the quarter. We think it will reinforce the results we got from our initial experiment with pairing.

Team Environment

A maintenance team environment should be a mixture of personal and team space to enhance the interactions and collaborations that should occur within the team. We suggest starting by simply eliminating some of the typical cubicles and moving tables and some casual furniture into the resulting space.

Community workstations should be of the highest specification possible and should be made available specifically for pair programming and code reviews.

Feedback and Refactoring

Analyzing bug statistics is essential to identifying areas of code that need to be refactored. This form of customer feedback is an important part of targeting improvements and stopping code entropy.

Refactoring should always be on an engineer's mind when analyzing a problem or an enhancement request. The engineer should wonder, "How can I make this area of the code work better?" as opposed to "How can I get this problem fixed quickly?" (the Band-Aid approach). We give our engineers a lot of freedom to replan an enhancement or bug fix and to turn it into a refactoring effort. For some customer issues, we cannot afford the time to do the refactoring effort because of commitments to restore times. However, it is part of the process that engineers, along with analyzing a problem, identify whether the area of code they are working on is a candidate for refactoring.

Conclusion

In concluding, we focus on two points. First, how has Extreme Maintenance helped our engineering group, and second, what things will we be doing in the future to improve on the practices to refine the model that is presented by XP?

Our metrics (although not particularly extensive) seem to show some quantitative improvements in productivity during the period in which pair programming was being used to address specific deliverables or bug fixes for a major customer. This productivity increase has continued beyond the initial experiment. This is perhaps attributable to the fact that more people seem to be using the pair programming and open collaborative spaces we created during that period. As the graph in Figure 20.3 shows, during the period of this effort (the week of November 2, 2000 through the end of November) we saw a measurable peak in productivity over and above the previous several months. This was an improvement of 67% based on the next most productive five-week period, and by looking at the trend line, we see continued improvement.

The graph in Figure 20.3 shows several things. First, the new bugs represent issues that the team must address. An eight-week running average trend line would show that this averages to four issues a week. Second, the number of closed issues represents the number of issues that are resolved in a patch to the customer. This patching cycle represents our XP iteration and is on the order of two to three weeks (note the closure peaks).

One of the greatest success stories concerns improvements in visibility. This is, in our opinion, the greatest single benefit to the entire team. By having a big storyboard set up where we prioritize tasks and discuss progress daily, we are encouraging best practices, giving people an opportunity to see what others are working on, and giving management the chance to gauge actual progress. It's all about improving communications!

Figure 20.6 shows the dramatic improvements in our workflow queues as a result of using the storyboard. In February 2001, when we installed the board, it focused people's attention on the fact that they were allowing issues to go unverified for significant amounts of time. We also saw a dramatic increase in the number of issues that people started to actively work on. It is felt that visibility alone was a strong motivational factor in this turnaround. In the future, we are looking to see how to scale this practice across multiple development sites.

How can XP help us improve even more? First, improving the pair programming initiative is something that we feel can improve our lack of cross-training among the many modules of the code base. Granted, it is not a practice for which this is intended, but it is felt that it is a useful side benefit to a real problem as the team grows smaller. Engineers have accepted the benefits, but we are still in the process of structuring a more general approach to ensuring that the practice of pairing becomes part of the IONA culture. The current plan is to have each new bug, enhancement request, or refactoring effort signed up for by an individual, and to have that individual then be responsible for grabbing a partner to work through the issue. Our technical leads feel comfortable with this approach, and we intend to propose it to the whole team early in 2001.

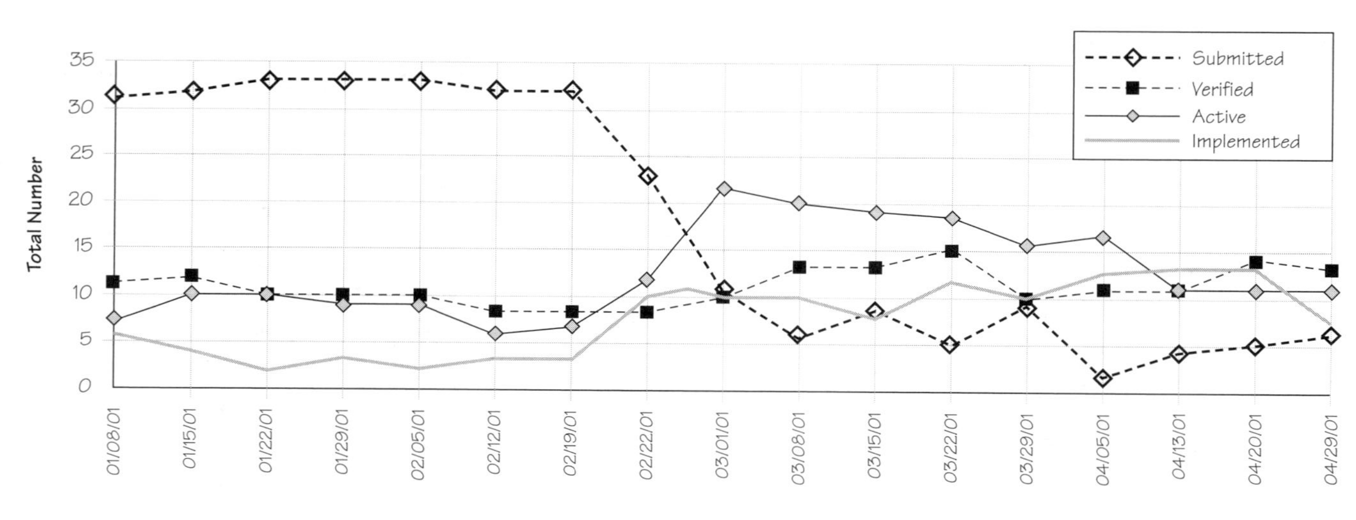

FIGURE 20.6 Workflow queues

Second, metrics are critical to the replanning game, but it is difficult to get engineers to contribute. To plan how long it will take to complete a story, you need to know how long it took to complete a similar piece of work, based on the estimates of the engineer to whom the work is assigned. "As the basis for your planning, assume you'll do as much this week as you did last week" [Beck+2000]. Kent Beck and Martin Fowler call this rule "Yesterday's Weather," and we think it is an appropriate analogy.

We are currently running an internal project to improve our ability to enter metrics into our defect tracking system and report on them automatically. The volume of issues makes it difficult to track using a simple spreadsheet, but we do it anyway. Our operations lead speaks to each developer and notes how they have progressed on the work they are doing. The limited metrics we have indicate that it takes an engineer, on average, two ideal weeks to fix a bug [Beck+2000]. This matches exactly the suggested length of time to implement a story in the XP model. By measuring the calendar time with the defect tracking system, we can measure the calendar time it took to resolve an issue, and ultimately measure the velocity of the team [Beck+2000]. This information is invaluable in planning what we will do in the next patch or release iteration.

It is felt that XP represents an extremely viable and successful model for teams involved in maintaining and enhancing any code base. It provides mechanisms for dealing with the dynamic environment that exists in a software development project (customer support issues, feature requests and enhancements, and so on) and yet provides a very structured approach to identifying the features of deliverables as part of planning or replanning efforts. It encourages improvements in engineering practices through mentoring and pair programming, and creates an environment that encourages people to think outside the box, to look for solutions to problems rather than Band-Aids for issues.

We encourage others to look at XP if they are having problems with team productivity and quality in a maintenance environment, or if they see significant communications and prioritization problems or difficulty delivering to schedules in their teams. It appears to have provided our engineering teams with a boost in productivity, quality, and improvements in engineering practice, and an overall feeling of empowerment. Our customer services and sales teams as well as the CEO have all commented on the dramatic improvements.

References

[Beck2000] K. Beck. *Extreme Programming Explained.* Addison-Wesley, 2000.

[Beck+2000] K. Beck, M. Fowler. *Planning Extreme Programming.* Addison-Wesley, 2000.

[Fowler1999] M. Fowler. *Refactoring: Improving the Design of Existing Code.* Addison-Wesley, 1999.

[Jeffries+2000] R. Jeffries, A. Anderson, C. Hendrickson. *Extreme Programming Installed.* Addison-Wesley, 2000.

[Moore1999] G. Moore. *Crossing the Chasm.* Capstone Publishing Ltd., 1999.

Acknowledgments

The authors would like to acknowledge the help of Kent Beck in working with the Orbix Generation 3 team and the invaluable insights into the development process he provided that have motivated our teams to adopt XP.

About the Authors

Charles Poole has been a senior engineering manager at IONA Technologies for three years. He is currently working on IONA Technologies Web Services Integration Platform and is based in Santa Clara, California. He was formerly a senior consultant and principal consulting architect with various U.S. government agencies and in private industry. Contact him at charles.poole@iona.com.

Jan Willem Huisman is currently working with IONA Technologies in Dublin, Ireland, as an engineering manager responsible for the maintenance team for the Orbix Generation 3 product. He has extensive experience in software quality control and software development. Contact him at jan.willem.huisman@iona.com.

Part III

XTT: Extreme Technology Transfer—Introducing XP and AMs

Extreme Programming and other agile methodologies consist of prescribed practices. Some of these agile practices are based on previously established best practices. Practitioners and educators feel confident in using and teaching these best practices. In other cases, agile practices alter or depart from best practices. These are the harder practices to adopt and to have the confidence to teach. The authors in this section share experiences and techniques for teaching agile practices and transitioning teams to their use.

Part III begins with chapters written by university educators who have used various XP practices in the university classroom. First, in Chapter 21, Owen Astrachan, Robert Duvall, and Eugene Wallingford discuss their experiences in integrating XP into their classes. These educators have developed an innovative form of "pair programming" by having the instructor play the role of the driver. Jointly, all the students in the class play the role of the navigator and guide the teacher to a successful program implementation. Additionally, they have increased the number of "releases" required of their students to provide more timely and increased feedback. Last, they have introduced refactoring as a means to improve understanding of programs and design patterns.

In Chapter 22, Mike Holcombe, Marian Gheorghe, and Francisco Macias describe their experiences in integrating XP into their senior-level course on software engineering projects. In this course, the students build real projects for real clients. Customer satisfaction and high quality are essential because maintenance is virtually impossible as the students graduate and leave their projects behind. The authors report success and a positive student response. Dean Sanders shares students' mostly positive perception of XP and XP's practice of pair programming, based on a pilot course, in Chapter 23. David Johnson and James Caristi share similar experiences in their software design course in Chapter 24. These two educators describe their successes and offer some suggestions for future use of XP in a software design course.

Chapter 25 presents the experiences of Ann Anderson, Chet Hendrickson, and Ron Jeffries in running their tutorial on user stories and the planning game. This chapter is extremely valuable for both educators and developers.

Joshua Kerievsky contends that XP's values of feedback and communication support continuous learning. This learning can enable personal and process improvement. In Chapter 26, Joshua suggests that XP be augmented with a learning repository and organizational support for study groups and iteration retrospectives.

The concepts of the XP release planning practice can be difficult to sell and internalize with students and professionals, including developers and businesspeople. In Chapter 27, Vera Peeters and Pascal Van Cauwenberghe present a playful but effective interactive game to teach these concepts. While planning the game, participants experience first-hand user stories, estimation, planning, implementation, functional tests, and velocity.

In Chapter 28, Moses Hohman and Andrew Slocum discuss an innovative practice they term "mob programming," a variant of the XP pair programming practice. With mob programming, groups larger than two work together to refactor code. Employing this practice, their team has strengthened its use of other XP practices, such as pair programming and automated unit test cases. They have also further embraced the XP values of communication and courage.

"Show me the money." Some managers and practitioners remain skeptical of agile practices and methodologies. They desire proof before transitioning from their "trusted" practices. In Chapter 29, Laurie Williams, Giancarlo Succi, Milorad Stefanovic, and Michele Marchesi offer an empirical model for assessing the efficacy of agile practices and the impact of their use in creating quality software.

Chapter 21

Bringing Extreme Programming to the Classroom

—*Owen L. Astrachan, Robert C. Duvall, and Eugene Wallingford*

Part III

In this chapter, we discuss several features of Extreme Programming (XP) that we have used in developing curricula and courses at Duke University and the University of Northern Iowa. We also discuss those practices of XP that we teach as part of the design and implementation process we want students to practice as they develop programming expertise and experience. In theory the academic study of programming and software development should be able to embrace all of XP. In practice, however, we find the demands of students and professors to be different from professional and industrial software developers, so although we embrace the philosophy and change of XP, we have not (yet) adopted its principles completely.

Introduction

XP [Beck2000] and other light or agile methodologies [Agile2001; Fowler2000A] have gained a significant foothold in industry but have not yet generated the same heat (or light) in academic settings.

Significant interest in pair programming in an academic setting, and a resulting interest in XP, has been fostered by the work of Laurie Williams [Williams2000; Williams+2000]. However, the general tenets of XP are less known, and the engineering background of many academic computer science programs facilitates adoption of process-oriented methodologies such as the Personal Software Process (PSP) even early in the curriculum [Humphrey1997; Hou+1998]. However, we have had preliminary success in adopting and adapting principles of XP (and other agile methodologies) in classroom teaching and in the methods we teach and instill in our students. Although academic requirements, goals, and methods differ from those in industry, we have found that many aspects of XP can be incorporated into the design and implementation of a university-level computer science and programming curriculum.

What's Extreme about XP?

As explained in [Beck2000], XP takes good practices of professional software development to extreme levels. XP introduces a planned and coherent methodology without becoming overly dictatorial or secretarial. The four values of XP are given as communication, simplicity, feedback, and courage.

As we explain in this chapter, these values form the foundation of our approach. Thus, we think we're following the spirit of XP, although we're certainly not following every XP practice (testing, pair programming, planning game, and so on) [Hendrickson2000].

From these core XP values, five principles are given as fundamental to XP. Our approach uses each of these principles: rapid feedback, assume simplicity, incremental change, embracing change, and quality work.

Ten "less central principles" from [Beck2000] are given, of which we concentrate on the following four: teach learning; concrete experiments; open, honest communication; and local adaptation.

For example, as instructors, we often face a tension in developing good (often small) example programs for students. The tension arises because we want to develop simple, focused examples that teach a specific concept, yet we also want to show our students programs that are masterpieces of good design—programs that are fully generic and robust, and exemplify the best practices of object-oriented design and programming.

XP advocates that we design the simplest possible solution that works well for the current set of requirements, not those that we imagine will exist in the future. This helps relieve some of the tension of designing overly generic or optimized programs when creating example code.

Additionally, with this new mind-set, we can now add new features to that example and show students how the code changes. In other words, we can give the students a peek into the process of creating programs. When we call this process refactoring, we can discuss a program's design in more concrete terms [Fowler2000B].

In this chapter, we report on three aspects of XP that we have employed very successfully. We have used XP in our introductory programming courses for majors, in advanced courses on object-oriented software design, and in programming courses for nonmajors. These three aspects are as follows:

- Pair (teacher/class) programming as part of lecture
- Small releases from student groups
- Refactoring to understand programming and design patterns

Our Clients

Embracing change within a university setting is different from industry because our clients are different. In fact, when using XP, we are meeting the demands of two different client/customer groups.

- We strive to develop programmers who appreciate simplicity and elegance, who love building software, and who understand the contributions of computer science to software design. The process we mentor and teach must resonate with our students and scale from introductory programming courses to more advanced courses in software architecture.
- We want our curriculum, assignments, and materials to be adopted and adapted by educators all over the world. Our materials must be simple and elegant, and support adaptation and refactoring to meet local demands. The process and materials must resonate with educators at a level different from the resonance we hope for with students.

Our student clients take several courses each semester. They devote 20% to 40% of their time to a course on programming, depending on the demands of other courses and the interest level we can maintain in our courses. We assume that students live and breathe solely for our courses, but we are also not surprised that other professors in other departments hold similar views about their courses. Thus, it is difficult for groups of students to meet frequently or for extended periods of time outside of class.

The structure of the work students do in our courses varies from traditional lecture to structured (time-constrained) labs, to unstructured group and individual activity in completing assignments. Our XP-based material typically takes more time to prepare and requires us to use XP practices to produce it.

Lecturing Using Pair Programming

We use a didactic form of pair programming in our large lecture courses. The instructor is the *driver*, while the class as a whole (from 40 to 180 students) works together as the second member of the pair programming team, which we call the *navigator*. A typical scenario, used from beginning to advanced courses, is outlined in the following two sections. First we explain the process from a student view; then we elaborate on the process from a faculty developer perspective.

Student View

- A problem is posed that requires a programming solution. The problem and its solution are intended to illustrate features of a programming language, elements of software design, and principles of computer science and to engage students in the process.
- A preliminary, partially developed program is given as the first step to the solution. Students read the program and ask questions about it as a program and a potential solution.
- The instructor displays the program on a projection screen visible to the class (each student has a written copy) and adds functionality with input from the class. This involves writing code, writing tests, and running and debugging the program. The instructor

drives the process, but the class contributes with ideas, code, and questions.

- The final program is added to the day's Web site for reflection and completeness and for those students unable to attend class. Both the initial and final programs are part of the materials available to students.

We have tried a variety of standard active-learning techniques in this form of pair programming: calling on random students to contribute, breaking the class into small groups to provide solutions, and making pre- and post-class-work questions based on the programming problem.

Educator View

The instructor who drives a programming problem and solution must develop a complete solution beforehand and then refactor the solution into one that meets the needs of the instructional process as described in the previous section. This process may take more preparation time and require more responsibility from the instructor during class time than a traditional lecture.

- The instructor finds a problem and develops a complete program/solution to the problem. The solution is developed using XP, but the goal is a simple, working program, which isn't always the right instructional tool.
- The program must be refactored until it is simple enough to be understood by the student client while still achieving the intended didactic goals. This simplification process is often easier in introductory courses because the programs are smaller. In some cases, especially in more advanced courses, a problem and its solution must often be completely reworked or thrown out when they're too complex to be used in a one-hour lecture.
- Parts of the program are then removed so the program can be completed as part of an instructor/class pair programming exercise. The instructor has an idea of what the solution could be, but the solution developed during class isn't always the one the instructor pared away. Instructors must be comfortable with accepting and using student input, going down knowingly false trails for instructional purposes.

Small Releases Mean Big Progress

Students in our nonmajor's programming course as well as our first- and second-year major's courses sometimes work on large projects in groups, in which they may be given as much as three weeks to complete the project. The projects are not designed to require students to work full-time for the duration of the assignment; instead, the schedule is typically padded to allow them time to work out group meetings, to do other course work, and to learn the topics necessary to complete the assignment. Typically, the assignment is discussed repeatedly in and outside of class during this time, but rarely do most curricula require students to demonstrate their progress until the final deadline. This practice has caused mixed success in these large projects—sometimes groups fail to deliver even a compiled program!

This past year, we have changed to requiring many small releases before the final project is completed, giving the students only a few days to a week to submit part of the final product. We then work with our teaching assistants to look at these releases and provide groups with feedback while they are still working on the project. Using this practice, every group successfully completed the project, and the quality was much higher than what we experienced in previous semesters.

Student View

Many students abuse the time given in a large project by ignoring the project until the last minute and then coding in long spurts until it is finally done. This style of working gives the computer science department a reputation for being hard and requiring all-night coding sessions. Although this process may make sense in the context of juggling all the demands placed on a student, it leads to many problems when creating a good software project.

- Communication between group members is generally very tenuous unless they are all in the same room. Because no one is certain when a specific feature will be worked on, it is hard to count on a feature getting done, let alone planning to use it, improving on it, or adding to it.
- One way of dealing with the communication problem is to meet once at the beginning of the project and break it into chunks that can each be managed by one student working alone. The students then meet again at the end of the project and attempt to

integrate their individual parts into a working whole. The first step goes well, but, unfortunately, the last step rarely does for average groups.

- When dividing the work, some students may have much more to do than others in the group, either because some features were not understood well enough when the project was planned or because one student got very excited about a part and added many extra features. Additionally, most students do not understand the details of the other parts of their project.

Making small releases has helped relieve these problems simply because it requires the group to communicate more often. Not only can the course staff better monitor the group's progress, but so can the students. Because they had to integrate their code more often, they typically had something that they could run while they were working.

Students reported that this led to even more intragroup communication because having a running program gave them more to discuss with their group members: how to improve specific features, curiosity about how other parts of the project were implemented, and plans to determine what parts remained to be done.

Students also reported that they were actually proud of their projects. Many more groups were inspired to add more features as they worked with their programs to make them easier to use or more interesting. In one case, students were asked to complete a game that could be run from a Web page. One group told other students in their dorm about the Web page and soon had a large user community. As people played, they made suggestions for new features. The group published new versions of the game as often as every 20 minutes! Many of these features were not part of the specification for the game but ended up being extra credit.

Educator View

The instructor developing small releases for large projects must do some more work to take advantage of these benefits. First, one must decide what will be required for each release and schedule these deadlines as if they were real, including minimizing conflicts with the university schedule. In essence, each release becomes an assignment in itself. This extra work is balanced in some sense because it may make it possible to better plan the order of topics in the course.

Additionally, each release must be checked and feedback given to the group as quickly as possible. This is even more important because these mini-assignments build toward a single final project, and feedback after the assignment is over is all but useless to the group. In our courses, we typically meet with the group as a whole once a week during the project, demonstrating their project, discussing its design, and planning for the next deadline. In fact, the role of the course staff is often crucial to realizing truly big progress from these small releases.

For example, in our advanced programming course, we have asked students to complete a LOGO interpreter and programming environment [Papert1980]. They had three and a half weeks to complete the assignment, and we gave them six deadlines: Three required written submissions, and three required running code. The first two deadlines attempted to get students to think about the project by asking them to explain specific design issues and use cases with respect to the project [Cockburn2001]. For each of the next three weeks, they turned in successively larger releases of their project, the last being the final version. In each case, they were told to focus on getting the current, smaller set of requirements finished rather than trying to show that they had started, but not finished, all parts of the project. Finally, after the final version was submitted, each student in the group was asked to complete an individual project postmortem, reflecting on the group experience [Kerth2001].

An unexpected benefit of these small releases was that the course staff was able to grade the projects more quickly and give better feedback because they already knew the details of the code. They had learned the details as the project was built instead of having to learn them after the fact. Teaching assistants reported that student groups were more open when talking with them if they started from the beginning of the project as opposed to only starting a dialogue after the project was complete (and the student's grade was more clearly on the line). This resulted in faster, higher-quality grading.

Refactoring for Learning Design

We use refactoring both to improve the quality of student programs and to help students understand the basic tenets of object-oriented software design.

For many years, we used a form of apprentice learning in which we provided simple, elegant designs that students implemented in solving problems [Astrachan+1997]. The idea was to instill a sense of elegance by experiencing our designs. However, students were not able to internalize the design principles simply by filling in a finished design. Students would not use the principles in our designs because they could not appreciate them as being useful in solving problems: They appreciated the designs only as rules to follow to receive a good grade.

Now we ask students to develop the simplest (to them) working solution they can to solve a problem. We then ask them to change their solutions to accommodate changes in the problem specification. We help them understand how to refactor their solutions to incorporate design patterns and fundamental software design principles that they are able to appreciate in a more visceral way because their solutions can be refactored to accommodate the changes.

For example, we start with a series of examples from [Budd1998] that introduce, first, a simple bouncing-ball simulation, then a game that fires cannonballs at a target, and finally a pinball game. During these examples, we build the inheritance hierarchy shown in Figure 21.1 for the balls used in each game, in which each kind of ball responds differently to the `move()` message.

The students are then asked to allow the balls to decelerate, or not, in any of the programs (according to friction or some other property). Initially, they create an additional subclass for each kind of ball, leading to the hierarchy shown in Figure 21.2.

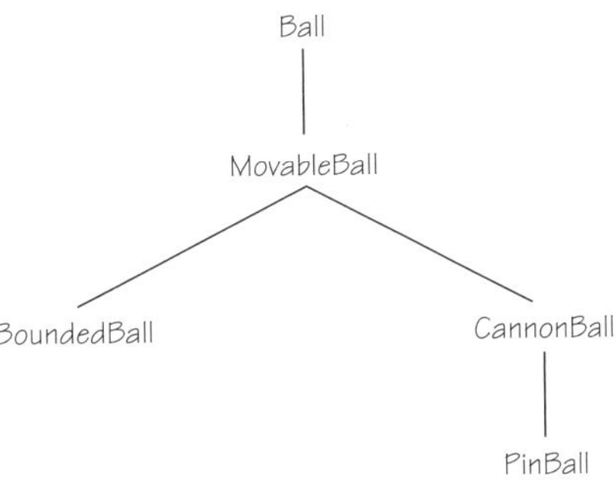

FIGURE 21.1 Initial ball inheritance hierarchy

Part III

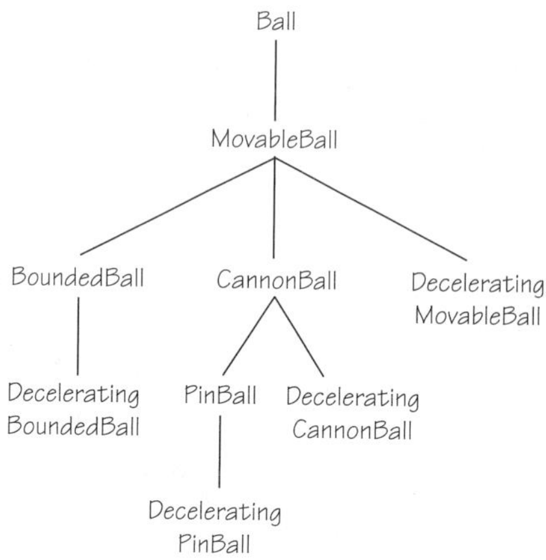

FIGURE 21.2 First attempt at extending the ball inheritance hierarchy

For most students, this is a simple solution, easy to understand and implement. However, the students also realize that there is a lot of duplicated code, because each decelerating subclass changes `move()` in the same way. In particular, it is easy to motivate that a change made to one subclass will need to be made in all the subclasses. Moreover, any new kinds of balls will need a decelerating subclass in addition to their own.

Students understand that this is not an ideal solution and are primed to find a better way to solve this problem. Because all balls adhere to the same interface, they can be substituted for each other. A movable ball can be used where a cannonball can or where a decelerating pinball can. Using this principle, we show students how to implement a decelerating ball that takes another kind of ball as an argument and delegates the bulk of its work to that ball, and how to add its decelerating behavior. We show the students the diagram, shown in Figure 21.3, that characterizes our solution and ask them to refactor their first solution to fit this model.

In this case, they are using the decorator pattern but do not know it as such [Gamma+1995]. After going through another example, we show them the general pattern, but by then they have internalized it and can explain when it is useful. Instead of telling them the pattern and ask-

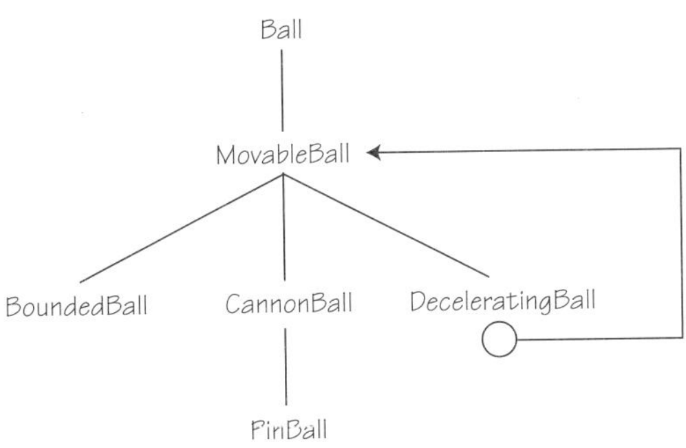

FIGURE 21.3 Refactored ball inheritance hierarchy

ing them to understand it from some abstract description, we have shown a concrete example and motivated them to find a better solution (which just happens to be one for which we already have a name).

Conclusion

No single practice of XP stands on its own; instead, it must be reinforced by the practices of XP [Beck2000]. For example, designing for the current requirements as simply as possible works only if you are willing to pause to refactor any part of the code as needed. And you can feel comfortable refactoring code only if you collectively own and understand all the code. Pair programming helps promote this collective ownership. In this chapter, we have discussed several ways for academics to embrace the changes espoused by advocates of XP.

Currently, our students do not necessarily practice XP when they program outside of the classroom. We have introduced some of the ways in which our students differ from professional programmers currently practicing XP. Instead, we have attempted to design our curricula and methods to help students practice certain aspects of XP automatically and to understand how these practices can improve the way they think about programming and program design by giving them a view of how programs are constructed.

Thus, we feel our efforts are certainly in the style of XP even if we are not doing all 12 practices. However, we feel that more growth is still possible by incorporating some additional practices. Here are some that we are beginning to experiment with.

- We would like to emphasize testing more in our advanced programming courses. Using tools like JUnit (see http://www.junit. org), we would like to automate the testing process so that students test their code each time they compile. If something did not pass a test, we hope they would be motivated to fix it immediately rather than ignoring it. Initially, we feel that we would have to write these tests for them to get them into that habit.
- All instructors advise their students to design (or plan) before writing their code, and sometimes beginning students even follow that advice (but it is hard to avoid the lure of the computer). We have begun to incorporate the planning game, along with metaphor (or vision), to make this phase of the project more useful, fun, and concrete for the students. Instead of simply asking students to create a UML diagram, we ask them to make stories, or use cases, and create a project Web page that acts as an advertisement of the team's vision of the project.
- It is especially hard with group projects to make sure that everyone in the group understands the entire project. To promote better understanding of the overall project, we would like to move students around within and without their group. Additionally, this would force groups to take on new members during the project and have some plan and materials to get new members up to speed on the project's design.

References

[Agile2001] *Manifesto for Agile Software Development.* http://agilemanifesto.org/. 2001.

[Astrachan+1997] O. Astrachan, J. Wilkes, R. Smith. "Application-Based Modules Using Apprentice Learning for CS2. *Twenty-Eighth SIGCSE Technical Symposium on Computer Science Education,* February 1997.

[Beck2000] K. Beck. *Extreme Programming Explained.* Addison-Wesley, 2000.

[Budd1998] T. Budd. *Understanding Object-Oriented Programming with Java*. Addison-Wesley, 1998.

[Cockburn2001] A. Cockburn. *Writing Effective Use Cases.* Addison-Wesley, 2001.

[Fowler2000A] M. Fowler. "Put Your Process on a Diet." *Software Development*, December 2000. http://www.martinfowler.com/articles/newMethodology.html.

[Fowler2000B] M. Fowler. *Refactoring: Improving the Design of Existing Code.* Addison-Wesley, 2000.

[Gamma+1995] E. Gamma, R. Helm, R. Johnson, J. Vlissides. *Design Patterns: Elements of Reusable Object-Oriented Software.* Addison-Wesley, 1995.

[Hendrickson2000] C. Hendrickson. *When Is It Not XP?* http://www.xprogramming.com/xpmag/NotXP.htm. 2000.

[Hou+1998] L. Hou, J. Tomayko. "Applying the Personal Software Process in CS1: An Experiment." *Twenty-Ninth SIGCSE Technical Symposium on Computer Science Education*, 1998.

[Humphrey1997] W. Humphrey. *Introduction to the Personal Software Process.* Addison-Wesley, 1997.

[Kerth2001] N. Kerth. *Project Retrospectives: A Handbook for Team Reviews.* Dorset House, 2001.

[Papert1980] S. Papert. *Mindstorms.* Basic Books, 1980.

[Williams2000] L. Williams. "The Collaborative Software Process." Ph.D. diss. University of Utah, 2000.

[Williams+2000] L. Williams, R. Kessler. "Experimenting with Industry's Pair-Programming Model in the Computer Science Classroom." *Computer Science Education*, March 2001.

About the Authors

Owen L. Astrachan is professor of the practice of computer science at Duke University and the department's director of undergraduate studies for teaching and learning. He has taught programming in a variety of environments for more than 20 years, each year searching for a simpler, more agile approach in helping students understand computer science and the craft of programming. Professor Astrachan is an NSF CAREER award winner, has published several papers cowritten with undergraduates on using patterns in an academic setting, and is the author of the textbook *A Computer Science Tapestry: Exploring Programming and Computer Science with C++*, published by McGraw-Hill. He won the Distinguished Teaching in Science award at Duke in 1995, and the Outstanding Instructor of Computer Science award while on sabbatical in 1998 at the University of British Columbia. Owen can be reached at ola@cs.duke.edu.

Robert C. Duvall is not an actor, but a lecturer in computer science at Duke University. Before moving to Durham, North Carolina, he did his undergraduate and graduate work at Brown University, where he helped move the curriculum from a procedures-first approach using Pascal to an objects-first approach using Java. He has also taught with Lynn Stein's Rethinking CS101 project at MIT. Primarily, he enjoys using graphics, object-oriented frameworks, and patterns to make current research understandable and usable by novice programmers. Robert can be reached at rcd@cs.duke.edu.

Eugene Wallingford is an associate professor of computer science at the University of Northern Iowa. He has been writing object-oriented programming for more than ten years, in CLOS, Smalltalk, C++, Java, and Ruby. He spent many years doing research in artificial intelligence, where he built applications that used domain knowledge to solve problems in legal reasoning, product design and diagnosis, and ecological systems. Eugene still does some work in AI but spends more of his time studying the structures of programs and helping students learn how to write programs. His work with programming and design patterns developed in tandem with a view on how programs grow in the face of changing requirements, which in turn found a compatible philosophy in Extreme Programming. Eugene can be reached at wallingf@cs.uni.edu.

Chapter 22

Teaching XP for Real: Some Initial Observations and Plans

—Mike Holcombe, Marian Gheorghe, and Francisco Macias

Part III

Fourth-year students run their own software house, in which they carry out real projects for real business clients. This year we have introduced them to Extreme Programming (XP), and in this chapter we examine the initial impact that XP has had on their business. The philosophy has been adopted with much enthusiasm and seems to have delivered in a variety of contexts, including maintenance and new projects. Some plans for a more rigorous experiment looking at the possible benefits of XP are also described.

Introduction

Teaching computer science and software engineering students is greatly enhanced if they can be introduced to the real issues relating to software design through the mechanism of projects for *real business clients.* For more than ten years, we have required students in their second year to take part in team projects in which the teams compete with each other to produce a solution for a businessperson's current problem. Each student is required to work on this project for 100 hours during the 12-week semester, which equates to nine to ten hours per week. Typically, 80 students are in the class, and there are three business clients, each with a specific problem relating to their business. Each student team is allocated to one of these clients. The teams comprise five students, and each client deals with five or six teams. At the end of the semester, the clients evaluate all the software solutions produced and select the best one for use in their organization. The winning students receive a prize.

This framework transforms the students' learning because it emphasizes two of the most problematic issues when teaching software design: how to communicate with a client and capture the real requirements, and how to deliver a high-quality, bug-free system.

It is hard to introduce either of these dimensions into the curriculum using projects specified by academics. Students know that once the software has been marked, it is usually thrown away. With our approach, which we call the "Software Hut," students are much more motivated because they know that someone *wants* their work and *will use it*. They also learn a lot about the way businesses work. It is always the most popular course and the one that they say teaches them the most. (More details can be found in [Stratton+1998; Holcombe+1998; Holcombe+1999].)

A recent extension of this approach occurs in the fourth year, when the students run their own software company and spend approximately one-third of their time working in it. The company, which they call Genesys Solutions (formerly called VICI), has a wide variety of clients requiring database systems and e-commerce applications.[1] About 25 students work in the company. The students run the company, make all major decisions, operate their own premises and network, and carry out R&D as well as specific industrial projects. As part of this, the students negotiate the details of a contract with a client: cost, delivery, and the detailed requirements specification.

As you might expect, estimation and planning is a major issue in running the company, and one of things we are trying to do is to collect suitable data on projects that would help us do this better. The estimation of resources for XP-driven projects needs to be considered in a different way from traditional projects, so we are starting from a posi-

1. See the Genesys Solutions Web site at http://www.genesys.shef.ac.uk.

tion where we need to think about things rather differently. We believe that this student-run company is a unique innovation but one that the students are incredibly enthusiastic about. (As an aside, a number of former members of this company have successfully set up their own real software houses.)

Problems That Motivated Changing to Extreme Programming

These sorts of projects are not without their problems, but we do not want clients coming back with complaints about software quality and inappropriate functionality, and we cannot afford to spend all our time on maintenance. Consequently, we must ensure that we deliver extremely high quality solutions. The Genesys company can do some maintenance, particularly where the client wants some new functionality, but we have to focus hard on software quality and, in particular, thorough testing of the product. The students are steeped in conventional software engineering methodologies by the time they reach the fourth year, but these have not been able to guarantee the level of quality we need, and in many cases these methods get in the way.

This year we decided to introduce the fourth-year class to Extreme Programming. None of them had heard of it before, but the response was overwhelmingly positive, and they decided to apply the ideas, as far as they could, to all their projects.

Introducing XP into the Company

Two types of projects existed when we started: major testing and debugging of existing projects, and new development.

In past projects, we had organized ourselves so that the teams would test each other's software, thus relying on the view of many test experts that independent testing is the most effective approach. This didn't work, because the teams' main priority was to their own project, and with deadlines fast approaching, each team concentrated on its own development work at the expense of testing another team's system. Coupled with the problem of teams trying too hard to satisfy late changes in their client's requirements, this was a clear recipe for disaster. Thus, when the academic year ended, we were unable to deliver software of the appropriate quality. (After the end of the year, the students graduate and leave, so we do not have the flexibility of extending deadlines or the benefits of continuity in the teams, because next year's company comes from the next cohort of students.)

We discussed these problems with the next cohort when they arrived in September 2000, and then looked at the ideas behind XP, primarily using [Beck2000] and the main XP Web sites. It was immediately clear to them that this new technique could be a big improvement on what had been done before. They therefore decided to adopt this way of doing things as far as possible.

The idea of pair programming was well received and has proved extremely effective in debugging code. The construction of functional test sets from the requirements also had a big impact on the process. It highlighted the need for suitable testing software, so both test generation and test application tools had to be built for the specific applications. Because these tools were based on generic concepts, they can be adapted to other projects. We describe some work on developing extremely powerful test case generators in [Holcombe+2001]. However, we still have problems estimating the amount of time and effort needed to complete projects, and this area needs further research.

The other important influence was in the management of client expectations, and this is now realized to be a vital factor. Delivering a high-quality basic system, rather than one with lots of extra, mainly unnecessary features, was instructive. The students are enthusiastic about satisfying their client's requirements, but sometimes they try too hard, and the project is then at risk because they cannot deliver it all in time and with high quality.

For brand-new projects, we introduced the students to a new approach for organizing stories and creating provably powerful test sets. This approach was tried on a Web-based project and immediately produced excellent results. It was both simple to use and powerful in its ability to capture the essence of the system. However, the projects are still ongoing, so it is perhaps too early to make any firm conclusions.

Risk Management

Part of any successful company activity is the management of risk. In both Genesys and the Software Hut, this is an important activity. XP raises a number of different issues with the traditional design-led approaches. We have, in the past, carried out two phases of risk analysis. At the start of the project, the teams are asked to carry out a risk analysis for their project; then they record the results and create their work plan in light of these results. After seven weeks, there is a second risk analysis exercise, which is influenced by the problems and successes of the project during the intervening period. The plan is then altered to suit the circumstances. At this stage, the scope of the project is usually reduced because some of the desirable requirements in the original plan are downgraded to being optional. With XP this process may need to be more continual, and it is an area we wish to consider.

Future Experiment

This coming semester (February 2001) will see the start of the next Software Hut exercise. As usual, three clients will each deal with four to six teams. We plan to divide the teams into two groups, one of which will be given some reinforcement in traditional software design techniques, and the other will get a crash course in XP. We will then monitor the progress of the two cohorts of students, some using XP and others not, as they attempt to build their solutions.

We will do the monitoring by studying the way the students manage their projects. Each team must produce and maintain realistic plans, keep minutes of all their project meetings, and be interviewed weekly. We will also get all their working documents, requirements documents, analysis, test cases, designs, code, and test reports. These will provide many further opportunities for measuring the attributes of their output, ranging from function and object point analysis to bug densities. The XP experiments suggested by Ron Jeffries will be helpful in this respect.[2]

At the end of the semester, the clients will evaluate and mark all the delivered solutions. They use a structured marking scheme that we construct for them, which provides a final level of measurement of how well the solutions performed in terms of usability, installability, functionality, robustness, and so on. These are the key attributes because they will be applicable to all the solutions no matter how they were built. We will use this information in a statistical analysis to see whether

2. See the XProgramming Web site at http://www.xprogramming.com.

there are any significant differences in the quality of the final products between XP and traditional "heavyweight" methods.

Finally, we will require each student to give both a team evaluation and a personal commentary on how the project went, describing the strengths and weakness of what they did and how they did it. In the past, this has been useful in identifying issues and problems with approaches to software development.

After delivery, we will be able to track the performance of the delivered systems to gain further information about their quality in their working environment.

The three clients are as follows.

- Client A is an organization that brokers waste. A waste exchange provides a facility for industrial companies to offer their waste products to other companies that might be able to reclaim something of value from it. The waste exchange maintains a database of current waste products and arranges for the exchange and payment of deals in waste. The project is to build a Web-based system that interfaces with the existing database and gives clients the opportunity to browse the database.
- Client B is a small start-up company in the bioinformatics industry requiring software for data analysis. Various new algorithms for processing and analyzing genomic and protonomic data have been developed by the company, and they now require a set of programs that can automatically apply these algorithms to data that is continually being placed on Web sites directly from the scientific experiments.
- Client C is a legal practice center that provides specialist training for the legal profession. One aspect of this training is postacademic qualifications and deals with the experiential learning related to legal practice in solicitors' offices. The client needs a computerized assessment system to provide a mechanism for tracking and evaluating each student's performance in the course.

The overall arrangements are described in Figure 22.1.

In all of this, the students will be basing their approach on what they have learned in the course so far. In the first year, they will have taken part in a group project that involves building a small software system

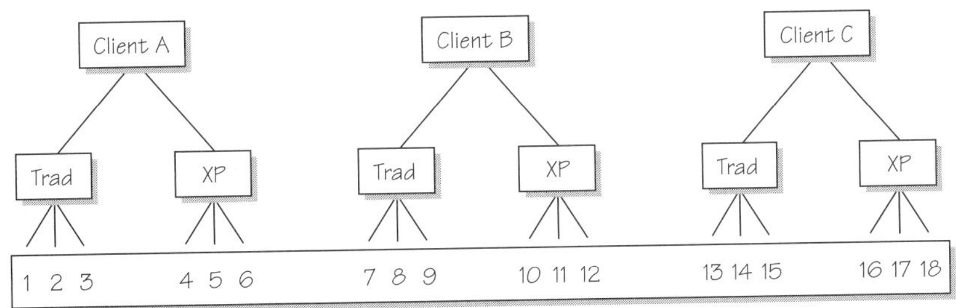

FIGURE 22.1 The organization of the teams and clients

specified by the course lecturers. The students do this as one-sixth of their work over the year, and it integrates what they have been taught in formal lectures dealing with requirements and specification, Java programming, and systems analysis and design (essentially UML). This exercise helps them start understanding some of the issues relating to working in teams, keeping accurate records, and producing high-quality documents; some of the problems in dealing with clients (a role played by their academic tutors) and the problems of delivering quality; and the need for thorough review and testing activities.

Before they start on the Software Hut projects, they attend a practical course on teamwork, organized by the university's Careers Services Department.

They will then be split into two cohorts, the XP teams and the Trad (traditional) teams, for further specific training in a methodology and an approach to software construction.

One area that we must address concerns the advice we give about the form of the project plan. The XP-based plans will be very different from the traditional approach, and it will be a new phenomenon for the tutors to be managing a set of projects that are at very different stages at any one time. The students will also compare notes to some extent, and we hope that the teams using XP will be discreet about what they are doing so they do not influence the other teams too much. We have found in the past that the competitive element has minimized this.

Part of this trial run will be learning about the sorts of metrics and data we need to enable us to carry out proper comparisons. We will then be able to run better experiments.

Conclusions and Further Work

Clearly, it is early and there is much work to be done. What is different about our approach is that the student teams are building real systems for real clients. Thus they face, immediately, the issues of communicating with their client and trying to understand the client's business context and their problem. *This is vital.* Normal student project experiments are rarely valid, because the whole exercise is something of a sham and everyone knows this. Nobody wants to be able to use the products in real life. The Software Hut approach also creates the desire among nearly all the students to do it properly because they realize that delivering software full of bugs or with an unusable interface just will not do. They have some professional pride and don't want to let the university down. We are convinced that this means that we can really carry out legitimate empirical experiments in controlled conditions and that the results will be meaningful.

This is only the start. We are bound to see, as XP evolves, the emergence of different ways of doing it, using different tools, methods, and notations. This will give us further opportunities to test the ideas in what we call our "Software Engineering Observatory": the Software Hut, for detailed comparative experiments, and Genesys, where we are investigating how new ideas and methods can be introduced into a working software company.

References

[Beck2000] K. Beck. *Extreme Programming Explained.* Addison-Wesley, 2000.

[Holcombe+1998] M. Holcombe, A. Stratton. "VICI: Experiences and Proposals for Student-Run Software Companies." In *Projects in the Computing Curriculum.* M. Holcombe, A. Stratton, S. Fincher, G. Griffiths, eds. Springer, 1998.

[Holcombe+1999] M. Holcombe, H. Parker. "Keeping Our Clients Happy: Myths and Management Issues in 'Client-Led' Student Software Projects." *Computer Science Education*, Volume 9, Number 3, 1999.

[Holcombe+2001] M. Holcombe, K. Bogdanov, M. Gheorghe. "Functional Test Generation for Extreme Programming." *Proceedings of XP2001*, Sardinia, Italy, 2001.

[Stratton+1998] A. Stratton, M. Holcombe, P. Croll. "Improving the Quality of Software Engineering Courses through University Based Industrial Projects." In *Projects in the Computing Curriculum*. M. Holcombe, A. Stratton, S. Fincher, G. Griffiths, eds. Springer, 1998.

Acknowledgments

We would like to acknowledge our colleagues Tony Simons, Tony Cowling, Gerald Luettgen, and Kirill Bogdanov for many useful discussions and suggestions. We would also like to thank our clients who agreed to work with our students on their problems.

About the Authors

Professor Mike Holcombe is head of the Verification and Testing Research Group in the Department of Computer Science, University of Sheffield, and dean of the faculty of engineering. He is the author of five research monographs and edited works, and around 100 papers on subjects in software engineering, theoretical computing, pure mathematics, and bioinformatics.

Dr. Marian Gheorghe has been interested for more than 20 years in computational models, formal language theory, and software engineering. He has written more than 40 papers investigating the power and properties of various computational models as well as their use in defining efficient parsing strategies or specifying and testing dynamic systems.

Francisco Macias received a B.E. degree in geology from the Instituto Politecnico Nacional in Mexico, and an M.S. degree in computer sciences from the Universidad Nacional Autonoma de Mexico. He worked for one year at Olivetti in software production. After six years as a lecturer in Mexican universities, he joined the Department of Computer Science of the University of Sheffield. He is pursuing a Ph.D. in the Verification and Testing Research Group.

Chapter 23

Student Perceptions of the Suitability of Extreme and Pair Programming

—*Dean Sanders*

Part III

Senior students were asked to write opinion papers about the use of Extreme Programming (XP) in a software engineering class and the use of pair programming in an introductory programming course. Most of the students opposed using XP in the software engineering class but favored the use of pair programming in an introductory programming course. A pilot study uncovered some reservations about using pair programming early in a computer science curriculum. The students' comments are insightful and should be considered before introducing either of these practices into the curriculum.

Introduction

The first portion of this chapter summarizes the opinions of senior students about the use of Extreme Programming in a software engineering class and the use of pair programming in an introductory programming course. The second portion of the chapter describes the perceptions of students who participated in a pilot study of the feasibility of using pair programming early in a computer science curriculum.

This chapter does not discuss the value of Extreme Programming or pair programming per se. Instead, it provides insight into the minds of those who will be directly affected if either of these topics becomes an important component of the curriculum. The students' opinions show considerable insight.

Perceptions of XP

Students in the author's software engineering course work in small teams to develop the requirements for, to design, and to implement the first build of a project for an external client. A few projects are for clients outside the university, but most are sponsored by other faculty members.

In addition to the project, the students are required to complete two research/writing assignments during the semester. One of these is an opinion paper that is due near the end of the course. The opinion paper is always on a relevant topic that has not yet been covered in the course, to avoid influencing the results. By the time they write the paper, the students know that their opinions do not have to agree with the instructor's opinions, which removes a possible source of bias.

During the fall semester of 1999, all students were required to write an opinion paper that addressed the question "Should Extreme Programming be adopted as the life cycle model for the project portion of this course?" During the fall semester of 2000, the students were given a choice of topics, including the same question about Extreme Programming. The students were given a few references as a starting point and were required to include additional references in their papers.

The numbers and reasons that follow must be viewed in light of the characteristics of the students as they pertain to this topic. This was the first time that most of the students had studied team dynamics and software life cycle concepts. Students entering this course had no prior instruction in systems analysis, software design, or software engineering. Fewer than 25% of them had had an internship or significant industrial experience. Although all the students had been required to work in small informal groups to complete major projects in other courses, this was the first time that they had worked with a client other than the instructor for the course.

The results were consistent across the two semesters. Of the 40 students who addressed this question, 14 (35%) were in favor of adopting

XP and 26 (65%) were opposed. Although there was little support for using XP on the project, there was very strong sentiment for studying XP as an alternate life cycle model. The numbers are interesting, but the reasons for the opinions are more enlightening.

Support for Extreme Programming

The primary reasons that were given to support using XP as the life cycle model for the project in software engineering can be organized into four categories: (1) progress is more visible, (2) communication within the project is improved, (3) complexity is easier to manage, and (4) testing is improved. Each of these reasons is discussed later in this chapter.

Most of the proponents cited visible progress as a major justification for using XP in the project. One student wrote:

> *Students are used to being able to see progress when working on a project. Extreme Programming allows the student to produce a program a little at a time. By seeing this progress, the students will feel more comfortable with the process.*

Another wrote:

> *If XP were used, we could develop less paperwork in the beginning so we could start writing code. It is much easier to see progress when you can use something that you can see work.*

As indicated by the preceding two statements and other similar responses, students have learned to equate progress with functioning code. Extreme Programming is a better match for their perception of progress.

A few students included improved communication among their reasons for using Extreme Programming. Although most of these comments appear to have been motivated by problems with individual project teams, one student added a new insight.

> *XP keeps the clients continuously in contact with the teams during the process and included in all of the decisions that are made in the project. This gives the students the opportunity to build on their interview skills.*

The statements pertaining to reduced complexity focused on the small size of each build. These comments were from members of teams who failed to manage the complexity of their projects.

Some students mentioned the testing aspects of Extreme Programming. The most compelling statement was made by a student who wrote:

> *Generally, testing is not emphasized strongly in the college curriculum and yet it is so very important in the real world. An XP approach would give students an opportunity to develop the skills for designing and running thorough tests.*

Opposition to Extreme Programming

The students had several reasons for not adopting XP. These reasons fall into five major categories: (1) narrowing of the course content, (2) inadequate preparation for XP, (3) scheduling conflicts, (4) insufficient estimation skills, and (5) unrealistic cycle times.

The most persistent and compelling arguments against the use of Extreme Programming were based on course content. The students felt that they needed to understand the issues and processes associated with requirements elicitation, systems analysis, and software design before they began to use Extreme Programming. The following four quotes demonstrate the students' thinking.

> *XP isn't for beginners. It assumes that the developers already know the tricks of the trade concerning design and that they know their own abilities.*
>
> *Students entering the class have little knowledge of developing software and need to learn about requirements, specification, design, implementation, and integration. The best way to learn these different steps is to do them, so XP wouldn't be the best choice, because the XP model doesn't seem to be concerned with any division of these steps.*
>
> *One of the other life cycle models is perhaps better because they work slowly through the specification and design phase, allowing for developers to learn the importance of documentation and global thinking about a software system.*
>
> *The process of XP requires some prior knowledge of software development life cycles to fully understand the concept behind it and why it would be useful.*

The students that mentioned scheduling conflicts approached the issue from two perspectives. Some pointed out that modern students must divide their time between course work and other obligations, such as work and family. Others mentioned difficulties in scheduling frequent sessions with the clients, who have their own agendas. One student captured the essence of this problem by writing:

> *The chances that software engineering students can work on their individual portion of the project every day are very slim. Instead of a workplace environment with focus on only those projects, the students have other obligations along with their multiple classes.*

A few students were concerned about other issues. Some mentioned that they lacked the experience to make accurate time estimates as required by XP. In a related theme, some were concerned about the short cycle times for each build. In both cases, the primary concern seemed to be a perception of decreased quality. This concern was expressed well by the student who wrote:

> *As a result of prior programming classes, students will have more than likely adopted the build-and-fix method of developing software. This is fine when the projects are small, but in a large project and without self-discipline, the "iteration process" of XP could quickly degrade into the build-and-fix model as students feel the need to hurry up and finish.*

Perceptions of Pair Programming

During the fall semester of 2000, the students were required to write two opinion papers chosen from a short list of possible topics. One choice was to address the question, "Should pair programming be taught in the introductory programming courses in our department?"

Twenty of the students chose to address this topic. Fourteen (70%) of the students favored teaching pair programming and six (30%) were opposed.

Once again, the numbers and reasons that follow must be viewed in light of the characteristics of the students as they pertain to this topic. Starting with the first programming course, the students were allowed to work in pairs to develop programs, but the partnerships were casual and unstructured. The pairing was gradually discouraged as they progressed through the curriculum. Some of the students had participated in these informal pairings, while others had not. In addition, many of the students had had recent contact with beginning programmers by working as teaching assistants or laboratory assistants.

Support for Pair Programming

The students who advocated the use of pair programming tended to echo the supporting themes that appear in the literature, including increased learning and comprehension, enhanced communication and teamwork, improved time management, improved self-reliance, improved problem solving and strategic thinking, and more opportunities to experiment and consider alternative solutions.

Some of the students drew from their personal experience to advocate pair programming as a way to increase retention. One student wrote:

> *Fewer students would abandon their computer science major if pair programming were taught here. I know several students who started out as computer science majors and switched their major because they did not think that they were smart enough to program. Pair programming would put more students at ease because it uses the attitude that two brains are better than one.*

Another student, who had failed his first attempt at a programming course, wrote:

> *Speaking from experience, when first learning a computer language, it seems like learning Chinese. I did not realize that you had to adapt yourself to a different level of intellect and think on a different plane. If I would have been paired with someone, together we could have helped each other adapt to this way of thinking.*

Another raised an interesting point concerning pair programming.

> *The beginning programmer finds it difficult to clearly document code. With a partner looking on in pair programming there would be a constant pressure to write code that another can read.*

Opposition to Pair Programming

Most of the students' arguments against using pair programming in the introductory courses were based on what could happen if pair programming practices were not strictly followed by all participants. Several of the arguments expressed the concern that pair programming would not be effective unless both members were competent. The following quotes capture the essence of these arguments.

When people who know a lot are put with people who know nothing, the person who is supposed to be watching for errors doesn't know what an error would look like.

When assignments would be handed out, the more experienced programmer would do all the work so they wouldn't get a bad grade on the assignment.

Some students expressed reservations about whether or not pair programming would be practiced without direct supervision. The following quote expresses this thought very well.

Pair programming requires that two people work on the project at the same time. This would involve work outside the classroom and for people to find time that they are both available. They wouldn't work in pairs if they were supposed to outside of class. One would do this part and the other would do that part. And that wouldn't be pair programming, that would be modular programming.

A few of the concerns dealt with some of the realities of a beginning programming class. What happens when strangers form an incompatible pair? What happens when one member of a pair withdraws from the course or simply stops participating?

Finally, one student expressed a concern about an apparent conflict between the goals of pair programming and the goals of an introductory programming class.

A programming group turning out "products" at an early stage in the learning process is a bad way to look at teaching. The product of a student's efforts is knowledge and understanding, not a chunk of code with a minimal number of errors.

Part III

Suggestions from the Students

A few students expanded on the assignment and suggested ways to incorporate pair programming into the beginning programming courses. Most of these suggestions were variations on the theme that pair programming can be used successfully only in a closed laboratory environment. A few suggested that the instructors would have to develop more challenging assignments and adjust their grading criteria.

The most provocative comment came from the student who offered the following suggestion.

> *The time taken for a student to complete a program would be nearly cut in half, allowing the professor to assign more programs. This would aid the students' knowledge by allowing them to complete more programs.*

A Pilot Study

The reported classroom experiences with pair programming tend to involve upper-division students [Wells2001; Williams+2000A]. Is pair programming a reasonable practice for students in lower-division courses? This author conducted a pilot study to assess the feasibility of using pair programming in a data structures course.

During the summer term of 2001, the data structures course had a small enrollment that was very representative of the diversity of students who normally take the course—representative in terms of age, gender, ethnicity, family obligations, job schedules, majors and minors, and grade point averages. The first day of the semester, the students were asked to read two articles on pair programming [Williams+2000A; Williams+2000C] and were told that pair programming was to be used for all programming assignments during the semester. The students were then required to write a few sentences that described their initial impressions of pair programming. As was the case with the students in software engineering, the students were generally enthusiastic but expressed a few concerns about scheduling, personality clashes, and work habits.

Because this course lacked a separate laboratory component, some regular class periods were converted to closed laboratory sessions. The initial stages of each programming assignment were completed in the laboratory sessions. The instructor (this author) monitored the students' application of pair programming and made suggestions for improvement. After a few laboratory sessions, the teams were allowed to complete the assignments on their own time, but they were still expected to practice pair programming.

The students completed two questionnaires about their experience with pair programming—one after the first assignment and one at the end of the semester. As one would expect, their perceptions changed.

Initially, communication difficulties and schedule conflicts were seen as the major difficulties. By the end of the semester, most of the communications difficulties had been resolved, but finding time to meet and work outside of class was still a problem. As the semester progressed, a new difficulty arose in pairs of significantly differing abilities. The stronger student in each of these pairs grew frustrated with having to explain everything to the weaker student.

When asked to describe the positive benefits of pair programming, the results were consistent with those reported in the literature [Williams+2000C]. Most students reported improved relations with their partner, more efficient defect avoidance, and apparently shortened development times as the primary benefits.

Finally, the students were asked whether pair programming was feasible for use in the data structures course during the regular semester. Early in the summer, the unanimous answer was "yes," but the early enthusiasm waned. The majority believed that pair programming was a valuable practice but that it should be delayed until a later course. They strongly recommended that the pairs be of roughly equal ability and that all pair programming activities occur in laboratory sessions.

Conclusion

Any process is difficult to implement if the participants lack faith in the process. A thoughtful group of senior computer science majors have expressed their opinions concerning the use of Extreme Programming in a software engineering class and the use of pair programming in an introductory programming class. Most of those students feel that Extreme Programming should be taught as a lecture topic, but using it for a project should be delayed until the students become more proficient in the traditional phases of software development. Most also believe that pair programming should be used in the introductory programming courses, but many feel it might be better to defer pair programming to a later course. Indications from a pilot study support the opinion that pair programming is a valuable practice, but it should not be introduced early in the curriculum.

Although student opinions should not dictate changes to the curriculum, they provide valuable insight that should be considered. Their opinions are particularly valuable as we consider changing the way that they are expected to work and interact with one another.

References

[Beck1999] K. Beck. "Embracing Change with Extreme Programming." *Computer,* Volume 32, Number 10, October 1999.

[Biggs2000] M. Biggs. "Pair Programming: Development Times Two." *InfoWorld,* Volume 22, Number 30, 2000.

[Conrad2000] B. Conrad. "Taking Programming to the Extreme Edge." *InfoWorld,* Volume 22, Number 30, 2000.

[Extreme2001] *Extreme Programming.* http://ootips.org/xp.html. November 14, 2001.

[Nosek1998] J. Nosek. "The Case for Collaborative Programming." *Communications of the ACM,* Volume 41, Number 3, March 1998.

[Siddiqi2000] J. Siddiqi. *An Exposition of XP But No Position on XP.* http://computer.org/seweb/dynabook/index.htm. 2000.

[Wells2001] J. Wells. *Extreme Programming: A Gentle Introduction.* http://www.extremeprogramming.org. November 14, 2001.

[Williams+2000A] L. Williams, R. Kessler. "All I Really Need to Know About Pair Programming I Learned in Kindergarten." *Communications of the ACM,* Volume 43, Number 5, May 2000.

[Williams+2000B] L. Williams, R. Kessler. "Experimenting with Industry's 'Pair-Programming' Model in the Computer Science Classroom." *Journal on Software Engineering Education,* December 2000.

[Williams+2000C] L. Williams et al. "Strengthening the Case for Pair Programming." *IEEE Software,* Volume 17, Number 4, 2000.

Acknowledgments

The author thanks his students for providing well-considered, insightful responses to his questions and for keeping him from becoming too complacent.

About the Author

Dean Sanders is a professor of computer science at Northwest Missouri State University. He received a B.S. degree from Western Michigan University and M.S. and Ph.D. degrees at Michigan State University. His primary interests are computer science education, software design, and software engineering.

Chapter 24

Extreme Programming and the Software Design Course

—David H. Johnson and James Caristi

Part III

This is a report on an effort to simulate the practices of the Extreme Programming (XP) methodology in a software design course. Two teams of 11 members followed many of those practices in developing their semester projects. Included is a description of which practices were required of the development teams, which were encouraged, and which were not easily simulated. Near the end of the semester, the students were asked to answer a number of questions about how well each practice had served the process. Summaries and examples of their responses along with the instructor's observations are presented as an evaluation of this approach. Suggestions for what might be done differently to better simulate the XP methodology are included.

Introduction

The computer science curriculum at Valparaiso University has included an upper-level course in software design for almost 20 years. The goals of the course have remained fairly constant over time, while the development methods emphasized have changed drastically to keep up with the latest advances in methodology. We have always sought to simulate as much as possible a "real world" environment. Our students work in teams on substantial projects that are proposed by a client. The instructor sets the list of activities each team should go through in the development process.

This chapter reports on our recent use of XP as the guiding methodology. It includes input from our students on their reactions to the various components we attempted to simulate and suggests ways to make the course activities fit XP more closely.

Procedures

Students cannot devote 40 hours per week to a single class, and they are not, in most instances, seasoned programmers. Twelve XP "practices" are listed in Chapter 10 of [Beck2000]: the planning game, small releases, metaphor, simple design, testing, refactoring, pair programming, collective ownership, continuous integration, 40-hour week, on-site customer, and coding standards. To accommodate our restrictions, we tried to simulate only those practices that were feasible in our situation.

There were two groups of 11 students, each working on one of the following projects: a MathML editor and a floor plan drawing tool. Once into the project, each team had two 50-minute periods and one two-hour period per week in a computer lab where we could simulate an XP working environment. Some XP practices were not simulated. We were unable to provide on-site customers for either project. Neither did we have students attempt to estimate the time it would take to complete a task (planning game). Estimates would be guesses at best, because most of our students had limited experience in implementing the types of tasks their projects required. Other practices—such as developing a guiding metaphor, continuous integration, small releases, and refactoring—we chose to *encourage* but not require. What we did require was that the teams develop coding standards, write unit tests, program in pairs, and practice collective ownership.

The student teams were responsible for devising the details of how they would proceed within these guidelines. Near the end of the course, all students completed a questionnaire concerning their impressions of XP (see the sidebar Questions Used in the Survey). They also wrote a short paper in which they were asked to evaluate the experience in light of what they now thought it might be like to work professionally as a developer.

Questions Used in the Survey

Extreme Programming—Your Reactions

Please answer the following questions concerning our use of the Extreme Programming method. You need ***not*** sign this sheet unless you so desire. The answers will in no way affect your course grade.

Coding Standards. Your group established coding standards near the beginning of the process. Did you follow those standards in the code you wrote for the project? If so, was it difficult? (If you did primarily other things than develop code, indicate so.) What percentage of your group followed the standard? Do you think it was easier to read and modify others' code as a result of the standards?

Unit Testing. Did you ever really write unit tests before starting to code a class? (Or even in conjunction with coding the class.) Did you ever use the tests developed by the group as you changed or refactored code? (If not, give some reason.)

Collective Ownership. Was there a feeling of group ownership of the project code? How did you like the fact that anyone in the group could change code you had written? Was that a help or hindrance to the progress of the project?

Pair Programming. Did programming in pairs make the process go more quickly or do you think it slowed you down? Were you able to split the work equitably or did one person tend to dominate? Did working in pairs help you to better understand the project as a whole? Were you ever able to learn more about an area originally unfamiliar to you by working with someone with more experience? Did one partner tend to work on an immediate problem while the other focused on strategy? Was there anyone that you just could not work with? If you tried pairing and it did not work, what went wrong and how do you think it could be fixed? Did you like programming in pairs? That is, give an overall thumbs-up or thumbs-down to it.

Customers. XP projects ideally have a client/customer on the team. We faked this. Would your team have benefited from having the customer more accessible? Were there enough "stories" to guide your work?

Refactoring. Refactoring is the process of changing a software system in such a way that it does not alter the external behavior of the system but improves the internal structure. It is a disciplined way to clean up code that minimizes the chances of introducing bugs. Were you involved in refactoring any code written by your group? (I know you all changed code to get it to work the way you wanted it to. That is not necessarily refactoring.) Describe. Was the resulting code in your opinion better from the maintainability standpoint? That is, do you think a person coming "cold" to the code would be better able to understand what it did reading the refactored version? In what way was the structure of the code improved in your opinion?

Multiple Small Releases. One of the basic tenets of XP is to get a stripped-down version working and release it. Then add a few features and release the updated version. The process continues in this manner until the final release. Did your group continuously integrate code so that you had a simple working version early in the term that could have been "released" with the proviso that more features would be added in future releases? If yes, did having a "working version" help with making desired additions? (Describe how in your opinion.) If no, why not?

Observations and Student Reactions

Metaphor Definition

XP projects need a guiding metaphor to help everyone on the project "understand the basic elements and their relationships" [Beck2000]. We provided both groups with an initial story and suggested a metaphor. We also mentioned possible future enhancements such as chat capabilities, in which the basic elements of each project could be exchanged. We did not require that the group explicitly develop their own version of a metaphor.

About halfway into the semester, we asked the students to give a one-sentence description of what their team was constructing. Their responses showed that in most cases the enhancements had become an integral part of their perception of what they were doing. For both teams, this fuzziness appeared to make it harder to get started with a simple first version. It might work better to require students to develop a simple metaphor themselves and then ask them every so often to recall what it is.

Coding Standards

One of the first things that we asked each team to do was to develop and publish coding standards to be followed by all team members. Almost all students reported that they followed their standards and that 60–80% of their group members did also. Almost all felt that the standards made it easier to read any team member's code and that they enhanced the attitude of group ownership of the code.

Part III

Stories and Preliminary Design

One student in each group was elected manager. This person was responsible for leading group planning sessions, identifying tasks, and coordinating all activities. The fact that this person was a peer made it somewhat unrealistic, but both managers performed quite well.

We felt that, as novices, our students needed some structured activities in order to make a start. A metaphor might be enough for an experienced programmer who has done similar things before, but beginners need something more. We provided a big "story" and several smaller ones, and asked that each group create a concept diagram [Larman1998] and then turn that into a class diagram. The students may have viewed this task, as one put it, "like a big pain in the . . .," but their thinking changed when they saw how much the diagrams helped keep their group on track. From our perspective, even considering the fact that student responses in the evaluation may lean toward what they thought we wanted to hear, the diagrams did help create within each group a better sense of what they were building. The group that had more trouble with their project looked back at this part of the process and speculated that more care in making the diagrams and determining class responsibilities would have helped.

Unit Testing

Unit testing is fundamental to the XP process. We used the JUnit testing framework and spent several lab periods getting somewhat familiar with it.[1] We asked our students to write tests, gave a number of demonstrations, and encouraged them to write tests *before* coding the class. A number of tests were written, but no one would admit to writing one before the class code was written! There was little indication that tests that were actually written were used extensively. Part of this is due to the fact that automated tests for graphical applications are harder to write, and the teams could and did run quick visual tests to verify that a method was working. But the fact remains that automated unit tests were not used very much.

Probably the fundamental reason for this lack of unit testing is that our students have not been trained in writing them. The idea that writing tests helps in designing a class is not a natural one for them. Their tendency is to want to get the job done and see some "results." And in an academic environment, where the life cycle of most student projects ends after the program works, there is little to point out the value of having a suite of tests available. Our efforts to demonstrate how to incorporate tests in the normal coding patterns had little effect, and we believe that no matter what one might do at this point in our curriculum, the results would be much the same.

Unit testing should be incorporated into the curriculum at least as soon as objects are introduced and earlier if possible. Then testing would become a programming habit whose value would be taken for granted (like coding standards). We have taught coding standards for some time, so they now come naturally to students. (When asked whether it was difficult to follow the coding standards adopted by their team, students typically responded, "No, that is the way I program normally.") Testing, if taught early and often in the curriculum, would become just as natural. The benefit would be better code, an admirable goal no matter what development method is chosen.

Pair Programming

Following the XP practice, we asked our students to code in pairs at one computer. Our students are used to working in small groups, but none had experienced pair programming. We suggested that one way

---

1. See the JUnit Web site at http://www.junit.org/.

they could work would be for one partner to code tests or class methods while the other worked on strategy. After a time they should switch roles. We also encouraged them not to work with the same partner every day.

It is hard to judge just how good a simulation of an XP environment this turned out to be. The students did quite well in pairs even though they might not have followed the XP model exactly. As mentioned earlier, testing was an afterthought for them in spite of our instructions. So instead of having one partner start by implementing some tests while the other developed a strategy for implementing the responsibilities of the class, they would first work on strategy and planning together. Then one partner would start to type while the other checked for typos and syntax errors, while at the same time asking the partner questions about how and why something was done. We asked our students to give us their impressions of pairing, and we believe that their responses show that it served both the student and the project well.

There were several areas in which 80% or more of our students felt that pair programming helped. For instance, they overwhelmingly reported that pairing helped them understand the project as a whole. These were some responses.

> *Some parts I would not have understood at all. But after a couple days working with someone on it, I was much more comfortable.*

> *Talking a lot helps you know the project code inside and out.*

Most felt that they had learned more about an unfamiliar area by working with someone who knew more. The few who did not respond positively reported that neither of them knew much about their tasks, so a lot of time was spent with the documentation.

One of the criticisms of XP is that it cannot be efficient to have two skilled programmers working on a single task when they could be working separately on two. Most of our students do not agree. About two-thirds thought pairing made the process go faster, while another quarter thought sometimes yes, sometimes no. Only a couple felt that pair programming was wasteful. Part of the speedup perceived by most of the students was probably due to having more than one person catching syntax errors and typos. As one commented:

> *Having someone looking over your shoulder and asking questions and pointing out errors early saved time.*

They frequently responded that the design of a class was a joint effort that benefited from more than one perspective.

> *It helped bring up more ideas . . .*

> *A second person can . . . introduce more ideas . . .*

Those who were more skeptical of pair programming felt that the communication process really slowed them down.

> *But communication of those ideas takes time.*

> *Slowed me down since I had to make sure my partner understood what was going on.*

Even these statements indicate that pairing helps with overall team communication.

In an effort to obtain student perceptions of how well the teams worked together, we asked them to comment on whether one person tended to dominate the pairing. Here the students were divided roughly evenly in their opinions. As mentioned earlier, only a few responded that they split the work along the lines of one partner coding a method while the other focused on strategy. So it is probably quite natural that the "better" programmer would dominate. Few reported any personality difficulties that seriously impaired their work. These results demonstrate what Beck claims in [Beck2000], that pair programming "is a subtle skill, one that you can spend the rest of your life getting good at." We made many process mistakes, such as not developing tests in a timely manner. So a good question might be, "Was there enough learning to justify our approach?"

Even with the mistakes made, we are satisfied that we have made a good start in using pair programming and the XP software development process in general. We asked our students to give a positive (thumbs-up) or negative (thumbs-down) assessment of pair programming. Fourteen gave it a thumbs-up (some even two thumbs-up), three said it depends on the project, and five just did not like it. The following comments from those who liked it indicate that they felt they learned a lot and that pairing helped the team work together better.

> *Project B was tight.*
>
> *Gave a chance to work with other styles of programming.*
>
> *I did like it; getting multiple ideas and then going with the best helped avoid unnecessary trial and error.*
>
> *It made the project more fun.*
>
> *Focuses on understanding how the given class functions.*

There were some valid criticisms and useful suggestions. Several reported that they were unable to accomplish very much in our two 50-minute periods, although they were much happier with what they could achieve during the two-hour lab period. Even when the pair continued on the same task, a certain amount of start-up time was needed whenever they reassembled. Toward the end of the semester when the teams were hurrying a bit, the better programmers tended to become more dominant and especially found at this time that having a partner slowed the process.

The few who remained unconvinced about the merits of pair programming said:

> *I found that it slowed the process. Working individually causes everyone to have to carry their share of the load.*
>
> *I code better alone. So do most of our better programmers. If I don't know what I am doing, pairs can help, though.*
>
> *I would still prefer to work independently, though it was good to try something different.*
>
> *The only time it worked well was in the lab, where you had time to get things done. It might work better in a workplace environment, where the XP protocol could be held more closely.*

Even these thumbs-down votes show an openness to later reevaluation of the process.

On the whole, we were pleased with the way our students used pair programming. What we did was not a perfect simulation of the pair programming process, but almost all students came to see its potential as an important part of the development process.

Multiple Small Releases

Neither of our groups produced a simple working version of their project for early "release." The group working on the floor plan drawing tool came the closest. Because their output was primarily graphical, they did build an early integration of their three windows to test it. They did a lot of testing of the type "If it doesn't look the way it is supposed to, fix it." In their view, they had a working version quite early, and subsequent work enhanced the current version.

The group doing the MathML editor was unable to integrate until near the end of the project, and they underestimated how difficult this would be. Too many members of the group had never had any experience implementing many of the elements of the project they were dealing with. Perhaps this is where a full-time customer on the project would have helped this group establish simple early-release criteria so that some of the integration problems at the end could have been solved in a simpler context.

Collective Ownership of Code

We required that both groups open all code to all team members so that anyone could improve existing code as long as they did not break it. Most class members reported that there was a feeling that the whole group owned all the code. They were more split on whether this was helpful, however. It seemed to work better in the group that could do more visual testing. Students responding positively to group ownership made comments such as these.

> *People would refactor others' code and make it more efficient. It was definitely a help to the group.*

> *If you were going through and found something that could be refactored, it could be done right then.*

I had no problem with others changing my code, as long as I could still understand the code. The open ownership of code seemed to help the project.

The few who thought it hindered progress said things such as, "It was helpful if you had done something wrong, so someone else could fix it, but annoying if someone changed something you thought was right."

Refactoring

We spent a number of class periods demonstrating systematic refactoring according to [Fowler1999]. Although both groups made changes in their code that amounted to some sort of refactoring, the lack of automatic tests prevented them from doing this in any systematic manner. They also ran out of time in the semester. The amount of refactoring they did was a result of the fact that they were doing pair programming. The need to make bad code better is clearer when lots of people are reading it.

Part III

Reflections

In spite of the problems in simulating an XP environment in a single academic course, we believe that our course served our students well as a good introduction to the methodology. Some of the problems we encountered can be solved. For instance, the team could be asked to formally develop a metaphor for the project and be required to rearticulate it periodically. As unit testing is incorporated into the curriculum from the beginning, that should enable testing to be a natural activity for students. If unit testing is new to the students, more time needs to be devoted to this topic before work on the project starts. If actual customers are not available, the instructor should help each team develop a simple set of criteria for an "early release." This should stimulate more refactoring and enable a more advanced form of pair programming to take place. To enable implementation of the planning game, and to improve students' abilities in planning and estimation, Watts Humphrey has suggested [Humphrey1997] that from the first course, students be required to estimate how long the assignment is expected to take and compare that with how long it actually took. We have started implementing this practice in our curriculum, and we expect to be able to do the planning game successfully in future software design courses. Splitting our four hours in the lab into two periods instead of three would help teams use the time better.

These suggestions would serve to smooth some of the rough spots that we found. Our student responses and our own observations agree that our XP-like process resulted in good team communication and a broader knowledge of the project as a whole. Those results alone indicate that an XP-based approach has merit in the context of the software design class.

References

[Beck2000] K. Beck. *Extreme Programming Explained*. Addison-Wesley, 2000.

[Fowler1999] M. Fowler. *Refactoring: Improving the Design of Existing Code*. Addison-Wesley, 1999.

[Humphrey1997] W. Humphrey. *An Introduction to the Personal Software Process*. Addison-Wesley, 1997.

[Larman1998] C. Larman. *Applying UML and Patterns*. Prentice Hall, 1998.

About the Authors

David H. Johnson has over 20 years' experience teaching most aspects of the computer science curriculum. His approach to the software design course has evolved over the years to the point where XP is emphasized. This includes having students use the XP approach in their semester-long projects. His enthusiasm for XP has only been increased by adapting it to the learning environment. He says it makes the entire development process, problems and solutions, clearer for students. He can be reached at David.Johnson@valpo.edu.

James Caristi has published research in computer simulation, expert systems, and theoretical mathematics. In 1990 he received the Sears-Roebuck Foundation Teaching Excellence and Campus Leadership Award, and in 1999 he received the Distinguished Teaching Award of the Indiana Section of the Mathematical Association of America. He has been involved in many software consulting projects and worked with X-ray astrophysicists at NASA on improved X-ray detectors and parallelizing simulations. Jim has been converted to the cause of agile methods, especially XP. He can be reached at James.Caristi@valpo.edu.

Chapter 25

The User Stories and Planning Game Tutorial

—Ann Anderson, Chet Hendrickson, and Ron Jeffries

Part III

The User Stories and Planning Game Tutorial is an interactive exercise-based tutorial. The students, in small groups, experience exercises in release planning, iteration planning, story writing, acceptance test definition, and story estimation. Lessons are drawn from discussion by the group, rather than from lecture by the tutorial leaders.

Tutorial Overview

The User Stories and Planning Game Tutorial was presented at both XP Universe (XPU) and XP2001. This chapter is a summary of the combined tutorial experiences. The tutorial had very little lecture; instead, small groups performed a series of interactive exercises. Each exercise was followed by a discussion with the entire group.

The goal of the tutorial was to familiarize participants with the aspects of Extreme Programming (XP) that involve stories, estimation, and planning. Participants gained experience in writing and explaining user stories, assisting customers in producing stories, estimating stories for release planning, selecting and explaining stories for iteration planning, breaking down stories into tasks, and estimating tasks.

Exercises

The tutorial consisted of four short exercises: (1) planning, (2) defining acceptance tests, (3) estimating stories, and (4) writing stories. Each exercise enabled the participants to learn by doing. The exercises can be done in any order; in fact, we have tried several different orders. The order described is the one we like best. Each exercise was completed (including discussion) in two hours or less. None of the exercises require any previous knowledge of XP or any programming skills. The participants did the exercises in small groups of approximately eight people.

Planning

Purpose

This exercise gives participants experience in project planning. A project is planned using three different methods, with each method producing a substantially better plan.

Description (Part 1)

The participants were told that they are in charge of planning a very important project. The project has to be completed in six months. The project has 45 critical features, which are represented by 45 small cards. The cards have the number of the feature (1 to 45) in the center of the card. The cards also have other numbers in each corner of the card, but these numbers are not explained. The participants are told to lay the cards out in six columns, where each column represents one month of the project.

Events

This part of the tutorial was always chaotic. The participants wanted to know what the other numbers meant. Everyone seemed to have a hard time deciding what to do. The participants were always looking for the secret. After the instructors repeatedly refused to tell them what the other numbers meant, the participants finally managed to get the cards on the table in six columns.

The groups spent a lot of effort trying to find the best plan. Some groups used numeric order. Some groups tried a wedge shape, where they plan to get less done in the first month but gradually increase productivity. Some groups tried to use the other numbers on the card. The number of different approaches was a testament to their creativity.

Once every group had a plan, the instructors went around to each table and told the group how much work they completed during the month. We used an incredibly complicated algorithm, but it always had the same effect. The group did not manage to get all the work done that they planned to complete. The cards that were not done were removed from the first column. These cards needed to be worked into the remaining five months.

This was repeated for two more iterations. The participants became really frustrated by this exercise. They were attempting to get work done, but they always had cards that were not completed. Finally, when they were just about ready to lynch us, we told them the secret.

Description (Part 2)

Planning a project is hard when you don't know the cost of a feature. The instructors had been using the small numbers on the right side of the card to determine the cost of the feature (how long it takes to implement). We randomly decided to use either the upper number or the lower number, but it didn't matter which one we picked. Each group had been completing ten units of work per month.

Now that the groups know the cost of the features and how many features they can complete in a month, they create another project plan. Management (in this case, the instructors) still wants the project in six months, but each group gets to pick their project ship date.

Events

One of the first things every group did is to figure out that it is impossible to get all 45 features done in six months. It would take nine months to complete all the features. The project plan was much better than the previous plan because they had information about how much work they could get done and when the project would be completed.

In this version of the exercise, we let each group decide in which iteration they wanted to ship the project. Some groups would ship at the end of the full nine months; others would ship sooner. Once everyone chose a ship date, we told the groups the second secret: The numbers on the left side of the card represent the value of each feature.

Using the value numbers, each group announced how much business value they shipped. We then displayed a simple spreadsheet and graph that showed the results. We assumed that the development costs for each group were $20,000 per month. The values of the features were in thousands of dollars. Then we showed what a profitability graph would look like for different ship dates. It was always surprising how well the groups did who shipped early. True, the ones who waited until the end finally won out, but shipping just once, early in the project, turned out to be a very good strategy.

Figure 25.1 shows a sample of how three different ship dates impact profitability. All three groups have the same monthly development cost. Group 1 decided to ship after month 4. One month later, this group had recovered their development cost and started earning profits. Groups 2 and 3 waited until months 6 and 9 to ship. Although both of

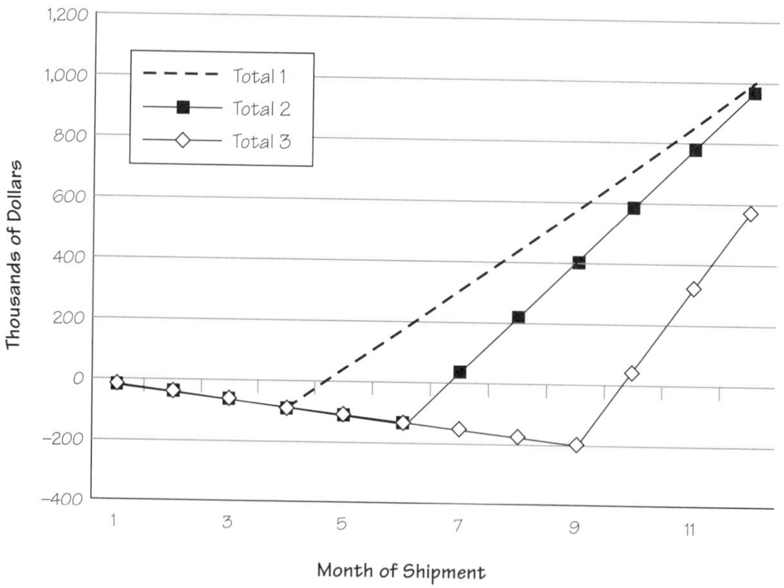

FIGURE 25.1 Early versus late shipment, unknown story value

these groups shipped higher value than group 1, they also had higher development costs to recover.

Description (Part 3)

The second part of the planning exercise let the participants produce a better plan. However, it still isn't the best plan. Now that the groups know both the cost and the value of a feature, they can lay out the cards to produce the best possible plan.

Events

None of the groups had a problem figuring out which features to do first. They all decided to do the high-value, low-cost cards first. The project plans were very similar. However, the groups still did not agree when to ship their projects. The release dates still tended to vary. Some groups wanted to wait until they got everything done. Some groups wanted to ship earlier.

We used the spreadsheet again in this part of the exercise. All the groups shipped a more valuable product except the group that waited until they had all the features completed. The profitability graph shown in Figure 25.2 is similar to the previous graph in Figure 25.1, except that the slopes for the groups that released in months 4 and 6 are a little bit steeper. Because both of these groups shipped with less than all the features, using this approach let them maximize the value of the features that they did complete. The group that shipped all the features in month 9 still eventually had the highest profitability, but shipping early was still a very good strategy.

Description (Part 4)

Knowing cost and business value enables the groups to produce the best possible plan. Then they need to figure out the best possible ship date.

Events

In the first three parts of this exercise, we allowed the participants to select only one ship date. In this part of the exercise, we let the participants experiment with multiple releases. Then we used the spreadsheet to show the impact on the profitability graph, shown in Figure 25.3.

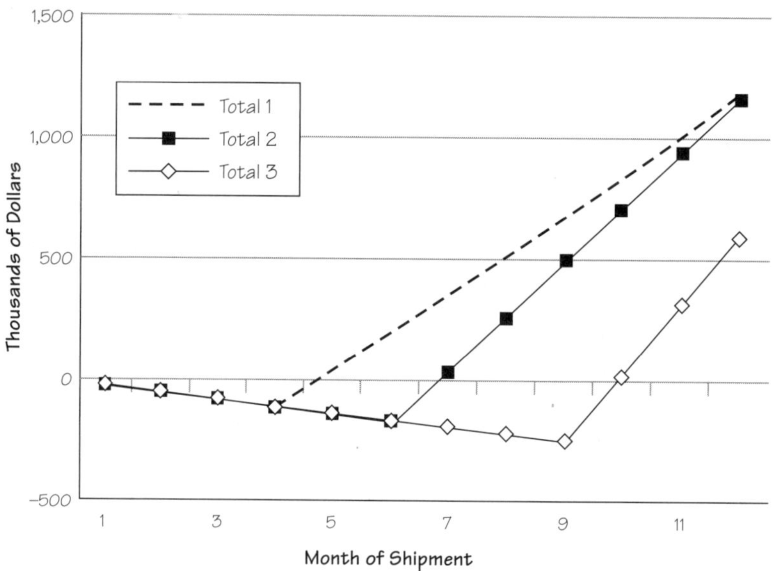

FIGURE 25.2 Early versus late shipment, optimal story value

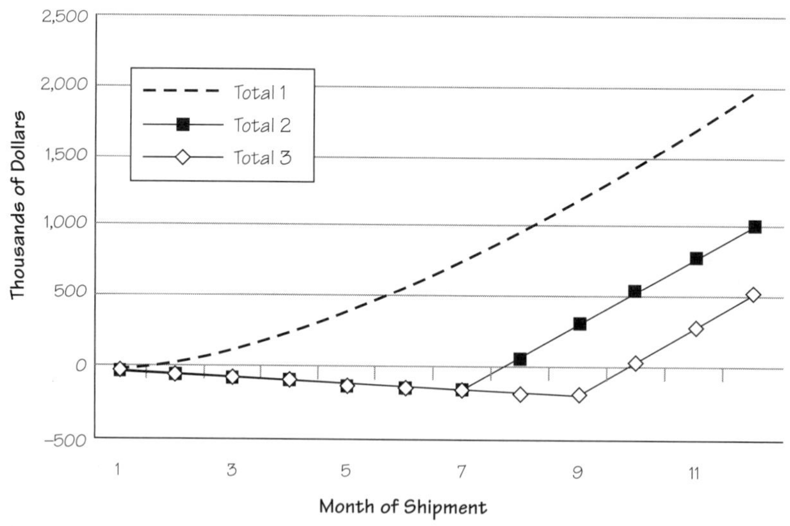

FIGURE 25.3 Incremental shipment, optimal story value

Summary

To create an optimal project plan, you need to know the relationship between cost and business value. This exercise demonstrated a simplified version of project planning. We eliminated all the uncertainty. We knew exactly how much work each group could get done. We knew exactly how much each feature would cost. We knew exactly how much value each feature would provide.

The bad new is that you won't know this exact information for your project. The good news is that it won't matter that much. Think about it. All you need is the ability to make comparisons between cards. This card is worth more than that card. This card is harder to implement than that card. Knowing the cost and value of a feature, relative to other features, is sufficient to let you create a good project plan.

Defining Acceptance Tests

Purpose

Acceptance tests are an important part of Extreme Programming, but all too often they are ignored. This exercise enables participants to become familiar with acceptance tests.

Description

As part of the preparation for the tutorial, the instructors got together and brainstormed ideas for applications. The criteria for the application were that it had to be interesting, nontrivial, and understood by both Europeans and Americans (because XP2001 has a large concentration of European attendees). The application that we selected was an electronic teller.

Then we wrote the user stories that described this application. We wrote about 40 user stories in just under an hour. The goal was to get a fairly large volume of stories. However, the goal was *not* to write especially high quality stories. We purposely wrote stories that were duplicates of other stories, included contradictory requirements, were too vague, and were much too large.

We gave each group of participants a copy of these stories and gave them 45 minutes to define the corresponding acceptance tests. The participants were told to write the acceptance tests on the back of the story cards.

Events

In this exercise all the participants played the role of the customer. Again, many of the groups had a hard time getting started. Some of the groups read all the stories before writing acceptance tests. Some of the groups split into two smaller groups, with each of the smaller groups taking about half of the story cards. A few groups just started writing tests.

The instructors gave warnings every 15 minutes, but other than that, all they did was observe and answer questions. Very few groups asked any questions about the stories, even though we were standing close enough to hear them talk about what they didn't understand.

At the end of the time limit, none of the groups had acceptance tests for all the stories, but all the groups had some acceptance tests. The groups shared their acceptance tests with all the participants.

Many of the groups had similar tests. The acceptance tests that were written tended to use the same approach.

The groups also tended to write tests for the same stories. This was true even though the story cards were shuffled and were not given to the groups in the same order. One story that all the groups wrote a test for was "Allow customer to make a deposit." A sample acceptance test for this story follows.

```
Acceptance test
    Establish account
    Make deposit
    Verify balance is correct
```

Several teams had variations of this same basic test. It was interesting to note that the acceptance tests tended to be vague. Even though the developers knew that they prefer to get acceptance tests that are more explicit, when the groups were writing the tests, they kept making the tests too fuzzy. An example of a more specific version of the same acceptance test follows.

```
Acceptance test
    Establish account
        Account number = 1231234556
        Account owner = John Smith
        Starting balance = 921.53
    Make deposit
        Deposit amount = 51.21
    Verify balance is correct
        Updated balance = 972.74
```

The groups also tended to have difficulty writing acceptance tests for the same stories. One story that none of the teams managed to write an acceptance test for was "Transform electronic teller into an armored car and have it drive to bank to make pickups." The stories that the groups were unable to write acceptance tests for were the stories that we considered lower-quality stories.

Summary

The participants already knew how to define acceptance tests; they just needed practice and reminders about what makes a good acceptance test. The stories that the groups had problems with were either too large or too vague.

Estimating Stories

Purpose

The ability to estimate how long a story will take is one of the keys to being able to plan your project. The purpose of this exercise was to learn how to estimate a user story.

Description

We used the user stories from the previous exercise in this exercise too. The participants were given 45 minutes to estimate all the stories. This gave them a little more than one minute per story.

Events

By this time the participants were used to the chaos. Most of them just started doing the estimates, although they did have questions about what kinds of units they needed to use. We told them they could use any units that they wanted.

At the end of the time limit, all the groups had an estimate for how long they thought the application would take to implement. The estimates had a fairly large range, although all the groups were fairly certain that their estimates were correct, plus or minus 10%.

Just as in the previous exercise, where groups had difficulty in writing acceptance tests for certain stories, the same stories were hard to test. In both exercises, the reason for the difficulty tended to be that the story was too large or too vague.

Writing Stories

Purpose

The purpose of this exercise was to learn how to write user stories.

Description

The groups were given a one-page description of a course-scheduling application and were asked to write all the stories for this application. They were told to take turns, with one person at a time writing a story while the others asked questions and made sure the story was estimable and testable. The time limit for the exercise was 45 minutes.

Events

They wrote the stories just as if they knew how. By this time, the groups were much more relaxed and were even having fun.

The exercises tend to build on one another—what you learn in one exercise is used and reinforced by the other exercises. In the previous exercises, the participants learned to think about acceptance testing and estimation. They also made a strong correlation between story "quality" and the ability to do acceptance testing and estimating. The participants knew the difference between a good story and a story that needs work.

At the end of the time limit, the groups shared their stories. Different groups had very different ideas about the systems that they would be implementing. Some groups were writing the stories for a batch system. Some groups wrote stories for an interactive Web-deployed system. The one-page description we gave them didn't specify any type of user interface, so they were free to do anything they liked.

Conclusion

This tutorial succeeded far beyond our expectations. When we came up with the proposal for this tutorial, we had a lot of uncertainty about how well it would work. We wanted people to learn about XP and have fun doing it. We thought the best way to accomplish those goals was in this format—actively trying to do some task, followed by a review of what worked and what did not. Fortunately, the participants agreed.

Much of what made this an excellent tutorial was the enthusiastic participation we got from the students. Thanks to everyone for taking part so enthusiastically.

Chapter 26

Continuous Learning

—Joshua Kerievsky

Part III

Continuous learning is part of the spirit of Extreme Programming (XP), implied in its values and implemented, to a certain extent, in its practices. I've learned that to be really good at XP, teams can go even further with their practice of continuous learning. In this chapter, I describe specific continuous learning tools, including learning repositories, study groups, and iteration retrospectives, which apply to programmers, coaches, and entire XP teams.

Introduction

The spirit of continuous learning is at the heart of XP. Customers and developers learn continuously from iteration planning; developers learn continuously from pairing, swapping pairs, testing, and refactoring; coaches learn continuously by communicating with everyone; and entire teams learn continuously from feedback generated by the XP process.

Thus, although continuous learning isn't a stated value or practice of XP, it is inherent to XP. In practice, this means that XP teams and individuals on those teams gradually learn and improve.

Experiencing the pace of these learnings led me to look for ways to shorten the learning curve. I discovered that by using a few powerful learning tools, a team could improve at a much faster rate. These tools include using a learning repository and conducting regular technical study groups and iteration retrospectives.

Teams Take Learning for Granted

Because continuous learning isn't an articulated value or practice, customers and developers often take learning for granted. It's something that is just supposed to happen.

You might imagine that if a team truly appreciates the XP values of feedback and communication, continuous learning will result. But in practice, this doesn't necessarily happen. Either teams don't associate feedback and communication with continuous learning, or they don't reflect enough to realize that they need to learn. This is understandable. Imagine if XP's 40-hour workweek principle were not articulated but only implied. Do you think teams would strive to work just 40 hours?

I've noticed that XP teams often miss the chance to learn in ways that could significantly improve their performance. XP teams are very code-centric and focused on making functional software. When reflection and learning happen, it's often in a watered-down, haphazard way.

Learning on an XP project today can be a bit like the practice of refactoring was before Kent Beck described it as an XP practice and turned up the knob on this practice to 10. Before XP, programmers would refactor their code when they felt like it, or maybe after code was shipped or released, but not all the time. By articulating refactoring as a practice and defining the importance of doing it continuously ("mercilessly"), XP challenged programmers and teams to improve their process.

Economic Incentive for Learning

Continuously refactoring, like all the other XP practices, can be shown to have a direct effect on the economics of software projects. If a team refactors continuously, their code will be easier to understand, extend, and maintain. As a result, the team will be more efficient, and that will enable them to get more done in less time. Bang, there's your economic incentive.

So is there also a direct economic incentive for practicing continuous learning? You'd better believe it.

Judy Rosenblum, who spent five years as Coca-Cola's chief learning officer and three years as Coopers & Lybrand's vice chairwoman for learning and education, says that learning must be connected directly to business. Organizations have to make learning a strategic choice. And to make that happen, organizations need leaders who see how important learning is to the continued health and success of their organizations. Such individuals must effectively embed learning into their organization's processes and projects, as Rosenblum explains.

> *Someone has to decide to make learning not just an individual experience but a collective experience. When that happens, learning isn't just something that occurs naturally—it is something that the company uses to drive the future of the business.* [Webber2000]

You might think this is completely obvious—of course organizations need to keep learning! But is learning a main topic in executive meetings? Is it believed to be as important as marketing, sales, and human resources? Most organizations would like to say, "Yes, we value learning," but in practice, they don't. They hope teams will learn, and they send people to training classes a few times a year, but they don't understand that continuous learning can have a huge impact on their bottom line. Instead, they overemphasize action.

Judy Rosenblum addresses this oversight.

> *The sense of urgency creates a bias for action. And that, in turn, prevents organizations from taking the time to learn. You have this phenomenal asset—your organization's collective experience—but this bias for action keeps you from focusing on it.* [Webber2000]

A Bias for Action

XP teams, especially new or inexperienced ones, are often too action-centric. Customers want to keep producing stories and writing acceptance tests, while developers want to keep testing, coding, and refactoring. But when does the process improve? Don't the customers want to get better at what they do: writing stories, planning, interacting with their customers, communicating with development, trimming fat from stories and tasks? And don't developers want to improve at refactoring, pair programming, design, automated testing, patterns, integration, or the simple art of knowing when to ask for help?

Certainly they do. But do they make time to improve? You might think that they don't need to, that learning will just happen over time. But I've been frustrated by the slowness of this process, which is largely due to the lack of time devoted to group learning.

For example, I can learn three hugely valuable things in one day, but my team isn't going to know about these learnings because the process doesn't include time for sharing them.

You might argue that XP does include time for sharing, because XP advises that teams conduct daily stand-up meetings, in which participants physically stand up and give summaries of what they're working on and how they're doing. Isn't that a good time for sharing learnings? Absolutely not.

Stand-up meetings are meant to be quick events—they aren't appropriate for conducting learning sessions, in which reflection and dialogue are requisite. So when would be an appropriate time? More to the point: What is the simplest, most cost-effective way to share learnings?

A Learning Repository

My preference is to use a simple, security-free, browser-based learning repository, such as Ward Cunningham's Wiki.[1] I say security-free because I've seen tools that have too many security bells and whistles, and I've seen how no one enters content into these tools simply because they are too burdensome to use.

So your learning repository must be simple to use, but just installing it and asking folks to use it isn't enough, either. Teams need to establish usage conventions. For example, a team can decide that developers will quickly jot down learnings on index cards as they work, and when they integrate their code, they can integrate significant learnings as well. Do-

1. See http://c2.com/cgi/wiki?WikiWikiWeb.

ing this will rapidly produce a valuable learning repository. Here are just a few examples of what a team might record.

> *Database Layer XML Refactoring (Jan. 27, 2001): While working on the new XML framework, Eric and I discovered that the database layer had been given new responsibilities that really didn't belong there—the mixture of responsibilities complicated the original design. So we've refactored the XML code out of the database layer and placed it into the new XML framework code. —Bob*

> *Tapping Your Finger: A Pair Programming Technique (Jan. 30, 2001): I discovered that instead of annoying my pair by telling her that she missed something, I can just tap with my finger on the offending spot in the code and give my pair the chance to figure out what was missing or incorrect. My pair, Mary, really liked this. It could be a good pair programming technique for everyone on the team. —Sandra*

> *Getting Stuck and Unstuck Thanks to the Customer (Feb. 1, 2001): Today Karen and I discovered that the task we had signed up for was actually way more complicated than we'd thought. We asked Rob (the coach) for help, and that triggered a ten-minute meeting with the customers, which resulted in a great idea from Jim (a customer) about a far simpler, better implementation. It sure helped us to ask a question rather than continuing to program. —Jerry*

Group Learning

Once teams produce enough learning content, they will need to reflect on and discuss it. There are two good places to do this: For technical matters, the best place is a programmers' study group; and for team, people, or process matters, the best place is in an iteration retrospective. As you will see later, study groups and retrospectives are powerful learning tools, both of which take time away from programming. Some may worry about this lost time. This is fear talking, saying, "We have to act, we don't have time to learn or reflect."

Such fear is quite common on XP projects, particularly when it comes to refactoring. Under pressure, many developers skip refactorings to go faster. They don't yet know that this will eventually slow down the entire team as the code becomes bulkier and more brittle.

It's not easy to understand that you have to slow down to go fast. Taking time to refactor seems as if it may slow you down, but it will actually make you go faster. Taking time to reflect and learn may also seem as if it's slowing you down, but it, too, will make you go significantly faster.

Nevertheless, a coach or team may still be uncomfortable taking the time to conduct group learning sessions because, unlike refactoring, this work doesn't have a directly visible effect on the code. But although the effect of group learnings on the code is indirect, it is nevertheless highly beneficial.

For example, I once worked with an XP team that had experienced a few bumpy iterations. They had not been refactoring enough, and after these bumpy iterations, it became harder to implement new code, given the heavy accumulation of code smells. One day I discovered a particularly potent design smell and pointed it out to my pair. He said that he had known about that problem for a few months. This alarmed me. I wondered, was he the only one who knew about this? Did other programmers or the coach know about it? What other potent smells were out there but unknown to the entire team?

It was clear to me that every programmer on the team needed to at least be aware of the system's potent smells. This would enable them all to pay attention to these smells and consider how to refactor them out of existence. So we began a process of documenting these potent smells on index cards, which we stacked on the group table. Doing this work enabled the group to learn, and those learnings eventually led to direct action.

Learning Capabilities

But not everyone on a team will be able to spot particularly potent smells, or even know what to do with them once they are spotted. There is a capability issue here.

What if a system was originally designed to let Java directly output HTML, but it is clear to a few programmers that this approach is far from ideal? And what if no programmer on the team knows how XSLT could replace the Java/HTML code to radically simplify the system?

Well, given the burdensome nature of this Java/HTML code, the team might try to refactor it a few times. But if they don't come up with an entirely new approach, the code will continue to be a burden.

OK, what if one person on the team does happen to know about XSLT? Then the team has a chance to greatly simplify their system. But how did this one person know XSLT? Perhaps this person is a continuous learner, someone who regularly reads industry magazines to stay up on new technology developments. It's a good thing for the team that at least one person happens to be a continuous learner.

But this is certainly far from optimal. I want teams to continuously learn because doing so will help them produce simpler systems, faster than ever. Peter Senge, author of the profoundly important, best-selling book *The Fifth Discipline: The Art and Practice of The Learning Organization*, had this to say about team learning.

> *Most of us at one time or another have been part of a great "team," a group of people who functioned together in an extraordinary way—who trusted one another, who complemented each others' strengths and compensated for each others' limitations, who had common goals that were larger than individual goals, and who produced extraordinary results. I have met many people who have experienced this sort of profound teamwork—in sports, or in the performing arts, or in business. Many say that they have spent much of their life looking for that experience again. What they experienced was a learning organization. The team that became great didn't start off great—it learned how to produce extraordinary results.* [Senge1990]

The two most powerful learning tools that I suggest for use by XP teams to support the practice of continuous learning are study groups and retrospectives.

Study Groups

I'll begin with study groups. You may be amazed, as I often am, that there are programmers today who have never read Martin Fowler's book *Refactoring: Improving the Design of Existing Code* [Fowler1999]. There are even programmers on XP projects who have never studied the refactoring catalog in this book, even though they are supposed to be refactoring all the time! Martin's book is one of those hardcover classics that everyone is supposed to read, but they don't because they perceive it to be too imposing or hard to understand, which is far from the truth.

So if programmers on XP projects don't know the refactoring catalog, how good do you suppose they'll be at refactoring? They can get better by pair programming with developers who do know the refactoring catalog, but that can be a slow process, which may still fail to introduce them to important refactorings. In addition, if these programmers don't know anything about other areas of software development, such as design patterns and good domain-modeling practices, how good do you think they'll be at building a well-designed system?

To continuously improve programmers' technical abilities, I recommend study groups. A programmers' study group meets regularly in a comfortable place to delve into important technical topics. These topics can come from the group's learning repository, from books or articles, or even from a guest participant.

Ken Auer's XP company, Role Model Software, allocates time once a month for technical group learning sessions, which Ken calls "strategic focus time."

Attendance in a study group is optional, but having the meetings regularly, such as once per iteration, is vital. I recommend that groups meet for two hours if they want to delve deeply into a subject, though one-hour meetings are fine for covering topics quickly.

There are roles to be played in a study group and certain important safety rules and rituals to follow. Absolutely no one should play the role of lecturer or teacher in a study group. The group meets to conduct group learning. If someone is expert in a certain technical area, that individual ought to help others learn, not show off or talk down to participants.

Those who find it burdensome to study important books or articles on their own may be surprised to discover that group study can make learning easier and more insightful.

If you'd like to start a programmers' study group and learn how to run it successfully, I suggest that you study my pattern language on this subject, which is called Pools of Insight: A Pattern Language for Study Groups [Kerievsky1999]. You might even begin your first study group by studying the patterns in that language, as several groups have done.

Retrospectives

Study groups address programmers' needs for continuous technical learning, but when does the entire XP team—customers, developers, and coach—come together to reflect and learn about how to improve? The whole team gathers during release and iteration planning meetings, but the primary purpose of those meetings is planning, not learning. So what happens when something in the current process isn't working well? Too often, there is simply no time to air the problem, discuss it, and resolve it.

What is commonly missing is the practice of holding retrospectives. Norm Kerth, author of the book *Project Retrospectives: A Handbook for Team Reviews* [Kerth2001], describes a retrospective as an end-of-project review, involving everyone who participated on the project in examining the project to understand:

- What happened
- What the community could learn
- What the community could do differently next time

The continuous learning approach to retrospectives means they come not at the end of a project, but at the end of every iteration. Conducting iteration retrospectives enables teams to quickly adjust and improve their performance because they are continuously revisiting these questions.

- What worked well?
- What did we learn?
- What should we do differently next time?
- What still puzzles us?

Norm gives very clear guidelines for successfully conducting retrospectives. I'll do my best to summarize them here, but you'll probably enjoy reading his book, which is destined to become a classic.

Norm recognizes that people have a fear of retrospectives—because they have a fear of being attacked, of being made to look foolish, of getting a poor performance review, or of hurting someone's feelings. Yet no retrospective can succeed if people are afraid or if there is an atmosphere of blame, criticism, sarcasm, or even humor at other people's expense. Therefore, Norm lays down specific ground rules that help establish a safe environment for conducting a retrospective. Perhaps the most important of these ground rules is Kerth's Prime Directive of Retrospectives, which states:

> *Regardless of what we discover, we understand and truly believe that everyone did the best job they could, given what they knew at the time, their skills and abilities, the resources available, and the situation at hand.* [Kerth2001]

Once the group understands these safety ground rules, it's time to break out some butcher paper. This is paper that is usually 30 feet long and six feet high. Norm likes to hang this stuff from the walls, break it up into sections of a timeline (for example, three sections could signify each week of a three-week iteration), and then have teams go off and identify key events or things that happened during each section. People then add their identified events and happenings to the various sections of the timeline, which is next mined for stories and team goals. Norm suggests that professional facilitators help lead this process. In fact, he believes it is vital that the facilitator be an outsider and not a member of the team involved in the retrospective.

The final part of a retrospective is perhaps the most important. This is when the participants take the lessons learned during the retrospective and turn them into concrete ideas for improving their development process. This is hard work. I would add that it is particularly hard on XP projects, because it is easy to think you've found a deficiency in the XP process, when all you've really found is a faux deficiency. Chris Collins and Roy Miller describe how "process smells" can be identified during retrospectives, and they advise people to be careful about how they choose to fix them.

> *The key to retrospectives is to make sure you are solving the correct problem. Sometimes the tendency is going to be to add a practice to the process, where the real problem is in how you are implementing one of the twelve practices.* [Collins+2001]

So how much time should it take to run one of these iteration retrospectives? If we spend too much time on them, we'll lose vital development time. I asked Norm about this, and his answer surprised me. He said that even for a three-week iteration, he would begin with a retrospective that lasts two and a half days. I thought that was excessive, but Norm explained that groups need to learn how to do retrospectives. When beginning to perform retrospectives, they need lots of time. As time goes on, they will get better and better at it, until it takes perhaps only half a day. I marveled at the simple good sense of this advice: Take time early on to get good at doing retrospectives, and you won't need much time to do them in the future.

A Continuously Learning Coach

We've talked about ways for the programming team to continuously learn and ways for the team as a whole to continuously learn, but what about an XP team's coach?

It is critical that an XP coach be a continuous learner, because the coach is the leader of the team. If the coach doesn't value learning, the team won't either.

A coach must lead by example. This means that the coach must seek out and obtain coaching and mentoring from the best sources available.

The coach must also ensure that continuous learning happens on a regular basis. And it can take quite a bit of courage to not cancel a programmers' study group meeting in the face of a looming release date.

Coaches must strive to learn about their customers' needs, team or personality conflicts, new technologies, and the latest wisdom about XP and other lightweight methods.

I recently learned of an excellent continuous learning technique for coaches from Rob Mee, who is an XP coach at Evant, a merchandise management company in San Francisco. Rob has learned that the best way for him to continue to learn about the system his team is building is to program. So Rob programs to learn, and says he now uses 50% of his time to do so.

Conclusion

Continuous learning isn't a new part of XP, but a core part of it, implied but not directly articulated. It is a practice that can help a good XP team rapidly become a great XP team. Try it and see what you learn.

References

[Collins+2001] C. Collins, R. Miller. Adaptation: XP Style. Submitted as a paper to XP2001.

[Fowler1999] M. Fowler. *Refactoring: Improving the Design of Existing Code.* Addison-Wesley, 1999.

[Kerievsky1999] J. Kerievsky. *Pools of Insight: A Pattern Language for Study Groups.* http://www.industriallogic.com/papers/kh.html. 1999.

[Kerth2001] N. Kerth. *Project Retrospectives: A Handbook for Team Reviews.* Dorset House, 2001.

[Senge1990] P. Senge. *The Fifth Discipline: The Art and Practice of The Learning Organization.* Currency Doubleday, 1990.

[Webber2000] A. Webber. "Will Companies Ever Learn?" *Fast Company Magazine*, October 2000.

Acknowledgments

I'm always indebted to my wife, Tracy, who endures my writing stints and does a superb job of copyediting. I'd also like to thank Norm Kerth for his interview, and Ward Cunningham and Eric Evans for reviewing this work.

About the Author

Joshua Kerievsky is a software development coach, programmer and author. After programming on Wall Street for nearly 10 years, in 1995 he founded San Francisco Bay Area-based Industrial Logic (http://industriallogic.com), a company that specializes in XP. Since 1999, Joshua has been programming and coaching on small, large and distributed XP projects and teaching XP to people throughout the world. He regularly speaks about XP, has authored numerous XP articles, simulations and games and is hard at work on the forthcoming book, *Refactoring to Patterns* (http:// industriallogic.com/xp/refactoring/).

Chapter 27

The XP Game Explained

—Vera Peeters and Pascal Van Cauwenberghe

Part III

The XP planning game, velocity, and user stories are hard to explain and "sell" to developers and businesspeople. How can we better explain these concepts? The XP specification, estimation, and planning methods sound too weird and simple to work. How can we prove or show that they work, without committing ourselves to "just do it" on a real project? If the project is to succeed, we need to get developers and businesspeople working as one team. How can we get them to talk, cooperate, and trust each other?

The "XP Game" is a fun and playful simulation of the XP development process. No technical knowledge or skill is required to participate, so we can form teams with both developers and businesspeople. The element of competition helps the players bond with their teammates. At the end of the game, everybody has experienced how user stories, estimation, planning, implementation, and functional tests are used. They have seen how the "velocity" factor is used to adjust the schedule. Developers and customers have gotten to know and respect each other.

Introduction

Lesire Software Engineering had been using "developer-only Extreme Programming" for a few months. Refactoring, unit tests, simple design, and pair programming had resulted in measurable improvements in the software process.

When the company wanted to transition to "full" XP and expand the use of XP beyond the development team, it faced a number of problems.

- Poor communication between business and developer teams.
- No understanding of user stories, the planning game, and velocity.
- Distrust of the planning game and velocity. How could such simple methods deliver credible plans and schedules?

Presentations, discussions, training, and coaching did not completely resolve these issues. Developers and businesspeople reluctantly agreed to try the XP experiment, without much hope of success.

Then Vera Peeters, Lesire's XP coach, exclaimed, "Let's play a game!"

Let's Play!

The players are divided into small teams (four to eight players). Each team consists of developers and customers. A coach assists each team, to explain and guide the game and to answer questions. The team can earn "business points" by performing simple tasks. The team with the most business points wins.

The coach gives the team a small set of prewritten story cards. These cards describe simple tasks, such as "Build a two-story house of cards," "Throw a six five times using two dice," and "Find a missing card from a pack of cards."

The team members (acting as developers) estimate how long it will take them to "implement" the tasks. The coach is available to answer questions about the stories. The team may choose a time between ten and 60 seconds. Or they may declare that it's impossible to implement the task in 60 seconds. When all the stories have been estimated, the cards are handed back to the coach.

The team (now acting as a customer) must create a release plan: They choose the stories to implement and the order of implementation. Each story is worth some business points. The team tries to maximize the number of business points they can earn. The total time to implement all selected stories may not exceed 180 seconds, the fixed iteration time.

The team members (acting as developers) must now implement each planned story in turn, in the order defined by the customer. An hourglass is used to measure the implementation time. When the implementation is "accepted" by the coach, the team earns the business points of the story. When the hourglass runs out, the iteration ends. If the team has finished all the stories before the end of the iteration, they may ask the customer for another story.

At the end of each iteration, there is a debriefing, discussing the problems, solutions, and strategies. The "team velocity" is explained and calculated. For the next iteration, the team must use velocity instead of time as a measure of how much work they can do.

The simulation typically runs over three iterations. It takes from one and a half to two hours, including debriefing and discussion sessions.

Open the Magic Bag

At the start of the game, a bag with game props is emptied on each team's table. The bag contains dice, playing cards, colorful paper, balloons, pieces of string, folded hats and boats, story cards, planning/scoring sheets, a pen, and an hourglass.

This jumble of colorful, childish props reassures the players that this is not a serious event. They will not be judged; they can relax and enjoy the game. They are open to bonding with their teammates and to absorbing something new. It's just a game, after all.

Tell Us a Story

The story cards contain simple and small tasks such as "Find a missing card from a deck" or "Inflate five balloons to a size of 40 cm." No special knowledge is required to understand how to carry out these tasks.

And yet, the cards alone do not contain enough information to estimate the complexity of the tasks. The players ask the coach (acting as their customer) more questions about the tasks—for example: "Are we allowed to perform the task as a team?" "What do you mean by throw a six five times? Do we need five consecutive sixes?" The coach clarifies the meaning of the stories and explains what conditions must be fulfilled to accept the story.

This reinforces the idea that user stories aren't specifications but "a promise to talk." It's all right to ask the customer questions. Get as much information as you need to make good decisions. Ask the customer—they know! Or at least they can find out the answer.

Estimating: How Hard Can This Be?

One of the most difficult aspects of working with velocity is convincing developers to estimate consistently. The velocity factor includes all the variable parts of team performance: experience, knowledge of the problem domain, team size, adding and removing team members, interruptions, and so on. If the planning game is to result in realistic schedules, stories should be estimated consistently in terms of their relative required effort. Developers should not try to adjust their estimates.

The coach asks the players to estimate by comparing with other stories. If a story looks twice as difficult as another story, estimate it at twice the difficulty. The mix of stories proposed in the documentation contains stories that are suited to demonstrating this. For example, folding eight boats will probably take twice as long as folding four boats. There are also several stories that have the same complexity. For example, throwing a six five times is obviously exactly as difficult as throwing a four five times.

But it's not always that easy. Building a two-story house of cards is more than twice as difficult as building a one-story house. And finding two missing cards from a full deck is about as difficult as finding one, if you sort the cards.

Estimating how long it takes to perform these little tasks is difficult. Developers already know estimating is difficult. For some customers, it might come as a surprise to learn how hard it is.

One way to improve the estimates is to do short experiments, called "spikes." You could implement these simple stories completely as a spike. With real stories, this is not possible, so we give the players only a limited time (for example, 15 minutes) to come up with their estimates.

Insanely Short Iterations

XP recommends short iterations, so the XP Game uses *really* short iterations: 180 seconds. These 180 seconds include only the "pure" implementation time, without counting any preparations or the time to perform acceptance tests.

These 180 seconds are the "budget" the players can allocate when making their release plan: The total estimated time of all the chosen stories must not exceed 180 seconds.

If all the chosen stories have been implemented and there's time left, the customer may choose some more stories. The iteration ends after exactly 180 seconds, not a second more, not a second less. If the team is still working on a story, this story is abandoned. This emphasizes the fixed iteration time, during which the customer can change only scope and priority.

When the iteration is about halfway through, the team compares their actual implementation to their plan: Are we ahead, behind, or right on schedule? Should we warn the customer that they might have to reduce scope?

We used to measure time with a stopwatch, but an hourglass is more fun, more tactile, and more visible. We don't care about one-second precision; we need to know if we're halfway or almost done. It turns out that even with such simple tracking tools as a list of story cards and an hourglass, we can give the customer pretty accurate and useful feedback on our progress. The sight of the last grains of sand sliding down the hourglass reminds the players that time is finite and increases the pressure to finish the implementation of their story.

Planning with Risk

Most of the stories depend only on skill and teamwork. We can expect the team to perform consistently on these tasks.

But some stories depend on luck. How can you estimate how long the dice stories (for example, "Throw three ones with two dice") will take? You can compute the odds; multiply by the time it takes, on average, to throw the dice. The answer might be "On average, it will take about 30 seconds to throw three ones with two dice."

When you're planning, you need to take this uncertainty and risk into account. If the estimate is 30 seconds, it might as well take ten or 60 seconds, depending on your luck. When you have two stories that will earn you about the same business value, but one is riskier than the other, which one do you choose? Some people choose riskier stories with a higher payoff; some people prefer the stories with a lower risk. The important thing is to explicitly take the risk into account when planning.

Customers learn that it's not always possible to come up with definite estimates. Developers learn that it's hard to plan when story estimates include uncertainty.

Silly Little Games

The stories are silly little games: throwing dice, sorting cards, finding missing cards, building a house of cards, folding a paper hat, inflating balloons. You can invent your own additions, but all these stories have some features in common.

- They add to the relaxed, playful atmosphere.
- They are not a bit technical, so everyone on the team can join in and contribute.
- They are difficult enough to require some concentration and team effort to complete quickly.
- They are not too difficult, so the players can concentrate on the XP concepts we want them to experience and learn.

The team decides before each game how they will perform the task (in team or solo) and who will perform the task. Players sign up for tasks; tasks are not assigned to them.

All the planned games are played one at a time, in the order chosen by the customer. This reinforces the idea that the whole team is responsible for all the stories.

It's fun to see grown men and women working so hard to fold paper hats or build houses of cards—or design and execute a six-way parallel sort of a deck of cards!

Playing to Win

The element of competition is important to the game. Everybody in the team cooperates to implement as many stories as possible, as fast as possible. They want their team to earn more points than the other teams. Putting developers and businesspeople in one team makes them work together, maybe for the first time.

Don't create teams with only developers or only businesspeople. We don't want to see who's "smartest"—we want to foster cooperation.

Acceptance Testing: Don't Trust Developers

Most of the questions the players ask about the stories are related to the acceptance criteria of the story. The coach (acting as the customer) tells the players how he will test whether a story is implemented correctly. For the balloons, there are pieces of string to measure whether the balloon is big enough. For the paper-folding stories, there are prototypes of the boat and hat to be folded.

Some stories look so easy that no explanation is necessary. But what do we mean by a "sorted deck of cards?" Is the ace the first or the last card? Do we need to put the different suits in some order? The team has to agree with the customer/coach up front to estimate the difficulty of the story.

When the team has implemented a story, the coach explicitly performs the acceptance test: The sorted deck is verified; the folded hats are compared with the prototype; the balloons are measured with the piece of string. When the implementation doesn't pass the test, the team must continue the implementation. Even the simplest tasks can be implemented incorrectly, so an acceptance test failure underscores the importance of testing.

Trading Places

During the game, the whole team switches between developer and customer roles. The coach emphasizes this fact by displaying a banner, which reads, "We are the customer" or "We are the developers." If the players must switch roles, even briefly (for example, when they ask for more stories from the customers), the coach explicitly makes them switch roles.

This makes it clear that the customer and developer roles are distinct. Each shares some part of the responsibility to succeed. Both have well-defined tasks. Developers should never make customer decisions; customers should never make developer decisions.

Switching roles lets everybody experience all aspects of the cooperative game of software development. Developers and customers experience what "the other side" does during a project. This increases the respect each group has for the work of the others.

Velocity: How Much Did We Get Done?

This is the trickiest part of the simulation: explaining the concept of velocity after the first iteration.

After each iteration, each team announces the number of business points earned and the sum of the *estimated* durations of the implemented stories. These numbers are easily found on the planning sheets. Let's call the sum of the estimated durations *X*. Note that we don't know the actual duration of each story, because we use an hourglass.

What we want to know is, how many stories can we implement in one (180-second) iteration? Well, we just did such an iteration. How many stories did we implement? We implemented some stories requiring *X* amount of work. How much work will we be able to perform next time? The *Yesterday's Weather* rule says, probably about the same amount as in the previous iteration. That's if we don't take sick leave, holidays, interruptions, team learning, reuse, refactoring, and a thousand other details into account.

Let's give *X* a name: "Velocity." Velocity measures how much work the team can do per iteration. If we want to finish the next iteration on time, each team will schedule its Velocity's worth of stories.

If Velocity is effort per iteration, the story estimates don't represent time, but estimated effort. We no longer estimate in seconds, but in "points" or whatever you like as a unit of programming effort. How can we estimate using this made-up unit system? We estimate by comparing with other stories: If a new story is about as difficult as an implemented story, give it the same number of points. If it looks twice as difficult, give it twice the points. These points really express the relative complexity of the stories. Maybe a good name would be "complexity points." The important thing is to estimate consistently.

What about all these pesky factors that influence how much work the team can do? We let the velocity take care of them. If the team learns about the domain or reuses more code, they get more done. Their measured velocity rises; they take on more work. If new members join the team or people go on holiday, the measured velocity decreases, and the team takes on less work. It really is that simple! The most difficult thing is *not* to take all those factors into account when estimating.

Does this really work? In the simulation, the teams typically underestimate the stories in the first iteration and end with a velocity lower than 180, which indicates that few teams can estimate even these simple stories accurately. In the second iteration, they get to ask for more stories (because they get better at doing the implementations) and increase their velocity. By the third iteration, they get pretty close. In real life, the authors have experienced that the velocity stabilizes after only a few iterations. This has been observed in teams that worked for several iterations on the same project and in teams working on different projects in the same domain, using the same tools. Expect your velocity to change dramatically if you change your team, problem domain, tools, or environment.

Sustainable Playing

Each iteration has a fixed size of 180 seconds. Before implementing each story, the players devise their strategy. The hourglass is started when the implementation starts. When the team thinks it has completed the story, the hourglass is stopped. The hourglass only measures real implementation time.

The implementation time is very stressful, because the players try to complete a task in only a few tens of seconds. The players can relax a bit between implementations and discuss their design and strategy. This simulates the XP practice of sustainable pace or "no overtime": Developers work with full concentration on some task, go home, relax, and come back the next day, ready to perform another task.

Despite the concentration and stress of the story implementations, the players don't feel tired after three iterations. That's because they enjoy what they're doing, and they get time to relax between tasks.

Conclusion

The XP Game is a fun and playful way of simulating the XP process. It enables the participants to experience, in a relaxed environment, several of the XP practices: user stories, estimation, the planning game, acceptance tests, short releases, sustainable pace, progress tracking, and velocity. It is ideally suited as a follow-up to a tutorial on these practices. The competition, team effort, and fun aspects make it a great team-building tool: Playing the game improves trust and communication between developers and businesspeople.

The XP Game has been played in companies transitioning to XP, during XP tutorials, and at software engineering conferences. The participants always have fun and feel they have learned more about the XP practices.

And Lesire Software Engineering? They're still doing XP and delivering working software to their customers. Developers and businesspeople are working together and enjoying it.

Acknowledgments

We thank all those who played and coached the XP Game for helping us improve the game and for the fun we had doing the game.

We thank Gerard Meszaros for making us think about what we were trying to teach.

We would like to thank Lesire Software Engineering and the XP2001 and XP Universe conferences for letting us play.

About the Authors

Vera Peeters is an independent consultant with more than ten years of experience in implementing object-oriented systems in a variety of domains. For the last two years she has been working with XP, helping her customers transition to XP, coaching XP teams, and giving lectures and presentations about XP. Vera is involved in the organization of the Dutch and Belgian XP user groups.

Pascal Van Cauwenberghe is the CTO of Lesire Software Engineering, where he leads the software development teams. He has been designing and building object-oriented systems for more than ten years.

The XP Game is free and available from http://www.xp.be.

Chapter 28

Mob Programming and the Transition to XP

—*Moses M. Hohman and Andrew C. Slocum*

Part III

Extreme Programming (XP) development practices emphasize the importance of developer communication. Our team is currently in a transition toward using many of XP's suggested lightweight practices. As part of and to facilitate this transition, we have been developing a collaborative method we call "mob programming." The term "mob programming" is whimsically derived from the term "pair programming" and indicates the practice of refactoring code in groups larger than two developers. The purpose we identify for this refactoring focuses less on writing code that we will use later and more on encouraging healthy discussion. In this chapter, we describe our process and its precursors as they have evolved over time. We report the successes realized and the failures suffered in the context of the values of XP.

Introduction

The benefits of pair programming are documented: better, simpler code written in less time; improved interdeveloper communication and feedback; and shared code ownership, to cite a few [Williams+2000; Cockburn+2001]. We have undertaken an experiment on our development team to see if some of these benefits remain when the programming group grows beyond two people. This experiment evolved from regular developer lunch meetings originally run in a presentation format, with one member of the team presenting code familiar (usually only) to him or her. At the time, we were not employing XP practices but had vague plans to do so at some point in the future.

Since then, the team as a whole—not just the developers—has begun to take the first steps toward XP. We now have iterations and some form of continuous integration; we are writing unit and acceptance tests; and we have dabbled in pair programming. Because our team is unfamiliar with and therefore unsure of XP's benefits, it is useful for us to find ways to experiment with and eventually to reinforce beneficial XP development practices.

To this end, we have identified long-term and short-term goals. Regular developer meetings cannot achieve all these goals on their own. However, we intend for the meetings to facilitate this achievement in the context of a broader set of XP practices. In the long term, we want to decrease individual code ownership, to encourage pair programming, and to improve unit test coverage. We want to improve the overall quality of the code we write. Formal mentoring is not an option, so instead we want to provide greater opportunity for developers to work together, enabling them to exchange information about coding standards, helpful programming patterns, and design decisions. Finally, we hope that working together regularly will build our sense of ourselves as a team.

In the short term we want these meetings to be fun and interactive. We want the format to respond to our needs and interests as they evolve over time, so that the meetings do not feel forced. We also typically set a small practical goal before ourselves to provide something as a focus for our attention. In the beginning this practical goal was the short presentation but has recently evolved into what we have capriciously termed "mob programming," the refactoring of a small piece of code in groups larger than two people.

The formation of this weekly ritual has been an iterative and ongoing process as we continue to strive for a format that feels "natural." We have by no means arrived at this desirable goal, but we hope that an account of our experiences is nonetheless interesting to the reader. Therefore, we begin with a historical description of our efforts. With this picture, we move on to compare an idealized view of mob programming with the values of XP and to discuss the lessons we have learned that help mob programming be more productive. Before concluding, we discuss some of the problems we have encountered during our experiments.

Description of Methods

Early Days

In early January 2000, we began a series of weekly developer lunches, whose purpose is best described by quoting the e-mail one of the authors sent to the developer team.

> *Here is the basic idea I propose (subject to any modifications you guys feel are necessary of course): each week . . . someone will give a short (30 min), informal presentation of some piece of development work. . . . The presentation will be followed by group discussion of the material for another half an hour or so. . . . Loosely, these talks will hope to serve to: familiarize us all (esp. new people!) with the . . . architecture, help those giving the talks to come up with new ideas about how to solve architectural problems, and give us a chance to all talk shop together as a group. I imagine that more familiarity with what everyone does might also help when we try . . . [pair] programming . . . in the coming months. . . . You should try to show some real code . . . I emphasize that the point of these talks is to provide an opportunity for informal group discussion. Don't worry about making a powerpoint* [sic] *presentation . . .* [Hohman2000]

When these meetings began, individual code ownership was the rule. Developers who had been around for a while were pushing for the adoption of XP techniques (such as unit testing and pair programming), and new developers had a hard time getting a handle on the already present code base. Frequent and regular code discussion was unanimously received as a good idea.

Our goals were similar to the broader goals of XP. We wanted to increase developer communication, both to increase morale and to aid in the dissemination of crucial knowledge about our software. We wanted to decrease individual code ownership. With a broader knowledge of the overall architecture, each of us would be less afraid to change

Part III

"someone else's" code. We wanted to encourage more feedback within the group on design and coding decisions. And we wanted a lightweight solution. Formal presentations, arduous preparation, and prescribed meeting content were not going to be accepted by the group. We wanted to provide a forum for people to talk about issues they already found interesting.

First Light

The presentations were boring. They resulted in little actual feedback or informal discussion. The first half hour mercilessly took over the second half hour, because the second half hour was often awkwardly silent. After a couple of months, we had already discussed every part of the application, at least at a general level. We needed to make a change. The presentation format did not serve our goals. We needed to increase the emphasis on group discussion.

For a couple of meetings, we completely dropped any official agenda whatsoever and just had lunch together. Discussions arose naturally, often with different parts of the group discussing different topics. However, as often as not, these topics were not related to our work. There was little focus, and as a result, people began to lose interest and leave after they had eaten. A total lack of structure was not good either.

To re-create focus, we wrote a simple utility to pick one Java class at random from our source tree. The day before each meeting, we would pick a couple of classes and announce them to the group. At the meeting, we would project the code on the wall and discuss it. The idea was that, over time, we would have the opportunity to discuss code from all parts of the application while avoiding the arduous presentations.

By looking at the code one class at a time instead of one module at a time, we did not have to worry about running out of material after two months. Familiarity with a particular module could grow over time. In this format the person who had written that particular class still did a lot of the talking; however, we did notice that these meetings elicited more discussion than our original format.

Looking at code at the class level was more instructive than at the module level. At module granularity, a half-hour presentation can cover only the barest summary of the screens, the business logic, and the high-level architecture. Also, module presentations become less helpful and less interesting over the life of the project. As the code complexity of a module increases, the level of detail of a presentation must decrease.

At the class level, developers can see the similarities between modules. Many of our design patterns apply across the application, and a discussion of one module's use of a pattern can explain an entire layer of the application. Additionally, common utility classes can be hard to find or are implemented several times. Class-level discussions with all the developers present can reveal or prevent this kind of redundancy.

Which Brings Us to the Present

One day, a few months ago at the time of this writing, we were particularly distressed by the quality of code under discussion. So we decided to go ahead and make a few changes right then and there. We were not particularly careful, and there were no unit tests written for the class, so we ended up breaking the build. To restore the build to health, someone had to spend time throwing away the changes we made. However, we had learned something. Changing the code during the meeting made the discussion more interesting, perhaps because it forced people to think, and when people think, they tend to have more to say. We decided we were on to something, so we subsequently added structure to make the process safer and to improve on the idea. This process is still a work in progress, so here we present only our current view of its ideal execution.

Some period of time before the meeting—the most effective period is a few days—one or two classes are picked from the source tree for discussion. The person who runs the selection utility vetoes generated code and code destined to be removed soon from the source tree. The remaining results are then filtered based on level of interest, until there are one or two worthwhile candidates. Two people ("previewers") spend time together looking over these classes to make sure that there is enough material for an hour to an hour and a half's discussion. If there is not, they replace one of the selections. These two people also examine the unit test coverage and augment it if necessary. Finally, these two developers begin to brainstorm issues for discussion and possible refactorings. When the previewing phase is over, the two e-mail the code in the body of an e-mail message to all the developers on the team so they have a chance to glance over it themselves before the meeting.

The day of the meeting, the group meets in a closed room to avoid outside distractions. For the first 20 minutes or so, we eat and engage in social discussion. Then we begin.

Developers play different roles in the process. One role is the "driver," a person who types, compiles, and tests the code. Because we split into two groups, there are two drivers, one at each of a pair of laptops. We connect these laptops to projectors that display the code on opposite walls, giving each group some focus. We intend that all developers share the driver role (though this does not often occur; see the section Shortcomings). Second, the person or persons who originally wrote the code (or are familiar with it) take on a special role as "narrators," providing a description of the code, its purpose, and how it fits within the context of the rest of the application. Finally, the rest of the group participates by offering suggestions and feedback. These people form the mob, probably the most difficult role to play and the least understood of the three.

At the beginning, the narrator tells the group about the code and its history. Then we split into two groups, one at each laptop/projector, and discuss ideas for refactoring. We discuss with our hands as well, typing in our suggestions to communicate them more clearly. If the refactorings we agree on are simple enough, we carry them out. After about half an hour, or when we feel it is time, the two groups rejoin and discuss the changes each group has made. We then decide which to keep (if any) and which to throw away.

The Intended Benefits of Mob Programming in the Context of XP

The four stated "values of XP" in Kent Beck's *Extreme Programming Explained* are communication, courage, feedback, and simplicity [Beck2000]. Mob programming provides an opportunity for maximal feedback and communication. During meetings, the entire team shares ideas about all aspects of code design. For part of the meeting, we split into two groups small enough that everyone can be involved in the discussion at some level. Then when we regroup, each developer has an opportunity to share those discussions with everyone else on the team. By looking at a different piece of randomly chosen code each week, all developers get feedback on coding and design decisions they have made in the past, without being singled out. Also, during refactoring and wrap-up, our peers review the programming decisions we make during the meeting. Naturally, discussions that begin during mob programming can continue outside the meetings, fostering an atmosphere of greater communication. We also hope that working together in this way may make us more open to pair programming outside the meetings.

Mob programming also fosters the value of courage. At one time, we merely looked at code during meetings. Now we change it on the spot, as soon as we see something that can be improved. It is important that we actually change code during the meeting, because this active engagement of the material promotes thought and discussion instead of passive spectatorship. We also encourage throwing away the code at the end of the meeting if the group feels that the changes made are not an improvement. We try to rotate the roles of driver and narrator throughout the group so that each developer has an opportunity to be courageous. Honest, open discussion is promoted during meetings, so opinions that may not be expressed outside of meetings (such as a deeply divided opinion within the group about a design decision) are confronted.

To be able to change code courageously, good test coverage is necessary. The test coverage of our code increases as a function of the meetings, because the previewers must make sure it is adequate before the meeting begins. Also, while we are changing code during meetings, the value and practice of testing can be reinforced.

Finally, our meetings value simplicity. The atmosphere has always been informal. We incrementally add structure only when we feel it is necessary. For example, we have found that we must preview the code. If we do not, the meeting is often spent debugging someone's application configuration, trying to get one test to succeed. Such episodes try everyone's patience and are totally unproductive. Also, by ensuring that there are already working tests, previewing makes it much easier to add tests as needed while refactoring. Finally, it is important that a couple of people have already looked at the code in some detail before the meeting, because the person who wrote the code may not be present and thus be unable to play the narrator role. Having a couple of people who understand the present state of the code helps start discussion. E-mailing the code in the body of an e-mail message to everyone in the group has also been successful in acquainting people with the code before the meeting so that people are more ready to begin discussion. We have found this much structure to be useful. We are always ready to remove any structure that turns out to be unnecessary.

We note finally that we have experimented both with two groups/projectors and one group/projector. One projector is a little easier to manage logistically. However, because our group is composed of about ten developers, having only one point of focus can make it difficult to include everyone in the process. With two projectors, we can try several different, generally more engaging formats. We can follow the format described earlier: split into two teams, each of which comes up with its own refactoring of the code, which is then compared with the other team's and discussed. We have found this format to be the most successful. We have also tried having one team refactor and the other team write tests. This latter format suffers from the problem that to refactor, you need working tests. Conversely, once you have written the necessary tests for the next refactoring step, often you must wait for that refactoring to occur before it makes sense to write additional tests. One team ends up waiting for the other. In any case, having two points of focus involves more people and shares the roles played more broadly within the group. Also, having two groups increases the diversity of ideas that are presented during the meeting.

Shortcomings

At the time of this chapter's final revision, we have practiced mob programming about ten times. It has not been an unmitigated success. In this section, we discuss the problems we have encountered.

First of all, we have had trouble following our own guidelines. For instance, it has always been clear that good preparation, in the form of previewing, has a strong effect on the quality of the meeting. However, only once or twice have we found someone sufficiently motivated to complete this preparation thoroughly. This points to a potential weakness of our practice. Mob programming, in some ways, stretches the principle of doing what is natural. For a quality meeting, some discipline is necessary. We are still searching for a degree of discipline that works for our team. It is not clear whether the team will eventually find preparation more natural, or whether we will find a way to avoid preparation. This is an important point. It is not just our guidelines that evolve, but also the team itself. This should not make us uncomfortable. Shooting at moving targets is an integral part of the XP experience.

We have also discovered that people find it difficult to remain focused, especially those who are not driving. The mob plays a role that is not as well defined as the driver role, so it is easy for a mob participant to feel useless during mob programming. Having more than two programmers in a group leaves the other members of the mob to daydream, to have other, unrelated conversations, and so forth. Unless everyone in the room feels engaged in the practice, the mob inevitably becomes unruly. How, then, could we change the format of mob programming so that we engage everyone? We have not yet found an answer to this question. The lack of engagement may be exacerbated by the fact that the team does not seem to have bought the idea of mob programming completely. At this point the costs are clearer than the benefits. We will expand on this greater issue at the end of this section.

When searching for ways to improve mob programming, we have so far found it difficult to get feedback from the rest of the team. This may just be because we have not been practicing it for very long, and people have not made up their minds one way or the other. However, we also wonder if perhaps this is because the group sees one of the authors (Moses) as the motivating force behind the meetings. We have some evidence that people feel reluctant to criticize the process because criticism may be construed as criticism of Moses.

The Role of "Coach"

One inadequacy of our chapter so far is that we have completely ignored an important role in the whole process, and that is the role of "coach" (to use Beck's terminology). This role, during and surrounding these weekly meetings, has consistently been played by Moses. All the developers on the team see these meetings and especially see mob programming as "Moses' baby."

Moses has made a number of probably classic coaching mistakes that can be summarized as leading too directly. When no one volunteers to act as a previewer, he does it himself. This can lead to this work being done at the last minute and not very thoroughly, because the burden is not shared. Because Moses is excited about seeing these ideas put into action, he often takes too active a role in the process. He is usually one of the drivers during mob programming.

This is clearly problematic. These meetings, in whatever format, will never work if they are not a creative and experimental process for the team as a whole. We have begun to see improvement in this area, however. Several months ago, the meetings would not occur if Moses were out of town or otherwise too busy to organize the meeting. Today this is no longer true. More regularly we observe other developers suggesting and implementing new ideas for improvement, both during the meetings and outside of them. Progress toward group ownership of this process takes time, and we believe we are beginning to see it happen. New ideas may take us completely away from our current format, but succeeding at mob programming in particular is certainly not the point anyway. It is far more important, and more in line with our goals, that we succeed at doing something owned by the group, developed interactively without one person at its center.

Sometimes, after a particularly unproductive meeting, we wonder whether we should continue having these meetings at all. If they began as unproductive presentations and have resulted in chaotic attempts at mob programming, have we really found anything of value? We believe that the answer is undeniably yes. We base this judgment on our observations of the changes in team behavior not only during developer meetings, but also during our day-to-day operation.

At the first meetings, no one talked except the presenter. Today our meetings are chaotic because everyone talks, and people are usually talking about code. They may not be talking about the code under discussion, but they are talking about code. The fact that at our last meeting four people other than Moses began a discussion criticizing mob programming and seeking a remedy is significant. These people saw the meetings as theirs to control.

Outside the meetings, frequent informal discussion has become markedly more common, even commonplace. We have also become bolder. Recently we used a developer meeting to discuss our level of commitment toward XP practices compared with our current level of achievement of those practices. We decided to speak with our project manager to put a plan in place to carry out the last half of our current release in three two-week iterations, with tasks estimated by the team instead of by a manager. For the first time in the history of our project, most of the development team participated in the planning and feature estimation part of our development process. Our team has become noticeably more courageous, more collaborative, and more open.

We can thus see our meetings, in whatever format, as a "generative" process—a process that "produces the generated quality indirectly" [Gabriel1996]. Meeting together every week to invent and experiment with practices of our own design has changed us as a team. We have not only gotten better at designing and carrying out these practices, we have become closer and more capable as a team. These benefits cannot be attributed solely to our weekly meetings, but the meetings have played an important role.

Finally, we add that when we actually followed our guidelines for mob programming, the process went relatively well. Also, during periods when we have done less mob programming, we have found that less progress was made toward better and more complete testing.

We have decided to continue to pursue mob programming with two improvements. One, we will complete the necessary preparation. Two, the coach will coach more indirectly, yet more firmly (for example, more consistently enforcing the preparation). We have also decided, as a team, to alternate mob programming with other formats. We want to give mob programming a chance to succeed if it can, while experimenting with alternatives.

Part III

Conclusion

Our experiment with mob programming, still in its infancy, has so far received mixed reviews. The undeniable benefits of the practice have been more indirect. Communication has been noticeably enhanced. Test coverage is improving. The meetings themselves are becoming more productive, regardless of format. There is a growing sense of ownership of the meetings by the team as a whole. We view these meetings as a work in progress. We do not view the process as it exists today dogmatically, but as a lightweight method of encouraging shared values. If mob programming does not work, we will try something else. We hope, however, that sharing our experiences may help others searching for ways to facilitate the transition to a more people-centered, communication-focused process like XP.

References

[Beck2000] K. Beck. *Extreme Programming Explained*. Addison-Wesley, 2000.

[Cockburn+2001] A. Cockburn, L. Williams. "The Costs and Benefits of Pair Programming." In *Extreme Programming Examined*. G. Succi, M. Marchesi, eds. Addison-Wesley, 2001.

[Gabriel1996] R. Gabriel. *Patterns of Software: Tales from the Software Community*. Oxford University Press, 1996.

[Hohman2000] M. Hohman. Personal e-mail communication. January 2000.

[Williams+2000] L. Williams et al. "Strengthening the Case for Pair-Programming." *IEEE Software*, Volume 17, Number 2, July/August 2000.

Acknowledgments

The authors would like to thank the other members of the ThoughtWorks Cat development team (especially Eric Altendorf, James Newkirk, and Alexei Vorontsov, for their insightful comments), Martin Fowler, Rebecca Parsons (both also of ThoughtWorks, Inc.), and Robert Martin of Object Mentor, Inc., for helpful discussions.

About the Authors

Moses M. Hohman is a software developer for ThoughtWorks, a custom e-business software development consulting firm. Currently, he works out of the recently opened Bangalore, India, office, where he mentors new software developers and teaches a course on agile software development at the Indian Institute of Information Technology Bangalore. He received an A.B. in physics from Harvard University and a Ph.D. in physics from the University of Chicago. Contact him at mmhohman@thoughtworks.com.

Andrew C. Slocum is a software developer for ThoughtWorks. He received an M.S. in computer science from Case Western Reserve University. He is interested in making agile development work on large and distributed projects. Contact him at acslocum@thoughtworks.com.

Chapter 29

A Metric Suite for Evaluating the Effectiveness of an Agile Methodology

—Laurie Williams, Giancarlo Succi, Milorad Stefanovic, and Michele Marchesi

Part III

Recently, a new class of software development methodologies has been emerging. These methodologies, termed the agile methodologies, are adaptive rather than predictive, and they are people-oriented rather than process-oriented. Advocates of agile software development methodologies profess that these methods are superior for dealing with change and, therefore, for providing customers with what they want, when they want it, and with acceptable defect rates.

The software engineering community has begun to examine these methodologies to judge their impact on the creation of quality software. However, software development organizations often lack the ability to quantitatively analyze the effectiveness of their software development methodology. Additionally, these organizations are frequently unable to assess the efficacy of new practices integrated into their current methodologies. In this chapter, we propose a framework for an empirical investigation of the effectiveness of agile methodologies. Through industrial use of this framework, we, as a software community, can gain valuable information on the prudent use of agile methodologies.

Introduction

The software engineering community has begun to examine agile methodologies to judge their impact on the creation of quality software. Such an interest can be seen in the literary, corporate, and academic inclusion of such methodologies as Extreme Programming [Beck2000], Adaptive Software Development [Highsmith1999], Crystal [Cockburn2001], Scrum [Rising+2000], and others.

Any software development process has to deal with the inevitable change, to satisfy rapidly evolving requirements and technologies. Recent growth in Internet and entrepreneurial software assets accentuates the need to handle such unavoidable change. The software engineering community has begun to examine and implement lightweight, agile methodologies [Cockburn2001]. Advocates of these methodologies profess that these methods are superior for dealing with change and, therefore, for providing customers with what they want, when they want it, and with acceptable defect rates.

As we said, quite a few emerging methodologies can be classified as agile. The creators of these methodologies met in Snowbird, Utah, in February 2001 to find common ground. As a result, they formed the Agile Alliance [Beck+2001]. These individuals state their uniting principles this way.

> *We are uncovering better ways of developing software by doing it and helping others to do it. We value:*
>
> - *Working software over comprehensive documentation.*
> - *Individuals and interactions over processes and tools.*
> - *Customer collaboration over contract negotiation.*
> - *Responding to change over following a plan.*

These principles and the details of the agile methodologies sound promising, particularly given the tumultuous conditions of the software industry. However, the practices of these methodologies diverge significantly from processes that have been viewed as trusted, commendable, predictable processes, such as the Personal Software Process [Humphrey1995] and the Rational Unified Process [Jacobson+1999]. There is a need to quantitatively study the effectiveness of this new class of methodologies to assess whether they are, indeed, improvements over the more traditional practices.

Software metrics and models are invaluable for characterizing software processes and assessing their effectiveness and improvement. A well-defined set of product and process metrics can support a quantifiable, objective assessment of the costs and benefits of the agile methodologies. In this chapter, we propose an experimental framework for this assessment. Through industrial use of this framework for empirically investigating the effectiveness of agile methodologies, we, as a software community, can gain valuable information on prudent use of these methodologies.

Agile Methodologies

Each of the agile methodologies has its own practices, which may be similar to other methodologies or unique. However, the members of the Agile Alliance have identified 12 uniting principles [Beck+2001].

1. Our highest priority is to satisfy the customer through early and continual delivery of valuable software.
2. Welcome changing requirements, even late in development. Agile processes harness change for customers' competitive advantage.
3. Deliver working software frequently, from a couple of weeks to a couple of months, with a preference for the shorter timescale.
4. Businesspeople and developers work together daily throughout the project.
5. Build projects around motivated individuals, give them the environment and support they need, and trust them to get the job done.
6. The most efficient and effective method of conveying information with and within a development team is face-to-face conversation.
7. Working software is the primary measure of progress.
8. Agile processes promote sustainable development. The sponsors, developers, and users should be able to maintain a constant pace indefinitely.
9. Continuous attention to technical excellence and good design enhances agility.
10. Simplicity—the art of maximizing the amount of work *not* done—is essential.

11. The best architectures, requirements, and designs emerge from self-organizing teams.
12. At regular intervals, the team reflects on how to become more effective, then tunes and adjusts its behavior accordingly.

Empirical Investigation

Case Study

We propose that industrial organizations structure a case study with related surveys to provide quantifiable, empirical results. In a case study, key factors that affect outcome (such as the transition to an agile methodology) are identified. Then, specific, predetermined outcome measurements are tracked and analyzed. Case studies are generally performed in a "typical project," and they can be thought of as "research in the typical."

Often, a more preferred research technique is to run a formal experiment. Formal experiments can be referred to as "research in the large," and their results have greater external validity or applicability to many settings [Kitchenham+1995]. However, formal experiments generally require a control group (a group that uses the organization's existing development methodology) and an experimental group (a group that uses the new methodology), often replicating the same or very similar projects.

It is very difficult to affordably run formal experiments in industry [Fenton+1998]. As a result, we suggest that organizations structure a case study that compares pre-agile metrics with post-agile metrics. "Although they cannot achieve the scientific rigor of formal experiments, case studies can provide sufficient information to help you judge if specific technologies will benefit your own organization or product" [Kitchenham+1995]. We propose a multiproject study as defined by Basili, Selby, and Hutchens [Basili+1986], whereby the case study examines objects across a single team and a set of projects. It is beneficial for the projects to be as similar as possible in complexity and scope and for as many of the same people to be involved in the pre- and posttransition studies.

Surveys could be used to poll a set of data from the software engineers involved in the study. Pretransition and posttransition surveys could assess their reaction. Additionally, surveys could be used to measure customer satisfaction with software releases.

Empirical Study Hypotheses

The overall "effectiveness" of a new methodology is multifaceted. As a result, in designing the case study, we define several hypotheses. Each of our six targeted areas of investigation is now stated in terms of a null hypothesis that assumes there are no significant differences between agile and more traditional methodologies. The empirical investigation will determine whether the data is convincing enough to reject these null hypotheses.

Productivity and Cycle Time

1. There is no productivity or cycle time difference between developers using an agile methodology and developers using a more traditional methodology.

To assess developer productivity, organizations need to measure things such as the amount of time necessary to complete a task in relation to a size measure, such as lines of code or function points. The results need to be compared with the productivity results of engineers on past projects or compared, in aggregate, with software engineers not using the new methodology. Cycle time is a matter of survival for many companies. As a result, the cycle times to complete tasks, releases, and projects must be compared.

Externally Visible Prerelease Quality

2. There is no difference in externally visible prerelease quality between code produced using an agile methodology and code produced using a more traditional methodology.

We can assess this statement by examining the number and severity of functional test cases and the amount of time spent to fix these prerelease defects. To do this, the development team needs to record the amount of time they spend fixing a defect once an external test group reports it.

Externally Visible Postrelease Quality

3. There is no difference in externally visible postrelease quality between code produced using an agile methodology and code produced using a more traditional methodology.

We can assess this statement by examining the number and severity of customer and field defects and the amount of time spent to fix these released defects. To do this, the developers need to record the amount of time they spend fixing a defect once the code has been released.

Additionally, an important aspect of externally visible software quality is reliability. Measures of reliability widely used in software engineering include the number of failures discovered and the rate of discovery [Mendonça+2000]. Service Requests (SRs) are requests for changes (because of defects or the desire for enhanced functionality) by customers after product release. The literature on SRs has partially overlapped that of software reliability, because SRs often refer to occurrences of faults that also affect the reliability of software systems. Wood suggests that the models used for describing software reliability can be used also for the overall analysis of SRs, without any major loss of precision [Wood1996].

We also propose that the SRs be analyzed in relation to appropriate growth models to assess changes in product reliability. Software Reliability Growth Models (SRGMs), formal equations that describe the time of the discovery of defects, give additional insight into the defect behavior of the software product and the effort necessary for achieving the desired quality. The SRGMs can be used to compare the reliability of the pre-agile development process with the new methodology being introduced.

Responsiveness to Customer Changes

4. Developers using an agile methodology will be no more responsive to customer changes than developers using a more traditional methodology.

A significant professed advantage of agile methodologies is that the development team has the potential to improve its ability to adapt to customer changes and suggestions *during* product development. This could be done when the developers are asking for clarification on a requirement, which improves their understanding of the requirement. Alternatively, the development team could incorporate customer changes postrelease as the proposed change is prioritized into future product development.

Midrelease changes are very difficult to quantify. There is a fine line between simply clarifying a requirement and correcting or changing a requirement. The postrelease changes could be quantified by:

- Counting the number of future requirements that relate to changing previously released functionality.
- Counting the SRs that deal with altering previously released functionality.
- Calculating the percentage of SRs that deal with altering previously released functionality that are handled by the development team, as Highsmith proposes [Auer+2002].
- Recording the amount of time spent by the development team changing previously released functionality as a percentage of the total development effort.

It would also be advantageous to run a short customer-satisfaction survey after each release. As an organization transitions to an agile methodology and learns to improve its responsiveness to and understanding of customer requirements, customer satisfaction may improve.

Part III

Internal Code Structure

5. There will be no difference in internal code structure between code produced using an agile methodology and code produced using a more traditional methodology.

We believe that the project source code contains a wealth of information about the quality built in by the team members. Based on a set of design metrics, appropriate software engineering models can be built to link internal design aspects of the software product with its defect behavior, future maintenance costs, and ability to be easily enhanced. Increasingly, object-oriented measurements are being used to evaluate and predict the quality of software [Harrison+1998]. A growing body of empirical results supports the theoretical validity of these metrics [Glasberg+2000; Basili+1996; Briand+1995; Schneidewind1992]. The validation of these metrics requires convincingly demonstrating that (1) the metric measures what it purports to measure (for example, a coupling metric really measures coupling) and (2) the metric is associated with an important external metric, such as reliability, maintainability, and fault-proneness [ElEmam2000]. Note that the validity of these metrics can sometimes be criticized [Churcher+1995].

As proposed by Succi in [Succi+2001], the relatively simple and well-understood CK metrics suite proposed by Chidamber and Kemerer [Chidamber+1998] can be used to assess the internal structure of product code. Riel also advocates these metrics in *Object-Oriented Design Heuristics* [Riel1996]. This set of six metrics shows good potential as a complete measurement framework in an object-oriented environment [Mendonça+2000]. Important quality data can be mined from the source code based on these metrics, preferably with the use of automated tools. These are the six CK metrics.

- *Depth of inheritance tree* (DIT) for a class corresponds to the maximum length from the root of the inheritance hierarchy to the node of the observed class. The deeper a class is within the hierarchy, the greater the number of methods it is likely to inherit, making it more complex to predict its behavior. Deeper trees constitute greater design complexity but also greater potential for reuse of inherited methods.
- *Number of children* (NOC) represents the number of immediate descendants of the class in the inheritance tree. The greater the number of children, the greater the likelihood of improper abstraction of the parent and of misuse of subclassing. However, the greater the number of children, the greater the reuse.
- *Coupling between objects* (CBO) is defined as the number of other classes to which a class is coupled through method invocation or use of instance variables. Excessive coupling is detrimental to modular design and prevents reuse. The larger the number of couples, the higher the sensitivity to changes in other parts of the design; therefore, maintenance is more difficult.
- *Response for a class* (RFC) is the cardinality of the set of all internal methods and external methods directly invoked by the internal methods. The larger the number of methods that can be invoked from a class through messages, the greater the complexity of a class. If a large number of methods can be invoked in response to a message, the testing and debugging of the class becomes com-

plicated because it requires a greater level of understanding from the tester.

- *Number of methods* (NOM) is a simplified version of the more general weighted methods count (WMC), as usually done [Basili+1986]. The number of internal methods is extracted instead of forming a weighted sum of methods based on complexity. The number of methods and the complexity of the methods involved is a predictor of how much time and effort is required to develop and maintain the class. The larger the number of methods in a class, the greater the potential impact on children because children will inherit all the methods defined in a class. Classes with larger numbers of methods are likely to be more application specific, limiting the potential for reuse.
- *Lack of cohesion in methods* (LCOM) is defined as the number of pairs of noncohesive methods minus the count of cohesive method pairs, based on common instance variables used by the methods in a class. High cohesion indicates good class subdivision. Lack of cohesion or low cohesion increases complexity, thereby increasing the likelihood of errors during the development process. Classes with low cohesion could probably be subdivided into two or more classes with increased cohesion.

Part III

Job Satisfaction

6. Developers using an agile methodology will be no more satisfied with their job than developers using a more traditional methodology.

We view employee job satisfaction to be of prime importance because happier employees are also less likely to leave their job. Therefore, improved job satisfaction means less risk of losing team members during project development. To assess job satisfaction, we suggest that a short survey be administered to the development team before transitioning to the agile methodology. Additionally, we periodically readminister the survey to the team as they transition.

In analyzing the data to assess these hypotheses, we must consider how well the software developers actually adhered to the practices of the chosen methodology. It is very important to set the results in the context of which practices were actually performed by most of the programmers. This is not to say that a team will succeed only through following the practices. Instead, we want to be able to find relationships and draw conclusions knowing what the team has actually done and how they have adapted and enhanced the methodology to meet the requirements of their project.

Conclusion

Some anecdotal evidence suggests success of the agile methodologies in producing higher-quality software in less time. In this chapter, we set up a framework and measurement plan for an objective assessment of these methodologies. Our goals are to provide insight into the effectiveness of the new practices in helping organizations meet their business objectives and in developer satisfaction and confidence and related managerial issues. In particular, certain environments and certain projects may be better suited for an agile methodology than others. The authors are interested in collecting and analyzing the results of industrial experiments related to agile methodologies. Anyone interested in running such an experiment is invited to contact the authors.

References

[Auer+2002] K. Auer, R. Miller. *Extreme Programming Applied*. Addison-Wesley, 2002.

[Basili+1986] V. Basili, R. Selby, D. Hutchens. "Experimentation in Software Engineering." *Transactions on Software Engineering*, Volume 12, 1986.

[Basili+1996] V. Basili, L. Briand, W. Melo. "A Validation of Object-Oriented Design Metrics as Quality Indicators." *IEEE Transactions on Software Engineering*, Volume 22, 1996.

[Beck2000] K. Beck. *Extreme Programming Explained*. Addison-Wesley, 2000.

[Beck+2001] K. Beck, M. Beedle, A. Bennekum, A. Cockburn, W. Cunningham, M. Fowler, J. Grenning, J. Highsmith, A. Hunt, R. Jeffries, J. Kern, B. Marick, R. Martin, S. Mellor, K. Schwaber, J. Sutherland, D. Thomas. *Manifesto for Agile Software Development*. http://agilemanifesto.org. 2001.

[Briand+1995] L. Briand, K. El Emam, S. Morasca. "Theoretical and Empirical Validation of Software Metrics." 1995.

[Chidamber+1998] S. Chidamber, D. Darcy, C. Kemerer. "Managerial Use of Object-Oriented Software: An Explanatory Analysis." *IEEE Transactions on Software Engineering*, Volume 24, 1998.

[Churcher+1995] N. Churcher, M. Shepperd. "Comments on 'A Metrics Suite for Object-Oriented Design.'" *IEEE Transactions on Software Engineering*, Volume 21, 1995.

[Cockburn2001] A. Cockburn. *Agile Software Development*. Addison-Wesley, 2001.

[ElEmam2000] K. El Emam. "A Methodology for Validating Software Product Metrics." *National Research Council of Canada Technical Report NCR/ERB-1076, NRC 44142*, June 2000.

[Fenton+1998] N. Fenton, S. Pfleeger. *Software Metrics: A Rigorous and Practical Approach*. Brooks/Cole Publishing, 1998.

[Glasberg+2000] D. Glasberg, K. El Emam, W. Melo, N. Madhavji. "Validating Object-Oriented Design Metrics on a Commercial Java Application." *National Research Council of Canada Technical Report NCR/ERB-1080, NRC 44146*, September 2000.

[Harrison+1998] R. Harrison, S. Counsell, R. Nithi. "An Evaluation of the MOOD Set of Object-Oriented Software Metrics." *IEEE Transactions on Software Engineering*, Volume 24, June 1998.

[Highsmith1999] J. Highsmith. *Adaptive Software Development*. Dorset House, 1999.

[Humphrey1995] W. Humphrey. *A Discipline for Software Engineering*. Addison-Wesley, 1995.

[Jacobson+1999] I. Jacobson, G. Booch, J. Rumbaugh. *The Unified Software Development Process*. Addison-Wesley, 1999.

[Kitchenham+1995] B. Kitchenham, L. Pickard, S. Pfleeger. "Case Studies for Method and Tool Evaluation." *IEEE Software*, Volume 12, Number 4, July 1995.

[Mendonça+2000] M. Mendonça, V. Basili. "Validation of an Approach for Improving Existing Measurement Frameworks." *IEEE Transactions on Software Engineering*, Volume 26, 2000.

[Riel1996] A. Riel. *Object-Oriented Design Heuristics*. Addison-Wesley, 1996.

[Rising+2000] L. Rising, N. Janoff. "The Scrum Software Development Process for Small Teams." *IEEE Software*, Volume 17, 2000.

[Schneidewind1992] N. Schneidewind. "Methodology for Validating Software Metrics." *IEEE Transactions on Software Engineering*, Volume 18, 1992.

[Succi+2001] G. Succi, M. Stefanovic, M. Smith, R. Huntrods. Design of an Experiment for Quantitative Assessment of Pair Programming Practices. Presented at XP2001, Italy. 2001.

[Wood1996] A. Wood. "Predicting Software Reliability." *IEEE Computer*, Volume 29, 1996.

Acknowledgments

We thank Shari Lawrence Pfleeger for her comments on an early draft of this chapter.

About the Authors

Laurie Williams is an assistant professor of computer science at North Carolina State University. Dr. Williams has a Ph.D. in computer science from the University of Utah, an M.B.A. from Duke University, and a B.S. in industrial engineering from Lehigh University. She worked for IBM for nine years in engineering and software development before obtaining her Ph.D. Dr. Williams is recognized as an expert on the technique of pair programming. She is currently writing a book for Addison-Wesley entitled *Pair Programming Illuminated,* to be published in 2002. She can be reached at williams@csc.ncsu.edu.

Giancarlo Succi is a full professor of computer science and director of the Center for Applied Software Engineering at the Free University of Bozen-Bolzano. He holds a Laurea Degree in electrical engineering (University of Genova), an M.S. in computer science (SUNY Buffalo), and a Ph.D. in computer and electrical engineering (University of Genova). Dr. Succi researches and consults on XP, AMs, object orientation, software product lines, software metrics, and empirical software engineering. He can be reached at Giancarlo.Succi@unibz.it.

Milorad Stefanovic is a software developer at IBM Canada in Toronto. He holds an M.S. from the University of Alberta.

Michele Marchesi is a full professor of computer science in the Department of Electrical and Electronic Engineering of Cagliary University in Italy. He started to program almost 30 years ago and has been using object-oriented programming for more than 15 years. His main fields of interest are OO languages, software development processes, connectionism, and financial applications of engineering. He was the program chair of the first three International Conferences on Extreme Programming and Agile Processes in Software Engineering, held in Sardinia, Italy, in 2000, 2001, and 2002. He authored a book on Smalltalk language and edited, with Professor Giancarlo Succi, the book *Extreme Programming Examined*, published by Addison-Wesley in 2001. He is the author of more than 200 papers published in reviewed journals and conference proceedings. Michele can be reached at michele@diee.unica.it.

Part IV

XR: Extreme Reality—Real-Life Experiences

Part IV reports on a series of experiences in applying XP. The goal is to guide future applications of XP by showing what went well and what did not work.

This is a first step toward establishing a body of knowledge about XP in which different experiences can be classified and compared. To ease the comparison, the authors have been required to follow a fixed set of headings as follows:

1. Research hypotheses, in which the goals of the trial of XP are described
2. Description of the context of the experience, detailing the environment where XP (or a portion of it) was tried
3. Results from the experience, with numeric quantification of the outcome, whenever possible
4. What actions were taken as a result of the experience

We have also encouraged the authors to follow a rigorous and factual style in reporting their XP experiences.

A comparison with what happens in medical studies may help in understanding the purpose and the scope of our work. Usually, a drug becomes available for general use at the end of a four-phase process. We think that a similar approach would benefit software engineering in general and especially XP. These are the four phases.

- Phase 1—The drug is tested to determine whether it is harmful; in our case, we would like to know if a given methodology would be extremely harmful for an organization to try. We think that in XP we have already completed this phase.
- Phase 2—The drug is administered to volunteers to determine whether it has the beneficial effects it claims to have. We are at exactly this step in XP. We are "administering" the XP practices to the "volunteer" organizations that think that XP would benefit them.
- Phase 3—The drug is tested on a large scale, to perform a general, unbiased evaluation of its effects.
- Phase 4—The drug is released for general use but still under scrutiny for possible unexpected results and contraindications.

However, the first trials of novel techniques are usually performed by those adept at such techniques, those who have a direct interest in showing that the tried technique does indeed work. Remember, we are in phase 2 of our experimental study. Therefore, the language is often emphatic, and the reporters are clearly biased toward XP. This does not limit the validity of the study, because some of the results are definitely positive, while others require more careful investigation, and a few denote a negative impact, especially in the managerial aspects.

Table IV.1 summarizes the results.

Taking the same experimental approach as with medical studies, we think that now is the time to move in two directions.

- Extend these phase 2 experimentations, to broaden the scope in situations where people are not sure how to apply XP, such as with large or geographically dispersed teams.
- Initiate phase 3 experimentations—that is, systematically apply the XP approach to cases where it appears it would be useful.

TABLE IV.1 Results of Real-Life Experiences with XP

Chapter	Authors	Hypotheses	Context	Results
30	Hodgetts and Phillips	1. XP increases the rate of development. 2. XP reduces development costs. 3. XP increases the correlation of software to business needs. 4. XP reduces the release cycle. 5. XP increases the product quality.	Internet start-up; typical enterprise technology, including ASP, J2EE, relational db.	All hypotheses have been verified.
31	Kini and Collins	1. XP works well in general. 2. XP is easily accepted by the customer. 3. Some practices have worth when requirements or conditions change. 4. Most practices are not difficult to implement.	XP-based company, with specific hardware and infrastructures for XP. Four developers and one tester.	All hypotheses have been verified; areas of improvement include a formalization of the in-house XP process.
32	Schalliol	1. The story cards and the resulting code are a sufficient guide for the project. 2. Dividing application functionality into story cards is learned once and then reapplied for all subsequent iterations.	J2EE development project that switched to XP halfway through its three-year life.	Each hypothesis raises some concerns. 1. There is a lack of the "big picture," perhaps because of the size of the project. 2. It is not always true, because sometimes the division is not "obvious."

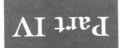

Table continued on next page.

TABLE IV.1 *Continued*

Chapter	Authors	Hypotheses	Context	Results
32 (*cont'd.*)	Schalliol	3. It is easy to identify the single customer who drives the planning game for the XP process. 4. Such a customer can drive the planning game and is the primary author of all functional tests.	Fifty-person team: about 30 developers, eight quality assurance testers, and eight analysts. Overall, about 500,000 lines of executable code.	3. The large size of the application would require more than one customer in charge of leading the project. 4. The customer often was uneasy in defining the acceptance tests. 5. There were also aspects in which XP worked really well.
33	Elssamadisy	1. XP provides customers with positive feedback via quick releases. 2. XP "manages expectations" more easily because of constant customer involvement. 3. XP results in a better-quality product, delivered on time to customers. 4. XP eliminates integration problems caused by the presence of several subteams.	Large distributed leasing application; typically about 25 developers, ten business analysts, ten quality assurance people. About 600,000 lines of executable code in 6,500 classes.	All the hypotheses have been verified. In large teams, though, there are problems in meeting, applying pair programming, staying within the 40 hours a week, and defining suitable metaphors.

34	Griffin	1. XP makes the development team more responsive to business needs. 2. XP increases the speed of releases and reduces the error rate. 3. XP improves the development cycle flow.	Provision of secure transaction settlement services for business and consumer e-commerce sites. Multitier architecture with ASP, Java/EJB, Oracle db, and XML.	All the hypotheses have been verified. However, the company was not happy with the "performance" of the XP team—no overtime, no stress, and so on. Therefore, the team was dismissed at the end of the project.
35	Johansen, Stauffer, and Turner	1. Adhering to the principles of XP would help overcome the major deficiencies usually encountered on "regular" projects. 2. XP creates a stronger team and an experience that is remembered with pleasure.	Small software development company. Eight-month, six-developer project, delivering a major upgrade to an enterprise software system.	All the hypotheses have been verified in general. However, the management and one of the developers felt that working more would have helped the project to deliver more.
36	Gittins, Hope, and Williams	1. The incremental addition of XP practices provides significant benefits to the overall development process. 2. There are difficulties of various kinds, which can be discovered using qualitative statistical methods.	Medium-sized software company committed to implementing XP.	Both hypotheses have been verified, with a careful analysis of the outcome of each XP practice.

Chapter 30

Extreme Adoption Experiences of a B2B Start-Up

—*Paul Hodgetts and Denise Phillips*

This chapter presents the results of adopting XP at an Internet business-to-business (B2B) start-up. We discuss our motivations and goals for adopting XP and the context under which the adoption efforts were evaluated. Then we present the results in terms of objective metrics and subjective evaluations. The results indicate that the project conducted under XP demonstrated significant improvements.

Escrow.com faced extreme challenges as a new Internet start-up. The business-to-business e-commerce market was, and remains, immature and rapidly changing. Time-to-market was critical to establish the business and gain market share. Quality was essential for the company as a provider of regulated online transaction settlement services.

This chapter discusses our experiences in adopting XP. Escrow.com was in a unique position to compare nearly identical projects conducted under both XP and non-XP processes. By collecting a small set of simple metrics, we were able to measure the relative success of the adoption effort. As we'll see, even under difficult circumstances, this adoption effort produced tangible improvements over the prior project.

Extreme Programming has gained considerable fame and acclaim over the past several years. Although the published body of theoretical and how-to knowledge has grown quickly, more experience reports are needed to provide convincing evidence of XP's effectiveness in real-world project contexts. This report strives to contribute to this body of evidence.

Research Hypotheses

By October 2000, Escrow.com was experiencing severe and growing problems in its development efforts, including a dramatically slowed pace of delivery, increasing development costs, poor product quality, and a deteriorating state of the code base. Early process improvement efforts were largely unsuccessful at solving these core problems.

Senior management recognized that a fundamental change to the development process was needed. Spearheaded by a team of senior developers, research was conducted using XP. Afterward, we hypothesized that adopting XP would deliver the following benefits:

1. *Increased rate of development*, enabling the development efforts to keep pace with the increasing demand for new features
2. *Reduced development costs*, enabling a reduction in the size of the development team or deploying existing resources to new projects
3. *Increased correlation of software to business needs*, bringing the delivered releases in line with the requirements of the end users and eliminating unnecessary or low return-on-investment features
4. *Reduced release cycle*, enabling frequent releases of high-priority features
5. *Increased product quality*, reducing the quantity and severity of defects that delayed production releases
6. *Increased quality of implementation*, reducing the code entropy that hindered the addition of new features and increasing the maintainability of the code base

Existing project management and change control practices produced metrics that measured developer effort and defect discovery rates. Combined with code analysis, this data enabled objective measurements of the improvement from adopting XP.

Description of the Context of the Experience

Escrow.com is a provider of online settlement services. Escrow.com's services are delivered via Internet-based enterprise systems, using typical enterprise technologies including Active Server Pages (ASP), the Java 2 Platform, Enterprise Edition (J2EE), and relational databases.

To attack the emerging business-to-business e-commerce market, Escrow.com began development of a flexible and full-featured transaction-processing engine. This project, creatively dubbed "Version 2," or "V2," was conducted using many elements of "traditional" defined processes, and required significant expenditures for personnel, tools, and technologies. The V2 project is used as the baseline for our process improvement comparisons.

To address problems with the V2 project, Escrow.com radically retooled its development process and culture. The resulting project, called "Version 3," or "V3," used XP as its development process and is the focus of this experience report.

The XP adoption efforts at Escrow.com were conducted under actual production circumstances. Because of the immediate need to address problems and the company's small size, we had neither the time nor the resources to conduct a pilot XP project. The switch to XP was immediate and complete. Following a brief, two-week preparation period, all development was conducted using the full set of XP practices.

Based on our observations, the context under which XP was adopted at Escrow.com is similar to the development environments at many small to medium-sized companies. We believe our results can be generalized to similar development environments and projects.

Results from the Experience

In this section, we evaluate the results of the XP adoption efforts by using metrics gathered from both the V2 and V3 projects. The results are summarized in Figure 30.1.

We must point out that these comparisons were not made in the context of a controlled, scientific study and are therefore anecdotal. Some comparisons are based on subjective criteria. We nevertheless believe even anecdotal evidence in this context to be relevant and valuable, particularly because of the rarity of scientific studies conducted in actual production environments.

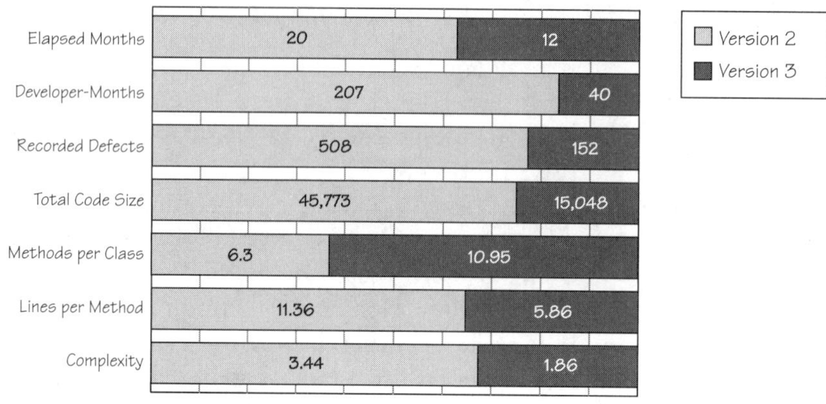

FIGURE 30.1 Version 2 versus Version 3 comparison of results

Comparing V2 and V3 Functionality

For the purposes of this evaluation, we must establish a comparison of the overall functionality of the V2 and V3 products. In the absence of objective function-point measurements, we must subjectively compare the two products.

In our subjective judgment, the V2 and V3 products were virtually equivalent in the total amount of functionality. Although the V2 product incorporated more complexity in its features, the V3 product targeted a wider set of simpler features.

Increased Rate of Development

The V2 project delivered its business value over a period of 20 months before the project was stopped because of the excessive costs of ownership.

The V3 project was suspended after nine months of development. At the established velocity, V3 would have delivered its total business value over a period of 12 months.

This result represents a 67% increase in the overall development velocity, as measured in terms of the rate of business value delivered over time.

Reduced Development Costs

The V2 project employed a total of 21 developers during its existence. The team size ranged from three developers to a maximum of 18 developers at its peak. The V2 project cost a total of 207 developer-months of effort.

The V3 project began with two developers. After four months, the team size was increased to four developers. Overall, using the estimated schedule, the V3 project would have cost a total of 40 developer-months.

These results represent an 80% reduction in developer-month effort and its corresponding personnel and overhead costs. We note that the V3 team was staffed by senior developers, and their expertise probably contributed to the productivity gains.

Increased Correlation of Software to Business Needs

The V2 project delivered features and technological capabilities beyond the requirements of the customer, at the expense of delivering revenue-generating features.

The V3 project's use of the planning game focused delivery only on clearly identified business requirements. As the expertise of the customer team increased, the development effort increasingly correlated directly to specific revenue-generating opportunities.

Reduced Release Cycle

The V2 project was unable to produce meaningful production releases in cycles of less than two to three months. The quality assurance cycle alone normally lasted two or more weeks.

The V3 project delivered production-ready releases in iteration cycles of two weeks. Because of the increased clarity and prioritization of the planning game, meaningful feature releases were produced in cycles of one to three iterations, representing a substantial improvement in the time between production releases.

The reduction in the release cycle enabled product managers to flexibly and quickly respond to changing business conditions. This was dramatically demonstrated by the rapid succession of changes to the product priorities following the introduction of XP. In January 2001, at the start of the XP adoption, two product lines were under development. In February 2001, two additional product lines were initiated, including the V3 product. In June 2001, development was stopped on V2, and another product line was suspended. Finally, in October 2001, V3 development was suspended, leaving one remaining active product line.

Increased Product Quality

For both projects, defects found in acceptance testing were tracked using a defect-tracking database. V2's policy was to verbally report minor defects without tracking, while V3 mandated that all defects be formally logged. Acceptance tests on both projects were manually executed, but the V3 project also used a suite of 1,230 automated unit tests. Acceptance testing on the V2 project was performed sporadically, while on the V3 project acceptance testing was performed repeatedly on all iterations.

The V2 project logged a total of 508 defects over its 20-month life cycle. Of these defects, 182 were logged during a difficult two-month period from September through November 2000. Another 123 defects were logged during the final one-month testing cycle before V2's last production release in June 2001.

The V3 project logged a total of 114 defects over its entire nine-month duration. All these defects were minor. Severe defects were discovered and fixed by the developers before concluding iterations. Assuming a linear increase in the number of defects had the project run to completion, V3 would have produced 152 total defects.

These results represent a 70% reduction in the number of defects discovered in acceptance testing. This reduction is even more significant when we take into account the lower defect severity levels.

Increased Quality of Implementation

Quality of design and implementation is difficult to measure objectively, because even the types of measurements are subject to debate in the software community. For these measurements, we chose a few relatively simple indicators of possible quality: total code size, the average size of classes, the average size of methods, and the average cyclometric complexity of methods. The total-code-size metric includes all types of sources (Java, JSP, ASP, and HTML), while the remaining metrics focus only on the Java sources.

Because the V3 project was suspended before completion, it was necessary to estimate the final total-code-size measurement, assuming a continuation of the observed linear growth.

Table 30.1 summarizes the comparison of these metrics.

Although these metrics are subject to differing analyses, when we combine them with our subjective reviews of the code base, we feel they represent an improvement in the quality of the implementation. The reduction in code size is indicative of a simpler implementation, assuming delivery of comparable functionality. The presence of a larger number of smaller methods per class, combined with the reduced complexity of methods, suggests an improved division of responsibility and behavior across methods.

What to Do Next

This chapter presents evidence that the V3 project produced significant measurable improvements over the prior V2 project. Many aspects of the two projects remained relatively consistent—the domain and feature sets, the tools and technologies, and the team. The primary difference between the two projects was the use of XP on V3. We must therefore conclude that XP contributed substantially to the improvements, a conclusion reinforced by our subjective day-to-day observations.

The XP adoption experiences at Escrow.com have proved to us that XP is particularly effective in today's fast-paced e-commerce environment, and we now make XP our process of choice. We plan to continue to measure and quantify the benefits gained as we adopt XP on future projects.

TABLE 30.1 Measurements of Implementation Quality

	Version 2	Version 3	% Change
Total code size	45,773	15,048	– **67%**
Average methods per class	6.30	10.95	**+ 73%**
Average lines per method	11.36	5.86	– **48%**
Average cyclometric complexity	3.44	1.56	– **54%**

Acknowledgments

We acknowledge and sincerely thank all our colleagues at Escrow.com whose efforts enabled these successes. In particular, we thank our former CEO, Russell Stern, for trusting our vision and enabling us to transform the business. We also must thank Robert Martin, Lowell Lindstrom, Brian Button, and Jeff Langr from Object Mentor, whose expert help proved invaluable. A special thanks to Beth Hechanova, Tamlyn Jones, and Paul Moore for their help as reviewers. Last, but certainly not least, we thank our families and friends for their limitless patience and support for our "extreme" endeavors.

About the Authors

Paul Hodgetts is the founder and principal consultant at Agile Logic, a provider of training, mentoring, and development services focused on agile development and enterprise technologies. Paul served as the director of product development and chief architect at Escrow.com during the V2 and V3 projects. Paul can be reached at http://www.AgileLogic.com.

Denise Phillips is an independent consultant working with companies to adopt agile development techniques and processes. She is the creator and instructor of the XP certificate program at California State University, Fullerton. Denise served as the senior enterprise architect at Escrow.com during the V2 and V3 projects. Denise can be reached by e-mail at dyp@pacbell.net.

Chapter 31

Lessons Learned from an XP Project

—*Natraj Kini and Steve Collins*

*This chapter is based on our experience while working for a software outsourcing company that was built around the XP methodology. One of the difficulties we had in adopting XP was that the original "white book" (*Extreme Programming Explained*), though inspiring and persuasive, was somewhat short on detail. We feel that it would be valuable to the XP community if groups doing real projects would provide detailed accounts of their experiences in applying XP. Finally, some issues took on additional significance for us because our client had outsourced their project to us.*

Part IV

Research Hypotheses

What facets of XP worked well and were easily accepted by the customer (including some practices that we expected that the customer wouldn't like)? What practices proved their worth when requirements or conditions changed? What practices were difficult to implement? What modifications did we make to some of the XP practices and why?

Obviously, we don't have definitive answers to these questions that can be extrapolated across all projects, but our account adds one more data point to the sample.

Description of the Context of the Experience

Our company was formed around XP, which meant that all our developers and our management were committed to XP from the conception of the company. The developers on this project had worked together on other XP projects for a few months, and some had long relationships during their careers, so we had a team that was ready to hit the ground running.

Our client for this project was also a start-up, which meant that they were more open to XP than a larger company with an existing methodology might have been. Many of our customers had backgrounds in development, so they were familiar with the shortcomings of conventional methodologies. They were also at a stage in their development where it was possible for them to remain on-site through most of the life of the project.

The XP-standard environment prescribed by Kent Beck proved its worth in this project [Beck2000]. We often had four pairs (including client developers) engaged on the four workstations in the corners of our development room. And much of the communication during the project happened indirectly as people overheard and responded to what an adjacent pair was discussing. The walls covered with whiteboard wallpaper also worked out well; they always held design scratchings and project notes. Even when we had online data such as bug reports, we put highlights up on the wall because they acted as a physical reminder of our priorities. Our wireless network and dockable laptops worked well too—they made it much easier for us to switch pairs and get together in another room for an impromptu design session.

We decided to allocate a specific and separate space for customers outside the development room. This helped them remain productive with their "real" jobs while still remaining accessible to the development team. It also meant that they didn't get in the way of the developers. Although we tried to be as open as possible, we also felt it necessary on occasion to meet in a separate room without customers present. Likewise, we made space available for the customers so that they could meet among themselves when they felt the need.

Results from the Experience

Billing and Contracts

Based on a recommendation from "Uncle Bob" Martin, we decided to bill by the iteration instead of by the hour to prevent any squabbling over hours worked. This also eased the time tracking burden on the developers and made it easier to swap developers when needed. More subtly, we felt that this helped show the client that we were sharing the risk with them and that we were invested in the project.

We found later that this also acted as a feedback mechanism—overtime is an effective cure for developer overreaching. We developers had nobody to blame but ourselves if our optimism resulted in long hours. Of course, this can be taken only so far—we still believe that we must go back to the customer and reduce scope when we find that the estimates are way off the mark.

The contract that we agreed on with our client did not attempt to nail down the deliverables for the seven-week life of the project—that isn't possible when you're going through iteration planning and changing direction every two weeks. We agreed on the size of the team and that we would augment the contract every two weeks with a list of stories for the next iteration.

Iteration Planning

We anticipated problems in convincing the customers to narrow iteration scope to a set of specific stories that made sense for both business and development. However, this negotiation actually went quite well—our customers were willing to listen to our reasons for wanting to do some stories ahead of others (though we tried to keep such dependencies to a minimum) and for giving high-risk stories a large estimate.

The customers loved the quick turnaround of the planning game. They were afraid that it would take us much longer to become productive than it did and were pleasantly surprised that we were able to identify the important stories as quickly as we did.

Team Size

Our team size for this project was four developers and one tester, whereas we had identified an ideal team size of eight developers and one tester and usually had at least six developers on previous projects.

We found that there were some advantages and disadvantages to this smaller team size. On balance, we'd probably still prefer to have six to eight developers in a team.

Pros

- We have struggled with whether everybody who is part of the development team should be in the planning game—progress sometimes bogs down with too many participants, but a lot of knowledge transfer does take place. This was not a problem here with the smaller team size.
- Communication and the coordination of schedules were easier.

Cons

- It was a little more difficult to recover when a developer had to leave for personal reasons.
- The overhead of tracking the project was more visible as a significant component of the total time spent on the project.
- We had a smaller spectrum of skills available among the developers.
- With a smaller number of stories in each iteration, we sometimes found that one of the assigned tasks was a bottleneck because other tasks depended on it.

Stand-up Meetings

How do you avoid discussing design during stand-ups? We had repeated problems in limiting the length of our daily stand-ups; the issues raised were often valid and needed further amplification.

One device that worked was to write on a whiteboard all the issues that people raised for discussion during the stand-up. Then, after the stand-up was completed, those who needed to be involved in each discussion could split into smaller groups and follow through on the "promise to have a conversation."

Another minor innovation was the use of an egg timer to limit stand-ups. We set the egg timer to ten or 15 minutes at the start of the meeting. Then the person who was talking at any time during the stand-up had to hold the timer in their hand. This acted as a reminder to the speaker to be brief and a reminder to others in the stand-up to avoid any private conversations while someone else had the floor.

We found that the client wanted a much more detailed status than we had planned to supply—they were used to the traditional spreadsheet view of project tasks with a percent complete for each task. We compromised with a daily status message that summarized the state of the project and the outstanding issues—most of the work to compile this daily message was done by one person at each stand-up meeting.

Pairing with Client Developers

We knew from day one that we would need to hand off our code to the customers in-house. For much of the project, their technical lead was on-site and worked with us. Four other, newly hired developers paired with us for different stretches of the last three weeks.

The objective of accelerating knowledge transfer by means of pairing worked very well. It also helped that XP is a cool new methodology that many developers are eager to experience. But that initial enthusiasm was probably sustained only because these developers were able to make constructive contributions. One developer didn't like the idea of pairing at all and quit when he found out that he would have to pair at least until the code was handed off to the client company.

Our experience with the technical lead was more complex. He was technically very capable and made several suggestions and observations that led us down unexplored paths. However, pairing with him was hampered by the fact that he was playing multiple roles, trying to get the most value for the client's investment while still acting as a developer. Therefore, he tried to steer us toward solving the difficult technical problems that he thought would crop up later, instead of focusing on the stories and tasks immediately at hand.

Finally, at the end of the sixth week, the team captain (our instantiation of the "coach" role) and another developer both had to leave the team unexpectedly. We introduced two new developers to the team and were able to deliver all agreed-on functionality on schedule, which further validated the worth of pairing and shared code ownership.

Story Estimates

During the first iteration, we felt the natural pressure to please the customer and bit off more than we could chew. We found that our attention to tracking and to promptly creating the acceptance tests as well as our discipline in sticking to our XP practices all suffered when we were under the gun. We continued to practice test-first programming but neglected to pair up when we thought that the tasks being tackled were simple enough that they didn't need the spotlight of a continuous code review.

As our customers came to trust us more in later iterations, we felt less pressure to prove that we were delivering value by stretching ourselves to the point that our discipline degenerated. We also learned from our failure to meet the optimistic velocity of the first iteration: We reduced our velocity by about 20% from the first to the fourth and last iteration and felt that the quality of our code improved as a result.

Bug Fixes

By the third iteration, a substantial fraction of our time was spent on resolving bugs from previous iterations. We found that we had to take this into account when estimating our velocity. Part of the problem was that our client was new to the idea that we could throw away work when we realized, after it had been completed, that it should be done differently. They saw these issues as bugs—we saw them as new stories in the making.

The "green book" (*Planning Extreme Programming*) suggests that significant bugs should become stories in future iterations [Beck+2001]. We probably should have tried harder to convince our client that this was the right course to follow—there's a natural tendency for the client to feel that bug fixes are "owed" to them.

One approach to bug fixes that worked quite well was to have one pair at the start of each new iteration working on cleaning up significant bugs—those the customer had decided definitely needed immediate attention. At times we had significant dependencies on one or two of the tasks in the new iteration. Especially in that situation, we found that it was an efficient use of our developer resources to have one pair working on bug fixes while these foundational tasks were tackled by others.

Overall, we were not satisfied with our handling of bug fixes during this project—we wanted to convert them into stories, but our customers always felt that they were "owed" bug fixes as part of the previous iteration, above and beyond our work on new stories.

Acceptance Testing

One thing we realized was the importance of a full-time tester to keep the developers honest. When we did not have a full-time tester for the first iteration, we got 90% of every story done, which made the client very unhappy during acceptance tests—they perceived that everything was broken. We also found that our tester provided an impartial source of feedback to the developers on their progress.

We made one modification to our process specifically to facilitate testing. Our tester felt burdened by having to ask the developers to interrupt their paired development tasks whenever she needed a significant chunk of their time. So we decided to assign the role of test support to a specific developer for each week of the project.

Because we had multiple customer representatives, we found that a couple of times one customer helped create the acceptance tests, but a different one went through them with our tester at the end of the iteration. This necessitated many delays for explanation during the acceptance testing and some confusion over whether acceptance tests had been correctly specified. We concluded that in the future we would strongly push for one customer to help create and approve acceptance tests.

Unit Testing

Our unit tests proved invaluable in ensuring the quality of our code—we found on numerous occasions that refactorings in one area of the code caused side effects elsewhere that we caught with our unit tests. Because we relied so heavily on the unit tests, the frequency and time to run them increased to the point that they took almost two minutes. Our first response was to do some refactoring to reduce this time. We then made use of the flexibility of Apache Ant's XML configuration to sometimes run only a specified subset of all the unit tests.

During one iteration, we implemented a story that required a multithreaded producer-consumer engine that was difficult to test using JUnit. We created pluggable stubs for each module of the engine so we could test any one module while simulating the functionality of the other modules.

Metrics

As a means of encouraging the creation of unit tests, we wrote a simple script that traversed our source tree daily and sent e-mail with details of unit tests written, organized by package and class.

We also used JavaNCSS (distributed under the GNU GPL), which generates global, class, and function-level metrics for the quality of code.

We automatically generated these metrics daily and wrote the results to the project wiki to help us determine what parts of the code were ripe (smelly?) for refactoring and whether test coverage was adequate.

In addition to these automatically generated metrics, our tester manually created a graph of the acceptances tests, showing acceptance tests written, run, passed, and failed. This information was available on the development room whiteboard with the tasks and status of the project. A snapshot of the current state of the project was thus available on the whiteboard, while a more detailed view of the project could be found on our project wiki.

The Grade Card

After each iteration, we graded ourselves on the main XP practices and a few other aspects of the process that we felt were important (tester-to-developer communication, clarity of the stories, accuracy of estimates). The scores showed us the areas where the development team needed to focus and provided some useful and immediate feedback into the process. They served as a check against our sacrificing the long-term benefits of sticking with the process for the short-term benefits of churning out more code. We found that our scores improved substantially with each iteration, with the lowest grade in the final iteration being a B–. We made these grade cards (see Table 31.1 for an example) available publicly on the wiki, although we did not invite the customer into the grading process. We will consider that step for future projects, at least after a couple of iterations, when some trust has developed between developers and clients.

Object-Oriented Databases

We were fortunate to be able to use an object-oriented database management system (OODBMS), rather than a traditional relational database management system (RDBMS), which enabled us to treat the domain model as identical to the persistence model and therefore to be agile when refactoring the code. It's much more difficult to refactor the model when the data representation cannot be changed at will.

Delivery Day

One aspect of XP that we had to rethink in our circumstances was the amount of documentation that was necessary. Because the client developers would be responsible for maintenance and enhancements, we

TABLE 31.1 Grade Card for the XP Project

Category	Grade
Met customer expectations	B–
Customer-developer communication	A–
Tester-developer communication	B–
Clarity of stories (planning game)	A–
Accuracy of estimates/risk assessment	B
Design simplicity	A
Tracking	A–
Unit tests	B–
Stand-up meetings	B+
Pairing	B
Refactoring	A
Build handoff to test	D

needed more documentation than for an in-house project. So we put together an overview of the design along with some automatically generated UML diagrams and made sure that all our classes had Javadoc comments. We also added some installation and release documents and a developer FAQ. For most outsourcing situations, this level of documentation is probably necessary.

The final iteration was completed on Wednesday of the seventh week, with the contract concluded on Friday. As delivery day approached, we noticed how different this was compared with past experiences at other companies. The developers all left before sunset on the day before D-day, and the atmosphere during the last couple of days was relaxed and cordial, even celebratory. For our final handoff to the client, we followed Alistair Cockburn's recommendation to videotape a design discussion. We pushed all our code and documentation over to their CVS repository, burned a CD containing the code and documentation, and celebrated with beer and foosball.

All in all, we were pleasantly surprised with the way our customers (both the developers and the businesspeople) embraced XP during this project. They had some knowledge of XP when we started and were eager to learn more. The CTO had previously worked on a similar application and had some definite ideas on how to handle the complexities of the project, but was still receptive to an incremental and iterative approach. We found that XP worked well when dealing with our technically sophisticated customers. Rather than going around in circles when we disagreed, we could prove (or disprove) our design ideas using the concrete feedback of our code.

What to Do Next

In retrospect, though a couple of our customers did read the white book, we felt that it would have been useful if we had created a brief "XP owner's manual," perhaps a few pages long. Such a document would include some items intended to educate the customer, such as the following:

- Planning game—Story creation, deferring in-depth discussion of each story until it is selected or needs clarification to be estimated
- Acceptance tests—Expected customer input; what happens at the end of an iteration

We would use other items as a checklist for discussion, such as the following:

- Bug fixes—Prioritizing bugs, possibly assigning them as stories
- Documentation and status—Determining how much documentation and reporting is essential

We also found that many aspects of our process worked better as we developed more trust in our relationship with our customers. With future projects, we would like to focus on whether projects with repeat customers do indeed bear out this observation.

References

[Beck2000] K. Beck. *Extreme Programming Explained.* Addison-Wesley, 2000.

[Beck+2001] K. Beck, M. Fowler. *Planning Extreme Programming.* Addison-Wesley, 2001.

Acknowledgments

We thank Kevin Blankenship and John Sims for making the Tensegrent experience possible.

About the Authors

Natraj Kini is a founder of Agile Development, based in Denver, Colorado, and specializing in the XP methodology. Natraj is excited about and scared by the forthcoming birth of his first child. He plans to apply XP wherever possible to the fathering experience: incremental steps with refactoring, automated testing, and pairing at all times. He can be contacted at ukini@yahoo.com.

Steve Collins is a founder of and senior architect for Agile Development. Steve started his career developing software in support of the Cray-3 supercomputer. Since his work at Cray, Steve has spent ten years engineering enterprise-class Web-enabled e-business solutions with a focus on J2EE technologies, XML, and OODBs. He can be contacted at sxcoll2@yahoo.com.

Chapter 32

Challenges for Analysts on a Large XP Project

—Gregory Schalliol

The author recounts the fundamental issues encountered by a team of eight analysts on a 50-person, multiyear development project that converted to an XP process. Those issues include the importance of comprehending the whole application in addition to the parts, the art of dividing the whole into meaningful story cards, the sometimes complicated role of the customer, and the place of more traditional analysis. In describing the team's responses to these issues, the author suggests what challenges analysts might expect in large XP projects.

Part IV

In Kent Beck's groundbreaking book *Extreme Programming Explained,* the word "analysis" does not appear in the index, and Beck explicitly warns against trying to use the methodology for large development projects [Beck2000]. I, however, am an analyst using XP on a large development project, and the point of this chapter is to show that I am not completely foolish for having played such a role.

Traditional wisdom would say that such a project is not a likely candidate for an XP approach, and the bulk of my chapter recounts the difficulties we encountered with XP on this project and the ways we dealt with them. Despite these difficulties, however, and despite our deviations from some core XP practices, I show how we experienced sufficient success to recommend similar methodologies for large projects in the future.

Research Hypotheses

In our effort to implement XP on this large project, we proceeded on the following assumptions.

1. The story cards and the resulting code that developed as part of the iterative, XP process would be a sufficient guide for everyone on the team to understand the whole application.
2. Dividing application functionality into story cards that would fit into our iterative plan could be learned once and then reapplied for all subsequent iterations.
3. We would be able to identify easily the single customer who would drive the planning game for this XP process.
4. The customer we identified would be able to drive the planning game and be the primary author of all functional tests developed to verify completion of new functionality.

Each of these assumptions or hypotheses is grounded in one or more of the core XP practices, so we felt confident that we could make these assumptions as part of our switch to this new methodology.

Description of the Context of the Experience

The case I discuss is a large Java 2 Platform, Enterprise Edition (J2EE) development project that switched to an XP approach about halfway through its three-year life. In the 50-person team on this project, there are about 30 developers, eight quality assurance testers, and eight analysts. The application being built is a comprehensive, "back-end" leasing system, a product that will manage everything from the moment a lease is booked through the eventual disposal of the leased assets. This includes all aspects of accounts receivable, asset management, and lease termination, not to mention the million-and-one possible ways the laws allow people to fashion a lease for renting something to someone. The application now consists of over 500,000 lines of executable code. Our initial customer/user is the leasing arm of a traditional, Fortune 500 company, but we are partnering with that first user to offer a more generic version of the application for the leasing industry as a whole.

Results from the Experience

Hypothesis 1

The first challenge I address is the difficulty we encountered because no holistic picture of the application was available to everyone during the development process. Although much planning and analysis had been performed before our project switched to an XP approach, once that approach was adopted, our primary roadmap was the set of story cards we developed and arranged in a large spreadsheet. At best, a more holistic picture of the application existed in the minds of those analysts on our team with extensive experience in the leasing business. But for those without such experience, which included most members of the team, the application appeared as a collection of independent parts, without a clear image of their connection in a whole. We refrained from developing any more up-front documentation or a graphic of the whole application to reap the purported benefit of XP's "agility." The story cards, we thought, would be enough of a guide.

But the absence of a readily available, holistic picture in this case contributed to a number of problems. Because leasing has exceptionally complex business logic, which is often counterintuitive, team members without direct business experience in leasing tended not to understand how their particular stories fit in with or depended on other stories in the whole scheme of things. Thus, when they were charged with implementing new stories, they often left out tests that would verify proper functioning of the newer stories in conjunction with the older ones previously developed. As the iterations accumulated and the complexity of the system grew, even our analysts with extensive leasing experience were frustrated by not knowing sufficiently how the parts were connected to be able to write sufficient tests to verify completed stories. So as you might expect, new cards were often "finished" in the eyes of their owners when, in fact, they were not.

When this became evident, we wrote new story cards to cover what we had missed. But there was a general feeling of frustration among card owners when they discovered they had missed some dependency and, at some times, minimal inclination to acknowledge that their card actually included the dependencies in question. A common response from many team members to the difficult task of developing and testing a new bit of functionality in all its entanglements with existing functionality was to quip, "Why don't we just use the XP approach?" The implication is that XP looks at the whole as a collection of atomistic stories—stories that can be treated as independent of one another. Although that may tend to be the case in some simpler applications, it was hardly the case in this one.

As the application grew in size and complexity with each new iteration, the amount of "analysis" required to compose a sufficient list of tests for each new story increased tremendously. Developers and analysts both tended to know the local functionality of a finite number of stories or sections of code, but hardly anyone had a comfortable grasp of how it was all connected, despite the extensive lines of communication among team members. For new members joining the team after the beginning of the project, the effort to understand the significance of the part without knowing the whole was especially daunting.

What was lacking, we think, was some easily accessible "picture" of the whole so that both developers and analysts adopting a new story could readily "see" what sort of connections with other parts they would have to test to complete the card. This would not have had to be a static picture that was produced before the first line of code was written. But at the very least, it would have had to be something that was available in an updated, cumulative form at the beginning of each iteration so that story owners could take their bearings and reliably estimate the scope of the stories and the requisite tests. No one could conceive of a usable "metaphor" to help "everyone on the project understand the basic elements and their relationships" [Beck2000], because leasing is too complex a business to be productively communicated through a simpler image. A more traditional picture or graphic was needed and would have helped us tremendously, but producing and maintaining it would have forced us to divert resources to the sort of design overhead that XP deemphasizes for the sake of agility.

To be sure, some of the difficulties here are the fault of the nature and size of our project. Less complex business domains are more easily described with metaphoric images, and less complex applications will have many fewer dependencies among stories. Nonetheless, we found ourselves too easily lulled into the belief that most stories are independent of one another [Beck+2001] and that we could find a useful metaphor for a very complex system. If XP is to be used for developing complex applications, we suggest some mechanism for constantly reminding everyone that functionality divided into distinct stories does not imply the independence of the stories. This is where a single, integrated "picture" needs to supplement a spreadsheet of separable story cards.

Hypothesis 2

Related to this problem was the difficulty we encountered in dividing the whole into story cards. To borrow an image from Plato, as well as from your own kitchen, you would think the division of the whole application into its story parts would be like cutting a whole chicken into its familiar pieces. Even though the joints may not be immediately visible, there are places to do the dividing that are more appropriate than others. But if you are cutting up the chicken for the first time, as I recall I once did in my parents' kitchen, you may encounter great difficulty because you do not know where the joints are.

It took us a good deal of practice to find the joints, particularly because we had many different cues for locating them. One cue we used was to divide into cards in ways that worked well in earlier iterations. Although this tended to work well early on, as the application grew in size and complexity, it became unreliable. The sort of functionality that was an independent chunk in iteration 4 had become, by iteration 14, intertwined with several other chunks that had been completed in the meantime. Thus, on more than one occasion, we discovered that we had missed testing one or more interactions because the list of story cards by itself did not include any built-in guide to interactions among past and present cards. Here again, a holistic picture of the whole application that would be updated regularly would have helped tremendously. Without this, we found ourselves devoting much time to continually reviewing and rewriting story cards to try to keep track of new functional interactions in the card texts. We eventually devoted one full-time analyst to developing and managing the story card list with our customer.

Another guide we used to distinguish story cards was to divide by bits of functionality that would produce some new, visible business value in the build we would deliver to the customer at the end of each iteration. The goal of this was to ensure that the customer could *see* ongoing progress. But dividing at these "joints" often turned out badly. For example, we played one story card early on entitled "Terminate lease billing schedule." At first glance, this distinct mechanism seemed like a perfect candidate for a story card because it encompassed a clear function that the customer could understand and actually use when finished. But as we began to implement it in a one-month iteration, we discovered that our desire to deliver the whole function at once led us to badly underestimate the time needed for the card. Luckily, the analyst for the card had devised her functional tests in such a way that we were able to divide the card into smaller cards along the lines of her functional tests. Thus, although the customer did not have the whole of the termination functionality available for use after one iteration, some testable part of it was finished. Over the next two iterations, the other, more granular cards were finished. In the process, however, we learned our lesson: not to divide automatically at joints of fully usable functionality. But this meant that we had to prepare our customer to be patient with partially finished business functions after certain iterations were completed.

From this experience, we perceived a precarious tension between two goals of XP. On the one hand, iterative development promotes the impression that the customer receives some level of a usable application at frequent intervals and can, as a result, decide to terminate a project at many stages and still walk away with an application having business value. On the other hand, the division of development into iterative chunks often makes it impossible to deliver functionality that the customer can actually use for his business at the end of any particular iteration. In the case of our "Terminate lease billing schedule" example, the chunk we delivered at the end of the first iteration could be used and tested, but from a business perspective, it was valueless without the other chunks that were completed in subsequent iterations.

In sum, dividing story cards well means not following any particular guide too rigidly. To return to the example of the joints of the chicken, if you insist on quartering a chicken, some of the cuts may be easy because they happen to fall at natural joints, but that last cut through the breastbone will create much additional toil. We found that trying to adhere too rigidly to dividing cards by deliverable functionality or by past experience often created more toil rather than less.

Hypothesis 3

Our customer/partner for this project devoted a team of its employees full-time to this project, but they were not on-site with our development team. This fact contributed to expected problems in the efficiency of communication between customer and developer, but these were not the most difficult challenges that confronted us in this area. Because of the breadth and complexity of the application, it was impossible for us to have the XP ideal of a customer who was also an end user. In a typical leasing business, the person responsible for managing accounts receivable for its customers is not the person who handles end-of-lease transactions or the person who books the original lease. The application we were building, however, required a "customer" who was simultaneously familiar with all these dimensions of the business and with how all of them needed to work together. Moreover, our customer's business was itself divided into multiple leasing divisions, and no two of them had identical business processes or requirements. To top that off, the way our customer did business often deviated from typical practices in the leasing industry as a whole.

This meant that our customer was in fact several distinct and different "customers," each having peculiar requirements that were not always compatible with one another. To be sure, much of this was due to the peculiar circumstance of our trying to build a custom product for one company and a generic product for an entire industry at the same time. Nonetheless, we suspect that more often than not, typical customers for larger applications will be more multifaceted than the ideal customer who speaks with a single voice.

To handle the competing "voices" among our various customers, we instituted "issue" cards in addition to development cards. The issue card stated the particular business function that needed to be addressed, and a team of business domain experts from our team and the customer's team met periodically to resolve how the functionality should be developed. When some agreement was finally reached, the issue card was then turned into the appropriate story cards. Here again, though, the complexity of our project added another weight that reduced the agility of XP on this project.

Hypothesis 4

The fact that our customer, despite its multifaceted nature, should determine the functionality of the system we built was never an issue, and they felt comfortable in that role. But when it came time for the customer team to develop the set of functional tests that would prove the completion of functionality they had requested, their comfort level was much lower. Part of this, we think, was due to the prevalent view among nontechnical professionals that computer applications are complex and difficult, so it's OK to use them but scary to peek at all under the covers. We made an extraordinary effort to convince our customer's team that they needed to not just specify the functionality to build, but also develop the tests to verify its completion. They eventually did so, but only after having relied on many, many samples from our own analysts for a long time. They were just not used to the analytic process a typical software analyst would go through when figuring out how many tests covering which functions would constitute a complete verification of this new card.

There was a clear difference, in our mind, between devising a business scenario and devising a functional test. In the former case, you make sure that, say, when you dispose of a particular asset from inventory, the correct accounting transactions are performed. In the latter case, you verify everything tested in the business scenario, but also verify the proper functioning of all negative and atypical actions that could occur in the process—widget action on screens, behind-the-scenes dependencies, and so on. Our customer team did not need much coaching to provide us with the business scenarios, but the functional test itself, in all its detail, required us to do much more training with the customer than we had anticipated. In this respect, we think the typical description of the ideal XP customer working directly with the developer, although surely true in some cases, is not typical and thus underestimates the need for the traditional analyst intermediary.

Where XP Worked Well

Despite the various ways in which we found XP in need of supplemental procedures and artifacts for our unusual project, we came to appreciate many of its basic practices. The fact that we were forced to articulate and develop the functional tests at the beginning of the development process in an iteration was very healthy. Too often, when functionality is designed first and tests devised only much later after development, there is a disconnect between the original design and the tests. Reducing this time to a short iteration makes that discrepancy less likely to arise.

The frequency of deadlines in the iterative process tended to keep us focused and productive on the particular cards we had adopted. We tried to find the optimal iteration length for our project, starting first with one-month iterations (which seemed a bit too long) and then changing to two-week iterations (which seemed a bit too short). Our individual focus was also encouraged greatly by the fact that owners of tasks were responsible for estimating those same cards. It was much more difficult for someone to acknowledge that something could not meet a deadline when that confession also implied that the person had estimated the task badly. We soon learned that task estimation and ownership need to extend not just to developers, but to all roles in the project.

The practice of giving individuals ownership of their own problems also made it possible for several individuals to employ their peculiar intelligence to solve many problems. One case in particular stands out. We attempted to implement one card dealing with a very complicated piece of functionality during iteration 6, and it soon became apparent that the original strategy we had developed would be cumbersome and, in the end, perhaps unacceptable. Seeing this, we assigned time to one of our business domain analysts to "think through" the card again and propose an alternative way of implementing the functionality. He figured out a substantially more elegant and efficient way to implement the functionality on the card—something that would not have been possible had we felt obliged to implement exactly what we had been told to do.

This case led us to introduce "analysis" cards in addition to regular development cards. For particularly complex bits of functionality, typically with many dependencies, we estimated analysis time for someone during an iteration to flesh out carefully all the test cases that would be needed for implementing the card in question. During the subsequent iteration, that card was played like any other card. The amount of time required to think through a sufficient list of functional tests for cards varied greatly from card to card, so we had to implement provisions like this to accommodate those differences.

What to Do Next

From our experience on this development project, we do not mean to imply that XP fails to work for large and complex application development. Instead, we only point out that many of the basic practices of

XP are quite useful in such projects, but they need to be supplemented with some "heavier" methodology to work well. A list of story cards, if it becomes too large and complicated, needs to be supplemented with a holistic "picture" to ensure that the cards are managed, updated, and ordered well. More importantly, you must carefully watch the dependencies among stories as the list and complexity of story cards grow. Metaphors can go so far, but the complexity they can communicate is limited. A "customer," if it has many facets, needs someone to facilitate communication among the camps, manage the reconciliation of incompatible voices, and provide business expertise from a global perspective. All these examples point to the fact that you should be prepared for reduced "agility" from XP, as well as unforeseen challenges, when it is implemented for particularly complex or large application development.

But our experience also speaks to the issue I raised at the outset of this chapter: Is there a place for analysis in XP? From the experiences I have recounted here, it should be apparent that our use of XP on a large and complex development project forced us to institute roles and procedures that are not clearly envisioned in the common list of XP practices and roles. Thus, it made sense for us to include a team of traditional analysts in this project to fill these and other related roles. Of particular importance in this case was the complexity of the business logic in this particular application. The customer's team on this project provided considerable guidance in defining what was built, but they needed assistance from business experts with a broader perspective and from traditional software analysts to articulate clearly and completely in a set of functional tests what the system needed to do.

To help avoid disagreements with our diverse customer and to articulate more completely the dependencies among parts described in story cards, we needed to produce more traditional artifacts in addition to the story cards and functional tests. For each story card, we developed a separate, more detailed description of the functionality involved, its business purpose, its impact on other parts of the application already developed, and any additional specifics needed to direct the developers. This document was accessible online to all parties involved and often helped resolve misunderstandings or uncertainties that could not be determined by examining the story card by itself. Were we to initiate a similar project of this size in the future, I suspect we would devote even more manpower to the production of more traditional artifacts of analysis so that the XP practices we found productive could be employed once again successfully at this scale.

References

[Beck2000] K. Beck. *Extreme Programming Explained.* Addison-Wesley, 2000.

[Beck+2001] K. Beck, M. Fowler. *Planning Extreme Programming.* Addison-Wesley, 2001.

Acknowledgments

It was my ThoughtWorks colleague Martin Fowler who encouraged me to communicate this experience to a wider audience, and it was my fellow analyst Terri Hollar who helped me articulate parts of that experience. I am indebted to both for their assistance, as well as to the rest of my colleagues on this project at ThoughtWorks for their continual support.

About the Author

Gregory Schalliol began programming in the 1970s before he took a career diversion into academic philosophy that only recently ended with his return to the software development industry. He worked for over a year at ThoughtWorks, Inc., as a business analyst on the project described in this chapter before becoming a project manager for implementation activities connected with this software application. Gregory can be reached at glschall@speakeasy.net.

Chapter 33

XP on a Large Project—A Developer's View

—*Amr Elssamadisy*

At ThoughtWorks we have adopted a modified version of XP that has been tailored through our experiences to suit a large project of over 35 developers, eight analysts, and seven quality assurance (QA) testers. This project, a leasing application that we internally called ATLAS, started three years ago with the standard analysis and design front-loading of traditional development projects. This chapter is written from a developer's point of view—the experiences and the techniques that were tried and either became habit because they were useful or never quite caught on. We take the different practices that are encouraged by XP in Kent Beck's Extreme Programming Explained *[Beck2000] and give our feedback on each practice. Then, in summarizing, we recommend what changes must be made to the XP process to be able to use this methodology and still produce quality code at a fast pace for a large project.*

Research Hypotheses

The project had a reference strategy—we had certain expectations in embarking on the XP process with this project. These expectations, although never explicitly communicated, were the following:

1. Give our client positive feedback via quick releases to get more buy-in.
2. Be able to "manage expectations" more easily because of the client's constant involvement in making decisions about functionality.
3. Have a better-quality product. Because this decision was made on a project that was on a death march, we hoped to not only revive it but make it a thriving project.
4. Get away from integration problems caused by several subteams working on their own functionality and then having the pieces "come together" at the end for a fully functioning product.
5. Finally, and most importantly, *deliver* a quality product on time that addresses our client's needs and will be used successfully by the business for years to come.

Description of the Context of the Experience

As briefly described in the introduction, this is an experience report of our work at ThoughtWorks, Inc., in delivering a large distributed leasing application. Therefore, the context of the experience is basically a large, real-world project with real clients, real developers, and real deadlines. Before starting on XP, the developers had little or no exposure to the development process and were working in a typical development environment, with the analysis already done and documented, and business sections split among independent teams. Our experience is applicable to any project in similar circumstances. These circumstances are as follows:

- A large development team (our specific numbers varied over time, but typically about 35 developers, eight business analysts, and seven quality assurance testers)
- A large application (currently about 600,000 noncommented source lines in 6,500 classes)

- Good communication between team members
- An open environment, with team members able to say what works and what doesn't

Results from the Experience

Ok, now we get to the good stuff. The team of developers and analysts consists of approximately 35 developers, eight business analysts, and seven QA testers. The developers rely on the analysts to be the customers of the project. There is a real customer, however, and the analysts work with them to collectively make customer decisions. Tables 33.1 and 33.2 show the elements of XP as discussed in [Beck2000] and briefly describe how each aspect was being used at different stages in the project. We use these tables to analyze our team's natural selection of practices and explain how textbook XP evolved on a large project to support a 50-person team that has taken a project to completion.

After examining these tables, we notice that almost all the practices have evolved over 18 months. Some have stabilized, because we see many "same as above" entries in columns such as Continuous Integration and On-site Customer. So, after 18 months on a 50-person team, what are our recommendations and lessons learned?

1. Have an iteration planning meeting at the beginning of each iteration, where the customer and developers split into groups all day to discuss the latest story cards and estimate them. At the end of the day, regroup to present your estimates and findings, and then have developer sign-up. This will keep the whole team in the know about what is happening without burdening everyone with an extremely tedious and long meeting.
2. Keep releases as small as possible—two weeks works for us—but at the same time be flexible when larger pieces need to be done over several iterations. Allow sign-up for a multiple iteration card, but always review progress at every iteration.
3. Write as many unit tests as you can—that is self-evident. You should also have an automated suite of functional tests to keep the test coverage at an acceptable rate. A QA team cannot be replaced, no matter how many tests developers write; we are flawed in our biased understanding of how the system works or should work.

TABLE 33.1 Use of XP Practices during the Project (First Six Practices)

	Planning	Release Cycle	Metaphor	Design Simplicity	Testing	Refactoring
1/2000	Large iteration planning meetings. Full team of developers and analysts met for an entire day to discuss new story cards and estimate. Most developers sign up for new functionality.	One month	None	Transitioning with an existing code base. Existing code still complex, but new code as simple as possible. This phase included throwing out and rewriting existing functionality that "someday might be used."	Unit tests started with some of the new code. Push being made to have a large test base. QA does all functional tests and has the authority to pass/fail a story card.	Refactoring done as needed when touching old code.
7/2000	Same as 1/2000, but definitely feels very inefficient. Most attendees not concentrating or participating. Long, drawn-out discussions. Fifty-person meeting is overwhelming.	One month	None	Designs continuing to be as simple as possible. Refactorings of existing designs being done. Code reviews being done to collectively discuss new designs so that the whole team is familiar with coding/design trends.	Better unit test coverage but still not full coverage. Coded Functional Tests (CFTs) to help test coverage.	Most developers are heads-down in delivering functionality, very little refactoring done. Code base getting worse at end-of-iteration crunch to deliver cards to QA.

1/2001	Try making iteration planning meetings faster—by doing more prep work with small groups of developers before the actual meetings.	Two weeks	None	Most of the designs built on existing designs—standards kept, code reviews tapered off because new types of designs/refactorings not being done.	Attempted to get rid of CFTs and replace with a screen scraper and failed—went back to CFTs. New unit tests being added, but coverage still lacking. QA starts to automate functional tests with screen scraper.	Refactorings being done much more often as code starts to spaghetti in some parts of the app. Major clean-ups being done because implemented simply, and then iteration deadlines caused code to grow without the important refactorings being done.
6/2001	Several meetings for cards/sets of related cards between developers interested in or knowledgeable about the functionality and analysts who are responsible for the story card.	Two weeks	None	Large part of the team and all of QA working on delivering version 1.0 to the customer. Code base split and new functionality being added without QA. More reliance on unit tests.	Test coverage seems to have stabilized at a level that is lacking. QA has been out of the loop with new functionality because of focusing entirely on version 1.0 delivery.	Refactorings on the release are minimal, while on the continuing product branch developers are refactoring more conscientiously after being forced to do larger, more painful refactorings earlier in the year.

Table continued on next page.

TABLE 33.1 *Continued*

	Pair Programming	Collective Ownership	Continuous Integration	40-Hour Week	On-site Customer	Coding Standards
1/2000	Because we decided to use XP, the entire team read (Beck2000) and were encouraged to pair program. Everyone tried it, and it caught on with most of the team.	In the initial phase, we were moving from function-oriented groups, so we did not feel collective ownership, but also did not feel protective of our code.	Online from iteration 1. See (Fowler+2000).	This was a proof-of-concept work, and we wanted the client onboard. So a lot of extra hours were put in to meet the deadline.	Business analysts are the on-site customer. Fifteen analysts on the team. The actual client was off-site, and the analysts communicated with them.	None, other than normal Java syntax.
7/2000	Pair programming still strong; developers are pair programming for new functionality, but bugs and maintenance have developers working solo. Some programmers stop pair programming altogether.	Ownership of code is completely diluted as more developers touch different pieces of the app. Very good communication takes place via informal chats, code reviews, and short stand-up meetings.	CFTs also added to the build process.	Cyclic hours hitting 50- and 60-hour weeks at the end of each iteration to try to pass the story card.	Same as above.	Biweekly code reviews give developers a chance to discuss ways that different subsystems are being implemented where we agree on informal ways of coding similar parts of the system.

1/2001	Pair programming definitely less because more of the coding is straightforward or because a developer is refactoring a piece of code.	Stand-up meetings are dropped for being inefficient, but code ownership remains diluted. Developers start specializing in parts of the system again.	Stable—same as above.	With two-week iterations, developer estimates become more accurate and closer to a 40-hour week.	Same as above.	Code reviews tapered off; saturation of design/coding standards.
6/2001	Definite trend of almost all new functionality being pair programmed and almost all debugging/maintenance being done by a single developer.	With specialization, there is a trend of a small set of developers knowing more about different parts of the code—so we tend to have them be more active in the continuing designs, but still have communal ownership of the code.	Stable—same as above.	Same as above.	Same as above.	Same as above.

4. Simple designs have helped us consistently release a working product to the customer. Frequent design meetings (lunch is the best way to gather the development team) are very helpful during stages of adding intense new functionality. This helps prevent implementing parallel and maybe incompatible solutions in different parts of the application.
5. Refactoring is the only way to be able to have simple designs as stated in item 4. Refactoring of designs is just as important as refactoring of the code. It will always be tempting to not refactor and to just patch a solution, but if it is patched too much, the team will be forced to make major refactorings later on.
6. Pair programming should be religiously followed when new functionality is added and should be skipped when fixing bugs or doing repetitive tasks that have already been "solved" before by a pair of developers.
7. Collective ownership goes hand in hand with communication. The team must figure out a way to communicate effectively. It may be no more than just informal discussions, which worked best for our team; otherwise, regular stand-up meetings that last for ten to 15 minutes are a good way to disseminate information.
8. With a large project, a group of individuals are needed to be the customer, to generate enough work for the large number of developers. This strictly depends on the where the business knowledge is.
9. Coding standards have been very informal, and this has not been detrimental to our progress. What is more important is communication of ongoing work through presentations. Code is not documentation enough—developers need to see the big picture also, and that cannot be relayed through code.

We also found that the following things didn't work for us.

1. Biweekly stand-up meetings were not efficient. We opted for informal communication with once-a-month iteration team meetings.
2. Full team meetings during the iteration planning meeting did not work. A day of small group meetings, with a 30- to 45-minute review of the cards at the end of the day, worked better.

3. One-month iterations were too long and were detrimental to code quality. We moved to two-week iterations, which are easier to track and make estimations more accurate.
4. The approach in item 3 does not work all the time for larger chunks of code, especially when refactoring a large part of the system. So exceptions are made when one card spans several iterations.
5. Metaphors are unrealistic in large projects. They are just too complex. Period.
6. A 40-hour week has never been an issue for us. Forty hours is the minimum, and we have not been adversely affected by working more than 40 hours, but then again, we are not pair programming 100% of the time.

What about the hypotheses? Where do we stand *after* completing the project that we set out to recover two years ago by going to XP? How does reality compare with our initial expectations? We initially listed five major points that we hoped to gain by using XP, and here is where we stand today looking back.

1. We received tremendous buy-in from our customer, which resulted from our involving the client very heavily in decision making throughout the development cycle.
2. "Managing expectations" was much easier because of the incremental releases. When things fell behind, we didn't just say, "Oh, we are six months behind." But as functionality slipped at the end of each iteration, the client knew and was part of the planning to adjust our plan to reality.
3. To be honest, the quality of the product is better but definitely not as good as we hoped. The main fault here is that we were *not* rigorous about adding tests.
4. Integration problems are not an issue anymore. Collective ownership has given developers the knowledge and ability to work on all the code, and small iterations have always kept the product in a condition to be delivered to the client.
5. We have successfully delivered two separate releases of the application as of February 2002. The application is live and in production, being used for the daily business operations of our client. This,

above all, is what we gained from XP. Without it, we would have never been able to sustain the momentum for such a large and complex application while at the same time remaining flexible enough to give the client what they *really* needed.

That's it. XP, or our evolved version of it, has done wonders for us as a team. We have already delivered our product to our client, where it is being used to manage their day-to-day business successfully. The users find real value in the product because, in the end, we have delivered something that they really want and need, not just what they thought they needed a little over two years ago.

What to Do Next

Basically, at least for the development teams at ThoughtWorks, Inc., we will do more of the same. Since originally presenting the information in this chapter at XP Universe, we have written a paper that is a continuation of this experience [Elssamadisy+2001]. It addresses problems that we found with XP and specific mistakes that we made, and recommends solutions for them.

Also, there is a lack of literature that addresses the database administrator (team) in XP. This is mainly because XP is targeted toward smaller projects in which the developers also do the database administration tasks. But when applying XP to larger projects, as we have, many issues need to be addressed and explored.

References

[Beck2000] K. Beck. *Extreme Programming Explained.* Addison-Wesley, 2000.

[Fowler+2000] M. Fowler, M. Foemmel. *Continuous Integration.* http://www.martinfowler.com/articles/continuousIntegration.html. 2000.

[Elssamadisy+2001] A. Elssamadisy, G. Schalliol. *Recognizing and Responding to "Bad Smells" in Extreme Programming.* http://www.thoughtworks.com/library/index.html. 2001.

Acknowledgments

None of this work could have been done without the great development team we have at ThoughtWorks, Inc. I wish to thank every person on the team for making the experience at TW so valuable and fun.

About the Author

Amr Elssamadisy is a software developer at ThoughtWorks, Inc.

Part IV

Chapter 34

A Customer Experience: Implementing XP

—Ann Griffin

The Internet company described here began implementation of XP as its development process in December 2000, in parallel with other significant organizational changes. This chapter describes the many physical and organizational changes that occurred both to enable XP implementation and as a result of XP implementation. Implementation challenges as well as benefits of the XP process are discussed, and recommendations are provided for those considering implementing XP.

Part IV

"The Company" was incorporated in December 1999 to provide secure transaction settlement services for business and consumer e-commerce sites. "Version 1," the consumer-to-consumer (C2C) initial "gold rush" system, was developed using a two-tier architecture of ASP/VBScript with Microsoft SQL Server. "Version 2" used the "ultimate" platform, a multitier architecture with an ASP front end, a Java/EJB middle tier, an Oracle database, and XML for external interfaces and "glue."

The Company's early systems development strategy, like that of many start-ups, was to complete product as quickly as possible. The development process was ad hoc, subject to frequent change, and without clear communication between the business and development teams. Despite considerable success with the first product release, by August 2000, the Company had difficulty delivering customer requirements on time, and the financial effects made it obvious that a more standardized development process was needed.

At that time, viewed within the Capability Maturity Matrix (CMM) [Zubrow+1994], the Company was at Level 1. To summarize Level 1:

> *At the Initial level, the organization . . . does not provide a stable environment for developing and maintaining software . . . The Benefits of good software engineering practices are undermined by ineffective planning and reaction-driven commitment systems.* [Zubrow+1994]

To correct this untenable situation, the Company decided to implement XP as its development process. Implementation began in December 2000.

Research Hypotheses

In this industrial experience, the research hypotheses are phrased in terms of business goals for introducing XP. Achieving the goals or not is equivalent to proving or disproving the research hypotheses.

The organization's goals were as follows:

- *Goal 1:* Make the development team more responsive to business needs and pressures by delivering software and features requested by business users.
- *Goal 2:* Increase the speed at which releases occur, and reduce the error rate in released versions.
- *Goal 3:* Improve the development cycle flow by increasing communications, clarifying roles, and expecting the development team to achieve set goals.
- *Goal 4:* Improve the Company's financial situation by delivering marketable products in a timelier manner.

Description of the Context of the Experience

Preparation

The Company hired Object Mentor to provide training and on-site mentoring. The first iteration and release planning games were scheduled for January 2001. The Company had the necessary human resources in-house, consisting of 14 developers, four product managers, and three quality assurance (QA) specialists. The Company created a lab area for pair programming, with walls for posting stories, and a large whiteboard.

Object Mentor coaches spent three days per week at the workplace, providing training, advice, and encouragement. They were heavily involved in guiding employees through the first release and iteration planning sessions. Their time with the Company decreased gradually to two days per week, and by early March 2001, their on-site time ended, although they were available by phone or e-mail as needed. The start and end of the first iteration was timed so that Object Mentor coaches would be on-site on those days.

Product managers, the on-site customers, were to be the connection point to internal and external stakeholders. They would write stories and determine which stories would go in a release, based on the Company priorities.

QA staff would write tests for stories instead of creating tests for already produced code, as they had done previously. QA tests would be available to developers at the beginning of each iteration.

The developers would experience the most upheaval in their day-to-day work. Supervisory developer positions were to be eliminated, although those in the positions were retained, but the perceived demotion engendered resentment toward XP. Developers would work in pairs, lacking the privacy of cubicles. They were expected to write tests before writing code, whereas previously, they wrote few, if any, tests and not until they finished a project.

One staff member would record all stories, tasks, estimates, and who was responsible for each task. She would provide accurate information on velocity for each developer, each story, and each iteration.

Iteration 1

Getting estimates for the first release took a day and a half, with developers forming four groups and each group providing an estimate for every story. The developers did not understand the big business picture the stories represented and became bogged down in issues of business and design.

Customers' early stories lacked sufficient detail to describe the problem clearly and did not always provide a business solution to the problem. Here is an early story.

> *Suggest using some status indicator for where participants are at in terms of agreeing/modifying/viewing a transaction in the event that other participants (multi-buyer/seller config) are unable or unwilling to acknowledge a transaction (or not even receive e-mail).* (Starteam, CR 352)

The product managers prioritized the estimated stories and grouped them into four iterations, making up the first release. Then they obtained task estimates for the stories in the first iteration, a process almost as difficult as the first high-level estimation process. Once the task estimates were done, sign-up followed quickly, and work began on the iteration.

The developers previously had made many business decisions, and this responsibility was taken away from them. Despite their stated desire for better business input, this was a rough transition. Many of them did not like pair programming or test-first design. In time, developers who remained uncomfortable with the process chose to leave the organization. The product managers, on the other hand, welcomed the increased communication and ownership of the business content.

At the end of iteration 1, the actual development time of 335 hours was much lower than the estimate of 598.5 hours. The developers delivered the cleanest code that had yet been tested by QA. The stories that were promised for the iteration were, with one exception, completed. Product managers were confident that the product delivered was what they had requested.

Iteration 2

Suddenly, business priorities changed drastically. All the stories previously scheduled for iterations 2, 3, and 4 were pushed aside as two new projects moved to top priority. The product managers were not prepared for this extreme change, so they had to rush to develop adequate stories and obtain estimates for them. Task estimates were approximately half the time of the original story estimates, so customers did not have sufficient stories prepared to load the iteration, having based their iteration velocity on the original story estimates. Actual times for iteration 2 tasks were still significantly lower than estimated task times: 178 hours actual versus 285.5 hours estimated (see Figure 34.1). Some scrambling ensued during the first week to add more stories to fill up the iteration. However, this experience proved that XP can handle rapid changes in business priorities.

Stand-up meetings settled into a regular routine, although the product managers had to be reminded to include QA in their story-writing activities and, especially, to inform QA of all changes to the story.

The specialization of the development team emerged as a challenge. Because developers signed up for tasks according to their specialties—front end (ASP), middleware (Java), or back end (Oracle)—work was not evenly distributed. Some developers were overloaded, but others did not have enough to do; yet they resisted working across areas of specialization. It did not make sense for customers to choose their stories based on the availability of developers, so management began discussing alternatives.

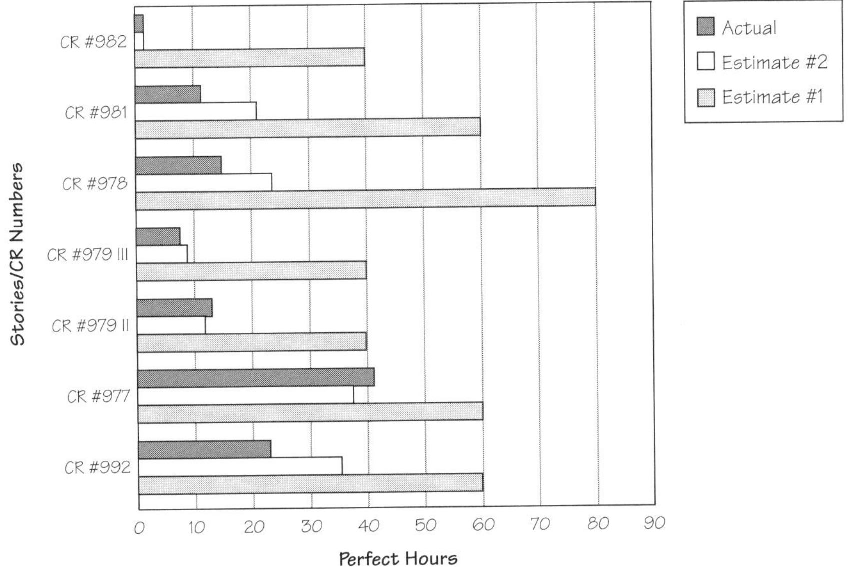

FIGURE 34.1 Actual times for iteration 2 tasks were significantly lower than estimated task times.

Part IV

Iteration 3

By iteration 3, most team members were more comfortable with the XP process. Iteration planning meetings shrank from one day to two to three hours. Product managers presented a high-level business overview to the development team at the planning meeting, laying the groundwork for stories to fit into a project. Stories were presented for estimation on flip-chart-size Post-it note pads rather than index cards. Story quality improved. Here is an example.

> *Action when participant clicks "disagree" on escrow instructions:*
>
> *—MUST show up on history log.*
> *—Change button text to "disagree/cancel."*
> *—Change message at the top of screen to:*
>
> *"A participant has disagreed with this transaction. This action has closed the transaction." (Starteam, CR 1265)*

Because estimates were still not very accurate, product managers routinely prepared more stories than they thought would be needed for the iteration, to ensure it would be filled up immediately. However, product managers had to allocate velocity to competing customer projects that continued to fluctuate in priority from one iteration to another.

Challenges and Changes

By the end of iteration 3, several problems had to be addressed: uneven workloads for developers because of their different roles, lower productivity than needed to achieve company goals because of inaccurate estimating, and continually shifting project priorities. Therefore, management broke the development team into three teams, each one led by a product manager and responsible for a specific project.

Two projects involved creation of a new code base, so those teams were better able to apply XP principles of unit testing than the team working on the legacy code. The team members working on the old code base were selected in part for their resistance to XP. They did not write unit tests and did little pair programming. This team initially appeared to make more rapid progress in stories completed than the other two teams. However, at release time, the advantages of XP became obvious. The XP-resistant team's code required a three-week test/fix/retest cycle before a release to production could be made.

Each team had separate stand-up meetings and separate planning meetings. The planning meetings became much shorter—about one hour—and more focused. The ability of developers to accurately estimate stories and tasks improved. One team's estimate was 103 hours, compared with an actual time of 72.1 hours, for iteration 10.

There was no longer competition between product managers for developer velocity, because each had their own team. Iterations were changed from two weeks to one week, although after about a month, they returned to two-week iterations because the weekly format took too much planning time.

Documentation

Initially, product managers used index cards, recommended by XP proponents. Because the Company used Starteam 4.2 as its version control and tracking software, stories on cards became CRs (change requests) in Starteam. Product managers eventually reduced use of index cards and focused on CRs. They were easier to track, easier for multiple users to access, easier to modify, and eliminated duplication of effort.

Stories posted in the lab for the developers were written on flip-chart-size Post-it note pads, with CR numbers and a title. Developers added tasks to each CR, their time estimates, and who was responsible for the task. Each task was checked off when finished.

Release notes contained the stories for a given release, but a traditional "feature guide" was created for external use.

Results of the Experience

Customers in a traditional development project count on schedule slippage. One of the Company's customers was surprised and pleased to learn that actual time came in at 120 hours for her project, with all stories finished ahead of schedule, instead of the estimated 200 hours. The customer, though, had slipped her own target date, and her inability to take advantage of the new available product contributed to the Company's financial struggles.

Executives enjoyed a new level of control over the end product of developers. Harder to accept was that "You still can't have it all at once." It was challenging to allow developers to set their own time estimates instead of operating to business agendas not based on the capacity of the development team.

The product management process was realigned to enable the product managers to drive the development process and to own the features under development.

The Company, at the time of writing, had passed its twentieth iteration of XP. In a space of five months, the organization leaped from Level 1 in the CMM to Level 4, in which:

> *An organization-wide software process database is used to collect and analyze the data available from the projects' defined software processes ... the process is measured and operates within measurable limits. This level of process capability allows an organization to predict trends in process and product quality within the quantitative bounds of these limits.* [Zubrow+1994]

Goals 1, 2, and 3 had been achieved, but goal 4 had not.

Goal 1: Making the Development Team More Responsive

The team changed priorities with very little notice and provided customers with what they requested.

The team demonstrated results and provided product for customers ahead of schedule.

Goal 2: Increasing Speed and Reducing the Error Rate

One team, at the time of writing, had created over 1,000 unit tests. A release required running all 1,000 tests, plus user acceptance tests. The increased degree of control of testing at all levels increased the degree of confidence in the product.

The quality of developer output increased significantly for those teams writing unit tests and programming in pairs. This is measured by the number of user acceptance tests that failed after release to QA, which was close to zero for those teams.

Goal 3: Improving Development Cycle Flow

Customer ability to determine development priorities increased the customers' confidence in their development unit.

Prioritization, at a corporate overall strategic level, a project level, or a story level, became easier as skill at estimation improved.

Creation of smaller development teams, with each team responsible for a specific product, increased velocity and job satisfaction.

The level of communication among customers and developers increased greatly. Before XP, communication between customers and developers was actively discouraged, exacerbated by environmental barriers of separate rooms and floors. With XP, communication between customers and developers became constant.

Goal 4: Improving the Company's Financial Situation

The Company did not achieve the improved financial position it sought. Factors other than XP, both internal and external, were more influential on the Company. The Company experienced several layoffs during the time period described, and its survival is not ensured at the time of writing.

Other Observations

Extreme flexibility places heavier responsibility on executives to produce adequate strategic plans. Responding to sudden changes is part of XP, but requiring extreme changes for each iteration is usually not sound business practice.

The lack of emphasis on documentation within XP does not take into account end-user needs for documentation, including user guides, integration kits, references texts, and fact sheets.

Part IV

What to Do Next

- Organizations considering XP may benefit from the Company's experience by considering these points.
- XP will provide a superior development methodology. It will not replace the need for market research, a strategic plan, and sound

business decision making, nor will it mitigate the effects of poor business practice.

- Training for all affected staff, from executives on down, is vital.
- Get buy-in from key participants, including the development team, *before* implementation. If you fail to do this, be prepared to pay a price that will undermine XP's performance in your workplace. Consider hiring a change management consultant to assist.
- Make the necessary physical changes to the workplace to foster two key tenets of XP: pair programming and constant customer-developer communication.
- Keep the customer in charge of what is developed and when.
- To demonstrate quickly the benefits of XP, implement it first on a new project with no legacy code.
- If implementing XP on software that has legacy code, be prepared to take extra time to write unit tests and to refactor that code.
- Reward people for their efforts.
- Create documentation that meets your corporate needs. Beware, however, of slipping back into the "old ways" of wanting all functionality defined before anything is developed.
- Collect data and share it.
- XP is not only for developers. It is essential that customers at all levels understand it and embrace it.

Acknowledgments

This chapter reflects a real workplace experience with XP, and many people have contributed indirectly to it by their actions and comments in the Company's XP environment. Contributions especially by Paul Hodgetts, Michael Kilcoyne, Denise Phillips, and Jeanne Bennett are gratefully acknowledged.

References

[Zubrow+1994] D. Zubrow, W. Hayes, J. Siegel, D. Goldensen. *Maturity Questionnaire*. Software Engineering Institute, 1994.

About the Author

Ann Griffin is a project manager who has worked on Internet, semiconductor manufacturing, and large-scale client-server projects. She came to the world of computing late in her career, having started as a psychologist and rehabilitation therapist, but became hooked on software development when she was asked to be a business expert (a "customer") for a government project in British Columbia, Canada. Her understanding of human behavior gave her a unique insight into some of the challenges experienced at the Company when it implemented XP. An enthusiastic proponent of the customer role in XP, she may be reached at anniegriffin@charter.net. She resides in Long Beach, California.

Chapter 35

Learning by Doing: Why XP Doesn't Sell

—*Kay Johansen, Ron Stauffer, and Dan Turner*

If there isn't much value in Extreme Programming (XP), why is it enthusiastically—some might say fanatically—embraced by some people? Yet if there is value, why do so many others dismiss XP so readily? The authors' recent experience in implementing partial XP may provide some insight. Through experience, they became convinced of the value of the XP principles but also learned the difficulty of selling those principles to others who are absorbed in the prevailing software development culture and have not experienced the XP culture.

During the year 2000, the authors were the team lead, senior programmer, and product manager for an eight-month, six-developer project to deliver a major upgrade to a small to medium-sized enterprise software system.

Ron and Kay had spent many years in the high-tech field and had experienced the frustrations that are all too common in the development world, including:

- Impossible deadlines
- Death marches

- Late, inadequately tested releases
- Unrealistic feature and functionality promises to customers
- Good ideas never implemented
- Successful products becoming unmaintainable because of years of patch-and-fix programming

Research Hypotheses

Ron and Kay decided to try XP on this project, to test whether adhering to the principles of XP would help them overcome the major deficiencies they'd encountered on many other projects. They also believed that using XP would create a stronger team and an experience that they would remember with pleasure.

By the end of the project, all three authors had learned that XP had given them the ability to schedule the release with surprising accuracy, clarify the requirements as the project went along, write good code without spending time on debugging, and have an enjoyable team experience without working a lot of overtime. This was only half of the story, however. To get the other half of the story, Dan performed retrospective interviews with the other team members and with upper management to determine their interpretation of the experience. Their opinions were mixed. Some of the developers liked XP, some of them didn't, and the project was not really viewed as a success by management. Some conclusions drawn from this "mixed review" are presented at the end of this chapter.

Description of the Context of the Experience

The story begins at a small software development company, whose cash flow problems had just brought on a company restructuring and a quest for venture capital. Over their two-year history, the company had struggled with limited market share and had acquired a mind-set of saying "yes" to every customer request. This kept them afloat, barely, but the resulting urgent time frames and unmanaged "featuritis" had damaged the original product design and quality. In 1999, the company hired a new VP of engineering, who championed the need for change and created a protected environment where the development team would have the opportunity to experiment with new methods.

When Kay joined the company shortly thereafter, her first concern was that Ron was the sole survivor of the previous development team—the only one who knew anything about the code. Pressed by the need to understand the code quickly, she encouraged Ron to adopt pair programming, which she'd read about on Ward Cunningham's Wiki, as part of that strange "extreme" programming method. Ron and Kay were both somewhat skeptical but didn't see any other way to handle the situation.[1]

Pair programming actually seemed to work.

They were able to come to solutions much more quickly together than they could individually. The code remained clean and consistent. When bugs slipped through and were discovered by customers, the bugs were usually in code that hadn't been pair programmed.

Based on this initial success with pair programming, they began to consider implementing other XP ideas. They were uncomfortable about the absence of testing on the project. They'd read about unit testing on the Wiki, and although they had never done it themselves or known anyone who had (surely it was too difficult and time-consuming a technique for use on products that have to be developed rapidly), they thought they could give it a try.

Their first attempts at unit testing failed abysmally. They hoped that *Extreme Programming Explained* [Beck2000] could help them when it came out that fall. Reading the book helped them understand that the XP principles supported each other, but it got them no nearer to applying unit testing to their project.

The breakthrough insight came when Kay attended Object Mentor's XP Immersion course.[2] She watched James Grenning and Michael Feathers demonstrate refactoring and unit testing on a small program. Then she got to participate for a week on a mock XP project team,

1. Ward Cunningham's Wiki is part of the Portland Pattern Repository, published by Cunningham & Cunningham, Inc. It is the first WikiWikiWeb and is located at http://c2.com/cgi/wiki.

2. XP Immersion is a registered trademark of Object Mentor, Inc. To find out more about XP Immersion, go to http://www.objectmentor.com.

coached by Ron Jeffries, pairing and getting a feel for JUnit and test-first programming.

Back at work, with this improved understanding, she quickly got VBUnit working and began practicing test-first programming. Kay and Ron soon discovered that having the test cases in place increased their confidence. They began to see the value of the immediate feedback, helping them focus on only one failure at a time and minimizing the tendency to get lost in multiple distractions. The tests did not seem to be slowing them down. They were learning the truth of Kent Beck's statement: "The mentality of sufficiency . . . creates its own efficiencies, just as the mentality of scarcity creates its own waste" [Beck2000].

Now it was time to put XP to the test. New programmers were joining the company, some of them quite opposed to the experimental ideas Ron and Kay were trying. Before they went any further, Kay and Ron asked for a separate team to be created that included those favorable or at least neutral to the XP ideas, and found a customer (the third author of this chapter, Dan).

The team had a mixed level of knowledge about and buy-in to XP, but at least no one was openly opposed to XP. Kay set the following policies for the project.

- All checked-in code will be either pair programmed or code reviewed.
- All code changes in the business objects layer will be supported by unit tests.
- A clean compile and clean run of the entire unit test suite must be obtained before checking in code.
- Attend iteration planning meetings every two weeks and stand-up meetings daily.
- At iteration planning, sign up for the same amount of work you completed last iteration.
- The customer chooses which stories are available for sign-up, with the amount of work not to exceed the combined amount the team completed last iteration.
- Only work on functionality required for stories you are currently signed up for.

- Should a story remain uncompleted at the end of the iteration, you may not sign up for the same story you had in the previous iteration (no second chance).
- Team members will not be asked to work more than 40 hours per week.

This was a limited version of XP, but most people in the engineering department perceived it as pretty radical.

The iterations began.

Dan, previously the company's director of client services, had spent a lot of time with our customers but wasn't sure how his new role as product manager would work out. As he began to work within the role of XP customer, he appreciated the structure the process provided and the ability it gave him to more effectively steer the project. He could see how XP encouraged open communication and information sharing among all team members, especially between the product manager and the developers. He appreciated the simplicity and flexibility of using cards and felt they made the planning and scheduling process "more real."

The developers were able to begin coding immediately because Dan worked out the requirements details as we went along. Kay appreciated this, coming from two previous projects where so much time had been spent on requirements and design that there was no time left to code—and the projects had therefore been canceled.

As the project progressed, Ron, Dan, and Kay learned how iterations set a rhythm and reduced the constant pressure they'd felt on previous projects. One teammate, who came to this team from a nondevelopment team, commented on how much moving to development *reduced* his stress.

Because this project was life or death for the company, implementing the 40-hour workweek took courage, but the authors learned that avoiding late-night programming sessions enabled them to be immediately productive the next morning and to spend much less time rewriting mistakes.

As it turned out, the team's initial velocity measurement was quite accurate in predicting how long it would take to complete the project, and they reached code complete precisely when the projections showed. To the authors, this was a great accomplishment, something they had not experienced on other projects. In addition, they were able to estimate for management the time it would take to do certain additional features, which management opted for, and the team was able to add the features in the estimated amount of time.

Results from the Experience

Events after completion of this project became rather surreal. At the shipping party, the team that actually worked on the project received no credit for shipping successfully. A new manager was hired to take care of this team. When layoffs came shortly thereafter, this team was the one that was let go, while the team that had missed all their deadlines but had worked more overtime was preserved.

Clearly, there was a difference in perception. The authors' perception was that their team had delivered superior performance, based on the fact that they accomplished the project according to the schedule they had gotten management's agreement on, and had team members who were happy and excited to work on the next project. The company's perception was that the team had delivered inferior performance—that they could have gotten the product out sooner if they had put more effort into it.

The differences in perception became more clear after the authors interviewed the other team members and management. The interview responses were surprising at first. Some of the developers said this project was the best work experience they had ever had; others felt the project was average at best. Some of the evidence the authors thought indicated success, such as the 40-hour week and delivering on schedule according to a measured velocity, were even considered negative factors by management and one of the developers, who thought the team showed a lack of commitment for not working overtime or faster than the estimates.

What most people agreed on was that the ruthless prioritization performed by the product manager helped the team stay focused on the most valuable functionality. The planning meetings always seemed to go well, and everyone got to feel the iteration rhythm. Even those generally opposed to XP did appreciate the predictability, sense of completion, and increased feedback that came from the short iterations.

In the end, the authors learned an important lesson: They learned that XP is best understood when actually tried.

The authors themselves didn't understand XP or fully believe it would be beneficial until they tried the practices. Even then, it took experiencing the practices with mentors at XP Immersion before the authors were really able to make progress on building new understandings.

The authors and the other developers who consistently tried the XP practices became convinced of their benefits and felt the practices were improving the software delivery process. Those who avoided the XP practices were never convinced of their value and never became comfortable with the practices, most notably test-first programming and pair programming.

Table 35.1 summarizes some of the differing viewpoints that were discovered in the retrospective interviews.

The authors also learned that it is hard to sell XP to management. Management did not participate in the team experience and thus saw even fewer advantages to the XP practices than the team members did, especially when it came to project scheduling. They did see that the team was doing something different. Management is usually under pressure, and this case was no exception. Under pressure, and looking from the outside, they do not usually perceive different ideas as good.

TABLE 35.1 Differing Viewpoints on XP Practices

Responses from Those Who Tried More of the XP Practices	Responses from Those Who Tried Fewer XP Practices
Writing tests saves debugging time and makes it possible to clean up the code.	Writing tests is too much work for too little benefit.
Pair programming results in better solutions sooner and promotes good discipline and effective teaming.	Pair programming is a waste of time except for teaching someone new about the code.
Adjusting the workload to match last iteration's velocity makes the schedule predictable.	Signing up for only as much as you did last time encourages slacking.
The 40-hour workweek results in better quality by removing pressure.	The 40-hour workweek demonstrates a lack of commitment.

What to Do Next

The authors proved to their own satisfaction that XP did indeed address those deficiencies they'd encountered on other projects, and they, along with many of the rest of the team, consider the team experience on this project the best they've ever had.

In future job assignments, the authors intend to create as XP-like an environment as possible but to have an increased awareness of the perceptions of others, especially those who are not involved with the team or are not trying the practices. An extra effort should be made to involve management with the process, because this won't occur naturally. The authors believe now that unless management (or anyone else) gets in and experiences the XP practices, they won't buy in to them, even if they may appear to for a while.

At some point, the authors hope to be able to work with a development team fully committed to XP, predicting that such an environment would prove even more productive and enjoyable than the partial XP they enjoyed on this project.

References

[Beck2000] K. Beck. *Extreme Programming Explained*. Addison-Wesley, 2000.

Acknowledgments

The authors wish to thank Alistair Cockburn for his encouragement to question assumptions, Object Mentor for XP Immersion, Zhon Johansen for additional help with the XP practices, and all those who participated in the project for being patient with our crazy ideas.

About the Authors

Kay Johansen has worked for ten years in software development, management, architecture, process, and software quality assurance. She cofounded the Utah XP users' group and teaches JUnit at the Utah Java users' group. She is currently employed with NTT/Verio. Kay can be reached at kjohansen@verio.net.

Ron Stauffer has spent the last ten years working with accounting systems, both as an end user and as a programmer. He can be reached at rkstauff@networld.com.

Dan Turner has worked for 20 years in both operations management and business consulting. He currently works as an independent consultant in process reengineering and ERP system implementation and optimization.

Chapter 36

Qualitative Studies of XP in a Medium-Sized Business

—*Robert Gittins, Sian Hope, and Ifor Williams*

This chapter introduces novel methods of gathering qualitative data, data collation, and data analysis and is designed to both improve research techniques and provide useful information to companies considering a move to Extreme Programming (XP). The work has been conducted to understand some of the problems encountered during early XP implementation. In particular, the chapter looks at the XP practices adopted by one software development company and reveals how some developers feel about and respond to change; discloses what their managers have to say about adopting XP practices; and considers both advantages and problems of introducing some early, selected XP practices.

Previous qualitative research into software development concentrated on nonjudgmental reporting, with the intent of provoking discussion within the culture being studied [Seaman1999; Sharp+1999; Cockburn+2000]. Such work provided observations and evidence, with collaborators deciding for themselves whether changes were required. The fieldwork study undertaken here followed the format of [Gittins+2000], whereby the researcher is immersed for a period in the software developer team. In this way, the active researcher becomes instrumental in the development and improvement of XP. Seaman described an empirical study that addressed the issue of communication among members of a software development organization [Seaman1999]. Sharp used combined ethnography and discourse analysis to discover implicit assumptions, values, and beliefs in a software management system [Sharp+1999]. Cockburn and Williams investigated the cost benefits of pair programming [Cockburn+2000]. Sharp, Robinson, and Woodman described a "cross-pollination" approach to inform and improve the development of software engineering through a deeper understanding of the software engineering community's implicit values and beliefs [Sharp+2000]. What has been reported has been done through the successful use of qualitative methods in the evaluation of software development approaches.

Now we look at XP and its evaluation by using qualitative procedures. What are the effects of applying XP in a software development business environment? To answer this question, qualitative research methods [Gittins2000] were explored and used to discover the problems dominating staff and management development. Productivity and efficiency are parts of a complex human dimension uncovered by this approach. The interpretation and development of XP's "rules and practices" in a medium-sized software development company, as well as the intricate communication and human issues affecting the implementation of XP, are discovered.

Research Hypothesis

The aims of the research were to discover the difficulties of applying XP in a changing software requirements environment and to use qualitative methods to uncover these difficulties.

This research expects to find that traditional evaluation techniques presently adopted in the analysis of novel software development methodologies such as XP will be improved by qualitative research and analysis techniques. Particularly, this research is moving in the direction of "soft computing" techniques that may be better used to evaluate qualitative data returned, for example, from the complex relationships that exist between the 12 XP practices.

During the process of investigation, the qualitative research uncovers the difficulties of applying XP in an environment of changing software requirements. Successes, failures, and evolving practices are discovered—how management and staff adapted during a period of rapid change, and why it was important to have a flexible management approach. The experiences of both management and staff were examined during a period when initial practices matured *and* new practices emerged.

The research project adopted some of the techniques historically developed from the social sciences [Gittins2000]: ethnography, qualitative interviews, and discourse analyses. An understanding of "grounded theory" was particularly important in this work, because grounded theory can provide help in situations where little is known about a topic or problem area, or to generate new ideas in settings that have become static or stale. Grounded theory was developed by Barney Glaser and Anselm Strauss in the '60s and deals with the generation of theory from data [Glaser+1967]. Researchers start with an area of interest, collect data, and allow relevant ideas to develop. Rigid preconceived ideas are seen to prevent the development of useful research. To capture relevant data, qualitative research techniques are employed [Gittins+2000], which include the immersion of the researcher within the developer environment. The use of guided interviews and the timely rotation of questionnaires was the chosen method of data collection.

Qualitative methods and data evaluation enabled the researcher to study selective issues in detail, without the predetermined constraints of categorized analysis. The researcher was instrumental in gathering data from open-ended questions. Direct quotations are the basic source of raw materials in qualitative research, revealing a respondent's depth of concern. This contrasts with the statistical features of quantitative methods, such as Goal Question Metrics [Basili+1984], recognized by their encumbrance of predetermined procedures.

In terms of qualitative interview procedures, Patton suggests three basic approaches to collecting qualitative data through open-ended interviews [Patton1990]. The three approaches are distinguished by the extent to which the questions are standardized and predetermined, each approach having strengths and weaknesses, depending on the purpose of the interview.

- "Informal conversation" interviews are a spontaneous flow of questions in which the subject may not realize that the questions are being monitored.

- ✧ The "general interview guide" approach, adopted extensively for this study, predetermines a set of issues to be explored.
- ✧ The "standardized open-ended interview" pursues the subject through a set of fixed questions that may be used on a number of occasions with different subjects.

In a series of interviews, data was collected using informal conversation and verbatim transcripts taken from general guided interviews.

To support data collected from the interviews, an extensive questionnaire (100 questions) was prepared to investigate the rules and practices of XP. Questions targeted the software development process, XP practices, and both managerial and behavioral effectiveness. Behavioral questions were based on Herzberg's "hygiene and motivation factors" [Herzberg1974], and ample provision was made for open comments on each topic. Because of the importance given to the XP working environment, a developer-area floor plan was provided with the questionnaire, giving respondents an opportunity to suggest improvements to the work area. Repeating the questionnaire every three months helped research and management by matching the maturing XP practices against developer responses.

Description of the Context of the Experience

The focus company for this research was SECURETRADING (ST), a medium-sized software company committed to implementing XP. ST comprised a team of nine developers committed to implementing XP in a progressive manner while conscious of the need to minimize disruption to the business process. (Reference material from companies, not specifically named in this work, is used in general terms to highlight some typical problems facing established companies. Traditional companies are those companies sensitive to their compartmentalized developer environment, fearful of disruption to key programmer staff members and control issues of looming production deadlines.)

When research began, ST had recently moved to larger offices, and their experience of XP consisted of some intermittent attempts at pairing developers. The relocation presented opportunities for improving the XP environment, reinforcing pairing proficiency, and selectively adopting XP practices. Flexibility in XP enables companies to cherry-pick those practices they regard suitable for implementation, in the order they see that best benefits their particular business environment.

Results from the Experience

The following is a commentary on XP practices and a brief summary of results taken from a selection of XP practices investigated at ST.

Pair Programming

Beck justifies the use of pair programming and why it works [Beck2000; Beck+2000]. Williams maintains that two programmers working together generate an increased volume of superior code, compared with the same two programmers working separately [Williams+2000A]. XP takes advantage of the benefits of pair programming reported for some time [Cockburn+2000; Williams+2000B].

Management at ST discussed the feasibility of implementing pairing with their development team, who unanimously agreed to buy in to the practice. The first questionnaire showed that some of the team were unhappy with pairing; 28% of developers preferred to work independently, 57% didn't think they could work with everyone, and 57% stated that pair programmers should spend, on average, 50% of their time alone. XP practices recommend that no more than 25% of a conditional 40-hour week be paired. Two developers summed up the team's early attitude to pair programming.

> *I feel that pair programming can be very taxing at times, although I can see the benefits of doing it some of the time.*

> *Not everyone makes an ideal pair. It only really works if the pair is reasonably evenly matched. If one person is quiet and doesn't contribute, their presence is wasted. Also, if a person is really disorganized and doesn't work in a cooperative way, the frustration can [disturb] the other participant!*

In fact, developers estimated that they spent approximately 30% of their time pairing, with partner changes occurring only on task completion, often spanning several days. Changes in pair partners were only infrequently agreed on and then mostly established in an ad hoc manner.

Part IV

This activity did not conform to the frequent partner swapping and partner mixing recommended by XP. Pairing practices matured with the introduction of a team "coach" and later a "tracker" [Beck2000]. Maintenance tasks were another problem, which routinely disrupted pairing. Here, control was reviewed and tasks better ordered to minimize this problem. In time, the impact of pairing activity on developers may be seen by comparing the data returned from the periodic questionnaire reviews and in the timeliness and quality of code released. Only from the results of broader and longer-term evaluations of this kind will the benefits of this evolving practice be understood.

Planning Games

Jeffries et al. detail each step in the planning game scenario [Jeffries+2000]. The "customer" duly chooses between having (a) more stories, requiring more time, and (b) a shorter release, with less scope. Customers are not permitted to estimate story or task duration in XP, and developers are not permitted to choose story and task priority. When a story is too complex or uncertain to estimate, a "spike" is created. Spike solutions are found by writing sample code that breaks down the problem into simple stories that are then easy to estimate, and they provide answers to complex and risky stories.

Planning games were introduced at ST soon after pairing practices were established. As an application service provider, which provides applications to a large number of clients, ST produced enhancements incrementally every two to four weeks in response to feedback from customers, sales representatives, marketing executives, and corporate management. Because of the number and distribution of project stakeholders, a true "customer on-site" model was not practical, and ST evolved a "customer proxy" model.

Commenting on the proxy model, the developer manager stated:

> *The inclusion of a representative from customer services has proven to be hugely beneficial, providing immediate feedback of the system's successes and failures on a day-to-day basis.*

Customers were given an on-site "proxy" who represented their interests during the planning game and during development. The customer proxy understood the customers' needs in detail and always acted in the best interests of the customers. A typical planning game involved several customer proxies and internal representatives from the sales, marketing, and operations departments. The stories to be implemented in subsequent releases were selected by consensus among stakeholders, during the planning game, to determine the order in which stories maximized business value. ST managers reported that they were pleased with the progress, development, and results of planning games. Reaching a consensus among interested parties often involved considerable discussion and was facilitated by the XP developer manager. However, the XP manager also played the role of "corporate management proxy" by communicating corporate strategy into the planning and by interpreting the story priorities in the context of corporate strategy. Qualitative research methods—in this case, the researcher immersed within the project team—played a useful role in abstracting and collating information.

Problem requirements routinely arose, and the team quickly adopted the spike mechanism for dealing with complex stories. Their method was to create spike solutions by logging a spike as a fully referenced story to quickly attack a problem. This effectively reduced a complex, inestimable story to a simple and easily understood group of stories. Results were very effective; spike solutions proved easy to develop, and consequently estimates for completion, derived at planning games, proved consistently accurate. In the early stages of implementation, it was common practice to combine the essential elements of both iteration and release planning games in one meeting. This practice worked for ST in the context of their limited, earlier projects. In addition, as confidence improved, planning games quickly matured into separate full-blown release and iteration planning games, and larger projects were soon brought online to adopt this and other XP practices.

Communication

A great deal of attention is necessary in providing an XP environment in keeping with the practices to support XP [Beck2000]. Key factors in communication are the use of whiteboards; positioning and sharing of desk facilities to smooth the progress of pair programming; stand-up meetings to broadcast knowledge and negotiate support; collective code ownership; and finally the principle of buying in to the concepts, rules, and practices of XP.

Interviews and questionnaires revealed many areas of concern among developers. For example, with respect to meetings, when developers were asked if meetings were *well organized, with results agreed on, recorded, and effectively communicated to everyone*, 86% of developers disagreed and added comments such as these.

> *Agreements at meetings are not set in concrete.*

> *Confidence is lost with meeting procedures when agreed action or tasks are later allowed to be interpreted freely by different parties.*

This type of qualitative feedback, provided from periodic reports, alerted management to address these concerns by concentrating their efforts on improving XP's planning game and story card practices. In part this was addressed by encouraging developers to agree on, and finalize with the client, the task description and duration estimates at timely planning game meetings. In addition, story cards were fully referenced and signed by the accepting developer, thereby becoming the responsibility of the initiating developer until completion. Only the "responsible" signatory of the story card was authorized to amend it. However, not all the issues have been fully addressed, and some problems with meeting practices remain at the time of writing.

The use and placement of whiteboards is said to be an essential supporting means of good communication in XP practices [Beck2000]. Mobile whiteboards were introduced by ST soon after pair programming practices gained momentum, and were used to record the story details agreed on at planning game meetings. At one point, story cards were physically stuck to the boards in prioritized order, with adjacent notes written on the board. This proved unpopular and developed into cards being retained but not stuck on the whiteboard. Tasks were written on the boards. Referenced tasks contained ownership, estimation, iteration, and priority, which were displayed in column format. On completion, the owner added the actual task duration. The information served to improve personal proficiency in estimation and in providing feedback toward establishing project velocity data for future planning games.

Stand-up meetings promote communication throughout the team. ST introduced this practice from day one. At ten o'clock every morning, a meeting allowed everyone to briefly state (standing promotes brevity) their work for the day and discuss problems arising from the previous day's activity. Anyone was free to comment, offer advice, or volunteer cooperation. The benefits of adopting stand-up meetings were far-reaching and seen by developers and management as an effective way to broadcast activities, share knowledge, and encourage collaboration among team members and management. ST meetings tended to degrade when reports migrated to topics of yesterday's activity rather than those planned for the day. This activity persists and may remain or need to be resolved and modified as their particular brand of XP develops.

Simple Design

Beck summarizes simple design with "Say everything once and only once" [Beck2000]. However, one developer revealed a common concern, which was recorded at a periodic interview.

> *Sometimes, it is a bit too simplistic, and issues seem to be avoided.*

XP states that it is important to produce a simple system quickly and that small releases are necessary to gain feedback from the client. ST didn't see themselves in a position to exhaustively implement the simple-design practice early in their XP implementation program. XP was introduced to maintain and enhance an existing system, which did not have automated acceptance or unit tests. This severely hampered the refactoring of legacy code *in situ*, and only when most of the functionality was migrated into XP clean code, did serious refactoring become possible.

Part IV

Testing

Acceptance tests are written in XP before the main code and give an early and clear understanding of what the program must do. This provides a more realistic scenario, as opposed to "after-the-code testing," which, unfortunately and for many reasons, neatly matches completed code. Time is saved both at the start of coding and again at the end of development. At ST, latent resistance to early testing became evident when the perceived closeness of a deadline loomed. Testing is perhaps the hardest practice to implement fully and requires above-average commitment from developers. An early questionnaire revealed that 71% of developers regarded unit testing practices in general to be "very poor." The developer manager commented on the early introduction of unit testing, saying:

> *If you already have a large, complex system, it is difficult to determine to what extent testing infrastructure is to be retrospectively applied. This is the most difficult aspect in our experience. Starting from scratch, it's much easier to make stories and code testable.*

With experience and the results of qualitative investigation, ST concluded that applying unit tests and acceptance tests to existing legacy code is counterproductive in the long term.

ST adopted the following additional policy with respect to testing.

- Start from a clean slate whenever a portion of the legacy system needs modifying.
- Write acceptance tests up front.
- Construct new applications with unit tests.
- Use small portions of legacy code in a new implementation only when necessary and appropriate.

Refactoring

Martin Fowler describes refactoring as "the process of improving the code's structure while preserving its function" [Fowler1999]. The use and reuse of old code is deemed costly. Developers are often afraid they might unwittingly break the software. XP advocates that refactoring throughout the project life cycle saves time and improves quality. Refactoring reinforces simplicity by its action in keeping code clean and reducing complexity. ST had not developed refactoring activities in line with XP at that time. Many developers expressed concerns with refactoring that are more commonly reported by traditional companies.

> *With more people, we could spend more time refactoring and improving the quality of our existing code base.*

The questionnaire revealed that 45% of developers considered refactoring sporadic or very poor. Many poorly developed practices blame resources as the key factor in restricting progress. In this instance, management has committed to facilitating change and improving their refactoring practices; future studies will monitor change and progress.

Collective Code Ownership

Kent Beck describes this concept as "Every programmer improves any code anywhere in the system at any time if they see the opportunity" [Beck2000; Beck+2000]. Collective code ownership is purported to prevent complex code from entering the system, and developed from the practice that anyone can look at code and simplify it. Although sometimes contentious, test procedures in XP are there to support collective code ownership and facilitate the prevention of poor code entering the system. Collective code ownership has the additional benefit of spreading knowledge of the system around the team. ST experienced growing pains in developing collective code ownership, as revealed by the comments of two developers.

> *I have conflicting interests in collective code ownership. I think it is very good when it works, but there are times when some code I have written seems to just get worse when others have been working on it.*

> *I like the idea of collective code ownership, but in practice I feel that I own, ... am responsible for, some bits of code.*

From the familiar traditional perspective of individual-ownership, it will be pivotal in the development of XP to record attitude changes during the transition to XP practices, when acceptance (or rejection) develops among staff and managers. Changing to collective-code-ownership may prove difficult where pride of work is inherently important to job satisfaction, and may need to be balanced by something equally important, perhaps in the form of stronger team awareness, belonging, and commitment. Collecting and reporting such qualitative factors, supports the evolution of this practice.

The Metaphor

A metaphor in XP is a simple shared story to encompass and explain what the application is "like," communicating a mental image so that everyone involved can grasp the essence of the project in a term universally understood. This may seem to be a relatively easy or lightweight activity to adopt. However, the value of this practice was not immediately evident to developers at ST, who experienced early difficulties in developing and applying suitable metaphors. Metaphor usage was consequently, and reluctantly, abandoned for future consideration.

What to Do Next

Established or "traditional" companies that are considering adopting XP have many more difficulties to overcome than younger, developing companies such as ST. Traditional development teams, in which developers are comfortably established, working in small offices in prohibitively cloistered environments coincide with management dilemmas. Such dilemmas include legacy software "owned" (ransomed) by one or two heroic developers at the cutting edge of their business. Other companies monitored by the researchers reported having some badly underperforming teams, and in some circumstances management resorted to consultants to resolve their problems, with no significant success reported.

Often with great reluctance, brought about by the constrictions of a traditional system, management allowed our research team to visit their developer offices. Stress levels were high in these companies. Common problems, described earlier for traditional companies, created high risks [Beck2000], quality was compromised, communication difficult, and control largely ineffective. The message here, to companies considering the change to XP, is that starting from scratch is easier than trying to introduce XP practices into an established company with many legacy problems. The ST developer manager reinforces this point, during their early attempts at developing XP projects, with his comment:

> *One of the key "discoveries" has been the relative ease to which XP has been employed on an all-new project, and the difficulty in applying XP retrospectively on an established system.*

In summary, a combination of qualitative and quantitative methods has helped identify uncertainties in applying XP practices in a medium-sized software development company—in particular, how one company interpreted and developed their own brand of XP, molded from their experiences, both successes and failures. Successes came from such areas as the use and development of spike solutions and finding ways to have a customer presence within the planning game activity. And failures were seen in developer reluctance to buy in to collective code ownership, and the difficulties of implementing a test-first strategy and adopting the practice of simple design. Partial success was seen in pair programming that posed early problems and then showed improvement in maturity, but of course the evolution of XP continues.

Clearly, the efficiency of XP applied within small and growing companies requires further investigation. XP practices support one another, and many complex interrelated human factors form part of an ever-changing scenario, all of which should somehow be considered in any evaluation process. Qualitative research techniques have helped us gather important data in this area. There are other problems, such as how XP practices relate to one another. It may not be enough to report the results of individual practices in isolation. Data analysis presents many challenges, and the investigation of software metrics, qualitative methods, and soft computing techniques have a practical working value that merits further work. Investigation into the use of soft computing techniques, particularly fuzzy logic, has already begun, attempting to provide richer results through improved analysis of both qualitative and quantitative data. We hope that by continuing this work, we will soon be able to provide some of the answers.

References

[Basili+1984] V. Basili, D. Weiss. "A Method for Collecting Valid Software Engineering Data." *IEEE Transactions on Software Engineering*, Volume 10, Number 6, 1984.

[Beck2000] K. Beck. *Extreme Programming Explained*. Addison-Wesley, 2000.

[Beck+2000] K. Beck, M. Fowler. *Planning Extreme Programming*. Addison-Wesley, 2000.

[Cockburn+2000] A. Cockburn, L. Williams. *The Cost Benefits of Pair Programming*. http://members.aol.com/humansandt/papers/pairprogrammingcostbene/pairprogrammingcostbene.htm. 2000.

[Fowler1999] M. Fowler. *Refactoring: Improving the Design of Existing Code*. Addison-Wesley, 1999.

[Gittins2000] R. Gittins. *Qualitative Research: An Investigation into Methods and Concepts in Qualitative Research.* http://www.sesi.informatics.bangor.ac.uk/english/research/technical-reports/sesi-020/. 2000.

[Gittins+2000] R. Gittins, J. M. Bass. *Qualitative Research Fieldwork: An Empirical Study of Software Development in a Small Company, Using Guided Interview Techniques.* http://www.sesi.informatics.bangor.ac.uk/english/research/technical-reports/sesi-021/. 2000.

[Glaser+1967] B. Glaser, A. Strauss. *The Discovery of Grounded Theory: Strategies of Qualitative Research.* Aldine Publications, 1967.

[Herzberg1974] F. Herzberg. *Work and the Nature of Man.* Granada Publications Ltd., 1974.

[Jeffries+2000] R. Jeffries, A. Anderson, C. Hendrickson. *Extreme Programming Installed.* Addison-Wesley, 2000.

[Patton1990] M. Patton. *Qualitative Evaluation and Research Methods, Second Edition.* Sage Publications, 1990.

[Seaman1999] C. Seaman. "Qualitative Methods in Empirical Studies of Software Engineering." *IEEE Transactions on Software Engineering*, Volume 25, Number 4, July/August 1999.

[Sharp+1999] H. Sharp, M. Woodman, F. Hovenden, H. Robinson. "The Role of 'Culture' in Successful Software Process Improvement." *Euromicro*, Volume 2, 1999.

[Sharp+2000] H. Sharp, H. Robinson, M. Woodman. "Software Engineering: Community and Culture." *IEEE Software*, Volume 17, Number 1, January/February 2000.

[Williams+2000A] L. Williams, R. Kessler. "All I Really Wanted to Know about Pair Programming I Learned in Kindergarten." *Communications of the ACM*, Volume 43, Number 5, May 2000.

[Williams+2000B] L. Williams, R. Kessler, W. Cunningham, R. Jeffries. "Strengthening the Case for Pair Programming." *IEEE Software*, Volume 17, Number 4, July/August 2000.

Acknowledgments

The authors gratefully acknowledge the funding and support of the EPSRC (award number 99300131).

The authors would like to thank SECURETRADING at Bangor, UK, for their cooperation and support.

About the Authors

Robert Gittins is a final-year Ph.D. student at the University of Wales Bangor, School of Informatics, Dean Street, Bangor, UK, LL57 1UT. Robert can be reached at the e-mail address rgittins@informatics.bangor.ac.uk.

Sian Hope is a senior lecturer at the University of Wales Bangor, School of Informatics, Dean Street, Bangor, UK, LL57 1UT, and can be reached at the e-mail address sian@informatics.bangor.ac.uk.

Ifor Williams is senior development manager at SECURETRADING, Parc Menai, Bangor, Gwynedd, UK. His e-mail address is ifor.williams@securetrading.com.

Part V

XT: Extreme Tools—How Tools May Help the Practices of XP and AMs

Part V is about tools that support XP and agile methodologies (AMs). In fact, there are not many such tools, because XP is based on simplicity, open communication, and coding, and it does not require complex project or documentation management.

So, the field of agile tools is still an open one, and a lot of research on it is being done. Testing and distributed development are perhaps the subjects about which most research takes place. In fact, the tools presented here are mainly intended to support automatic testing, especially in the case of Web applications and GUI testing.

In Chapter 37, Asim Jalis and Lance Kind introduce their solution for automatically generating "mock objects," which enable testing a distributed application without having all the external objects needed by the final application. The tool generates Java code and is available under the BSD open source license.

Chapter 38 is about automating acceptance tests, as has been done for unit tests. Tip House and Lisa Crispin argue that although acceptance tests have features that differ substantially from those of unit tests, their complete automation is indeed possible and desirable. They present a framework for automating acceptance tests in a Web environment.

Ivan Moore in Chapter 39 presents a tool able to verify the effectiveness and coverage of a test suite in a Java environment. The name of the tool is Jester, and it automatically generates deliberate errors in the code to check whether the test suite can intercept them. The approach is very interesting, and it is compliant with the practice of tuning and verifying test instrumentation, prescribed by any good quality assurance process. Jester is available under a "free software" license.

In Chapter 40, Martin Lippert, Stefan Roock, Robert Tunkel, and Henning Wolf present a tool that supports continuous integration in a Java environment. The tool, named JWAM, addresses the problem that arises when the integration on an integration machine takes too long and consequently the XP pairs must wait a long time for their turn to access this machine. JWAM IntegrationServer is an extension to a configuration management tool that works in a client-server architecture. It enables remote access to the integration server machine and makes possible incremental unit testing and integration of the code developed on the client. JWAM could also be used for distributed development and has been extensively tested in real development.

Finally, in Chapter 41, Giancarlo Succi, Witold Pedrycz, Petr Musilek, and Iliyan Kaytazov discuss how Holmes, an open tool that supports requirement and domain analysis and was originally intended to support the development of software product lines, can be customized to also support XP. The chapter also presents details of Holmes implementation.

Chapter 37

Automatically Generating Mock Objects

—Asim Jalis and Lance Kind

Introduction

In test-before-code environments, writing many quick and efficient unit tests helps projects adapt to change with high quality. One of the obstacles to getting good unit testing coverage occurs when the code starts touching external objects that have side effects. This problem is frequently solved by using mock objects.

We demonstrate a lightweight approach to mock objects and describe a tool that does most of the code generation work for you. Our focus is on simplicity and ease of implementation. Tests with simple architecture are easier to understand and modify and are more likely to be written.

Automated code generation takes the pain out of writing mock objects. Also it allows multiple mock objects for the same underlying system object. Each test can have its own custom-tailored mock object specialized for testing precisely the assertions made by the test.

We can create this rich family of mock objects without writing much code. The final impact on the code base is minimal, which keeps the tests comprehensible and minimizes code pollution.

Example of Using the Tool

Suppose that your boss wants you to write a tool that performs gets on HTTP servers. You decide to write a class called `HTTPGet`, shown in Listing 37.1, and following XP practices, you write your unit tests and code (in that order).

LISTING 37.1 The HTTPGet class

```
package xpPerspectives;

import java.net.*;
import java.io.*;

public class HTTPGet {

    static final String GET_REQUEST = "GET / HTTP/1.0\n\n";
    private Socket socket;

    void setSocket(Socket newSocket) {
        socket = newSocket;
    }

    public static void main(String [] arguments) throws
        IOException {
    HTTPGet httpGet = new HTTPGet();
        String response = httpGet.mainInternal(arguments);
        System.out.println(response);
    }

    public String usage() {
        return this.getClass().getName() + " <hostname>";
    }

    String mainInternal(String [] arguments) throws
        IOException {
        if (arguments.length != 1) { return usage(); }
    String host = arguments[0];
        connectToServer(host);
        return getRoot();
    }

    private void connectToServer(String host) throws
        IOException {
        // don't overwrite if socket is being mocked
        if (socket == null) socket = new Socket(host,80);
    }
```

```
private String getRoot() throws IOException {
        OutputStream output = socket.getOutputStream();
    output.write(GET_REQUEST.getBytes());
        InputStream input = socket.getInputStream();
        StringBuffer buffer = new StringBuffer();
        while (true) {
            int c = input.read();
            if (c == -1) break;
            buffer.append((char) c);
        }
        output.close();
        input.close();
        return buffer.toString();
    }
}
```

Here is one of the unit tests that you write.

```
    public void testGetRoot() throws Exception {
        HTTPGet httpGet = new HTTPGet();
        String response = httpGet.mainInternal(
          new String[] {"mastodon"});
        assertTrue(response.startsWith("HTTP/1.1 200"));
    }
```

Unfortunately, you find that sometimes the server (mastodon) is down and the test fails. Another time, you take the code home, and the test fails because you aren't on the intranet. Frustrating!

Then it occurs to you that instead of using an actual socket in `HTTPGet`, why not replace it with a mock socket that fools the tool into thinking it is talking to a real socket, when in fact it is talking to your mock socket.

In keeping with XP, you want to do the simplest thing that possibly works. So instead of going to the trouble of creating a complete mock socket class, you create an anonymous class in your unit test that extends the socket, as shown in Listing 37.2.

You are feeling pretty smug until your pair points out that your Web client's calls to the mock socket could be leaking through to the real socket. To trap all leaks, you write a guard class and extend your anonymous mock socket from your guard class, as shown in Listing 37.3.

Phew, that was a lot of work. But now you are ready to refactor your tests to use the guard object, as shown in Listing 37.4.

LISTING 37.2 Anonymous class for the mock socket

```
public void testGetRootUsingUnguardedMockObjects() throws
        Exception {
    String expectedResponse = "HTTP/1.1 200 OK\n";
    final ByteArrayOutputStream output =
        new ByteArrayOutputStream();
    final ByteArrayInputStream input =
        new ByteArrayInputStream(expectedResponse.getBytes());
    Socket mockSocket = new Socket() {
        public InputStream getInputStream()   { return
            input;  }
        public OutputStream getOutputStream() { return
            output; }
        public void close() { }
    };
    HTTPGet httpGet = new HTTPGet();
    httpGet.setSocket(mockSocket);
    String response = httpGet.mainInternal(
        new String[] {"mastodon"});
    assertEquals(expectedResponse, response);
    assertEquals(HTTPGet.GET_REQUEST, output.toString());
}
```

You and your pair are feeling pretty good about your tests because now they don't depend on servers being up and the Internet being accessible, and your unit tests run faster. But writing the guard object did take a lot of work. You wish there was a tool that did this automatically for you.

LISTING 37.3 Guard class for the mock socket

```
package xpPerspectives;
public class GuardSocket extends java.net.Socket {
    public GuardSocket() { }
    public java.io.InputStream getInputStream() throws
            java.io.IOException {
        throw new RuntimeException("unimplemented
            getInputStream() invoked");
    }
    // override all 41 public methods of java.net.Socket in
the same way
}
```

LISTING 37.4 Using the guard object

```
public void testGetRootUsingGuardedMockObjects() throws
        Exception {
    String expectedResponse = "HTTP/1.1 200 OK\n";
    final ByteArrayOutputStream output =
        new ByteArrayOutputStream();
    final ByteArrayInputStream input =
        new ByteArrayInputStream(expectedResponse.getBytes());
    GuardSocket mockSocket = new GuardSocket() {
        public InputStream getInputStream()   { return
            input; }
        public OutputStream getOutputStream() { return
            output; }
        public void close() { }
    };
    HTTPGet httpGet = new HTTPGet();
    httpGet.setSocket(mockSocket);
    String response = httpGet.mainInternal(
        new String[]{"mastodon"});
    assertEquals(expectedResponse, response);
    assertEquals(HTTPGet.GET_REQUEST, output.toString());
}
```

So we wrote one for you. To generate the previous guard object, use the following command:

```
java tools.GuardGenerator java.net.Socket
    xpPerpspectives.GuardSocket
```

In general use:

```
java tools.GuardGenerator <class to mock> <guard class>
```

Features of the Tool

The main features of the GuardGenerator tool are as follows:

- Generates guard objects from class files and does not require the source
- Through exception handling, tells the developer what methods need to be mocked
- Prevents tests from calling the real objects being mocked

- Enables easy creation of mock objects implemented as anonymous classes
- Creates mockable implementations of interfaces such as servlets

State of the Implementation

These are some limitations of the tool.

- It does not generate constructors.
- It does not mock classes or methods that are final.

It ships with unit tests and the example shown in this chapter.

Tool Accessibility

The tool is available at http://groups.yahoo.com/group/extremeprogramming-seattle/files/GuardGenerator.jar. It is available under the BSD license (http://opensource.org/licenses/bsd-license.html).

Chapter 38

Testing in the Fast Lane: Automating Acceptance Testing in an Extreme Programming Environment

—Tip House and Lisa Crispin

This chapter is about automating functional and acceptance testing in an Extreme Programming (XP) environment. We look at the central position of test-first programming and unit test automation with respect to other XP practices, examine what could be gained through a similar approach for functional and acceptance test automation, and discuss differences between unit and functional tests that affect test-first programming. We describe our framework for functional test automation and illustrate the method using a simple Web application and the WebART test tool.

Part V

Introduction

Test-First and Test Automation in Extreme Programming

The testing practice is a key component of XP. Not only is it one of the 12 core practices, but it also plays a vital role in at least five others. Continuous integration, refactoring, and collective code ownership would all be downright foolhardy in the absence of automated unit tests to validate code changes. And without those supporting practices, simple design and small releases would be impractical as well.

Two of the main ingredients of the XP testing practice are test automation and test-first programming, in which programmer pairs write unit tests first before they write the code. Not only does this ensure that unit tests exist to detect any defects in the code, it also focuses the programmers on potential defects immediately before coding, presumably eliminating many from coming into being at all.

This combination of test-first programming and unit test automation, coupled with the requirement that 100% of the unit tests pass before code goes into the repository, can practically eradicate unit- and integration-level defects from XP-developed software.

User-Apparent Problems and Unit- and Integration-Level Defects

What may be surprising is that even when the unit tests are comprehensive, automated, and pass 100%, the system may still be incorrect in the eyes of the customer. This is hard to appreciate in traditional software development, because the unit testing is so haphazard that the systems are literally teeming with low-level bugs. Examination of user-apparent problems in this environment almost always implicates unit- and integration-type bugs. But even when these low-level defects are eradicated, as is possible with XP, the user-apparent problems still remain. There may even appear to be more, because the real gaps between what the customer wants and what the system does are no longer masked by nonfunctional areas of the system.

With the goal of banishing the user-apparent defects in the same manner as unit and integration bugs, we asked the question, "Why not adapt the test-first pattern for acceptance testing, and write functional tests at the very beginning, even before writing unit tests? And why not then automate those functional tests, just like the unit tests, and require all code to pass 100% of them before going into the repository and after each integration, just like unit tests?"

Differences between Functional Tests and Unit Tests That Affect Test-First

We have looked at this question during the last couple of years while working on XP projects for several companies, and found that unit and functional tests differ in some important ways that affect how a test-first approach can be carried out.

Unit tests are written in the same language as the code they test. They interact with the programming objects directly, often in the same address space. A pair can switch seamlessly between writing tests, writing code, refactoring, and running tests, without even getting out of the editor. And the unit tests correspond almost exactly to the programming objects. It is perfectly natural for a pair of programmers to write the tests for the object they are about to code, and then make sure they all run 100% when they are done. And from then on those tests are invaluable in validating that the code is still working after a change.

But functional tests almost always run completely separately from the system that they are testing and require specialized tools, and often different languages, that are designed to specify and recognize behavior visible to a user instead of to another programming object. And functional tests correspond to the programming objects only very loosely. A single functional test almost always relies on many different programming objects, and a single programming object often affects the outcome of several unrelated functional tests.

It is not possible to switch easily between functional tests and coding the way it is with unit tests, nor is it desirable, because the functional tests will not run until all of the required code is ready, even when the piece the pair is working on is completed. For the same reason, the functional tests cannot be expected to pass 100% in refactoring or at the end of an integration.

Adapting Test-First to Functional and Acceptance Testing

Because functional tests do not fit naturally into programmers' workflows, do not help programmers focus on the details of the code about to be written, and cannot be relied on to immediately find defects as the code is being written or during refactoring and integration, we found it to be difficult for programmers to write and automate these tests before writing the code. It would be easier if the functional test automation were trivial, but we found that it often required almost the same level of conceptual, design, and programming skill as developing the system.

For this reason, we have found it best to have a team member dedicated to—or at the very least, focused on—functional and acceptance test automation. This team member pairs with the other programmers as well as the customer to systematically transform the user stories into executable functional tests during release and iteration planning, and then automates and runs the tests during the iteration proper. The high degree of interaction between the test automation programmer and other team members provides the benefit of focusing attention on potential user-apparent defects before their introduction, just as with unit testing. And the automation of functional and acceptance tests provides similar benefits near the end of an iteration as the required code is completed and then, especially, in subsequent iterations.

The current scope precludes further details of the method we use for transforming user stories into tests or how that is integrated with the other XP activities. We describe briefly instead the way we have been actually automating functional and acceptance tests for Web applications. Additional details, as well as information on the other topics, can be found in the upcoming book from Addison-Wesley tentatively titled *Testing for Extreme Programming*, or on our Web site at http://www.xptester.org.

Tool Features

Overview

The tools we use consist of a reusable framework coupled with a test automation tool. The goal of the framework is to provide a tool-independent method for automating the tests. One part of the framework consists of rules for designing and implementing the tests, and another is a set of Java classes that integrate with the JUnit tool and provide a convenient way to integrate functional and acceptance tests into the unit test automation when appropriate. A set of supporting utilities and modules, written in the scripting language of the test automation tool, interface the automation tool to the framework.

For a test automation tool, we use WebART, a tool for automated testing of Web-based applications. We are also experimenting with the use of other tools, such as HttpUnit.

Framework

The following rules guide the design and implementation of automated functional tests.

- *The tests must be self-verifying* to determine whether they passed or failed without human intervention.
- *Tests verify only the aspects of concern for a particular test*, not every function that may have to be performed to set up the test.

- *Verification is only of the minimum criteria for success.* It demonstrates the business value end-to-end, but not more than the customer needs for success.
- *Test data is separated from any actual code* so that anyone can easily extend the test coverage simply by adding cases—that is, without programming.
- *The tests are designed* so that they do not contain any duplication and have the fewest possible modules.
- *The tests are continually refactored* by combining, splitting, or adding modules or by changing module interfaces or behavior whenever it is necessary to avoid duplication or to make it easier to add new test cases.

Essentially, we specify the tests as a sequence of actions, parameters, and expected results. Table 38.1 shows some examples.

The actions are then implemented as test modules that perform the associated action according to the specified parameters and validate that the expected results actually occur. For instance, the login module would log in to the system using the specified user ID and password, and validate that the welcome screen results. The search module would search the toys category in Denver and validate that a list is returned that contains "KBToys." These modules are *generic* in the sense that a single implementation is used for all the tests for a given system.

The test modules interact with the system at the same level that a user does, over the same interface, using the test automation tool. They validate the fixed aspects of the system response first and then any specified variable aspects. For instance, the login module in the test in Table 38.1 might check for either the welcome page or an error message as the fixed portion of the validation, and then check that the variable portion (the welcome screen) was present. In this manner the

TABLE 38.1 Specifying Automated Functional Tests

Action	Parameters	Expected Results
Login	`User Id=Test1 Password=Pass1`	Welcome page
Search	`Category=toys Location=Denver`	Results list containing "KBToys"

same module can be used to test that the error message is present when a mismatched user ID and password are entered.

WebART

WebART is an HTTP-level tool for testing Web applications that is capable of functional testing as well as load and performance testing. The name comes from an earlier tool for online systems testing that was called ART, for Automated Regression Testing. It is based on a model of scripted user simulation, in which a script describes a sequence of user interactions with the system. Typical functional testing is done with a single simulated user executing a set of defined test cases, with validation of the results done on the fly by the script or by using a batch comparator and a result baseline file. Multiuser scripts are also possible in which the users' activities are synchronized for testing deadlock and other types of simultaneous user interactions.

Load and performance testing are accomplished by running large numbers of simulated users, either all executing the same script or executing a mixture of different scripts. All scripts are innately capable of execution by an essentially unlimited number of users, and a number of constructs exist in the scripting language to produce controlled variation among different users executing the same script. During a load or performance test, the system throughput, transaction rate, error rate, and response time are displayed and logged by the tool, and the load parameters (such as number of users, think time, and transaction rate) can be adjusted dynamically. Tests by up to several thousand users can generally be run on a single workstation (running Windows NT/2000/XP, Linux, AIX, or SunOs). For larger tests, the tool can be installed on multiple workstations and still controlled and monitored from a single point.

Example Usage

What follows is a very simple and condensed illustration of functional test automation. Our sample application is a telephone directory lookup Web site, http://www.qwestdex.com. This is not intended as any type of endorsement; it simply provides a stable, public application with characteristics that enable us to illustrate the tests.

We have found that spreadsheets are a convenient way to define and maintain test definitions. The test definitions for the example are shown in Table 38.2.

These are the actual definitions of the tests, in which the parameters and expected results are encoded in a form that can be directly interpreted by the test modules. For simplicity, all validation of expected results has been specified as checks on the presence of text strings, but the framework also supports validating the presence and attributes of links, forms, and tables.

The test modules are implemented using the WebART scripting language, and the Java framework can then be used to execute test definitions directly from the spreadsheet. The output from a test run is an HTML log file, as shown in Figure 38.1, that provides an overall pass/fail status for the test and individual outcomes on each test case.

It is possible to drill down to a particular test case by clicking the link for an individual test case. Figure 38.2 shows the GotoLogin case.

Likewise, it is possible to drill down to a particular validation, as shown in Figure 38.3.

TABLE 38.2 Test Definitions Maintained in the `qwmain.xls` Spreadsheet

Actions	**Parameters**	**Expected Results**
GotoLogin		VerifyText ("qwestdex.com Your Online Directory Expert","Please enter your password")
Login	`<uid=globners&psw=globners&>`	VerifyText("Tip House ")
GotoSearch		VerifyText("Select what you're looking for")
Search	`<cat=Woodworking Equip&city =cleveland&state=Ohio&>`	VerifyText("qwestdex.com found these businesses")
Logout		VerifyText("You have signed out ")

Part V

```
QWMAIN   PASS

   Date: 20020317  Time: 23:36:07
   Host: qwestdex.com

   PASS qwgotologin
   PASS qwlogin
   PASS qwgotosearch
   PASS qwsearch
   PASS qwlogout
```

FIGURE 38.1 Output from the `qwmain` tests

```
QWMAIN

   qwgotologin QWMAIN.iter1.0    PASS   Up
      Date: 20020317  Time: 23:35:40  Transaction: 0
      TestCase http://qwestdex.com/
      Validation: TSD
      Next Test Case
      Validation 0    PASS    Details
      Validation 0    PASS    Details
```

FIGURE 38.2 Output from the GotoLogin test case

```
QWMAIN

   QWMAIN.iter1.0
      Validation 0    PASS    Up
         Date: 20020317 Time: 23:35:34  Transaction:
         Description: Vtext:qwestdex.com Your Online
                      Directory Expert
         Next Validation

         Display
```

FIGURE 38.3 Validation output for GotoLogin

State of Implementation

The automation framework includes the Java classes required to execute test definitions directly, either from a text file or an Excel spreadsheet, once the test modules are implemented. It also provides all the supporting utilities and modules in the WebART scripting language that implement the test tool interface to the framework, and implementations in the WebART scripting language of the test modules from the earlier `qwmain` example.

The framework does not include the WebART tool itself.

The WebART tool includes a full set of functional, load, and performance testing features for Web applications, including a user manual.

Tool Accessibility

The framework is available for free at http://www.xptester.org/framework/.

The WebART tool can be purchased for around $900 U.S. from OCLC Online Computer Center in Dublin, Ohio. But there is a good chance that the tool will become open source or enter the public domain in some other form within the next year. Free evaluation versions can be downloaded at http://www.oclc.org/webart/downld.htm. These evaluations are fully functional, but they time out after a few months and have to be renewed.

About the Authors

Tip House is chief systems analyst at the OCLC Online Computer Library Center, Inc., a nonprofit organization dedicated to furthering access to the world's information, where he develops and supports test automation tools and document management systems for the Web. Although his main interest has always been software development, he also has a long-standing interest in software testing, software measurement, and quality assurance, having presented papers on these subjects at development, measurement, and testing conferences in the United States and Europe. He has achieved Certified Quality Analyst, Certified Software Quality Engineer, and Lead Ticket Auditor certifications, and managed the independent test function at OCLC during their three-year successful effort to become registered to the ISO 9000 standards. Tip can be reached at tip_house@oclc.org.

Lisa Crispin is the quality assurance manager for KBkids.com. She has been working as a tester on XP teams since July 2000. She is cowriting (with Tip House) a book on testing for XP, which will be published by Addison-Wesley in October 2002. Her article "Extreme Rules of the Road: How an XP Tester Can Steer a Project Toward Success" appeared in the July 2001 issue of *STQE Magazine*. She is a frequent presenter at software testing and quality assurance conferences such as STAR, Quality Week, and Quality Week Europe, and presented two papers at XP Universe 2001. Lisa has more than ten years' experience as a tester and quality assurance (QA) manager, testing Web applications, database software, case tools, client-server software, and 4GLs. She has introduced testing and QA to companies such as TRIP.com and introduced test automation to Fortune 100 companies.

Chapter 39

Jester—A JUnit Test Tester

—*Ivan Moore*

Extreme Programmers have confidence in their code if it passes their unit tests. More experienced Extreme Programmers have confidence in their code only if they also have confidence in their tests. A technique used by Extreme Programmers to gain confidence in their tests is to make sure that their tests spot deliberate errors in the code. This sort of manual test testing is either time-consuming or very superficial.

Jester is a test tester for JUnit tests; it modifies the source in a variety of ways and checks whether the tests fail for each modification. Jester indicates code changes that can be made that do not cause the tests to fail. If code can be modified without the tests failing, it indicates either that a test is missing or that the code is redundant. Jester can be used to gain confidence that the existing tests are adequate or to get clues about the tests that are missing.

Jester is different from code coverage tools because it can find code that is executed by running tests but not actually tested by them. Results of using Jester are discussed.

Part V

Introduction

Extreme Programmers have confidence in code if it passes tests and have confidence in tests if they catch errors [Beck2000]. Many Extreme

Programmers temporarily put deliberate errors in their code to check that their tests catch those errors, before correcting the code to pass the tests. In some project teams, a project saboteur is appointed, whose role is to verify that errors that they deliberately introduce into a copy of the code base are caught by the tests [Hunt+1999].

Jester performs similar test testing mechanically, by making some change to a source file, recompiling that file, running the tests, and if the tests pass, displaying a message saying what it changed. Jester makes its changes one at a time, to every source file in a directory tree, making many different changes to each source file. (The different types of changes made are discussed later.) Note that each change is undone before the next change is made—that is, changes are made independently of each other.

Jester can modify not only the code that the tests are testing, but also the test code itself. If a test is modified but does not fail when run, the test may be redundant or erroneous.

The initial version of Jester worked only for Java code with JUnit tests; the same approach can be used for other languages and test frameworks.[1] A version of Jester, called Pester, has been built for Python code and PyUnit tests.[2] Java and JUnit were chosen for the initial version because the author uses both, and JUnit is probably the unit test framework most widely used by Extreme Programmers [Gamma+1998].

The ideas of mutation analysis [Friedman+1995] or automated error seeding [Meek+1989] are not new, but Jester is able to be more widely applicable than other tools because of the widespread use of JUnit. For Jester, or any similar tool, to work, it needs to be able to run the tests programmatically, and that is what makes the use of JUnit so important to both the simple implementation of Jester and its wide applicability.

Features of the Tool

Jester modifies Java source code in very simple ways, which do not require parsing or changes to more than one source file at a time.

The modifications are as follows:

- Modifying literal numbers (for example, changing `0` to `1`)
- Changing `true` to `false` and vice versa

1. See http://www.junit.org.
2. See http://www.jesterinfo.co.uk, http://www.python.org, and http://pyunit.sf.net.

- Changing `if(` to `if(true ||`
- Changing `if(` to `if(false &&`

The last two have the effect of making the condition of the `if` statement always true or always false, respectively. The reason for these replacements, rather than the apparently simpler `if(true)` and `if(false)`, respectively, is to avoid needing to find the end of the condition, which would require some parsing and thus would not be as simple to implement. There is no possibility of making two changes that cancel each other out, because the changes are applied one at a time, being undone before the next change.

These simple modifications have been found to be quite effective, as shown later. Other modifications can be made by specifying them in a configuration file.

For any change that Jester was able to make without the tests failing, it prints the name of the file changed, the position in the file of the change, and some of the original source file—from roughly 30 characters before to 30 characters after—so that the change can be easily identified within the source file.

For each source file that Jester modifies, it prints a "score" indicating the number of changes that Jester made that did not cause the tests to fail.

Example of Using the Tool

Jester needs to know the JUnit test class (a subclass of `TestCase` that can be used by the JUnit `TestRunners`) and the directory that contains the source code that Jester is allowed to change.

The test class is the one that is expected to show any changes to code in the source directory. Typically, this test class would be the `TestAll` class of a package, and the source directory would be the subdirectory that contains the code being tested by that `TestAll` class.

This example use of Jester is for the Money samples of JUnit 3.2, which give a small example of how to use JUnit. There is an interface, `IMoney`, and two classes that implement the interface, `Money` and `MoneyBag`, and a test class, `MoneyTest`, which includes tests for both `Money` and `MoneyBag`. Including comments, there are about 400 lines of code.

Jester was invoked for this example as follows:

```
java jester.TestTester junit.samples.Money junit\samples
```

Jester made 47 separate modifications (including to the test class itself), ten of which did not make the tests fail; that is, they were changes that indicated possible missing tests or redundant code. This was a much higher percentage than expected. The version of Jester used ignores commented code. Because each modification requires recompilation and running all the tests, this took a long time to run, considering the amount of code. On a Pentium 133MHz (an old machine), Jester took 12 minutes to complete the run.

A description of the ten modifications that did not cause the tests to fail follows. Three of the modifications were in the `equals` method of the `Money` class:

```
public boolean equals(Object anObject) {
 if (isNull())
   if (anObject instanceof IMoney)
     return ((IMoney)anObject).isNull();
 ...
```

Jester reported that:

- `if (isNull())` can be replaced by
  `if (false && isNull())`
- `if (anObject instanceof IMoney)` can be replaced by
  `if (true ||`
  `    anObject instanceof IMoney)`
- `if (anObject instanceof IMoney)` can be replaced by
  `if (false &&`
  `    anObject instanceof IMoney)`

The first of these shows that either `isNull()` is always `false` in the tests (thus a test is missing for the case where `isNull()` is `true`), or it could show that it makes no difference to the running of the tests whether the `isNull()` branch is executed. In fact, there is no test of `equals` for a "`null`" `Money`. (The method `isNull` has been renamed `isZero` in JUnit 3.4). Without further examination of the code, the possibility that the branch of code does not make any difference to the correct running of code should not be discounted. This could happen, for example, if the `isNull()` branch was a behavior-neutral optimization.

The second and third modifications reported indicate that either that `if` statement is not executed or it makes no difference to the running of the code—that is, it doesn't matter whether the value of the condition is `true` or `false`. In this case, this code is not executed by the tests. A conventional code coverage tool would be able to spot this.

The other seven modifications that Jester made that did not cause the tests to fail were all for the `MoneyBag` class. One of these was changing the construction of a vector from `new Vector(5)` to `new Vector(6)`. This had no effect on the correct running of the code, because the effect of this number is on the initial internal size of the constructed vector, which can have an effect on performance but does not affect the vector's behavior. Another change was to modify the `hashCode` value of an empty `MoneyBag`. This has no effect on the correct running of the code and can be considered a "false hit" by Jester.

Three of the other modifications are similar to those for `Money`; they show that the `equals` method is not tested for "`null`" `MoneyBags`.

The remaining two modifications both relate to the `equals` method for the special case that two `MoneyBags` that contain a different number of `Money` objects are not equals. There are no unit tests for this special case code.

Jester has also been applied to parts of Sidewize, a browser companion built by Connextra.[3] It successfully identified where tests were missing and where code had become redundant and needed removing. However, it took considerable analysis of the results to identify whether the modifications reported by Jester represented missing tests or redundant code, or were simply false hits—that is, represented behavior preserving changes to the code.

Conclusion

Jester can reveal code that has not been tested or is possibly redundant. However, Jester takes a long time to run, and the results take some manual effort to interpret. Nevertheless, in comparison with a code coverage tool, Jester can spot untested code even if it is executed.

The value of using Jester is the benefit from discovering missing tests or redundant code minus the cost of using it. The cost of using Jester is the time it takes to run (mostly machine time) plus the time to interpret its results (developer time). The cost of missing tests can be

3. See http://www.sidewize.com.

enormous if there are bugs that would otherwise have been found. Redundant code can also be expensive because it wastes developers' time whenever it is read or modified (for example, to keep it compilable). Therefore, Jester's net value depends on the state of the code that it is used on.

Jester can modify not only the code that the tests are testing, but also the test code itself. If a test is modified but does not fail when run, the test may be redundant or erroneous.

State of the Implementation

Jester uses a simple text-based find-and-replace-style approach to modifying the original source code. This was simple to implement and has proved adequate so far. However, if Jester were to use a parsed representation of the source code (either using a parser on the source code or possibly working on class files), more sophisticated modifications, and better reporting of its modifications, would be easier to implement. Using a parsed representation would, for example, enable Jester to remove complete statements from methods and to report its changes per method rather than by character index/line number.

Tool Accessibility

Jester is publicly available under a "free software" license.[4] Efforts will continue to improve Jester—in particular, to provide results that are easier to interpret and to try to avoid false hits.

References

[Beck2000] K. Beck. *Extreme Programming Explained.* Addison-Wesley, 2000.

[Friedman+1995] M. Friedman, J. Voas. *Software Assessment: Reliability, Safety, Testability.* John Wiley & Sons, 1995.

[Gamma+1998] E. Gamma, K. Beck. "Test Infected: Programmers Love Writing Tests." *The Java Report*, Volume 3, Number 7, July 1998.

4. See http://www.jesterinfo.co.uk.

[Hunt+1999] A. Hunt, D. Thomas. *The Pragmatic Programmer.* Addison-Wesley, 1999.

[Meek+1989] B. Meek, K. Siu. "The Effectiveness of Error Seeding." *ACM SIGPLAN Notices*, Volume 24, Number 6, June 1989.

Acknowledgments

Many thanks to all those at the eXtreme Tuesday Club in London, England, for testing Jester and for comments on early drafts of this chapter; in particular, special thanks to Keith Braithwaite, Paul Simmons, Duncan Pierce, Tamara Galloway, Tim Bacon, and Aaron Oldfield. Also thanks to Connextra for providing a useful testing ground for Jester.

About the Author

Ivan Moore works for Connextra in London, England, as a senior developer and XP consultant. He has previously worked on a couple of successful IBM products: VisualAge for Java Micro Edition, in Ottawa, Canada; and VisualAge Smalltalk UML Designer, in London, England. He has written papers published at OOPSLA, TOOLS (U.S. and Europe), XP, and XP Universe; reviewed papers for OOPSLA and TOPLAS; and coedited a book on prototype-based object-oriented programming. He has a Ph.D. (on automatic restructuring of object-oriented programs, 1996), an M.S., and a B.S., all in computer science. Ivan can be reached at ivan@tadmad.com.

Chapter 40

Stabilizing the XP Process Using Specialized Tools

—*Martin Lippert, Stefan Roock, Robert Tunkel, and Henning Wolf*

One problem with the XP development process is its fragility. If developers use the XP techniques in an unintended way or not at all, the XP process is likely to break down: The misused techniques affect the other XP techniques in a negative way, breaking the whole process. We believe that it is possible to stabilize the XP process by using specialized artifacts to reify the XP techniques. We discuss the reification of the XP technique continuous integration *using the JWAM IntegrationServer as an example. We present our experience with this tool and analyze its effects on the other XP techniques.*

Part V

Introduction

Extreme Programming is a combination of a number of different techniques for developing software. These techniques are not independent, but instead influence and complement each other. Kent Beck shows their relationships in [Beck2000].

Over the past two years, we have used XP techniques in various development projects. We observed that the XP process is fragile: If one

XP technique is used in an unintended way or not at all, dependent XP techniques may be affected. The problem is that XP is based on discipline and experience. If a team lacks the necessary discipline or experience, the XP process is likely to break down. The role of an XP coach is therefore suggested by Beck. The XP coach has the required experience and tries to establish the XP values within the XP team.

However, this situation is unsatisfactory. Many small teams do not have the financial resources to pay for an XP coach, and even if they do, it is very hard to a get a good one. So far there have not been many successful XP projects that have produced skilled coaches.

Fortunately, there are other ways of transferring experience and knowledge. One is to reify successful routines and behavior in artifacts [Bødker+1991]. This is what cultures do: If a routine is executed over and over again in the same or a similar way, the culture will create an artifact that reifies this routine. A carpenter hammers nails into wood. The reification of this routine is the hammer. The hammer does not force the carpenter to use it as intended, or even to use it at all, but it helps the carpenter do his work effectively. Thus, the carpenter will, of course, use the hammer. At the same time, the hammer "helps" the carpenter remember how to hammer. This facility is more important for an inexperienced carpenter than for an experienced one. The hammer helps transfer the knowledge about how to hammer from the experienced carpenter to the inexperienced one. The hammer stabilizes the routine of hammering.

The idea of using artifacts to reify proven routines and practices is not only useful for XP projects without a coach. Even with an XP coach, the artifacts help stabilize the good practices and techniques. It is crucial to use artifacts as part of the game, but the artifacts and routines have to be complemented by a value system. Artifacts, routines, and value systems stabilize each other.

Here we focus on the continuous integration technique of XP. We present the JWAM IntegrationServer as one possible artifact reifying this technique and therefore stabilizing the XP process.

Reification of the integration Process in an Artifact

The dependency diagram in [Beck2000, p. 70], focuses on continuous integration, which is shown to be directly related to collective ownership, coding standards, testing, refactoring, pair programming, and short releases. If a team has problems with continuous integration, this is likely to cause problems with other XP techniques. But if continuous integration works well, it should support many other XP techniques.

When we started using XP techniques, continuous integration was one of the first we adopted. We tried to establish the technique as suggested in [Beck2000]. We used one physical integration machine for the whole team (about eight developers), which always keeps a consistent and running version of the system under development. However, this did not work as expected. We achieved only a few integrations per week, and the team's motivation was adversely affected.

The reason for the failure to establish continuous integration was easily found: Each integration took too much time (two to four hours). There were too many things to do, such as:

- Find out what changed on the client and on the server since the last synchronization of server and client.
- Merge the modifications done on the client.
- Compile server sources.
- Test server sources.

This had a further impact on other XP techniques, especially refactoring. Because integration was done infrequently, the refactorings were very large. We were therefore very often without running system versions, which hindered short releases. During the large refactorings, the test cases often broke down and had to be more or less rewritten after refactoring. This hampered the XP technique of testing.

We started to look for a more suitable integration method to restabilize our XP process.

We liked the idea of using an artifact to support continuous integration within our development team. But what sort of artifact would be suitable? Using one integration machine was unsuccessful, as were to-do lists.

We identified the following points as important for the continuous integration technique.

- Integration cycles must be very short. We consider a few minutes, no more, to be optimal. This enables us to realize smooth team development without adversely affecting other members of the team.

Part V

- Unit testing is essential. Ideal would be a tool that takes care of the correctness of all sources at every integration.
- The tool and the conventions should be as easy to use as possible.

We decided to develop a specialized tool, the JWAM Integration-Server, as an extension to CVS, to provide our developers with a smooth way of dealing with continuous integration. We would, however, like to emphasize that any other source code management system may be useful for reifying continuous integration with the right set of conventions and values.

Features of the JWAM IntegrationServer

Given the requirements and observations mentioned earlier, we developed a specialized tool to support the continuous integration process. This tool can be thought of as a unit testing addition to a normal version management system. It is based on two components.

- The IntegrationServer is a server process that runs on a server machine that is accessible to all developers. This server machine defines the reference machine and controls and manages the complete source code using a version management system.
- The IntegrationClient is a client-side tool that enables the user to update source code on the reference machine and obtain changed source code from it. The client tool works as the artifact for the developer and offers the user an easy-to-use interface.

The typical use case for this tool is that the developer has changed a number of pieces of source code and would like to integrate them to provide the other developers inside the team with the changes. This task is supported by the IntegrationClient, where the developer can list the changed files. The developer can then integrate them by simply pushing a button. This single action guarantees that:

1. The changed pieces of source code are transferred to the server reference machine.
2. The complete source code is compiled.
3. All test cases run on the reference machine.

Only if all three actions are successful and no failure occurs during unit testing are the updated pieces of source code accepted on the reference machine and the integration successful. If one unit test fails or an error occurs during one of the actions, the integration is canceled. As a result of a failed integration, the changed versions of the pieces of source code are rejected, and none of the code base is changed on the reference machine. Feedback about a successful or failed integration is reported to the developer sitting in front of the IntegrationClient tool.

Test cases are handled as normal source code by the IntegrationClient. The developer can add, modify, or delete test-case classes using the same tool as for every other piece of source code.

The other use case that often occurs is that another developer has changed some source code on the reference machine. In this case, the IntegrationClient shows all changed pieces of source code, and the developer has the opportunity to download all new or changed pieces of source code to the development machine.

Another interesting case is the occurrence of conflicts—for example, when two developers on the team have changed the same source code. In this case, the IntegrationClient indicates the conflict and does not allow the changed source code to be uploaded to the server. First, the developer has to download the changed version from the server, transfer the changes into this source code, and then integrate the new merged version.

Examples of Using the JWAM IntegrationServer

We have been using the tool since April 2000, and our experience during more than 3,000 integrations has been extremely positive. The tool is easy to use and enables changed source code to be easily integrated. An integration is done in less than ten minutes for large projects (thousands of source files) and in a few seconds for small projects (some hundred source files), with the XP idea of continuous integration being optimally supported. Results and possible errors are reported in a progress log.

Because the IntegrationServer incorporates an optimistic locking strategy, the first developer to integrate modified sources wins. If the integration is refused by the IntegrationServer, the developer who tried to integrate has to remove the problem. This leads the developers to integrate as fast as possible to avoid potential conflicts. Thus, the reification of the continuous integration technique in a tool as an artifact supports not only this technique but the refactoring technique as well. Developers are "forced" by the IntegrationServer to make small refactorings rather than large ones.

The fact that the IntegrationServer ensures a running version on the server supports the small releases technique, too. In principle, it is possible to deliver a new version every day. The technique of collective code ownership is also supported by the IntegrationServer because the developer that caused a conflict has to remove it—no matter which code has to be modified. Testing is supported by the IntegrationServer's testing facility. The developers know that the IntegrationServer will execute their tests over and over again and will avoid breaking their code. Developers thus experience the benefits of test cases and are willing to write test cases for their code.

In our experience, the IntegrationServer does not specifically support the XP techniques pair programming and coding standards. These techniques are supported by continuous integration as a technique and not by the IntegrationServer.

Related Tools

A number of different tools can be used as an artifact for the continuous integration process, such as CVS, Envy, or TeamStreams by Object Technology International [Rivières+2001]. The IntegrationServer "only" adds a special, extremely easy-to-use and smooth interface and automated testing of the integrated version, which makes it easier to use for XP projects. A similar functionality is offered by the open source project CruiseControl at http://www.sourceforge.org.

Other artifacts may be useful for reifying other XP techniques. The Refactoring Browser, for example, might be used for the refactoring technique.[1]

State of the Implementation

The tool is fully implemented and used for a lot of projects with up to several thousand classes. The described functionality is fully implemented as a pure Java client-server system.

1. Thanks to the reviewer who suggested this idea.

Tool Accessibility

The tool is used only within IT Workplace Solutions (http://www.it-wps.com) at the moment. The license model is still under construction. But feel free to contact us if you are interested.

Conclusion and Outlook

The reification of the continuous integration process using a specialized tool as an artifact works well. In particular, the shift from non-XP development to XP was stabilized by this tool.

The IntegrationServer is only a first step toward a set of artifacts stabilizing the XP process. In addition to presenting the IntegrationServer, this chapter is intended to provoke a discussion on other artifacts suitable for stabilizing the XP process.

References

[Beck2000] K. Beck. *Extreme Programming Explained*. Addison-Wesley, 2000.

[Bødker+1991] K. Bødker, J. Pedersen. "Workplace Cultures: Looking at Artifacts, Symbols and Practices." In *Design at Work*. J. Greenbaum, M. Kyng, eds. Lawrence Erlbaum Associates, 1991.

[Rivières+2001] J. Rivières, E. Gamma, K. Mätzel, I. Moore, A. Weinand, J. Wiegand. "Team Streams—Extreme Team Support." In *Extreme Programming Examined*. G. Succi, M. Marchesi, eds. Addison-Wesley, 2001.

Part V

About the Authors

Martin Lippert, Stefan Roock, and Henning Wolf are research assistants at the University of Hamburg, and professional software architects and consultants at IT Workplace Solutions. Among their current research interests are framework design and implementation, refactoring, Java, and Extreme Programming. They are senior architects of the JWAM framework and have gathered experience with Extreme Programming techniques over the past three years. They are project coaches for Extreme

Programming and software architectures and have given a number of talks, tutorials, and demonstrations on various topics of software engineering and XP at international conferences, including XP2000 and XP2001, ECOOP, ICSTest, and OOP.

Robert Tunkel is a student at the University of Hamburg and a software developer at IT Workplace Solutions.

Chapter 41

Holmes—A Heavyweight Support for a Lightweight Process

—*Giancarlo Succi, Witold Pedrycz,*
Petr Musilek, and Iliyan Kaytazov

In the last few years, we have noticed the appearance of a few new software process models, particularly for software product lines and agile methodologies. Examples of the former include the Rational Unified Process [Kruchten2000], FAST [Lai+1999], RSEB [Jacobson+1997], and Pulse [Bayer+1999]. The most well known example of the latter is XP [Beck2000]. Most of the processes for software product lines have associated tools that help adopt the process and automate the creation of various artifacts that are necessary within the different phases of the process.

The support for lightweight processes is mainly concentrated within well-known and existing development tools such as source code editors and Integrated Development Environments (IDEs). Examples of these are the applications/plug-ins that support the process of refactoring [Fowler1999] and unit testing. Some of these recently evolved into inseparable parts of IDEs. However, beyond the level of source code support, there is little tool support for lightweight processes.

We believe that the role of tool support goes beyond simple automation of tedious tasks. When the tool captures the essence of a process methodology, it can be successfully used to establish and institutionalize a given software process within a company. In this chapter, we discuss the requirements of a tool to support lightweight processes, and present a possible design and implementation of such a tool.

Requirements for a Tool Supporting Lightweight Processes

A tool supporting a lightweight process should not impose any extra work on a developer. After all, part of the wisdom behind lightweight processes is to trim unnecessary "administrative" overhead.

Along the same lines, we should not force users to learn new tools when existing tools already do their work with satisfactory results. For this reason, whenever possible there should be some way to integrate tools that have already been adopted and used with satisfaction.

A lightweight process reduces the differences between traditional roles among developers and increases the variety of tasks that people perform within the same project. For instance, the same group of XP developers deals with customers, writes user stories, prepares and runs test cases, collectively owns the code, manages the configurations, and so on.

A supporting tool should help trace and manage the different tasks in which XP developers are involved. The entire development process—from user stories and the planning game up to daily testing and down to frequent releases—should be maintained and even made visible to managers, with a complete and thorough lightweight approach.

Specifically, user stories should be easily mapped to the associated CRC cards, which in turn should be coupled with the relevant implementation and testing code—again, in a way that does not create any additional burden on developers. Everything should then refer to the different versions of the system under configuration. A change in the name of an entity in a user story, for instance, should be automatically reflected in a change of names in the associated CRC cards, and so on down to the code.

Moreover, the speed of development, the associated leftover bugs, and the time spent in fixing them and in refactoring should all be monitored to improve the estimation ability required in the planning game.

Holmes is a tool that tries to address these requirements. Developed with an incremental approach, it addresses the problem of developing products or product lines with a lightweight approach.

Structure of Holmes

Holmes incorporates five main sources of information: domain definition, domain characterization, domain scoping, domain modeling, and domain framework development. By "domain" we refer to the problem domain, which the software system should address. By "source of information" we refer to key information required to develop the final system. Notice that these sources of information constitute a core of data that can be mapped to any of the results of tasks of any software endeavor, from the initial conception to the actual implementation.

Applying Holmes in an existing context requires linking each phase of development to these five activities. In the case of XP, we would tie the user stories to domain definition, the planning game to domain characterization, and so on.

During domain definition, the boundaries of the domain are defined—information from the users and domain experts is collected and organized in an appropriate form: user stories, use cases, or more formal requirements specification. Also, a preliminary analysis that determines the feasibility of the project is performed.

All the domain terms that are entered in this phase and are used in the other tools of Holmes are recognized automatically and turned into hyperlinks (see Figure 41.1). Thus a software practitioner can easily refer to the description of a given domain term. Similarly, the products entered into classified information are automatically added in the phase of domain characterization (see Figure 41.2). Any modification to a term is automatically propagated to all occurrences of the term in the system.

Thus, any information that spans multiple phases is added only once. Given that model—keeping data consistent among all phases of the tool—support for CRC cards can be easily added, and the classes associated with a given CRC card can be linked to it.

Domain characterization analyzes existing products that address the same or similar problems, and evaluates the possibility of adding some of their features in the future. That information is used to determine how the product may evolve and the minimum set of features that should be implemented to provide the highest value to the user.

Domain scoping deals primarily with prioritizing what should be developed next. Different variations of the product are considered by including a different subset of all features required by the customer or

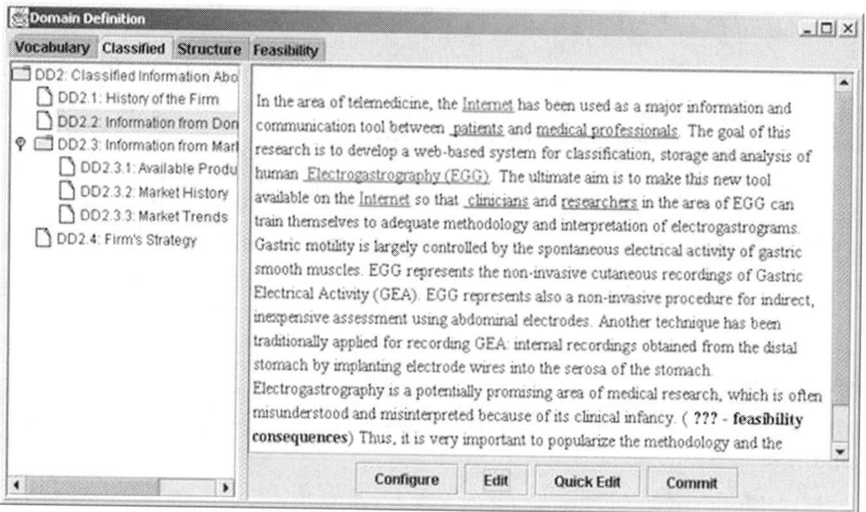

FIGURE 41.1 Domain definition

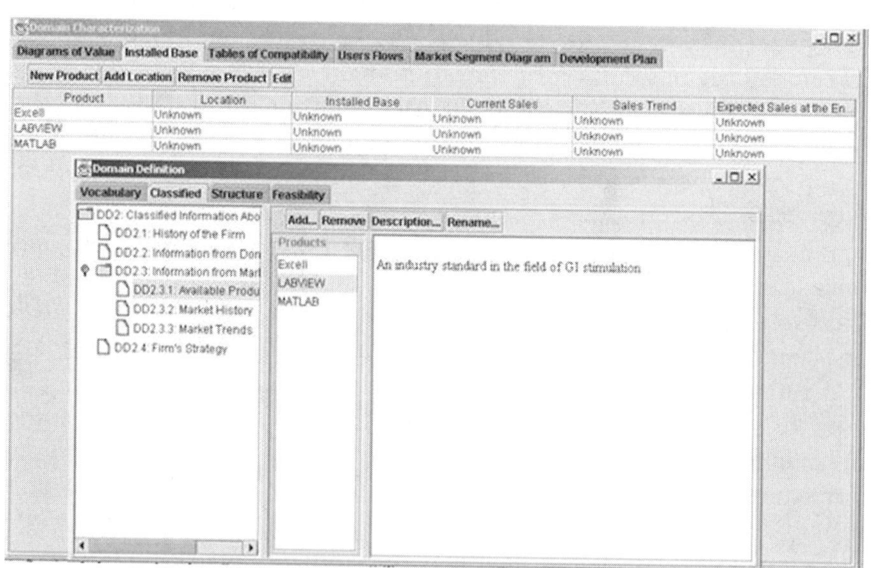

FIGURE 41.2 Adding the description of a new product

envisioned as possible future extensions. This is the crucial information for performing an informed planning game.

Domain modeling captures the requirements from the analysis of the product in the previous stages. It presents these requirements in the form of object-oriented modes, such as the CRC cards.

Domain framework development focuses on collecting the critical information for and from coding the final product. The framework consists of components that can be reused later in different parts of the software system. The reuse does not occur thanks to up-front decisions. Instead, having developed everything with a clean and coherent approach enables considering components for subsequent reuse.

A critiquing system permeates all the phases, enabling the system to provide customized semantics support for the different phases. The supporting system is customized with Prolog-based rules. It is within these rules that all the wisdom of XP can be put into practice.

The architecture of Holmes is completely open (see the next section for details), enabling complete integration of external tools. As mentioned, this is a key requirement for a lightweight introduction of Holmes.

Support for refactoring and unit testing can be provided by integrating some of the existing tools. Refactoring and unit testing can also take advantage of the critiquing system to reveal specific "patterns." Situations can be identified where refactoring and unit testing can be applied, and suggestions on how to perform them can be presented to developers.

Each part of Holmes can be logged for time elapsed and effort spent, and additional metrics can be extracted for subsequent business intelligence activities.

The Holmes Model of Tool Integration

Holmes Architecture

Holmes is built on a mixture of blackboard and implicit invocation architecture using a Linda tuple space [Gelernter1985], as implemented by Sun's JavaSpaces [Freeman+1999]. A tuple space is a form of virtual, shared, associative memory that generatively provides a repository for tuples.

One of its features is that an entity that is put in the tuple space continues to reside there as long as some other process does not take it from the space. The existence of an entity in the tuple space is completely decoupled from the existence of the process that created that entity and put it into the space. Therefore, a tuple space can be used as persistent storage that holds data to be exchanged among processes whose execution should not be constrained to overlap in time.

Another advantage of using a tuple space is that it provides an easy way to synchronize a number of processes that try to manipulate a set of shared objects. In that case, a process is given a random object among those that meet the criteria of the process. After the object is processed, it can be put back in the tuple space or disposed of, depending on the need.

In addition to time decoupling, a tuple space also provides space decoupling. In the JavaSpaces implementation, this is realized by using the Jini distributed technology. Every process that wants to access a JavaSpace uses the same uniform way of connecting to it, independent of whether the JavaSpace is executed on the same machine or somewhere else over a network.

Altogether, JavaSpaces supports the loose tool-to-framework integration that Holmes requires. Furthermore, the access method to any entity stored in JavaSpaces eliminates most of the difficulties usually associated with multiple users accessing a common resource. Certainly, such a method is not acceptable for any time-critical application, but strict timing is not an issue in our case.

The different tools incorporated in Holmes communicate using an algorithm similar to message-based communication (see Figure 41.3). In the proposed implementation, there are a few improvements over standard message passing. As mentioned earlier, the use of JavaSpaces waives the difficulty of properly initializing the communication channels between tools after they are started. JavaSpaces stores messages for as long as specified, including infinity. Other improvements are that the messages exchanged among the tools are objects, not data; a message queue implemented in Holmes is not susceptible to the number of tools that "subscribe" to the data posted on that queue.

The advantage of using messages as objects and not simple data is that an object encapsulates certain functionalities. Thus, the tools that communicate through objects are decoupled from the format of the data stored in the object, which actually represents a message. This flex-

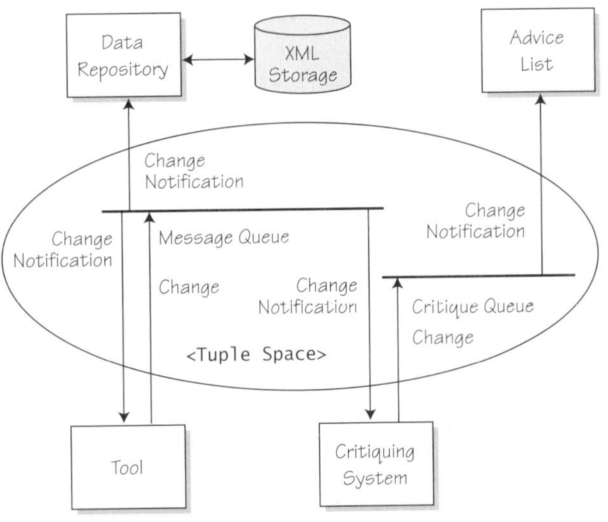

FIGURE 41.3 Holmes architecture

ibility is essential when dealing with diverse third-party tools, which use different output formats.

Implementing messages as objects turns them into functional units that perform the communication protocol. That way, changes made to the communication protocol leave the tools intact. The opportunity of using object-oriented design patterns, such as Adaptor, Visitor, and Strategy [Gamma+1995], leaves space for broad future evolution of the behavior offered by object-based messages.

Even though there are no clearly defined communication channels for exchanging messages among tools, the objects that represent these messages are organized into conceptual queues. These queues group messages belonging to semantically related data. A tool subscribes to queues that represent a flow of data the tool is interested in. A tool can act as either information provider or information subscriber. The way to enable that is to instantiate an object of type "writer" or "reader," respectively. All readers of a certain queue monitor JavaSpaces for specific types of messages. The order in which the readers subscribe to a queue is unrelated to the order in which they will actually read a message. In fact, that order is unpredictable and varies from message to message. Nevertheless, the sequence in which messages are posted to the queue is preserved when they are read. (For example, if message M1 is posted to a given queue before message M2, M1 will be read by a given reader before M2.)

Tools that act as information subscribers are not aware and do not depend on the type of tools that act as information providers, as long as they post messages that conform to the agreed interface.

The framework integrates the tools loosely in terms of time, type, and space. This implies a possible loss of performance, compared with structures supporting individual and clearly identified message channels among the tools.

Persistent Storage in Holmes

Holmes stores its data persistently through a number of tools, which are called repositories. Every repository stores semantically related information, just as queues group messages belonging to semantically related information. When a tool is started, all the other tools interested in the particular type of information provided by such a tool post a request for that information. If the repository responsible for that information is started and has activated its reader, it will notice the request, as will all other tools that monitor the queue, and will reply, posting the required data.

Similarly, when a tool makes a change to a certain piece of data, it posts the change on the queue. This gives all other tools, including the repository tool, a chance to update their copies as well. When the Holmes application is terminated, only the data contained in the repository tools is saved to persistent storage.

This way of storing data ensures that the repositories could hardly become a bottleneck in the system. The data, or parts of it, is distributed and duplicated among the tools that manipulate it. As explained, the use of JavaSpaces and objects as messages supports concurrent execution of multiple threads and polymorphic behavior on behalf of the tools.

Holmes data is stored using the Holmes Markup Language (HML), which is essentially XML [OMG1998; W3C1998] with a custom Document Type Declaration (DTD). The advantage of an XML-based format is that the data can be viewed in human-readable form by using a text or XML viewer. This maintains independence of the data from the particular tool that manipulates it. The human-readable structure also provides the capability of building DTD translators to convert from HML to other XML-based languages. Although it does not completely eliminate the need to build adapters (in this case, DTD translators), the effort is somewhat standardized and reduced. Obviously, the advantages of this approach rely on the growing popularity of XML as a data format, especially for product data management systems [Gould2000] and UML CASE tools.

References

[Bayer+1999] J. Bayer, O. Flege, P. Knauber, R. Laqua, D. Muthig, K. Schmid, T. Widen, J. DeBaud. "PuLSE: A Methodology to Develop Software Product Lines." *Proceedings of the Fifth ACM SIGSOFT Symposium on Software Reusability (SSR'99)*. 1999.

[Beck2000] K. Beck. *Extreme Programming Explained*. Addison-Wesley, 2000.

[Fowler1999] M. Fowler. *Refactoring: Improving the Design of Existing Code*. Addison-Wesley, 1999.

[Freeman+1999] E. Freeman, S. Hupfer, K. Arnold. *JavaSpaces Principles, Patterns, and Practice*. Addison-Wesley, 1999.

[Gamma+1995] E. Gamma, R. Helm, R.Johnson, J. Vlissides. *Design Patterns: Elements of Reusable Object-Oriented Software*. Addison-Wesley, 1995.

[Gelernter1985] D. Gelernter. "Generative Communication in Linda." *ACM Transactions on Programming Languages and Systems*, Volume 7, Number 1, 1985.

[Gould2000] J. Gould. "PDM/EDM/ERP/SCM ... Where Will It All End?" *Desktop Engineering*, Volume 5, Number 4, 2000. http://www.deskeng.com/articles/00/Feb/pdmedm/index.htm.

[Jacobsen+1997] I. Jacobson, M. Griss, P. Jonsson. *Software Reuse: Architecture, Process, and Organization for Business Success*. Addison-Wesley, 1997.

[Kruchten2000] P. Kruchten. *The Rational Unified Process: An Introduction*. Addison-Wesley, 2000.

[Lai+1999] C. Lai, D. Weiss. *Software Product-Line Engineering: A Family-Based Software Development Process*. Addison-Wesley, 1999.

[OMG1998] "XMI Revised Submission to the SMIF RFP." *OMG document ad/98-10-05*. http://www.omg.org/cgi-bin/doc?ad/98-10-05. 1998.

[W3C1998] "Extensible Markup Language (XML) 1.0." *W3C Recommendation REC-xml-19980210*. http://www.w3.org/TR/REC-xml. 1998.

Part VI

XEX: Extreme to the Extreme—Ideas on How to Extend XP and AMs

In Part VI, some ideas on how to extend the application of XP and agile methodologies (AMs) are presented.

First, in Chapter 42 Mark Paulk discusses how XP could be compliant with the Capability Maturity Model (CMM) for Software. In fact, XP addresses many CMM Level 2 and 3 practices and is even compatible with the requirements of Levels 4 and 5. On the other hand, CMM focuses on management and organizational issues that are not covered by XP. The conclusion is that a CMM-certified organization may actually use XP, provided that XP practices are thoughtfully implemented in an appropriate environment.

Chapter 43 is a deep explanation of the rationale and the value of the XP process from the perspective of quantitative risk analysis. Hakan Erdogmus and John Favaro first explain what the financial and real options are and how they can be evaluated; then they apply this theory to software development with changing requirements. They show in a quantitative way, perhaps with a depth never reached before in the software development field, why the XP process and practices can be more valuable than traditional big design up-front, from a risk management perspective.

Next, Chapter 44 deals with a big issue related to XP: Is it possible to use XP in a distributed environment? Although the usual answer is no, Michael Kircher, Prashant Jain, Angelo Corsaro, and David Levine present their experience and show how XP (or at least a substantial subset of it) can be applied by teams and developers working in different locations and even on different continents. Because distributed development is being used more and more, the information in this chapter is good news for many organizations.

Chapter 45, written by Ron Crocker, is also about one of the unresolved issues of XP: Is it possible to make XP scale to bigger projects than those with at most 10 to 15 developers? Ron analyzes the problem, identifies the reason why XP does not scale, and suggests a solution based on his experience with big projects with many interacting teams. Some rules and practices, which are beyond the scope of XP as currently defined, are proposed for inclusion in the methodology, not excluding other changes. In this way, the software development methodology would not be as agile as the original XP, but it would be able to scale.

Chapter 46 addresses another problem that could arise in applying XP in complex project settings. The issue occurs when the customer role is split between two figures: the prospective user of the system, who knows its technical requirements, and upper management (the *gold owner*), which knows the strategic and business goals of the system under development. In this situation, the planning game cannot be easily accomplished in the usual way, because whoever writes the user stories (the *goal donor*) has limited knowledge of the business value of each story. Martin Lippert, Stefan Roock, Henning Wolf, and Heinz Züllighoven propose a solution to this problem, based on their experience, that extends the classical XP roles.

Finally, Chapter 47 is about applying Semantic Analysis Patterns (SAPs) to XP. Based on his research, Eduardo Fernandez shows how knowing and applying SAPs can be a guideline in devising the system architecture, especially when global aspects such as distribution, security, and persistence must be addressed throughout the system.

Chapter 42

Extreme Programming from a CMM Perspective

—*Mark C. Paulk*

Extreme Programming (XP) has been advocated recently as an appropriate programming method for the high-speed, volatile world of Internet and Web software development. This popular methodology is reviewed from the perspective of the Capability Maturity Model (CMM) for Software, a five-level model that prescribes process improvement priorities for software organizations. Overviews of both XP and CMM are provided, and XP is critiqued from a Software CMM perspective. The conclusion is that lightweight methodologies such as XP advocate many good engineering practices, although some practices may be controversial and counterproductive outside a narrow domain. For those interested in process improvement, the ideas in XP should be carefully considered for adoption where appropriate in an organization's business environment because XP can be used to address many of the CMM Level 2 and 3 practices. In turn, organizations using XP should carefully consider the management and infrastructure issues described in the CMM.

Introduction

In recent years, XP has been advocated as an appropriate programming method for the high-speed, volatile world of Internet and Web software development. XP can be characterized as a "lightweight" or "agile" methodology. Although XP is a disciplined process, some have used it in arguments against rigorous models for software process improvement, such as the Capability Maturity Model for Software, a five-level model that prescribes process improvement priorities for software organizations, developed by the Software Engineering Institute (SEI). Many organizations moving into e-commerce have existing CMM-based initiatives (and possibly customers demanding mature processes) and want to know whether and how XP can address CMM practices adequately.

This chapter summarizes both XP and CMM and critiques XP from a CMM perspective. Although XP can be characterized as a lightweight methodology that does not emphasize process definition or measurement to the degree that models such as the CMM do, a broad range of processes can be considered valid under the CMM. As stated in the opening paragraph of this chapter, the conclusion is that agile methodologies such as XP advocate many good engineering practices, although some practices may be controversial and counterproductive outside a narrow domain, and that when thoughtfully implemented in an appropriate environment, XP addresses many CMM Level 2 and 3 practices. For those interested in process improvement, the ideas in XP should be carefully considered for adoption where appropriate in an organization's business environment, just as organizations considering XP should carefully consider the management and infrastructure issues described in the CMM.

The Software CMM

The Capability Maturity Model for Software [Paulk+1993; Paulk+1995] is a model for building organizational capability that has been widely adopted in the software community and beyond. The Software CMM is a five-level model that describes good engineering and management practices and prescribes improvement priorities for software organizations. The five maturity levels are summarized in Table 42.1.

TABLE 42.1 An Overview of the Software CMM

Level	Focus	Key Process Areas
5: Optimizing	Continual process improvement	Defect Prevention Technology Change Management Process Change Management
4: Managed	Product and process quality	Quantitative Process Management Software Quality Management
3: Defined	Engineering processes and organizational support	Organization Process Focus Organization Process Definition Training Program Integrated Software Management Software Product Engineering Intergroup Coordination Peer Reviews
2: Repeatable	Project management processes	Requirements Management Software Project Planning Software Project Tracking and Oversight Software Subcontract Management Software Quality Assurance Software Configuration Management
1: Initial	Competent people and heroics	

The Software CMM is intended to be:

- A commonsense application of process management and quality improvement concepts to software development and maintenance—the CMM practices are not rocket science (even the statistical process control concepts at Levels 4 and 5 have been successfully applied in other industries for decades).
- A community-developed guide—input from hundreds of software professionals was solicited in developing the current release of the CMM.

- A model for organizational improvement—which implies a set of priorities that may differ from those of any specific project, but which have been proven effective in organizational transformation.
- The underlying structure for reliable and consistent CMM-based appraisal methods—assessments and evaluations based on the Software CMM are widely used by software organizations for improvement and by customers for understanding the risks associated with potential suppliers.

Although the CMM is described in a book of nearly 500 pages, the requirements to be a Level 5 organization can be concisely stated in 52 sentences: the goals of the 18 key process areas (KPAs) that formally describe the model. The practices, subpractices, and examples that flesh out the model are informative material that guide software professionals in making reasonable, informed decisions about the adequacy of a broad range of process implementations—in environments as diverse as two- to three-person projects in a Web environment and 500-person projects building hard real-time, life-critical systems.

The informative material in the Software CMM is focused on large projects and large organizations, primarily in a custom development or maintenance environment. Even so, the degree of interpretation and tailoring required to use the CMM in radically different environments, such as small start-up companies, small projects, or e-commerce environments, is relatively minor so long as common sense is applied [Paulk1999; Johnson+2000]. The Software CMM's rating components are intended to be abstract enough to capture "universal truths" about high-performance software organizations, at least from a perspective of organizational excellence, and are listed in Table 42.2.

With the exception of Software Subcontract Management, which is not applicable if an organization does not do subcontracting, the key process areas and their goals should be applicable to any software organization. Companies that focus on innovation more than operational excellence may downplay the importance of consistency, predictability, and reliability, but performance excellence is important even in highly innovative environments. It is difficult to identify any goals in Table 42.2 that will not provide value to an organization, if thoughtfully implemented.

TABLE 42.2 Purpose and Goals of Software CMM Key Process Areas

	KPA Purpose and Goals
Tag	**Maturity Level 2—Repeatable**
Requirements Management	*. . . to establish a common understanding between the customer and the software project of the customer's requirements that will be addressed by the software project.*
RM Goal 1	System requirements allocated to software are controlled to establish a baseline for software engineering and management use.
RM Goal 2	Software plans, products, and activities are kept consistent with the system requirements allocated to software.
Software Project Planning	*. . . to establish reasonable plans for performing the software engineering and for managing the software project.*
SPP Goal 1	Software estimates are documented for use in planning and tracking the software project.
SPP Goal 2	Software project activities and commitments are planned and documented.
SPP Goal 3	Affected groups and individuals agree to their commitments related to the software project.
Software Project Tracking and Oversight	*. . . to provide adequate visibility into actual progress so that management can take effective actions when the software project's performance deviates significantly from the software plans.*
SPTO Goal 1	Actual results and performance are tracked against the software plans.
SPTO Goal 2	Corrective actions are taken and managed to closure when actual results and performance deviate significantly from the software plans.
SPTO Goal 3	Changes to software commitments are agreed to by the affected groups and individuals.
Software Subcontract Management	*. . . to select qualified software subcontractors and manage them effectively.*
SSM Goal 1	The prime contractor selects qualified software subcontractors.

Table continued on next page.

TABLE 42.2 *Continued*

Tag	KPA Purpose and Goals
	Maturity Level 2—Repeatable
SSM Goal 2	The prime contractor and the software subcontractor agree to their commitments to each other.
SSM Goal 3	The prime contractor and the software subcontractor maintain ongoing communications.
SSM Goal 4	The prime contractor tracks the software subcontractor's actual results and performance against its commitments.
Software Quality Assurance	*. . . to provide management with appropriate visibility into the process being used by the software project and of the products being built.*
SQA Goal 1	Software quality assurance activities are planned.
SQA Goal 2	Adherence of software products and activities to the applicable standards, procedures, and requirements is verified objectively.
SQA Goal 3	Affected groups and individuals are informed of software quality assurance activities and results.
SQA Goal 4	Noncompliance issues that cannot be resolved within the software project are addressed by senior management.
Software Configuration Management	*. . . to establish and maintain the integrity of the products of the software project throughout the project's software life cycle.*
SCM Goal 1	Software configuration management activities are planned.
SCM Goal 2	Selected software work products are identified, controlled, and available.
SCM Goal 3	Changes to identified software work products are controlled.
SCM Goal 4	Affected groups and individuals are informed of the status and content of software baselines.
	Maturity Level 3—Defined
Organization Process Focus	*. . . to establish the organizational responsibility for software process activities that improve the organization's overall software process capability.*
OPF Goal 1	Software process development and improvement activities are coordinated across the organization.
OPF Goal 2	The strengths and weaknesses of the software processes used are identified relative to a process standard.

TABLE 42.2 *Continued*

Tag	KPA Purpose and Goals Maturity Level 3—Defined
OPF Goal 3	Organization-level process development and improvement activities are planned.
Organization Process Definition	*. . . to develop and maintain a usable set of software process assets that improve process performance across the projects and provide a basis for cumulative, long-term benefits to the organization.*
OPD Goal 1	A standard software process for the organization is developed and maintained.
OPD Goal 2	Information related to the use of the organization's standard software process by the software projects is collected, reviewed, and made available.
Training Program	*. . . to develop the skills and knowledge of individuals so they can perform their roles effectively and efficiently.*
TP Goal 1	Training activities are planned.
TP Goal 2	Training for developing the skills and knowledge needed to perform software management and technical roles is provided.
TP Goal 3	Individuals in the software engineering group and software-related groups receive the training necessary to perform their roles.
Integrated Software Management	*. . . to integrate the software engineering and management activities into a coherent, defined software process that is tailored from the organization's standard software process and related process assets.*
ISM Goal 1	The project's defined software process is a tailored version of the organization's standard software process.
ISM Goal 2	The project is planned and managed according to the project's defined software process.
Software Product Engineering	*. . . to consistently perform a well-defined engineering process that integrates all the software engineering activities to produce correct, consistent software products effectively and efficiently.*
SPE Goal 1	The software engineering tasks are defined, integrated, and consistently performed to produce the software.
SPE Goal 2	Software work products are kept consistent with each other.

Table continued on next page.

TABLE 42.2 *Continued*

Tag	KPA Purpose and Goals
	Maturity Level 3—Defined
Intergroup Coordination	*. . . to establish a means for the software engineering group to participate actively with the other engineering groups so the project is better able to satisfy the customer's needs effectively and efficiently.*
IC Goal 1	The customer's requirements are agreed to by all affected groups.
IC Goal 2	The commitments between the engineering groups are agreed to by the affected groups.
IC Goal 3	The engineering groups identify, track, and resolve intergroup issues.
Peer Reviews	*. . . to remove defects from the software work products early and efficiently. An important corollary effect is to develop a better understanding of the software work products and of defects that might be prevented.*
PR Goal 1	Peer review activities are planned.
PR Goal 2	Defects in the software work products are identified and removed.
	Maturity Level 4—Managed
Quantitative Process Management	*. . . to control the process performance of the software project quantitatively. Software process performance represents the actual results achieved from following a software process.*
QPM Goal 1	The quantitative process management activities are planned.
QPM Goal 2	The process performance of the project's defined software process is controlled quantitatively.
QPM Goal 3	The process capability of the organization's standard software process is known in quantitative terms.
Software Quality Management	*. . . to develop a quantitative understanding of the quality of the project's software products and achieve specific quality goals.*
SQM Goal 1	The project's software quality management activities are planned.
SQM Goal 2	Measurable goals for software product quality and their priorities are defined.

TABLE 42.2 *Continued*

Tag	KPA Purpose and Goals
	Maturity Level 4—Managed
SQM Goal 3	Actual progress toward achieving the quality goals for the software products is quantified and managed.
	Maturity Level 5—Optimizing
Defect Prevention	*. . . to identify the cause of defects and prevent them from recurring.*
DP Goal 1	Defect prevention activities are planned.
DP Goal 2	Common causes of defects are sought out and identified.
DP Goal 3	Common causes of defects are prioritized and systematically eliminated.
Technology Change Management	*. . . to identify new technologies (that is, tools, methods, and processes) and transition them into the organization in an orderly manner.*
TCM Goal 1	Incorporation of technology changes is planned.
TCM Goal 2	New technologies are evaluated to determine their effect on quality and productivity.
TCM Goal 3	Appropriate new technologies are transferred into normal practice across the organization.
Process Change Management	*. . . to continually improve the software processes used in the organization with the intent of improving software quality, increasing productivity, and decreasing the cycle time for product development.*
PCM Goal 1	Continuous process improvement is planned.
PCM Goal 2	Participation in the organization's software process improvement activities is organization wide.
PCM Goal 3	The organization's standard software process and the projects' defined software processes are improved continuously.

Extreme Programming

Extreme Programming is a lightweight (or agile) software methodology (or process) that is usually attributed to Kent Beck, Ron Jeffries, and Ward Cunningham [Beck1999; Beck2000; Siddiqi2000]. XP is targeted toward small to medium-sized teams building software in the face of vague and/or rapidly changing requirements. XP teams are expected to be colocated, typically with less than ten members.

The critical assumption underlying XP is that the high cost of change has been (or can be) addressed by technologies such as objects/patterns, relational databases, and information hiding. As a consequence of this assumption, the resulting XP process is intended to be highly dynamic. Beck's book is subtitled *Embrace Change*, and the XP team deals with requirements changes throughout an iterative life cycle with short loops. The four basic activities in the XP life cycle are coding, testing, listening, and designing. The dynamism is demonstrated via four values: continual communication with the customer and within the team, simplicity by always focusing on the minimalist solution, rapid feedback via unit and functional testing (among other mechanisms), and the courage to deal with problems proactively.

Most of the principles espoused in XP, such as minimalism, simplicity, an evolutionary life cycle, short cycle times, user involvement, good coding standards, and so forth, are commonsense and appropriate practices in any disciplined process. The "extreme" in XP comes from taking commonsense practices to extreme levels, as summarized in Table 42.3. Although some may (improperly) interpret practices such as "focusing on a minimalist solution" as meaning hacking, in reality XP is a highly disciplined process. Simplicity means focusing on the highest-priority, most valuable parts of the system as currently identified rather than designing solutions to problems that are not yet needed—and may never be needed as the requirements and operating environment change.

XP can be summarized by 12 practices. Although many other practices can be considered part of XP, these 12 are the basic set.

1. *Planning game*—Quickly determine the scope of the next release, combining business priorities and technical estimates. The customer decides scope, priority, and dates from a business perspective, while technical people estimate and track progress.
2. *Small releases*—Put a simple system into production quickly. Release new versions on a very short (two-week) cycle.
3. *Metaphor*—Guides all development with a simple, shared story of how the whole system works.

TABLE 42.3 The "Extreme" in Extreme Programming

Commonsense Practice	XP Extreme	XP Implementation
Code reviews	Review code all the time.	Pair programming
Testing	Test all the time, even by the customers.	Unit testing, functional testing
Design	Make design part of everybody's daily business.	Refactoring
Simplicity	Always leave the system with the simplest design that supports its current functionality.	The simplest thing that could possibly work
Architecture	Everybody will work to refine the architecture all the time.	Metaphor
Integration testing	Integrate and test several times a day.	Continuous integration
Short iterations	Make iterations really, really short—seconds and minutes and hours, not weeks and months and years.	Planning game

4. *Simple design*—Design as simply as possible at any given moment.
5. *Testing*—Continually write unit tests that must run flawlessly; customers write tests to demonstrate that functions are finished. "Test, then code" means a failed test case is an entry criterion for writing code.
6. *Refactoring*—Restructure the system without changing behavior to remove duplication, improve communication, simplify, or add flexibility.
7. *Pair programming*—All production code is written by two programmers at one machine.
8. *Collective ownership*—Anyone can improve any code anywhere in the system at any time.
9. *Continuous integration*—Integrate and build the system many times a day, every time a task is finished. Continual regression testing means no regressions in functionality as a result of changed requirements.

10. *40-hour week*—Work no more than 40 hours per week as a rule; never work overtime two weeks in a row.
11. *On-site customer*—A real, live user on the team full-time to answer questions.
12. *Coding standards*—Rules emphasizing communication throughout the code.

The planning game and small releases depend on the customer providing a set of "stories," or short descriptions of features, that characterize the work to be performed in each release. Releases are two weeks apart, and the team and customer must agree on which stories (simple use cases) will be implemented within a two-week period. A pool of stories characterizes the full functionality desired by the customer, but only the subset identified as those features most desired by the customer for the next two-week release are being implemented at any time. New stories can be added to the pool at any time; thus the requirements can be highly volatile. But implementation proceeds in two-week chunks based on the most desired functions currently in the pool; thus the volatility is managed. An on-site customer is needed to support this style of iterative life cycle.

"Metaphor" provides the overarching vision for the project. This could be considered a high-level architecture, but XP emphasizes design while at the same time minimizing design documentation. Some have characterized XP as not allowing documentation outside code [Allen2001], but it is probably more accurate to say that because XP emphasizes continual redesign (via refactoring whenever necessary), there is little value to detailed design documentation—and maintainers rarely trust anything other than the code anyway. Design documentation is typically thrown away after the code is written. The only time design documentation is kept is when the customer can no longer come up with any new stories. Then it is time to put the system in mothballs and write a five- to ten-page "mothball tour" of the system. A natural corollary of the emphasis on refactoring is to always implement the simplest solution to satisfy the immediate need. Changes in the requirements are likely to supersede "general solutions" anyway.

Pair programming is one of the more controversial practices in XP because it has resource consequences for the managers who decide whether or not the project will use XP. Although it may appear that pair programming will lead to twice the resources, research has shown that pair programming leads to higher quality and decreased cycle time [Williams+2000]. For a jelled team, the increase in effort may be as little as 15%, while the reduction in cycle time may be 40–50%. For Internet-time environments, the increased speed-to-market may be well worth the increment in effort. Collaboration improves the problem-solving process, and the increase in quality will also have a significant impact on maintenance costs, which appears likely to more than pay for any added resource costs over the total life cycle.

Collective ownership means that anyone can change any piece of code in the system at any time. The XP emphasis on continuous integration, continual regression testing, and pair programming is intended as protection against problems here.

"Test, then code" is the phrase used to express XP's emphasis on testing. It captures the principle that testing should be planned early and test cases developed in parallel with requirements analysis, although the traditional emphasis is on black-box testing. Thinking about testing early in the life cycle is a well-known good software engineering practice, even if too infrequently practiced.

The basic XP management tool is the metric, and the medium of the metric is the "big visible chart." In the XP style, three or four measures are typically all a team can stand at one time, and those should be actively used and visible to the team. "Project velocity," the number of stories of a given size that can be done in an iteration, is one recommended XP metric.

When adopting XP—that is, the XP attitude toward process improvement—the recommendation is to adopt XP one practice at a time, always addressing the most pressing problem for your team. As one might expect, the XP attitude toward change is that it's "just rules"—the team can change the rules at any time as long as they agree on how they will assess the effects of the change. The advocates of XP recognize that XP is an intensely social activity, and not everyone can learn it. Having said this, it must also be recognized that XP is a "system" or "methodology" that demonstrates emergent behavior, and to gain the full benefit of XP, a reasonably complete set of the basic practices is needed.

XP, Process Rigor, and the CMM

The values of XP should be captured in any modern software project, even if the implementation may differ radically in other environments.

Communication and simplicity may be stated in other terms (coordination and elegance, for example), but without them, nontrivial projects face almost insurmountable odds. The XP principles of communication and simplicity are fundamental process design principles for organizations using the Software CMM also. When defining processes, organizations should capture the minimum essential information needed, use good software design principles (such as information hiding and abstraction) in structuring the definitions, and emphasize usefulness and usability [Paulk1999]. Rapid feedback is crucial to real-time process control; it has even been captured in previous centuries by aphorisms such as "Don't throw good money after bad," and in the quantitative sense can be considered the soul of Level 4. One of the consequences of the Level 1 to 2 culture shift is demonstrating the courage of our convictions by focusing on realism in our estimates, plans, and commitments.

Much of the formalism that characterizes most CMM-based process improvement is an artifact of large projects and/or severe reliability requirements, especially for life-critical systems. The hierarchical structure of the Software CMM is intended to support a broad range of implementations within the context of the 18 key process areas and 52 goals that compose the requirements for a fully mature software process.

As a system becomes larger, some XP practices become more difficult to implement. As projects become larger, emphasizing a good architectural "philosophy" becomes increasingly critical to project success. Architecture-based design, designing for change, refactoring, and similar design philosophies emphasize the need for dealing with change in a systematic fashion. Variants of these concepts, including architecture-based design and integrated product teams, may be more appropriate in large-project contexts, perhaps in conjunction with XP within teams. In a sense, architectural design that emphasizes flexibility is the goal of any good object-oriented methodology, so XP (with refactoring) and object orientation are well suited to one another. Multidiscipline teams are also problematic because XP is aimed at software-only projects.

The main objection to using XP for process improvement is that it barely touches the management and organizational issues that the Software CMM emphasizes. Putting in place the kind of highly collaborative environment that XP assumes requires enlightened management and appropriate organizational infrastructure. The argument that process discipline in the CMM sense—even to the point of a rigorous, statistically stable process—is antithetical to XP is unconvincing. XP has disciplined processes, and it is apparent that the XP process is a "well-defined" process. CMM and XP can be considered complementary. The Software CMM tells what to do in general terms but does not say how to do it, while XP is a set of best practices that contains fairly specific how-to information—an *implementation* model—for a particular kind of environment. XP practices may be compatible with the intent of a practice (or goal or key process area), even if they do not completely address it.

At Level 2, Requirements Management is addressed by stories, on-site customer, and continuous integration. Software Project Planning is addressed by the planning game and small releases. The XP planning strategy embodies Watts Humphrey's dictum, "If you can't plan well, plan often."

Software Project Tracking and Oversight is addressed by the "big visual chart," project velocity, and commitments (stories) for small releases. The commitment process for XP sets clear expectations for both the customer and the XP team at the tactical level and maximizes flexibility at the project's strategic level. The emphasis in XP on 40-hour weeks is a general management concern that is not addressed in the CMM but is considered a best practice. XP also emphasizes open workspaces, a similar "people issue" that is outside the scope of the CMM. Software Subcontract Management is not addressed by XP (and is likely to be not applicable in the target environment).

Although an independent Software Quality Assurance (SQA) group is unlikely to be part of an XP culture, SQA could be addressed by the culture of pair programming; ensuring conformance to coding standards is a typical SQA responsibility that is handled by peer pressure in an XP environment. However implemented, a CMM-based process has mechanisms for objectively verifying adherence to requirements, standards, and procedures. The XP reliance on peer pressure, although effective in most environments, may be vulnerable to external pressures, and this vulnerability should be considered at the organizational level.

Software Configuration Management (SCM) is partially addressed via collective ownership, small releases, and continuous integration. Although not completely and explicitly addressed, configuration management is implicit in these XP practices. Collective ownership may be problematic for large systems, where communication channels need to be more formalized to be effective, and could lead to SCM failures.

At Level 3, Organization Process Focus is addressed at the team level rather than the organizational level, but the philosophy behind adopting XP one practice at a time and "just rules" implies a focus on process issues. Because XP focuses on the software engineering process rather than the organizational infrastructure issues, this and other organization-level processes are areas that need to be addressed by organizations adopting XP, whether in a CMM-based context or not. Similarly, Organization Process Definition and Training Program are partially addressed by the various books, articles, courses, and Web sites on XP, but organizational assets are outside the scope of XP. As a consequence, Integrated Software Management cannot be addressed, because there may not be any organizational assets to tailor.

Software Product Engineering is well addressed in many ways by the XP methodology with metaphor, simple design, refactoring, the "mothball" tour, coding standards, unit testing, and functional testing. The lack of design documentation would be a concern in many environments, such as hard real-time systems, large systems, or virtual teams. In such environments, good designs are crucial to success, and the refactoring strategy would be high risk. For example, refactoring after a system has been proved to satisfy hard real-time requirements by a technique such as rate monotonic analysis would mean that the analysis would need to be redone—the assumption that change does not have a high cost would be invalid in such an environment.

Intergroup Coordination is addressed by the on-site customer and pair programming. XP's emphasis on communication appears to result in as comprehensive a solution to intergroup coordination as integrated product and process development (and could be judged an effective IPPD approach), although the software-only context ignores multidiscipline environments.

Peer Reviews is addressed by pair programming. Pair programming may be more powerful than peer reviews, in the sense of code reading and literate programming, although the lack of structure may lessen its effectiveness. The empirical data on pair programming is currently sparse but promising [Williams+2000]. Contrasting and comparing pair programming and peer review techniques remain an area needing empirical research as a basis for making informed trade-off decisions.

Few of the Level 4 and 5 key process areas are addressed by XP in a rigorous statistical sense, although Defect Prevention may be partially addressed by feedback during rapid cycles. Potential satisfaction of

TABLE 42.4 Satisfaction of Software CMM Key Process Areas by XP

Level 2 KPAs	Satisfaction	Level 3 KPAs	Satisfaction	High-Maturity KPAs	Satisfaction
RM	√ √	OPF	√	**Level 4 KPAs**	
SPP	√ √	OPD	√	QPM	—
SPTO	√ √	TP	—	SQM	—
SSM	—	ISM	—	**Level 5 KPAs**	
SQA	√	SPE	√ √	DP	√
SCM	√	IC	√ √	TCM	—
		PR	√ √	PCM	—

√ Partially addressed in XP
√ √ Largely addressed in XP (perhaps by inference, in the appropriate environment)

CMM key process areas by XP is summarized in Table 42.4, at least within the appropriate domain for XP.

Many of the key process areas partially covered or not addressed in XP are undoubtedly addressed in real projects. XP cannot survive without management and infrastructure support, even if it is not explicitly called out. It seems fair to say that XP focuses on the technical work, where the CMM focuses on the management work, but a concern with "cultural issues" is evident in both.

Conclusion

Most of XP consists of good practices that should be thoughtfully considered for any environment. Although the merits of any of these practices can be debated in comparison with other ways of dealing with the same issues, none of them should be arbitrarily rejected.

Putting these practices together as a methodology may be a paradigm shift in the same sense that concurrent engineering is. The concepts in concurrent engineering have been around for decades; integrating those concepts as a system results in a paradigm shift in how to build products. In a similar manner, XP provides a systems perspective on programming (if not the only one), just as the Software CMM provides a systems perspective on organizational process improvement. Organizations that want to improve their capability should take advantage of the good ideas in both and exercise common sense in selecting and implementing those ideas.

The Software CMM focuses on the management issues associated with putting effective and efficient processes in place, along with systematic process improvement. XP is a specific set of practices—a "methodology"—that is effective within its context of small, colocated teams. Both have good ideas that can be synergistic, particularly in conjunction with other good engineering and management practices. It is questionable whether XP, as published, should be used for life-critical or high-reliability systems. The lack of design documentation and the deemphasis on architecture would be judged risky decisions by most knowledgeable professionals, but one of the virtues of XP is that it can be changed and improved for different environments.

The risk in changing XP is that the emergent properties providing value in its proper context may not emerge. Still, the emphasis in choosing and improving software processes should be to let common sense prevail—and to use data whenever possible to provide insight when answering challenging questions.

References

[Allen2001] P. Allen. "XP Explained." *The Cutter Edge*, June 5, 2001.

[Beck1999] K. Beck. "Embracing Change with Extreme Programming." *IEEE Computer*, Volume 32, Number 10, October 1999.

[Beck2000] K. Beck. *Extreme Programming Explained*. Addison-Wesley, 2000.

[Johnson+2000] D. Johnson, J. Brodman. "Applying CMM Project Planning Practices to Diverse Environments." *IEEE Software*, Volume 17, Number 4, July/August 2000.

[Paulk+1993] M. Paulk, B. Curtis, M. Chrissis, C. Weber. "Capability Maturity Model, Version 1.1." *IEEE Software*, Volume 10, Number 4, July 1993.

[Paulk+1995] M. Paulk, B. Curtis, M. Chrissis, C. Weber. *The Capability Maturity Model: Guidelines for Improving the Software Process.* Addison-Wesley, 1995.

[Paulk1999] M. Paulk. "Using the Software CMM with Good Judgment." *ASQ Software Quality Professional*, Volume 1, Number 3, June 1999.

[Siddiqi2000] J. Siddiqi, ed. "Extreme Programming Pros and Cons: What Questions Remain?" *IEEE Computer Society Dynabook*, November 2000. http://computer.org/seweb/dynabook/Index.htm.

[Williams+2000] L. Williams, R. Kessler, W. Cunningham, R. Jeffries. "Strengthening the Case for Pair Programming." *IEEE Software*, Volume 17, Number 4, July/August 2000.

About the Author

Mark C. Paulk works at the Software Engineering Institute at Carnegie Mellon University in Pittsburgh, Pennsylvania. He can be reached by e-mail at mcp@sei.cmu.edu.

Chapter 43

Keep Your Options Open: Extreme Programming and the Economics of Flexibility

—*Hakan Erdogmus and John Favaro*

Financial evaluation and strategic analysis have long been considered two distinct approaches to evaluating new capital initiatives. An emerging valuation approach, known as real options, *attempts to align finance and strategy through a new perspective: The value of an asset lies not only in the amount of direct revenues that it is expected to generate, but also in the options that it creates for flexible decision making in the future. In general, the more uncertain the future is, the higher the value of flexibility embedded in an asset, whether financial or real. This perspective has significant implications for the economics of flexible processes. Applied to software development, it could imply that a lightweight process that is well positioned to respond to change and future opportunities creates more value than a heavy-duty process that tends to freeze development decisions early. Thus, the feasibility of Extreme Programming (XP) can be supported by the option value of flexibility inherent in it. What is the theory that underlies this statement? How does it relate to the fundamental assumptions of XP? How does it impact the value of an XP project? What are the implications of such value propositions for project decisions. If you are curious, read on . . .*

Introduction

Change: Ally or Enemy?

Kent Beck, during a workshop on XP for capitalists, provoked the audience by proposing that XP could create ten times more value than a heavyweight process. How can this ever be possible? Consider the two fundamental premises of XP.

A. Change is inevitable. Just about the only thing you can predict with some certainty is that *change will happen*. In *Extreme Programming Explained*, Beck emphasizes this point.

> *Everything in software changes. The requirements change. The design changes. The technology changes. The team changes. The team members change. The problem isn't change per se, because change is going to happen; the problem, rather, is the inability to cope with change when it comes.* [Beck2000]

B. Change is easy. The cost of change does not rise exponentially as the system grows. Contrary to popular belief, the rise in the cost of change gradually diminishes.
We don't question premise A. We take it as a given.

> *XP is a lightweight methodology for small-to-medium teams developing software in the face of vague or rapidly changing conditions.* [Beck2000]

Premise B is more controversial. We don't know whether it's true or whether it is universally true. We don't know whether it is a consequence of the 12 XP practices or of the advancements in software practice and technology in general. Thus, we will condition our conclusions and insight on the truth (or falsity) of premise B. For the time being, let's take it as a given as well.

Consider the following XP principles and practices.

1. Embracing change
2. Simple design
3. Small initial investment
4. Incremental change

5. Small releases
6. Continuous refactoring

How does one get from the premises A and B to the principles and practices 1 through 6? At a gut level, if change is inevitable, naturally the best way to manage it would be to embrace it. It all seems to make sense, but the cause-effect relationships between the premises and the resulting principles and practices of XP, as well as among the principles and practices themselves, are more subtle and complex than they first appear. True, a flattened cost curve would make 1 through 6 possible. But why would it also ultimately make XP more profitable? True, investing in a complex design would not make sense under highly volatile and vague requirements. But wouldn't this argument hold under an exponential cost-of-change curve even more strongly than it does under a flat cost-of-change curve? So again, how does XP create more value here?

The answer lies behind a crucial characteristic of XP: *flexibility.* Change is driven by uncertainty. At the heart of any process designed to cope with uncertainty is flexibility. Embracing change means treating uncertainty as an ally rather than viewing it as an enemy. Embracing change means embracing flexibility. Most of the principles and practices, indeed most things that are fundamental to XP, can be in one way or another traced back to flexibility. And flexibility creates value under uncertainty. The more uncertainty there is, the more value it creates.

What Is It with Flexibility, Anyway?

> *Flexibility can be viewed as an option.*
>
> —Nobel Prize Lecture in Economics, 1997

This simple yet provocative statement, made during the conferral of the most prestigious prize in economics, forms the point of departure for the discussion of the economics of XP.

Let's begin by considering a simple example of flexibility: a fully refundable plane ticket. Such a ticket gives its holder the flexibility to recover the full cost of the ticket in case of an unexpected event. In other words, the customer has the *option* to exchange the ticket for its cost on or before the travel date should such an event occur. The flexibility provided by the option is desirable if the future is uncertain—the more uncertain the future is, the more desirable the flexibility is. The customer can think of the ticket as a risky asset: If such an event occurs, without the flexibility, the ticket will be worthless; if everything goes well, the ticket will preserve its value.

A refundable ticket costs more than a nonrefundable ticket. Why? Because customers are willing to pay for the additional flexibility, which protects them in case of a negative development, or if they simply change their mind. The airline company demands a premium for this option over the price of a nonrefundable ticket because by offering a full refund, it risks flying with an empty seat and incurring a loss as a result. Customers, by agreeing to pay for the additional flexibility provided by the refundable ticket, implicitly believe that the value of the option, with respect to the amount of uncertainty they are facing, is comparable or superior to the premium demanded by the airline.

Options, Options Everywhere

Options arise everywhere in the business world. Here are some more concrete examples from software development.

- ✧ A pioneering Internet security project with a follow-on opportunity in the growing e-business market: Undertaking the pilot creates the option to be a player in an emerging market. This is an example of a *growth option* [Benaroch+2000; Favaro+1999; Taudes1998].
- ✧ Development of a framework for a future product line: The infrastructure investment enables efficient generation of a multitude of closely related applications without committing to a particular one. This is an example of a *platform option* [Erdogmus2001B; Favaro+1998].
- ✧ Abandoning a staged migration project midstream when budget overruns overtake the expected benefits: The ability to stop adds value proportional to the losses that would be incurred with continuing. This is an example of an *exit option* [Erdogmus+1999; Favaro+1998].
- ✧ Developing a prototype before the full application to resolve technical and user uncertainty: Investing first a small amount to learn reveals the feasibility of the larger investment. This is an example of a *learning option* [Sullivan1996].

- Waiting to see whether the Java technology gains acceptance before migrating a stable application to Java: Waiting before committing may be a cheap way to learn. This is an example of a *delay*, or *timing*, *option* [Benaroch+1999].

These strategic options, both technical and business-driven, commonly arise in the general software industry, but the topic of the discussion is Extreme Programming. What is the relationship of XP to the concept of such options?

XP as an Options-Driven Process

> *We need to make our software development economically more valuable by spending money more slowly, earning revenue more quickly, and increasing the probable productive lifespan of our project. But most of all, we need to increase the options for business decisions.* [Beck2000]

Beck's declaration makes it clear that the founders of XP also believe in the importance of creating business options—and believe that XP is capable of creating them. Some examples that should be familiar to the XP practitioner are the following:

- Checkpoints after every iteration, where the customer can make midcourse decisions
- Talented, trained personnel able to switch course rapidly with new or modified stories
- The ability to modify the project at a small cost through enabling technologies and best practices
- Waiting to see whether the customer really wants a feature before implementing it

The 12 practices and four values of XP are also a fertile source of business options.

- *Small releases* introduce decision points and opportunities to change course. At the end of a release, the customer has the option to continue, modify the course of the project, or stop, based on what has been learned from the previous releases. This flexibility increases the value of the project while reducing its risk.

Part VI

- *Refactoring* makes future options to modify the system more valuable by keeping the cost of change at bay.
- *Collective ownership* increases the chances of an option to improve the system to be exercised in a timely manner, which in turn increases its value.
- *Continuous integration* preserves business value. Anytime, you can stop and still have a working system that can be delivered to the customer with some inherent value. The option to exit is more valuable for the customer because of this salvage value.
- *Simplicity* creates options to modify the system. Complex code and design ossify the system. The simpler the code, the easier to modify it, and the higher the resulting option value.
- *Communication*, *feedback*, *pair programming*, *on-site customer*, and *testing* all help reveal information and resolve uncertainty. When uncertainty is not resolved, options cannot be exercised in a rational and timely manner, destroying the value of flexibility.
- *Courage* is required to exercise the options created. Without it, the options are worth nothing. Without courage, options virtually don't exist. Conversely, courage is also required to let go when it is revealed that an existing option is no longer likely to create business value.

All these points make a convincing argument that XP is a powerful options-driven process, capable of generating significant value. However, we also need an economic foundation for analyzing *why* and *how much* value is created by options. This brings us to one of the central activities of finance: valuation.

Valuation Basics: How to Quantify the Value of Capital Investments

Valuation is the process of estimating how much an asset is worth. An XP project is subject to the same fundamental principles of valuation as any other real asset, as summarized this way:

> *By adding up the **cash flows** in and out of the project, we can simply analyze what makes a software project valuable. By taking into account the effect of **interest rates**, we can calculate the **net present***

***value** of the cash flows. We can further refine our analysis by multiplying the **discounted cash flows** by the **probability** that the project will survive to pay or earn those cash flows.* [Beck2000]

That single paragraph contains references to most of the fundamental principles of valuation (shown in boldface, added for emphasis), so let's pick it apart now. Comprehensive coverage of the subject is beyond the scope of this chapter. In what follows, we provide an overview of only the most basic concepts as they relate to the current discussion. Suggestions for further reading are provided at the end of the chapter.

In finance, the costs and benefits associated with an investment are called *cash flows*. Investments are compared only on the basis of their cash flows. Cash flows are often represented in tabular form according to chosen time periods—for example, in years, quarters, or months. Usually, there is an original investment, C_0, represented as a negative number. Subsequent cash flows are denoted as $C_1, \ldots C_n$, spanning the time horizon in which the investment incurs costs and generates benefits.

Discounted Cash Flow and Net Present Value

The *present value* (PV) of a future cash flow is the value of the cash flow as though it were received today. How does one calculate the PV of a future cash flow?

Moving forward from present to future, an investment is expected to grow at a certain rate of return. Now turn it around: Moving backward from future to present, an investment shrinks with the same rate of return.

When moving back in time, the rate of backward adjustment is called the *discount rate*. The process of backward adjustment itself is called *discounting*. The general technique of valuing a capital investment project by summing its discounted future cash flows is known as *discounted cash flow* (DCF).

The DCF calculation doesn't usually include the initial investment, C_0. When that initial investment is included (represented as a negative cash flow), the *net present value* (NPV) is obtained: the benefits minus the costs. All of this is expressed in the following simple formula:

$$\text{NPV} = C_0 + \frac{C_1}{(1+k)} + \frac{C_2}{(1+k)^2} + \ldots$$

Here, the C's represent the cash flows, the subscripts represent the periods in which the cash flows occur, and k is the per-period discount rate. The NPV formula tells us whether the investment is worth more than it costs. The rule is that if NPV is positive, the investment is worth undertaking—it generates more value than it costs. If it is negative, it should be forgone—it generates less value than it costs. If it is zero, we are indifferent between undertaking and forgoing it.

A Valuation Example

We illustrate DCF and NPV in action by considering the development scenario illustrated in Figure 43.1. The horizontal line represents the time horizon extending to five years out. The outgoing arrows represent negative cash flows, or expected costs, including the initial investment (development cost) and the subsequent investments (maintenance costs). The incoming arrows represent positive cash flows, or expected benefits from sales revenues. The discount rate is given as 7% annual.

The straight net value of the investment is calculated simply by summing all the cash flows. In thousands of dollars, the calculation is as follows:

$$\text{Straight Net Value} = -1000 - (3 \cdot 200) + 400 + 800 + 400 + 200 = \mathbf{200}$$

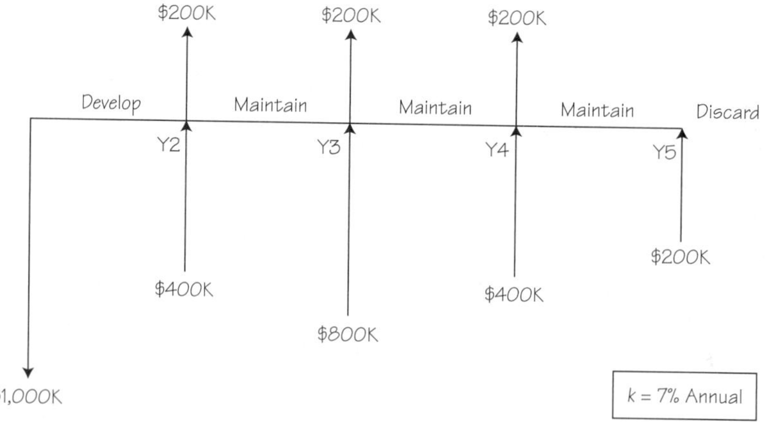

FIGURE 43.1 Cash flows of a software development project

According to this result, the net value is positive, and the project should be undertaken. However, the DCF approach yields a very different conclusion. The NPV, calculated using DCF, is as follows:

$$\text{NPV} = -1000 - \left(\sum_{t=2..4} \frac{200}{(1+0.07)^t}\right) + \frac{400}{(1+0.07)^2} + \frac{800}{(1+0.07)^3} + \frac{400}{(1+0.07)^4} + \frac{200}{(1+0.07)^5}$$

$$= \mathbf{-178}$$

The negative result tells us that the project is not worth undertaking. The cost of the investments exceeds the return on investment expected from the project. Therefore, if undertaken, the project would destroy value rather than create it.

It's All about Risk

Risk management is taken very seriously in XP. Clearly, then, risk has to be taken into consideration in any economic valuation of an XP project.

Software engineers have an intuitive view of risk that is related more to project management, even to sociology or psychology, than to finance. XP is no exception. Usually, risk is characterized by what can go wrong in the project, and the strategies for dealing with this problem have been limited to implementing the riskiest artifacts first. From the financial point of view, however, risk has a much more precise, well-defined meaning. Financial risk refers to the variability in the returns of an asset [Ross+1996]. It has two components:

- Systematic component—Market risk, a.k.a. systematic risk or nondiversifiable risk
- Unique component—Private risk, a.k.a. unsystematic risk or diversifiable risk

Private risk corresponds to the traditional software engineering view of risk. However, no business works in a vacuum—all businesses participate in a market and are affected by systematic risks that permeate the

TABLE 43.1 Private Risk Versus Market Risk in XP Projects

Private	Market
• Project canceled • System goes sour • Business misunderstood • Business changes • False feature-rich • Schedule slips • Staff turnover • Defect rate • Technology	• How much will the clients be willing to pay? • How much will skilled programmers cost? • How uncertain are fixed costs? Overhead? • How well is the economy doing? • Where are the short-term interest rates heading?

system in general and the sector in which they operate in particular. These systematic risks range from the overnight bank loan rate determined by the Federal Reserve Bank (in the United States) to the outbreak of war.

Table 43.1 contrasts the well-known risks identified for an *individual* XP project with the market risks that affect *many* projects. Market risks are often easier to tackle because they are priced by financial markets. Those are the risks that well-diversified investors are mainly worried about because diversification can minimize, if not completely eliminate, private risk.

Both market and private risk can figure into the simple NPV equation. When cash flows are estimated, effectively private risk must be taken into account. If things go well for the project, more will be earned. If things go badly, the cash flows will be smaller. So the private risk is accounted for in the *unbiased* estimates of cash flows in the *numerator* of a DCF term in the NPV equation. An unbiased estimate of a cash flow is calculated as a statistical expectation by considering as many scenarios as is feasible and the respective likelihood of these scenarios.

In contrast, market risk is accounted for in the *denominator* of a DCF term by adjusting the discount rate. The higher the market risk, the higher the discount rate. Figure 43.2 illustrates how the NPV equation accounts for private and market risk.

Corporations have developed practices to determine discount rates based on the returns of past projects and grouping of like projects into

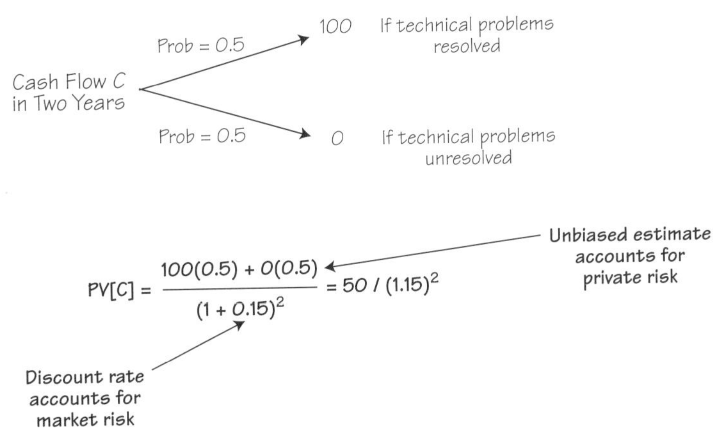

FIGURE 43.2 Accounting for private and market risk in the NPV equation

risk categories. In addition, many organizations specialize in the estimation of market risk, examining the historical returns of companies and deducing the amount of market risk borne to develop projections.

From Traditional Valuation to Real Options

Discounted cash flow is the foundation of modern valuation. It provides a method for capturing the value over time of operational benefits and costs associated with any investment so long as those benefits and costs can be cast in currency terms. We have seen that DCF techniques can deal with both project-specific, or private, risk (through unbiased expected cash flow forecasts) and systematic, or market, risk (through a suitably adjusted discount rate) associated with these operational costs and benefits.

DCF alone, however, is not sufficient for capturing *all* value inherent in a project. DCF can be used to evaluate the operational benefits from *business as usual*, often the case in a stable environment with well-understood and measurable costs and benefits, but it has little to offer to capture additional business value that is due to flexibility under uncertainty, such as strategic opportunities, learning, and the ability to respond to changing conditions.

Part VI

This orthogonal dimension of value generation requires techniques that can explicitly model *active management.* Although DCF works well only for deterministic projects with a linear timeline, projects that can be represented by a linear stream of expected cash flows, it does not work well for projects with future decisions that depend on how uncertainty resolves—for example, XP projects. For this purpose, we must turn to the intuition and more powerful techniques offered by the theory of option pricing.

Option Basics

In its most general form, an option refers to a future discretionary action. Financial options have been traded for centuries. They date back to seventeenth-century Holland, where tulip options were common. Investors bought options to buy and sell yet-to-be-developed tulip varieties.[1]

Options are a form of *derivative* [Hull1997]. The value of an option—that is, the price to be paid to acquire the option or the value it adds to an existing portfolio of assets—depends on the value of an underlying asset. For financial options, the underlying asset can be a stock price, an exchange rate, or a commodity spot price. For *real options,* the underlying asset is a real asset, typically a stream of future cash flows.

A large body of jargon is associated with the options trading industry. Fortunately, we need only the most basic terminology in this chapter. A *call option* refers to the right, without a symmetric obligation, to buy a risky asset at a preset price—called the *strike price* (a.k.a. *exercise price* or *exercise cost*)—on or before a future date, called the *expiration date* (a.k.a. *maturity date*) of the option.[2]

Figure 43.3 illustrates how an option works, with a simple example. Consider a call option on a stock whose *current price* is $50, with an *expiration date* after six months at a *strike price* of $45. Now let's consider two cases, where the stock price either goes up, to $75, or down, to $35, in six months. If the stock price goes up, the holder of the option exercises the option by buying the stock for $50 and selling it at its market value of $75, making a profit of $30. Otherwise, the holder of

1. Before long, the practice led to enormous speculation and a spectacular crash. To this day, speculative bubbles, such as the market crash in dot-com stocks in 2001, are commonly referred to as *Tulip Mania.*

2. The opposite is a *put option,* which refers to the right to sell an asset at a preset price on or before a future date.

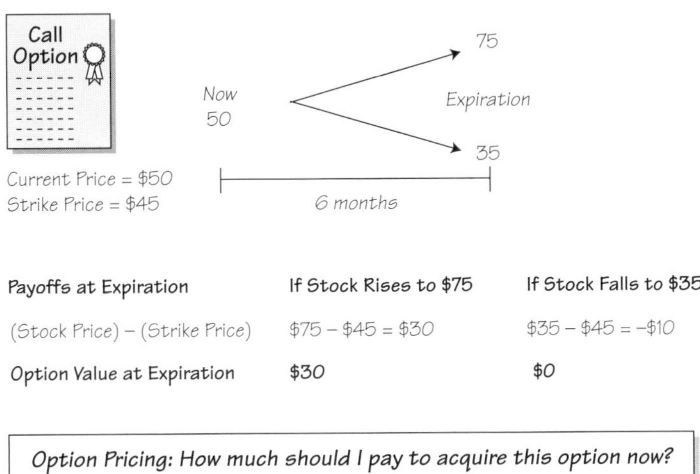

FIGURE 43.3 Call option example

the option does nothing, and the option expires worthless. Thus, the option is worth either $30 or nothing at maturity.

Five parameters determine the value of a call option, as shown in Figure 43.4. The arrows next to each parameter indicate whether a higher value of that parameter *increases* or *decreases* the value of the option.

Rational Exercise

The holder of a call option exercises the option only if the price of the underlying asset is above the strike price (the upper straight line in Figure 43.4), to avoid a loss. This practice constitutes a fundamental assumption of option pricing called *rational exercise.*

The rational exercise assumption is behind the behavior of an option's value in response to changes in volatility and the expiration date. As the volatility (total risk) of an asset and time horizon increases, the tendency of the asset's value to move away from its initial value also increases. Rational exercise prevents such an increased tendency to affect the maximum loss, thereby limiting downside risk, but without a symmetrical restriction on the size of the payoff in the case of a positive development.

From Financial Options to Real Options

So far the discussion has focused on the *financial* world of stocks and options; but the main interest of this chapter is in the *real* world of

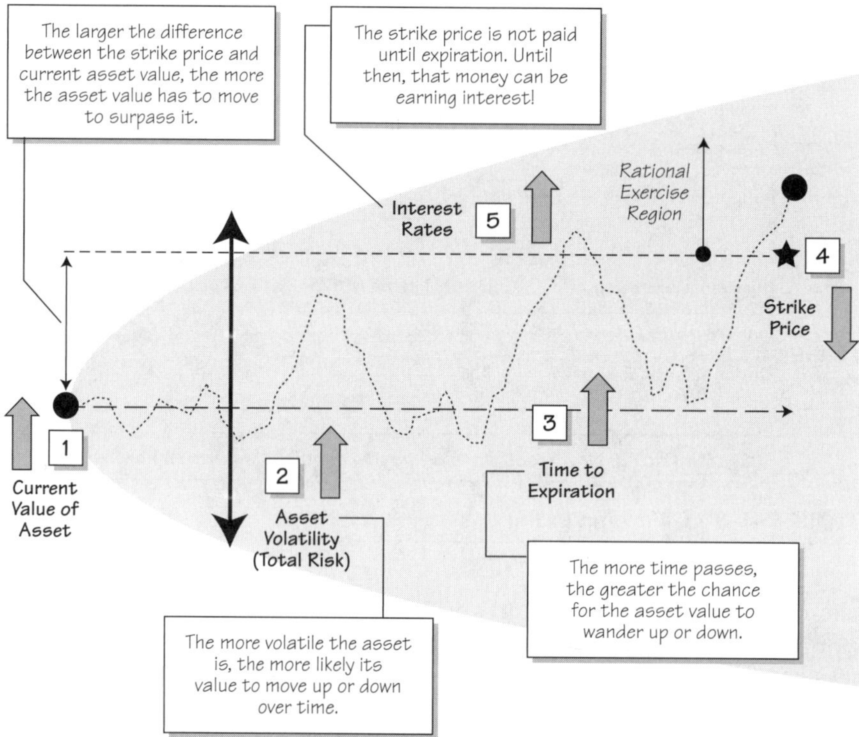
The larger the difference between the strike price and current asset value, the more the asset value has to move to surpass it.
The strike price is not paid until expiration. Until then, that money can be earning interest!
Rational Exercise Region
Interest Rates
5
4
Strike Price
1
Current Value of Asset
2
Asset Volatility (Total Risk)
3
Time to Expiration
The more time passes, the greater the chance for the asset value to wander up or down.
The more volatile the asset is, the more likely its value to move up or down over time.

FIGURE 43.4 Five parameters determining the value of a call option

projects—and processes that drive them. How do we make the leap from one to the other?

The term "real options" was coined in 1977 by Stewart C. Myers of the Massachusetts Institute of Technology (MIT), who first realized that financial option pricing techniques could be applied to the evaluation of projects. The essence of his insight is illustrated in Figure 43.5. The figure maps the five parameters affecting a financial option's value shown in Figure 43.4 to the analogous factors in real-world projects.

The analogy is not quite as simple as Figure 43.5 suggests. In the financial world, parameters such as the current price of a stock (parameter 1 in Figure 43.4) and its uncertainty (parameter 2 in Figure 43.4) are determined by the markets. In the world of real assets, however, it is

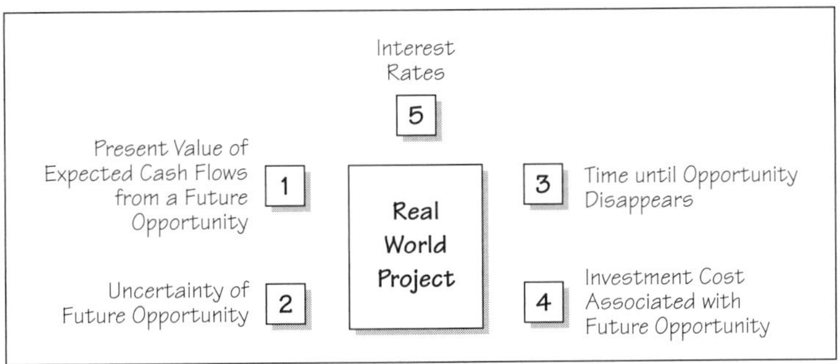

FIGURE 43.5 Analogy between financial and real options

usually necessary to estimate them through other means—often without much information to work from.

A full treatment of the relationship between financial options and real options is outside the scope of our discussion, but the main differences are summarized in Table 43.4 at the end of the chapter. For the purposes of this chapter, we take the analogy for granted and move on to the application of options to XP.

XP and Options

A basic understanding of how options work helps us understand how some of the basic XP value propositions can be justified using the fundamental tenets of XP. In this section, we examine two of these value propositions.

- *Proposition 1:* Delaying the implementation of a fuzzy feature creates more value than implementing the feature now.
- *Proposition 2:* Small investments and frequent releases create more value than large investments and mega-releases.

We begin with the technical premise of XP and its relation to the first proposition. Then we tackle the second proposition in the context of staged investments and learning. The option pricing models used to analyze each scenario are introduced just in time along the way.

The Technical Premise of XP

> *The software development community has spent enormous resources in recent decades trying to* ***reduce the cost of change****—better languages, better database technology, better programming practices, better environments and tools, new notations . . . It is* the *technical premise of XP.* [Beck2000]

XP challenges one of the traditional assumptions of software engineering: that the cost of changing a program rises exponentially over time, as illustrated in Figure 43.6.

The technical premise of XP is that this pathological behavior is no longer valid. Better technologies, languages, practices, environments, and tools—objects, database technologies, pair programming, testing, and integrated development environments come to mind—all help keep software pliable. The result is a cost-of-change function that resembles the dampened curve in Figure 43.7.

Why is a flattened cost curve important for an options-driven process? A flattened cost curve amplifies the impact of flexibility on value. It does so by creating new options that would not have existed under

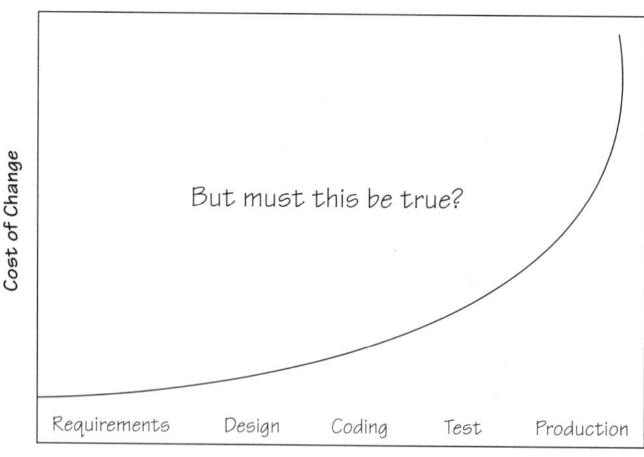

FIGURE 43.6 The traditional assumption about the cost of change

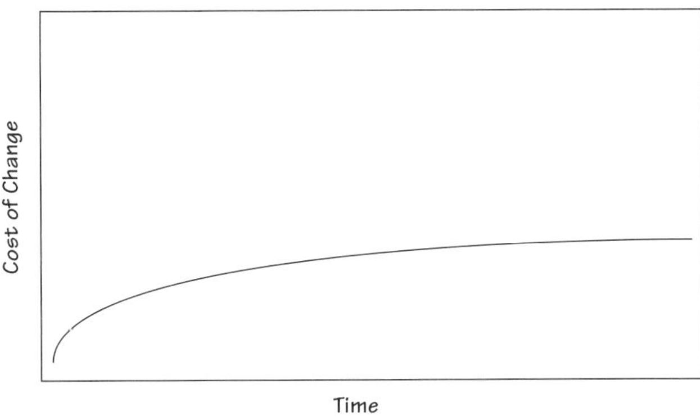

FIGURE 43.7 The technical premise of XP

an exponential cost function and by reducing the exercise cost, and therefore increasing the value, of existing options.

You Aren't Going to Need It: Now or Later?

> *We are traditionally told to plan for the future . . . Instead, XP says to do a good job . . . of solving today's job today . . . and add complexity in the future where you need it. The economics of software as options favor this approach.* [Beck2000]

One of the most widely publicized principles of XP is the "You Aren't Going to Need It (YAGNI)" principle. The YAGNI principle highlights the value of delaying an investment decision in the face of uncertainty about the return on the investment. In the context of XP, this implies delaying the implementation of fuzzy features until uncertainty about their value is resolved. YAGNI is a typical example of *option to delay*, an all too common type of real option.

Extreme Programming Explained provides an example of the application of options theory to YAGNI.

> *Suppose you're programming merrily along and you see that you could add a feature that would cost you $10. You figure the return on this feature (its present value) is somewhere around $15. So the net present value of adding this feature [now] is $5. Suppose you knew in your heart that it wasn't clear at all how much this new*

Part VI

feature would be worth—it was just your guess, not something you really knew was worth $15 to the customer. In fact, you figure that its value to the customer could vary as much as 100% from your estimate. Suppose further that it would still cost you about $10 to add that feature one year from now. What would be the value of the strategy of just waiting, of not implementing the feature now? . . . Well, at the usual interest rates of about 5%, the options theory calculator cranks out a value of $7.87. [Beck2000]

The scenario is illustrated in Figure 43.8.

The delay option underlying the YAGNI scenario is much akin to a financial call option, an option to acquire a risky asset on a future date. We will analyze the scenario using the famed Black-Scholes formula for calculating the value of a call option on an uncertain asset—the same formula used by Beck in *Extreme Programming Explained*. To understand in what way the cost of change affects the value proposition underlying the YAGNI scenario, we need to dig a little deeper into the option pricing theory.

Option Pricing 101

Three financial economists, Fisher Black, Myron Scholes, and Robert Merton, undertook the groundbreaking work on option pricing in the early '70s. Their efforts won them a Nobel Prize in economics in 1997. The equation published in a seminal paper in 1973 on the pricing of derivatives and corporate liabilities became known as the Black-Scholes formula [Black+1973]. The Black-Scholes formula revolutionized the

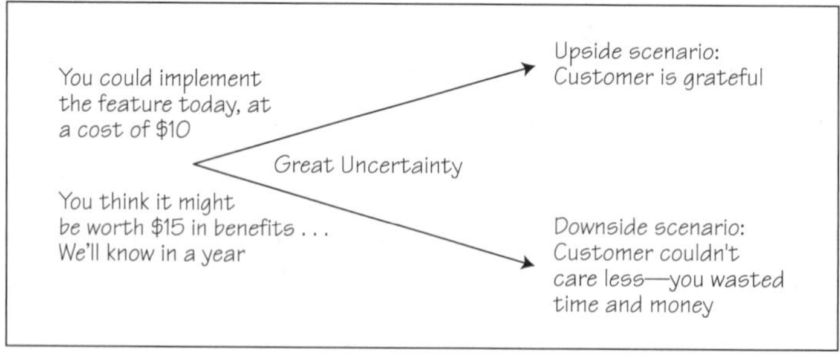

FIGURE 43.8 YAGNI scenario

financial options trading industry. Both the theory and the resulting formula in various forms are now widely used.

The Black-Scholes equation is illustrated in Figure 43.9. In the equation, C denotes the value of a call option on a non-dividend-paying asset with a strike price of L. M is the current value of the underlying asset, the asset on which the option is written. The option expires at time t. The risk-free interest rate is denoted by r_f, expressed in the same unit as t. The risk-free rate is the current interest rate on the risk-free asset, such as a short-term Treasury bill or government bond. Its value can simply be looked up in the business section of a daily newspaper. $N(.)$ is the cumulative normal probability distribution function, and "exp" denotes exponential function.

The parameter σ denotes the *volatility* of the underlying asset. Volatility is a measure of total risk, which subsumes both market and private risk. It is given by the standard deviation of the continuous rate of return on the asset's price (value) over time. Usually, this parameter is estimated using historical data. For a stock option, volatility can be estimated by calculating the standard deviation of the stock's past returns over small intervals spanning a representative period—for example, using weekly returns over the past 12 months. For real assets, estimation of volatility is much trickier, but sometimes market data can still be used. An example from software development is provided in [Erdogmus2001B].

The parameters M (the current value or price of the underlying asset), σ (the volatility of the underlying asset), t (the option's time to

$$C = N(d_1) \times M - N(d_2) \times L \exp(-r_f t)$$

$$d_1 = \frac{\ln\left(\frac{M}{L}\right) + t\left(r_f + \frac{\sigma^2}{2}\right)}{\sigma\sqrt{t}}$$

$$d_2 = d_1 - \sigma\sqrt{t}$$

C Value of call option on risky asset
L Strike (exercise) price
t Time to expiration
r_f Risk-free interest rate
M Current price of asset
σ Volatility (standard deviation of asset's rate of return)
$N(.)$ Cumulative normal probability distribution function

FIGURE 43.9 The Black-Scholes formula for the value of a call option

expiration), L (the option's strike price), and r_f(the risk-free interest rate) correspond to the five standard parameters of option pricing illustrated in Figure 43.4.

How did Black, Scholes, and Merton invent this magic equation? All earlier attempts at solving the option pricing problem involved calculating the net payoff of the option at expiration under the rational exercise assumption and then discounting this payoff back to the present to determine its current value. This approach required identifying the proper discount rate for the uncertain payoff. Essentially, the risk of an option is different from, and often much higher than, the risk of its underlying asset. Even if the discount rate for the underlying asset is known, choosing the proper discount rate for all possible payoffs of the option under different exercise scenarios is inherently problematic. Black, Scholes, and Merton succeeded not by *solving* the discount rate problem, but by *avoiding* it. Their solution is based on two key concepts:

- Replicating portfolio
- The law of one price, also known as no arbitrage

The first concept, *replicating portfolio*, states that the behavior of an option can be replicated by a portfolio consisting of a certain amount of the underlying asset and a risk-free loan to partially finance the purchase of the underlying asset. Thus, it is not necessary to buy options—one can create a *do-it-yourself* or synthetic option through a combination of the underlying asset and a loan. The option is then effectively equivalent to a *levered* position in the underlying asset. Indeed, the idea of financial leveraging has been known for a long time: Buying on margin has been widely practiced, especially during the stock market boom of the '90s.

The second concept, the *law of one price*, or *no arbitrage*, states that an efficient market lacks money machines. If one can replicate the behavior of an option exactly by a corresponding portfolio, the portfolio and the option are interchangeable for all practical purposes and thus must be worth the same. The two assets—the option and the replicating portfolio, with exactly the same payoffs under the same conditions—must have the same price. If the exact composition of the replicating portfolio, and therefore how much it is worth in the present, can be determined, then how much the option is worth in the present will also be known. Option pricing problem solved!

The original derivation of the Black-Scholes equation is based on solving a specific stochastic differential equation in continuous time. Cox, Ross, and Rubinstein provide a much simpler derivation originating from a discrete model [Cox+1979], which we will also take advantage of later in the chapter. In the YAGNI example, we will stick with the Black-Scholes model.

Evaluation of the YAGNI Scenario

Table 43.2 illustrates the application of the Black-Scholes formula to the YAGNI scenario.

The NPV of implementing the feature now is $5 (the $15 present value of expected benefits, minus the $10 cost of implementation). If the implementation is deferred for one year, at a volatility of 100%, the

TABLE 43.2 Calculation of the Option Value of the YAGNI Scenario

B-S Variable	Value	Explanation
M	15.00	B-S: Current price of underlying asset YAGNI: PV of benefits from proposed, deferrable feature implementation
L	10.00	B-S: Strike (exercise) price of the call option YAGNI: Cost of implementing proposed, deferrable feature
r_f	0.05	B-S: The risk-free rate of return YAGNI: The opportunity cost of implementation; the return that the implementation cost would earn if invested in a risk-free security
t	1.00	B-S: Years until expiration of the option YAGNI: Date on which feature implementation decision must be taken
s	1.00	B-S: Volatility of the underlying asset (standard deviation of the asset's rate of return) YAGNI: Volatility of the feature's benefits (the standard deviation of the return of feature's benefits)
C	**7.87**	B-S: Value of Black-Scholes call option YAGNI: Value of waiting one year before implementing the feature

Black-Scholes model yields an option value of $7.87, provided that the cost of implementation stays the same. Because deferring implementation incurs no initial cost, the option value equals the NPV of waiting a year before deciding whether to implement the feature. This value takes into account the possibility that the planned feature may be worthless in one year, which would force its implementation to be forgone, as well as the possibility that the actual benefit of the feature may very well exceed today's estimate of $15 (because of uncertainty), which would make the feature a much more profitable investment. The flexibility of deferring the decision increases the value created, because it helps limit the downside risk of the investment without a symmetric limitation on its upside potential.

Uncertainty is a key factor in this example. Figure 43.10 illustrates how the value created by waiting in the YAGNI scenario varies in response to the level of uncertainty, everything else being equal. Uncer-

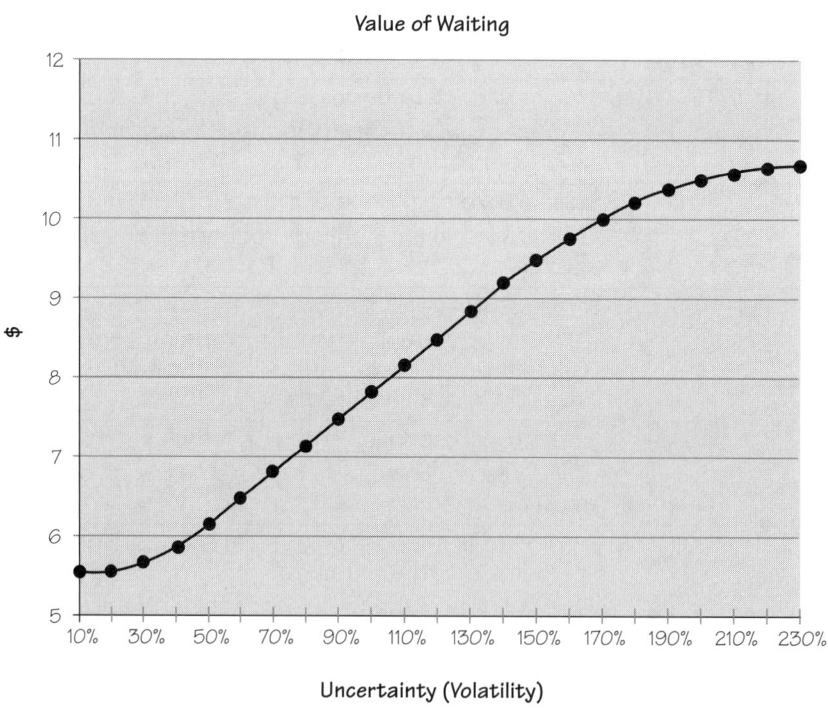

FIGURE 43.10 Sensitivity of the value of the YAGNI scenario to uncertainty

tainty is captured by the volatility of the feature's benefit. As the volatility increases, the option value of waiting also increases.

A Deeper Look at YAGNI

The YAGNI example discussed in the previous section assumes that the cost of change is constant over time. More insight can be gained through a closer look at the value of the YAGNI delay option under other cost functions. Consider the following two cost curves:

- A *traditional* cost curve, where the cost of change exponentially increases over time
- A *flattened* cost curve, where the cost of change gradually increases over time at a diminishing rate

An example of each type of cost curve is plotted in Figure 43.11. To see how the shape of the cost curves and waiting time affect the value created, we reevaluate the YAGNI scenario, using these sample curves.

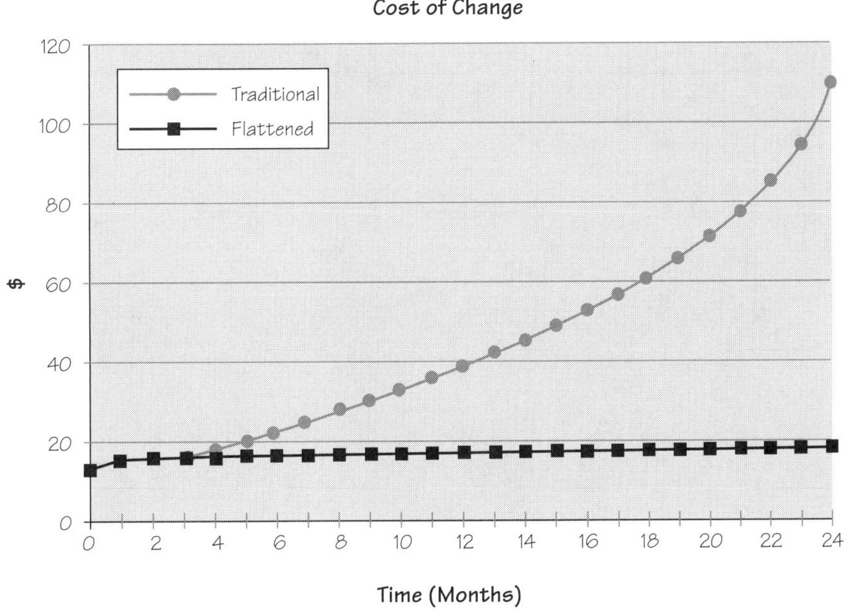

FIGURE 43.11 Sample cost curves: traditional versus flattened cost of change

Assume that the volatility of the feature's benefit is constant at 100% per year. Because this is per-period volatility, as waiting time (or the expiration date of the option) increases, cumulative volatility—total uncertainty around the benefit—also increases. The longer one waits, the more likely it is for the actual benefit to wander up and down and deviate from its expected PV of $15.

Figure 43.12 shows the result of reevaluating of the YAGNI option under the two cost curves. The option value, the value of waiting before implementing the feature, is shown for different waiting times for each curve. The dashed line represents the benchmark NPV of $5—the value of implementing the feature now, without any delay.

The bottom curve in Figure 43.12 reveals that under the traditional cost curve, waiting does not make much economic sense. Delaying the

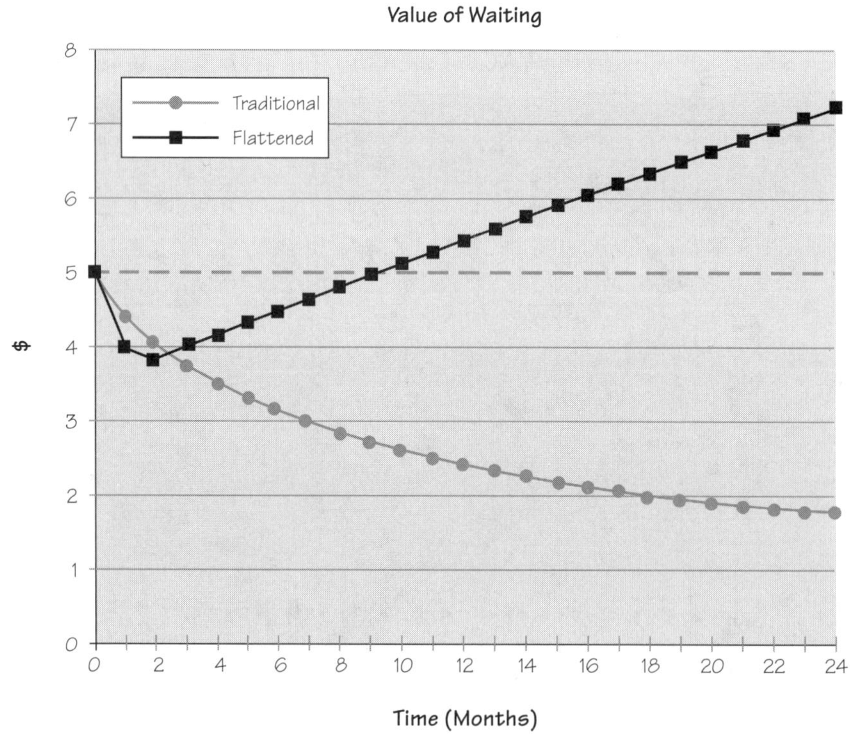

FIGURE 43.12 Option value of waiting under traditional and flattened cost curves

implementation decision destroys value because the increase in the cost of change overtakes the benefit of the flexibility to make the implementation decision later. As a result, the longer we wait, the less value we create.

Under the flattened cost curve (the top curve in Figure 43.12), however, the behavior is drastically different. If the uncertainty is expected to be resolved within a threshold waiting time, waiting is not profitable because of the initial ramp-up in the cost of change. After this initial, rapid ramp-up, the cost curve flattens, and waiting becomes increasingly profitable. The option value crosses over the $5 benchmark at approximately ten months, the threshold waiting time. Beyond this point, delaying the implementation decision creates more value than the immediate implementation of the feature.

In summary, the option pricing theory confirms that under the traditional cost model of change, decisions about system features should be committed to as soon as possible: Waiting is not desirable in this situation. However, under a flat cost curve, the timing of commitment depends on the level of uncertainty and when uncertainty about the benefits of the features is expected to be resolved. If uncertainty is high or it is expected to be resolved over the long term, decisions about system features should be committed to as late as is feasible; otherwise, they should be committed to now. Finally, under a constant cost function, commitment should always be made later rather than sooner. Figure 43.13 summarizes these conclusions.

Why Small Investment and Frequent Releases?

Another important principle of XP is to start with a small initial investment. How can XP afford to start a project with few rather than many resources? What is the rationale behind this principle? Consider this statement from the CEO of an international consulting firm, made during a discussion of the strategy of a start-up venture in Silicon Valley.

> *I'm convinced that successful new ventures—successful new anythings—come from* thinking big, but starting small. *Most big failures come from* thinking big and starting big *and getting into trouble financially or strategically because there hasn't been enough learning to translate the big idea into a workable idea before overcommitting the amount of money or how the big idea is*

implemented. Iridium—the Motorola satellite-based mobile phone venture—comes to mind as an example. Note how [the president of the start-up being discussed] is gradually building up his capital base through a series of small financing rounds rather than a big-bang financing that, had he been successful in getting it, probably would have led to poor use of the money because he hadn't learned enough about how to translate his big idea into a workable one.

—K. Favaro, CEO, Marakon Associates

In XP, the rapid feedback supplied by tight iterations resolves uncertainty, whether technical or business-related, and permits the results of the learning process to be incorporated into subsequent iterations. Tight implementation cycles and frequent releases provide decision points where the information that has been revealed can be taken advantage of to modify the course of the project. If the project is going badly, it can always be stopped. If it's going well, there is an option to continue with the next cycle. This process of continuous learning and acting based on the information revealed improves flexibility and minimizes risk. The cost of learning is limited to the small investment required to complete a small cycle, and its impact is therefore proportionately small. Taking proper action after learning increases value if the cost of learning is relatively small.

Type of Cost Function

Level of Uncertainty / Time Horizon	Traditional	Flattened	Constant
Low/ Short	Now	Now	Later
High / Long	Now	Later	Later

FIGURE 43.13 YAGNI scenario and the cost of change: implement now or implement later

In the rest of this section, we illustrate exactly how small investments and frequent releases increase the value created.

A Black Hole: Large Investment, No Learning

First consider the complete opposite of small investments and frequent releases: a scenario involving a large initial commitment, but no learning, no decision points. Essentially, this is a single-stage project with a large investment in the beginning and a mega-release at the end.

Figure 43.14 illustrates the scenario. The only decision in the scenario is that of go/no-go in the beginning. Alas, whether the large investment will pay off is not known *a priori*. Uncertainty about the success of the project is resolved only once the release has gone out the door, at the end. The probability of the project ending up worthless may be substantial because the course of the project could not be modified in the face of new information. There are no opportunities to take corrective action.

Now to lighten up things a little, assume that the probability of complete failure is zero. Throwing in a few numbers will make things more concrete.

- The large investment will cost $110 in present value terms.
- The total duration of the project is four months.

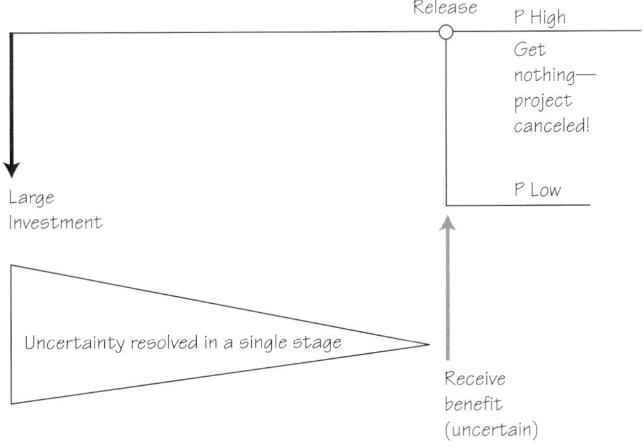

FIGURE 43.14 A single-stage project with no intermediate learning

Part VI

- ✧ The expected benefit of the whole project, again in present value terms, is $100.
- ✧ The benefit is subject to a monthly volatility of 40%.

Where multiple sources of uncertainty are present, the volatility measure collapses the different factors involved into a single factor. Each of these factors may have both a private and a market component. In this case, let's suppose that changing customer requirements are the sole source of uncertainty as with the YAGNI scenario, which again may be affected by both external and internal developments. What does the 40% figure imply? If the product were ready now, the customer would expect an immediate benefit of $100 in PV terms. Think of the 40% volatility as the standard deviation of the monthly percentage change in this expectation based on past experiences.

NPV in the Black Hole

The NPV of the single-stage project is simply the PV of the expected benefit, net of the PV of the large investment. Because all figures are expressed in PV terms, they have already been discounted. Thus, the NPV is calculated as follows:

$$\text{NPV} = 100 - 110 = -10$$

A negative NPV! The project does not look attractive. According to the NPV rule, it should not be undertaken, because it is expected to destroy rather than create value.

Remarkably, here we did not use the volatility of the benefit in the calculation of the NPV. This is because the benefit was already specified in *expected* PV terms—that is, the risk of the benefit is factored into the $100 estimate. Alas, such is not always the case. As we will see, the volatility plays a crucial role when the project involves decision points in the middle.

Light at the End of the Tunnel: Small Investments with Learning

Having established a benchmark for comparison with the single-stage project, let's now consider the alternative scenario, which is the real focus of the current discussion. This time, the same project is undertaken in multiple stages, each stage requiring a relatively small investment and resulting in a new release. This new scenario is illustrated in Figure 43.15.

Here are some characteristics of the new scenario. The releases progress in small increments. The stages can be ordered to implement the higher-value features first so that the PV of the total value realized is maximized (*earn early, spend late*). Moreover, each stage provides a learning opportunity. The customer can revise the estimates of future benefits and make an informed decision on whether to stop, continue as is, or modify the course of the project. The development team can similarly learn and steer technical choices and manage customer expectations according to the revised estimates. Uncertainty is gradually resolved in multiple steps.

Most remarkably though, each stage effectively creates a *real option* to undertake a subsequent stage. If the project is abandoned midstream, the value created during previous stages can at least be partially preserved: Only the investment associated with the last release will be completely lost. The additional value created by staging over the benchmarked single-stage scenario may be substantial. The more uncertain the expected benefits are, the higher this difference will be.

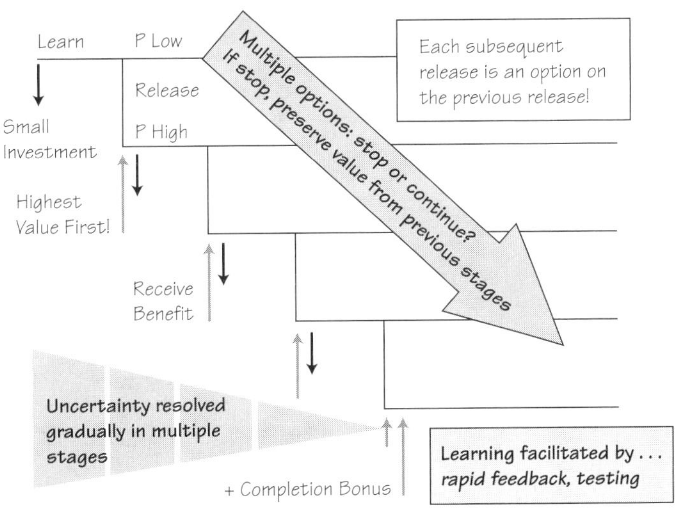

FIGURE 43.15 Staged project with small investments

Part VI

A Project with Two Stages

To see why, consider a seemingly small improvement over the simple single-stage scenario discussed in the previous subsection: a two-stage version of the same project with a single, midpoint decision.

Each stage covers half the original scope, takes half the total time, yields half the expected benefit, and incurs half the total cost of the single-stage project. Learning is incorporated into the scenario as follows. At the end of the first stage, the customer will revise the estimate of the remaining benefit, the expected benefit of the second stage, and decide whether to continue. Therefore, the second stage is conditional on the outcome of the first stage. Initially, the project benefits are subject to the same uncertainty as the benchmarked single-stage project, at a volatility of 40% per month. Though, unlike in the single-stage project example, this time the volatility will have a serious effect on value. Table 43.3 summarizes the setup of the two-stage project.

The costs and benefits in each column of Table 43.3 are stated in PV terms relative to the beginning of the period covered by the column. The risk-free rate is assumed to be a constant 5% per year, or 0.41% per month. The overall cost of 110 is the sum of the first-stage cost and the second-stage cost, but the latter is first discounted at the risk-free rate back two months from the beginning of the second stage.

The correct way to calculate the NPV of this scenario is by viewing the second stage as an option that will be exercised only if its expected benefits (estimated at the end of the first stage) exceed its expected cost

TABLE 43.3 Setup of the Two-Stage Project

	Stage 1	Stage 2	Overall
Flexibility:	Mandatory	Optional	
Purpose:	Learning	Completion	
Uncertainty:	More uncertain	Less uncertain	
Cost	55.2	55.2	110
Benefit	50	Stage 1 outcome	?
Volatility (per month)	40%	?	?
Duration (months)	2	2	4
Risk-free rate (per month)	0.41%	0.41%	0.41%

of 52.2. This contrasts with the DCF approach, which would view undertaking the second stage as a given.

To value the option underlying the two-stage project, we need a model that is richer and more accommodating than that of Black-Scholes. We will employ a closely related but more general model, of which the Black-Scholes model is a special case. Figure 43.16 demonstrates how to calculate the *expanded* NPV of the two-stage project—the NPV including the option value—using this model and an accompanying technique called *risk-neutral valuation*. The details of the calculation are given next.

Uncertainty in a Staged Project: The Binomial Model

The first step is to determine how to model uncertainty. The *binomial model* [Sundaram1997] is frequently used in option pricing to model uncertainty for solving problems with more complex structures than standard option pricing formulas can accommodate.

In the binomial model, the underlying asset of an option is modeled using a two-state, discrete-time random walk process. Starting from an

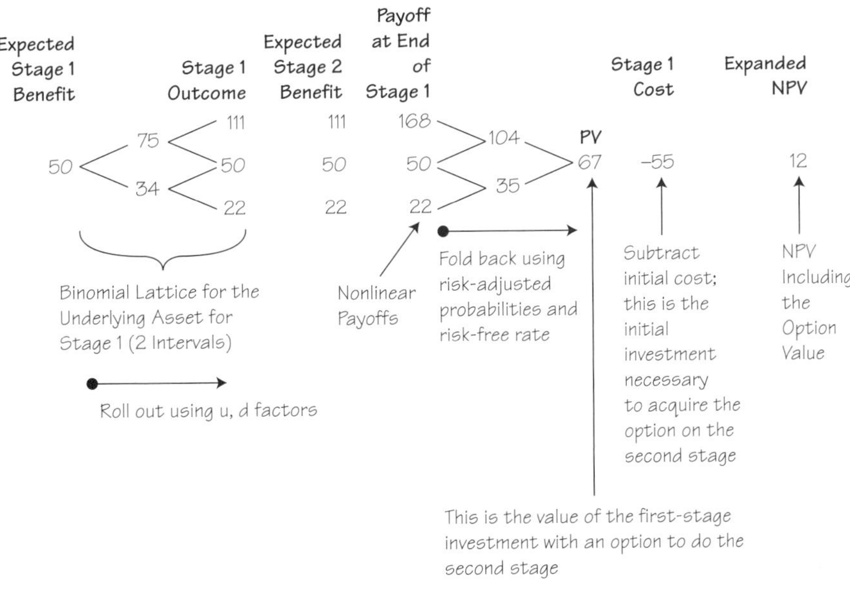

FIGURE 43.16 Valuation of the two-stage project

initial value, the asset moves either up or down in a fixed interval. The process is then repeated for successive intervals such that two consecutive opposite moves always take the asset to its previous value, generating a *binomial lattice*. The resulting structure represents the possible evolution of the asset in discrete time, starting with an initial value. It is essentially a binary tree with merging upward and downward branches.

In the two-stage scenario, the underlying, uncertain asset is the benefit of the first stage. The value of the overall scenario depends on the behavior of this asset. On the left side of Figure 43.16, a binomial lattice is shown for this asset. The root of the lattice is represented by the value 50, which is the specified expected PV of the first-stage benefit. Recall that the total duration of the first stage is two months. Suppose that at the end of the first month, enough information will exist to revise this estimate. Thus, we divide the duration of the project's first stage into two equal intervals, resulting in an interval size of one month.

The values of the subsequent nodes of the binomial lattice are determined using the volatility estimate of 40% per month. From the volatility, first we calculate an upward factor, u, that is greater than unity and a downward factor, d, that is smaller than unity. Over each interval, the value of the asset either increases by a factor of u or decreases by a factor of d. The upward and downward factors are chosen to be consistent with the volatility estimate, the standard deviation of the rate of percentage change in the asset's value. If the volatility is σ, u and d can be chosen as follows [Cox+1979]:

$$\mathrm{u} = \exp\,(\sigma\sqrt{\tau}) \text{ and } d = 1/u$$

where τ is the chosen interval size, expressed in the same unit as σ, and "exp" denotes the exponential function. In the current example, the volatility is 40% per month, and the selected interval size is one month. These choices yield the upward factor $u = 1.49$ and the downward factor $d = 0.67$. Before proceeding, we need to verify that the monthly risk-free rate of 0.41% + 1 = 1.0041 is greater than d and smaller than u, a condition that must be satisfied so that we can apply the principles of replicating portfolio and law of one price to the scenario.

Treating Nonstandard Payoffs

As shown in Figure 43.16, the PV of the stage 1 benefit is 50, which constitutes the root node of the binomial lattice. The lattice is rolled out beginning with this initial value and multiplying it repeatedly with the upward and downward factors to cover two intervals, which takes us to the end of the first stage. This process yields three terminal nodes—111, 50, and 22—each representing a possible stage 1 outcome. For each of these states, the expected stage 2 benefit equals the stage 1 outcome, as was stipulated in Table 43.3. This yields the estimate of the stage 2 benefit, conditional on the actual benefit of stage 1. Stage 2 will be undertaken only if its estimated benefit at the end of stage 1 exceeds its estimated cost of 52.2. Thus, applying the rational exercise assumption at the end of the first stage yields the following for each terminal node of the binomial lattice:

$$\text{(Net Value of Stage 2)} = \max\{0, \text{(Conditional Benefit of Stage 2)} - \text{(Cost of Stage 2)}\}$$

The overall net value, or payoff, at the end of the first stage therefore equals the following:

$$\text{(Outcome of Stage 1)} + \text{(Net Value of Stage 2)}$$

From top to bottom, the payoffs are calculated as 168, 50, and 22 for the three terminal nodes. Note that stage 2 will be undertaken only for the top node, the one with a payoff of 168. For the remaining nodes, the payoff simply equals the stage 1 outcome because the subsequent option on stage 2 is not exercised in those states.

Now comes the tricky part: recursively folding back the lattice to obtain the PV of the calculated payoffs. We perform this by invoking the same two concepts that underlie the Black-Scholes option pricing model: replicating portfolio and law of one price. Note that the Black-Scholes formula couldn't be used directly here, because the payoff function is not exactly the same as that of a standard call option: It does *not* simply equal the greater of zero or the maturity value of the asset net of an exercise price. We develop the general technique on the fly using the current example.

Calculating the Present Value of the Payoffs

Consider the top two terminal nodes of the binomial lattice in Figure 43.16 with the corresponding benefits of 111 and 50 and payoffs of 168 and 50. The terminal benefits of 111 and 50 are derived from the benefit at the parent node using the upward and downward factors $111 = 75u$ and $50 = 75d$. What is the expected discounted payoff at the beginning of the preceding interval? We can always attach probabilities to the upward and downward branches, calculate the expected payoff using these probabilities, and then discount the result back one interval using a proper discount rate. This procedure would have worked, except that (a) we don't know what those probabilities are, and (b) we don't know what the proper discount rate is. Besides, even if the probabilities were given, we would have to figure different discount rates for different branches, because the risk of the project changes after the option has been exercised. For large lattices, this procedure is simply impractical.

Instead, we appeal to the concept of replicating portfolio. According to this concept, the payoffs of 168 and 50 at the terminal states can also be realized artificially by forming a portfolio composed of a *twin security* and a fixed-interest loan. Assume now that there exists such a security—one whose movement parallels that of the benefit. The absolute value of the twin security is not important, but it must be subject to the same upward and downward factors. When the benefit moves up or down, the twin security also moves up or down by the same factor. Assume that the value of the twin security at the beginning of an interval is M.

The replicating portfolio is formed at the beginning of the interval this way.

- Buy n units of the twin security. This represents the position of the replicating portfolio in the underlying asset.
- Take out a loan in the amount of B at the risk-free rate of interest to partly finance this purchase. This represents the position of the replicating portfolio in the risk-free asset.

The worth of the replicating portfolio at the beginning of the interval then equals $nM - B$. If we can determine the value of n and B, we can calculate the exact value of the replicating portfolio (as we will see, we don't need to know the value of M). This is the right point to apply the law of one price: The value of the replicating portfolio must equal the expected value of the terminal payoff at the beginning of the interval, the price one would have to pay at that time to acquire the option to continue with the second stage at the end of the interval.

Now let's consider the possible values of the portfolio at the end of the interval. After one interval, the loan must be paid back with interest to receive the payoff. Regardless of what happens to the price of the twin security, the amount of the loan will be $B(1 + r_f)$, including the principle and the interest accrued. Here r_f is the risk-free rate, the total interest rate on the loan over one interval.

On the one hand, if the price of the twin security moves up to uM, the portfolio will then be worth $uMn - B(1 + r_f)$. For the portfolio to replicate the payoff, this amount should equal 168, the payoff after the upward movement. On the other hand, if the price of the twin security falls to dM, the portfolio will be worth $dMn - B(1 + r_f)$, which must equal 50, the payoff after the downward movement. Thus the law of one price provides us with two equations.

If the price moves up:

$$50 = \text{(Terminal payoff)} = \text{(Terminal value of replicating portfolio)} = \text{uMn} - \text{B}(1 + \text{r}_\text{f})$$

If the price moves down:

$$168 = \text{(Terminal payoff)} = \text{(Terminal value of replicating portfolio)} = \text{dMn} - \text{B}(1 + \text{r}_\text{f})$$

Because r_f, u, and d are all known, we can solve these two equations for B and n as a function of M, and then calculate the portfolio value at the beginning of the interval by plugging the solution into the expression $nM - B$. Fortunately, the unknown M is eliminated during this process, yielding a value of 104. This amount is precisely how much the option to continue with the second stage would be worth at the node labeled 75 in the binomial lattice. We can repeat the same procedure for the middle and bottom terminal nodes to obtain a value of 35, and then once again with the two computed values 104 and 35, regarding them as new payoffs, to reach the root of the lattice. In the end, we obtain a final root value of 67. This amount is precisely how much the option to continue with the second stage would be worth at the beginning of the project.

A Simple Procedure: Risk-Neutral Valuation

The procedure described in the previous subsection may seem somewhat cumbersome. Fortunately, there is an easier way. Solving a system of simultaneous equations to obtain the portfolio value at the beginning of an interval is equivalent to computing the expected value of the payoffs at the end of the interval using an artificial probability measure, and then discounting back this expected value at the risk-free rate by one interval. Figure 43.17 illustrates this simple technique.

In the middle portion of Figure 43.16, the portfolio values at the intermediary nodes and at the root of the binomial lattice are computed using the simplified procedure as follows. Starting with the terminal payoffs and recursively moving back in time:

$$104 = \frac{168 \cdot p + 50 \cdot (1-p)}{1 + r_f} = \frac{168(0.46) + 50(0.54)}{1.0041}$$

$$35 = \frac{50 \cdot p + 22 \cdot (1-p)}{1 + r_f} = \frac{50(0.46) + 22(0.54)}{1.0041}$$

$$67 = \frac{67 \cdot p + 35 \cdot (1-p)}{1 + r_f} = \frac{104(0.46) + 35(0.54)}{1.0041}$$

where: $p = \dfrac{1 + r_f - d}{u - d} = 0.46$ and $1 - p = 0.54$

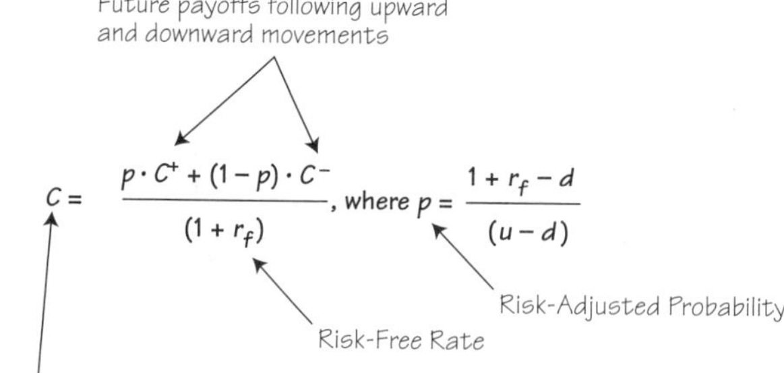

Future payoffs following upward and downward movements
$C = \dfrac{p \cdot C^+ + (1-p) \cdot C^-}{(1 + r_f)}$, where $p = \dfrac{1 + r_f - d}{(u - d)}$
Risk-Adjusted Probability
Risk-Free Rate
Option value is the expected value of future payoffs under the risk-adjusted probabilities discounted at the risk-free rate

FIGURE 43.17 Risk-neutral valuation in the binomial model

The quantities 1 and $1 - p$ here and in Figure 43.17 are referred to as *risk-adjusted*, or *risk-neutral*, probabilities. They are not the actual probabilities of the upward and downward movements of the underlying asset, yet they are used to compute an expected value (in Figure 43.17, the numerator in the equation on the left). The expected value is simply discounted back at the risk-free rate r_f. The artificial probabilities p and $1 - p$ depend on the spread between u and d, the upward and downward movement factors of the twin security. In a way, then, p and $1 - p$ capture the variation—or the total risk—of the underlying asset relative to the risk-free asset.

The general, recursive process of computing the present value of an asset based on replication and law of one price (no arbitrage) principles is referred to as *risk-neutral valuation*.

A number of features are remarkable about this technique. First, the value calculated does not require the actual probability distribution of the underlying price movement. Second, it does not require a discount rate, given the initial value of the underlying asset. Third, the procedure is independent of how the future payoffs are calculated. Because the rules used to calculate the payoffs don't matter, the process is the same for any payoff function.

Two-Stage Project: NPV with Option Value

The root value of 67 obtained in the previous subsection represents the PV of stage 1 and stage 2 combined, viewing stage 2 as an option on stage 1. This amount, however, does not account for the initial cost, the cost of stage 1, or the investment necessary to create the option on stage 2 in the first place. If we subtract this cost of 52.2 (which is already given in PV terms) from the calculated value of 67, we obtain an expanded NPV of 12, as shown on the right side of Figure 43.16. This value is an *expanded* NPV in the sense that it subsumes the value of the staging option.

Remarkably, the new NPV is not only positive, but also significantly higher than the benchmark NPV of the single-stage project, which was calculated to be –10. The difference of 22 is sizable compared with the total expected benefit of the single-stage project. Although they incur the same cost in PV terms, the two-stage project with learning creates a lot more value at the given level of volatility.

Impact of Uncertainty on the Option Value of Staging

The uncertainty of the expected benefit has a great impact on how much value is created when learning and additional flexibility are incorporated into the scenario. In the previous subsection, we calculated the expanded NPV using a volatility of 40% per month. This volatility captures the uncertainty of the benefit in terms of the variation in percentage changes in the estimate of the benefit from the start to the end of the first stage. What happens when this volatility increases or decreases?

Figure 43.18 plots the expanded NPV of the two-stage project as a function of volatility. As the volatility increases, the project value increases as well: The more uncertainty there is, the more important it is to have flexibility in the project. Remarkably, this effect was not observed in the single-stage project: As long as the PV of the benefit does not change, NPV remains constant. Although uncertainty also exists in the single-stage project, it was not accompanied by a discretionary, midproject action that depended on the uncertainty. Consequently, volatility has no further impact on the project value as long as it has already been accounted for in the PV estimate of the benefit.

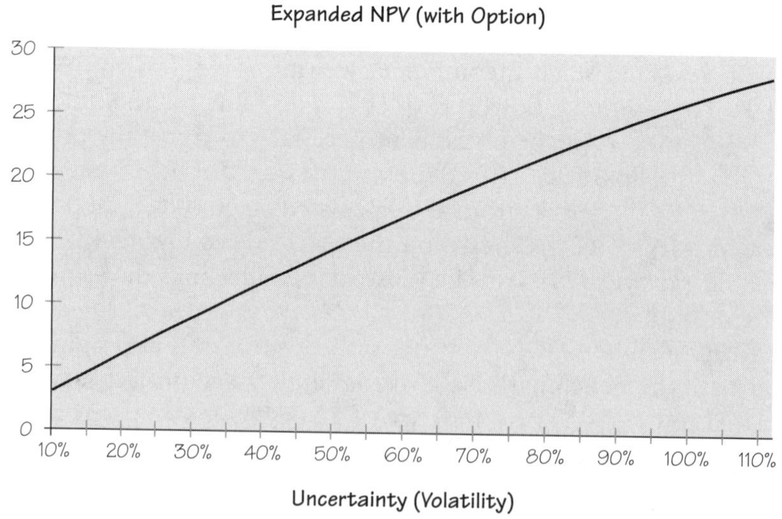

FIGURE 43.18 Effect of uncertainty on the value of the two-stage project

Implications of Real-Options Thinking

The flexible principles and practices of XP create several kinds of real options. These options enable us to view XP as a process that maximizes value. The insight gained can be expanded to other contexts as well, from risk and contract management to compensation and incentive systems.

A Different Attitude toward Risk Management

More careful, risk-averse companies get left in the dust.

—Dan Scheinemann, Cisco

We've seen that although project uncertainty may endanger the value of a project, uncertainty in the environment *increases* the value of real options embedded in a project. Risk-averse companies get left in the dust because they are not able to take advantage of external opportunities that accompany risk.

The most important implication of this argument is the need for an *expanded* view of risk management. The real-options approach refutes the notion that all risk is bad, that all risk has to be reduced, and especially, that all risk reduces value. This observation shifts the emphasis from the project-level idea of *contingency plans*, which have the connotation of something going wrong, to the idea of *contingent investments*, where it is economically justifiable to move toward risk, knowing that value is best maximized through active management [Favaro2002]. In other words, in an environment of high uncertainty, the emphasis shifts to *managing* risk from *reducing* risk. In fact, options theory goes one step further: It maintains that it is *total risk*, not only project-level or market-level risk, that needs to be managed.

Contractual Innovation

One of the most recent uses of options is in the design of innovative contracts with nonlinear payoffs. For example, a contract with a ceiling price or a floor price can be synthesized through a combination of buying and selling call and put options. In general, any set of contingent payoffs—payoffs that depend on the value of an underlying asset—can be priced as a combination of options on that asset. Thus derivative concepts can be used to engineer contracts using a mix of financial and real options, combined appropriately to manage risk. In Silicon Valley, these concepts are being used regularly to work out financing for venture capital start-ups and for licensing agreements. For an example of the use of contractual options in license agreements, see [Erdogmus2001A].

The options perspective can also be applied to XP contracts. In a white paper, Beck and Cleal [Beck+1999] note that XP contracts have characteristics of options in the sense that the features to be implemented are optional—they don't necessarily have to be implemented. That is, the scope of contracts is not predetermined.

XP contracts are not *fire-and-forget*. The customer and the development team have a set of decision points, which give them the ability to actively manage the contract. The customer exercises its options by asking the team to implement a set of features. As the team completes new features, the customer has to decide which new options to exercise next. These may be options that were in the original scope, options that were under consideration originally but not in the original scope, or newly discovered options. Thus, as successive iterations resolve uncertainty, the customer has decision points in which to intervene and maximize new opportunities while minimizing downside effects.

One surprising insight that can be gained from this perspective is that XP contracts add the most value when feature benefits are least certain. When a feature is *deeply in-the-money* (that is, the value of its immediate implementation is high), the feature should be implemented. Conversely, when a feature is *deeply out-of-the-money* (that is, the value of its immediate implementation is highly negative), it should not be implemented. However, when the feature is *at-the-money*, the NPV of immediate implementation is around zero, and the customer is uncertain of its benefits. In this latter case, the option to delay implementation may add a great deal of value, because the future is likely to resolve that uncertainty. This is precisely where the YAGNI principle makes the most economic sense.

Similarly, additional value can be created when the customer has a choice to implement the best of a set of alternative features. Such a choice is represented by a *best-of*, or *rainbow*, option. In an option on the *best of two assets*, the investor holds two options but is allowed to exercise only one of them, effectively creating a hedge. Options theory can demonstrate that best-of options have the most value when the underlying assets are negatively correlated—that is, if one asset goes up, the other goes down. Intuitively, this makes sense because it gives the holder of the option a real choice rather than a hypothetical one. In this light, XP contracts can also be seen as a portfolio of best-of options, where the customer is offered a set of suggested features plus the alternatives. A choice between contrasting alternatives is more valuable to the customer than one between related alternatives.

The Role of Discipline

The nonlinear thinking that underlies real options also has profound implications for information technology management in an increasingly uncertain environment.

An organization embracing this thinking systematically identifies leverage points where flexibility would be desirable, analyzes these leverage points, and structures projects with options that take advantage of them. Projects are continually refined to embed in them further options that increase their value.

An organization embracing the real-options approach becomes less averse to total risk. It recognizes that opportunity and risk go hand in hand. Consequently, it encourages and supports learning investments that explore new opportunities.

Paradoxically, an option derives most of its value from rational exercise. Therefore, if the organization is to move responsibly toward valid contingent investments with many embedded options, more rather than fewer projects will be started (although many of these will not be taken to completion due to rational exercise). To create and maximize value, decision makers need the discipline to abandon projects when their option value no longer justifies further investment. This attitude has serious repercussions in terms of how compensation and incentive systems should be redesigned. It will be important for management not to penalize teams for killing projects that aren't working out, moving from a philosophy of *killing careers* to a philosophy of *killing projects.* Project abandonment needs to have a positive connotation if done for the right reasons, not the negative connotation that it has in a myopic perspective of risk management.

An interesting anecdote for this line of thinking comes from the entertainment industry. A screenwriter is highly rewarded for the successful completion of a screenplay, even if a film is never made from it. The reason is the recognition of movies as high-risk, high-payoff projects. Simply the fact of creating the option to make a film (by developing a finished, professional-quality screenplay) is correctly recognized as having high economic value. The possibility that the option to make the film may not be exercised (or that the project may be abandoned in midcourse) is fully accounted for. By the same token, venture capital firms invest in a portfolio of highly risky projects. Most fail, but the few that succeed justify the investment in the portfolio as a whole.

It may seem that such an approach is destined to remain up at the relatively abstract levels of strategic planning and never be seen down in the trenches, where development is carried out. This is not at all the case. Recall that XP explicitly encourages technical experiments—mini-projects within projects, or *spikes* in XP terminology—that quickly test new ideas. These experiments ultimately are either incorporated into the main project if successful or abandoned otherwise. Developers are rewarded for this kind of creative exploration even if only a few of those experiments succeed.

In an options-oriented management system, the incentive and compensation package should be aligned with the concept of rational exercise—one of the cornerstones of option pricing. Such alignment encourages teams and individuals to undertake the kind of experimentation that will create valuable options for the project's or the firm's future—and to not fear for their jobs if some of those options are not realized. One of the four values of XP, courage, is fundamental here: To impact the creation of economic value, courage should imply not only the courage to create and exercise options, but also the courage to practice rational exercise in a disciplined way.

Conclusion

Software development takes place in an inherently uncertain environment, one that is constantly changing. In such an environment, continuous formulation and implementation of options enhances the capability to deal with the vast uncertainty through increased flexibility, exploitation of opportunities, and avoidance of pitfalls. By its very design, XP is well positioned to take advantage of this mind-set. The language of real options and the financial theory behind it demonstrate how the principles and practices of XP can guide a project toward value creation.

Final Remarks

Academics and practitioners frequently debate the suitability of the financial options analogy, and the techniques developed to price these options, to the valuation of real-options scenarios. The main differences between financial and real options are summarized in Table 43.4.

Two points are important to keep in mind here.

First, the existence of trading markets and assumptions about their efficiency, completeness, and liquidity are critical for financial option pricing techniques. These techniques are designed to treat risks that can be priced in such markets. The suitability of a specific option pricing technique to value a real-options scenario may thus depend on the nature of the uncertainty being treated and *how close to the market* the underlying assets are. In software development projects, where private risk is an important factor, the financial options analogy may be weak.

In cases where the financial option–real option analogy is weak, the option values yielded should thus be treated as *idealized values* computed under the assumption of the existence of a market equivalent that reasonably closely tracks the risk being tackled. Fortunately, sometimes risks that seem purely private at first can be market-priced, thanks to an expanding and vibrant securities market in the technology sector. For example, it was difficult to model the market risk associated with the growth option that Netscape had when it introduced the first browser, simply because it was the first of its kind and there weren't yet any other Internet companies on the market. This situation has changed. Netscape was rapidly joined by other Internet companies, with the result that there are now several Internet stock indexes that track the market risk and volatility associated with Internet investments. Another example is provided in [Erdogmus2001B]. For further discussion of the analogy between financial and real options and the limitations of this analogy, see the last sidebar in [Amram+1999].

Second, like all forecasts, the numbers used in options calculations will be more or less precise. The final numbers obtained are as good as the estimates used in their calculation. Where these estimates are unreliable, option values can still provide much insight if they are used in an

TABLE 43.4 Financial Options Versus Real Options

Financial Options	Real Options
Complete markets. Payoff structure can be emulated by a replicating portfolio.	*Incomplete markets.* Payoff structure often cannot be practically emulated by a replicating portfolio.
Traded asset. The underlying asset is traded in the financial markets.	*Twin security.* The underlying asset is not traded; instead, a proxy, or twin security whose value is correlated with the underlying asset, must be assumed. This also applies in DCF and NPV.
Observed current price. The current price of the underlying asset is observed.	*Lack of an observed current price.* The current price of the underlying asset is not observed. It must be estimated as a PV from a stream of future cash flows.
No discount rate. A discount rate is not needed to value the option because of the existence of an observed price and the use of replication and no-arbitrage assumptions.	*Discount rate needed.* A discount rate is often needed to calculate the PV of a stream of future cash flows as a substitute for the current price of the underlying asset.
No interaction. Financial options are self-contained contracts. They don't interact.	*Extensive interaction.* There are often complex interactions among different real options within a project or even across different projects. The behavior of one option affects the value of the other.
Sources of uncertainty constrained. Financial options involve one or two uncertain underlying assets.	*Multiple sources of uncertainty.* Real options often involve multiple underlying assets or assets with multiple sources of uncertainty.
Single ownership. Financial options have defined ownership.	*Shared ownership.* Real options are often shared among competitors. A company's exercise of a real option may kill or significantly undermine the same real option for a competitor and vice versa.
Value leakage. The holder of a financial option may be subject to the loss of benefits while waiting to exercise the option because of dividend payments or convenience yield that are available to the holders of the underlying asset, but not to the holders of an option. The rate and pattern of this can be estimated using historical data or using industry conventions.	*Competition, partnerships, and sharing.* The holder of a real option may be subject to the loss or amplification of benefits while waiting to exercise the option because of the actions of competitors and partners and shared ownership, all of which may be very difficult to quantify.

informed manner, especially along with comparative, sensitivity, and scenario analyses.

Further Reading

Introductory corporate finance texts provide more comprehensive discussions of basic valuation concepts—in particular, capital budgeting, discounted cash flow techniques, NPV, and the relationship between risk and return. Recommended texts are Ross et al. [Ross+1996] and Brealey and Myers [Brealey+1987].

Hull's book [Hull1997] provides an undergraduate-level overview of derivative securities (including options), the general techniques for their pricing, and derivative markets. Pindyck and Dixit [Pindyck+1992] offer a deeper and more theoretical exposition of option pricing theory together with the econometric foundations of the Black-Scholes and related models.

The seminal paper on option pricing is by Black and Scholes [Black+1973], which explains the original derivation of their and Merton's Nobel Prize–winning model. Cox, Ross, and Rubinstein [Cox+1979] provide a much simpler derivation of the same model, using the binomial model and the risk-neutral approach. The Black-Scholes model has many variations that have similar analytic solutions. The most relevant ones are discussed by Margrabe [Margrabe1978] and Carr [Carr1988]. Margrabe derives a formula for the option to exchange two risky assets, of which Black-Scholes is a special case. This formula can be used when the exercise cost of an option is also uncertain [Erdogmus2001A]. Carr provides a comprehensive discussion of Margrabe's formula and other, more complex variations, including compound options. Kumar [Kumar1996] provides a compact discussion of the impact of volatility on option value.

Sundaram [Sundaram1997] gives the best exposition of the binomial model and risk-neutral valuation. Smith and Nau [Smith+1995] explain the relationship between option pricing and decision trees, and demonstrate how the two models together can account for both market and private risk. These two articles are highly recommended for those interested in the practical application of option pricing to real assets.

Many excellent, high-level articles exist that discuss the use of option pricing theory in valuing options on real assets [Amram+1999; Luehrman1998; Myers1984]. Myers, who originally coined the term *real options,* explains how the real-options approach links strategy and finance. Texts that focus on applications of real options include Copeland and Antikarov [Copeland+2001] and Amram and Kulatilaka [Amram+1999]. Further applications can be found in two books by Trigeorgis [Trigeorgis1999; Trigeorgis1994]. The older of these is a self-contained textbook, and the more recent is an edited collection focusing mostly on applications.

Applications of real options to information technology in general and software development in particular have been addressed in many articles. Those addressing investment decisions in software development include [Erdogmus2001A; Erdogmus2001B; Favaro+1999; Boehm+2000; Erdogmus+1999; Favaro1996]. Sullivan et al. focus on applications to software design [Sullivan+1999], and the book by Clark and Baldwin focuses on applications to modularity in general in the context of hardware design [Baldwin+1999]. General applications to information technology investments are also available [Benaroch+1999; Benaroch+2000; DosSantos1991; Taudes+2000].

References

[Amram+1999] M. Amram, N. Kulatilaka. "Disciplined Decisions: Aligning Strategy with the Financial Markets." *Harvard Business Review,* 1999.

[Baldwin+1999] C. Baldwin, K. Clark. *Design Rules: The Power of Modularity.* MIT Press, 1999.

[Beck2000] K. Beck. *Extreme Programming Explained.* Addison-Wesley, 2000.

[Beck+1999] K. Beck, D. Cleal. Optional Scope Contracts. White paper. 1999.

[Benaroch+1999] M. Benaroch, R. Kauffman. "A Case for Using Option Pricing Analysis to Evaluate Information Technology Project Investments." *Information Systems Research,* Volume 10, 1999.

[Benaroch+2000] M. Benaroch, R. Kauffman. "Justifying Electronic Banking Network Expansion Using Real Options Analysis." *MIS Quarterly,* Volume 24, 2000.

[Black+1973] F. Black, M. Scholes. "The Pricing of Options and Corporate Liabilities." *Journal of Political Economy*, Volume 81, 1973.

[Boehm+2000] B. Boehm, K. Sullivan. "Software Engineering Economics: A Roadmap." In *The Future of Software Engineering*. A. Finkelstein, ed. ACM Press, 2000.

[Brealey+1987] R. Brealey, S. Myers. *Principles of Corporate Finance*. McGraw-Hill, 1987.

[Carr1988] P. Carr. "The Valuation of Sequential Exchange Opportunities." *Journal of Finance*, Volume 18, 1988.

[Copeland+2001] T. Copeland, V. Antikarov. *Real Options: A Practitioner's Guide*. Texere, 2001.

[Cox+1979] J. Cox, S. Ross, M. Rubinstein. "Option Pricing: A Simplified Approach." *Journal of Financial Economics*, Volume 7, 1979.

[DosSantos1991] B. Dos Santos. "Justifying Investments in New Information Technologies." *Journal of Management Information Systems*, Volume 7, 1991.

[Erdogmus2001A] H. Erdogmus. Management of License Cost Uncertainty in Software Development: A Real Options Approach. Presented at the Fifth Annual Conference on Real Options: Theory Meets Practice. UCLA, Los Angeles, California. 2001.

[Erdogmus2001B] H. Erdogmus. "Value of Commercial Software Development under Technology Risk." *The Financier*, Volume 7, 2001.

[Erdogmus+1999] H. Erdogmus, J. Vandergraaf. Quantitative Approaches for Assessing the Value of COTS-centric Development. Presented at the Sixth International Software Metrics Symposium. Boca Raton, Florida. 1999.

[Favaro1996] J. Favaro. A Comparison of Approaches to Reuse Investment Analysis. Presented at the Fourth International Conference on Software Reuse. 1996.

[Favaro2002] J. Favaro. "Managing Requirements for Business Value." *IEEE Software*, March 2002.

[Favaro+1998] J. Favaro, K. Favaro, P. Favaro. "Value Based Software Reuse Investment." *Annals of Software Engineering*, Volume 5, 1998.

[Favaro+1999] J. Favaro, K. Favaro. "Strategic Analysis of Application Framework Investments." In *Building Application Frameworks: Object-Oriented Foundations of Framework Design*. M. Fayad, R. Johnson, eds. John Wiley & Sons, 1999.

[Hull1997] J. Hull. *Options, Futures, and Derivatives*. Prentice Hall, 1997.

[Kumar1996] L. Kumar. "A Note on Project Risk and Option Values of Investments in Information Technologies." *Journal of Management Information Systems*, Volume 13, 1996.

[Luehrman1998] T. Luehrman. "Investment Opportunities as a Portfolio of Real Options." *Harvard Business Review*, 1998.

[Margrabe1978] W. Margrabe. "The Value of an Option to Exchange One Asset for Another." *Journal of Finance*, Volume 33, 1978.

[Myers1984] S. Myers. "Finance Theory and Financial Strategy." *Interfaces*, Volume 14, 1984.

[Pindyck+1992] R. Pindyck, A. Dixit. *Investment under Uncertainty*. Princeton University Press, 1992.

[Ross+1996] S. Ross, R. Westerfield, B. Jordan, G. Roberts. *Fundamentals of Corporate Finance*. Times Mirror Professional Publishing, 1996.

[Smith+1995] J. Smith, R. Nau. "Valuing Risky Projects: Option Pricing Theory and Decision Analysis." *Management Science*, 1995.

[Sullivan1996] K. Sullivan. Software Design: The Options Approach. Presented at the SIGSOFT Software Architectures Workshop. San Francisco, California. 1996.

[Sullivan+1999] K. Sullivan, P. Chalasani, S. Jha, V. Sazawal. "Software Design as an Investment Activity: A Real Options Perspective." In *Real Options and Business Strategy: Applications to Decision Making*. L. Trigeorgis, ed. Risk Books, 1999.

[Sundaram1997] R. Sundaram. "Equivalent Martingale Measures and Risk-Neutral Pricing: An Expository Note." *The Journal of Derivatives*, 1997.

[Taudes1998] A. Taudes. "Software Growth Options." *Journal of Management Information Systems*, 1998.

[Taudes+2000] A. Taudes, M. Feurstein, A. Mild. "Options Analysis of Software Platform Decisions: A Case Study." *MIS Quarterly*, Volume 24, 2000.

[Trigeorgis1994] L. Trigeorgis. *Real Options: Managerial Flexibility and Strategy in Resource Allocation*. MIT Press, 1994.

[Trigeorgis1999] L. Trigeorgis. *Real Options and Business Strategy: Applications to Decision Making*. Risk Books, 1999.

About the Authors

Hakan Erdogmus is a research officer with the Institute for Information Technology, National Research Council of Canada, in Ottawa. His current research focuses on software economics. He is the coauthor of several articles on the subject. He holds a Ph.D. in telecommunications from Université du Québec, Institut national de la recherche scientifique, and an M.S. in computer science from McGill University, Montreal. In 1997, Hakan was the program co-chair of CASCON, the annual conference of the IBM Center for Advanced Studies. He is the coeditor of an upcoming book entitled *Advances in Software Engineering: Comprehension, Evaluation, and Evolution*, reporting on the research activities of the Consortium for Software Engineering Research.

John Favaro is an independent consultant based in Pisa, Italy. He was general chair of the Sixth International Conference on Software Reuse in June 2000. He is European co-chair of the IEEE Technical Subcommittee on Reuse and is a founding member of the steering committee of the Society for the Advancement of Software Education. Recently, he has published articles on principles of strategy and valuation for IT investment, including "Value-Based Software Reuse Investment" in the special issue on reuse of *Annals of Software Engineering*

1998; that article became the basis for the material on options in *Extreme Programming Explained*. He has degrees in computer science from Berkeley and Yale.

Hakan and John cowrote the tutorial on the economics of XP given at the XP Universe 2001 workshop "XP for Capitalists," hosted by Kent Beck in Raleigh, North Carolina.

Chapter 44

Distributed Extreme Programming

—Michael Kircher, Prashant Jain, Angelo Corsaro, and David L. Levine

One of the key requirements of Extreme Programming (XP) is strong and effective communication between the team members. To enable this, XP emphasizes the need to physically locate the team members close to each other. However, for various reasons, that may not be feasible.

To address these situations, we propose a crosscutting idea called Distributed Extreme Programming (DXP), which inherits the merits of XP and applies them in a distributed team environment. Our experiences show that DXP can be both effective and rewarding in projects whose teams are geographically distributed.

Introduction

XP [Beck2000] is a lightweight methodology that has gained increasing acceptance and popularity in the software community. XP promotes a discipline of software development based on principles of simplicity, communication, feedback, and courage. It is designed for use with small teams that need to develop software quickly and in an environment of rapidly changing requirements. XP consists of 12 practices, which are planning game, small releases, metaphor, simple design, testing, refactoring, pair programming, collective ownership, continuous integration, 40-hour week, on-site customer, and coding standards. A careful analysis of these XP practices reveals certain key assumptions made by XP.

One assumption involves *physical proximity*. XP advocates a strong level of communication among team members. A key XP practice is pair programming. Pair programming is not just one person programming and the other observing. Instead, it is a dialog between people trying together to simultaneously design, program, analyze, test, and understand how to produce better programs. It is a conversation at many levels, assisted by and focused on a computer console [Williams+2000]. Therefore, a key assumption made by XP is strong and effective communication between the team members, enabling the diffusion of know-how and expertise throughout the group. To enable this communication, the literature on XP emphasizes that it is important to physically locate the team members close to each other. Ideally, the team members should all be in one room. This enhances the communication among team members through incidental overhearing of conversations [Beck2000] and minimizes any hesitation that the team members might have in communicating with each other.

Another important practice of XP requires *close customer involvement* through the entire development cycle. Different from traditional methodologies, XP stresses the role of an on-site customer and thus recommends having a representative of the customer working with the team all the time. The customer or one of its representatives thus becomes an integral part of the team. Therefore, a proper communication channel between the customer and the rest of the team can easily be realized if the customer is physically located on-site.

Thus, physical proximity of team members and close customer involvement are key assumptions made by XP. However, if physical proximity of team members or the customer is not feasible or desirable, will XP lose its effectiveness? In this chapter, we show how XP can be applied to software development and teamwork in a distributed team environment. Our crosscutting idea is whether it is really necessary for the team members to be physically located next to each other.

The next section describes our extension to traditional XP, which we call Distributed Extreme Programming (DXP). We describe the assumptions made by DXP, the rationale behind DXP, the challenges in DXP, and how to address these challenges. Then we present our experience report on using DXP, and finally we present our conclusions.

Distributed Extreme Programming

We define Distributed Extreme Programming as XP with certain relaxations on the requirement of physical proximity of the team members. DXP applies XP principles in a distributed and mobile team environment. In DXP, team members can be arbitrarily far apart as well as highly mobile. Some ideas about DXP have already been mentioned at the XP and Flexible Processes in Software Engineering XP2000 conference [Kircher+2001; Schuemmer+2001].

DXP addresses all aspects of XP, although to varying degrees. In general, certain things are irrelevant to the locality of the team, while others are totally bound to the fact that the team members are colocated. Table 44.1 summarizes some of the aspects that are relevant to DXP and some that are not.

From this table it becomes clear that for effective DXP, we need to address the practices of planning game, pair programming, continuous

TABLE 44.1 Relevance of XP Practices to DXP

XP Practice	Requires Colocated Team?
Planning game Pair programming Continuous integration On-site customer	Yes. These rely on close interaction among the businesspeople, including the on-site customer and technical people.
Small releases Metaphor Simple design Testing Refactoring Collective ownership 40-hour week Coding standards	No. These can be done independent of the fact that the team is centralized or distributed.

Part VI

integration, and on-site customer in a distributed team environment. In the section Addressing XP Practices and Values in DXP, we show how these practices are addressed.

Note that we consider refactoring, by itself, to not require collocation. The actual implementation of a refactoring relies on pair programming. However, the decision on whether to refactor does not require collocation. Even more concrete design tasks may best be initiated alone [Cowan2001]; we consider this to be part of the refactoring, while the implementation tasks fall under pair programming.

DXP Assumptions

To be effective, DXP assumes the existence of certain conditions and the availability of several tools and technologies. Beyond the assumptions of XP, including speaking a common language and general openness, DXP assumes these things.

- *Connectivity*—Some form of connectivity needs to exist between the team members. If communication is performed across long distances, it is assumed that the Internet is used as the communication medium. For company-local communication, an intranet can be used.
- *E-mail*—The ubiquitous availability and asynchronous nature of e-mail make it a key enabling technology for DXP. It can be used as a convenient means to exchange information and to schedule any DXP sessions.
- *Configuration management*—Effective management of programming artifacts mandates the use of some kind of configuration management tool. This in turn serves as a key enabler for collective ownership.
- *Application sharing*—To apply XP practices in a distributed environment, some form of application- or desktop-sharing software needs to be available to the team.
- *Videoconferencing*—For effective synchronous communication using audio and video among distant team members, some kind of videoconferencing support is needed [Steinmetz+1996].
- *Familiarity*—We expect that DXP can succeed only when team members know each other well and can view it as an extension of their prior work arrangements.

Why DXP?

XP stresses the need for physical proximity of team members. However, circumstances may prevent a team from working in physical proximity, thus mandating the need for using DXP. A company or a project may therefore be forced to adopt DXP for these reasons.

- *Situational constraints*—A company or a project may have little choice because of the existing physical distribution of development teams. Many projects are sanctioned with teams residing in different locations, sometimes across the globe.
- *Individual constraints*—An individual may not be able to work at the main project location, at least temporarily. It thus becomes important that the individual continue to stay part of the development activities even while being physically separated.

Even if a company or a project is not constrained by circumstances, it may still choose to adopt DXP. This is because, in addition to maintaining the benefits of XP practices, DXP offers some additional benefits.

- *Cost*—A growing trend in the software industry is to outsource all or part of a software project because of cost. It is often much cheaper to develop software in some countries, such as India or China. As a result, several projects are distributed across two or more countries.
- *Convenient customer involvement*—DXP makes it easier to involve the customer, even if they are unable to be at the development site. With traditional XP, the customer would have to stay on-site. This has the drawback of removing the customer from their own company environment. In DXP, however, this problem does not arise because the customer need not be on-site and can simply be available to the development team through, for example, videoconferencing.
- *Mobility*—In many organizations, some team members need to travel frequently to, for example, maintain customer contacts or attend conferences. DXP offers a smooth integration of mobile team members. Mobile team members can stay connected with the rest of the team by using mobile equipment such as a notebook with a small camera and a broadband or dial-up connection. The team members can then participate in the development activities for part of the day or even for just a few hours.

DXP thus addresses circumstantial constraints of companies and projects, and offers tangible benefits beyond those offered by XP.

Challenges in DXP

In relaxing the XP requirement of physical proximity, DXP faces several challenges.

- *Communication*—An important aspect of communication is to know how the other person reacts to what we say. To judge a reaction, typically we read this information from the body gestures, facial expressions, and voice patterns of the other person. In DXP, because the two people are not physically next to each other, how can they receive this information?
- *Coordination*—When two or more team members working together on a project are in two different physical locations, coordination among them becomes a challenge. This can include synchronizing availability, adjusting for time differences, and coordinating distribution and integration of activities. In addition, document and application sharing among the team members can also be a challenge.
- *Infrastructure*—Both communication and coordination among team members in DXP depend heavily on the infrastructure. This includes the available hardware and software as well as the bandwidth of the connecting network. A poor infrastructure can make it very difficult to make up for the physical proximity that may be missing in DXP.
- *Availability*—Distributed team members may be available at different times. Some of them might be working on multiple projects and thus be restricted by time. Others might be constrained by personal limitations. In addition, the availability of distributed team members can also be affected by different time zones.
- *Management*—The manager of the team needs to have a high degree of trust in their subordinates if the subordinates are often remotely located. Direct managerial control over distant subordinates can be difficult to execute, so new strategies may need to be defined.

Addressing the Challenges/Solution

DXP offers many challenges. However, each of these challenges can be addressed and in most cases overcome.

- *Communication*—Given a close-knit team, good communication can take place among members without requiring physical collocation. For example, assuming that you know the other person pretty well, a video picture of your partner might be sufficient to be able to tell what they are thinking and how they react to your comments. The team members can use many different forms of communication to bridge the physical distance. For example, they could convene a video- or phone conference or could send each other e-mail. In addition, actual meetings could be convened periodically to enhance interpersonal relationships among team members, thus easing remote cooperation. When deciding on a particular form of communication, we need to consider many different factors. These include the cost of equipment and its usage, travel costs, cost of time, available bandwidth, and the effectiveness of the particular form of communication with respect to the tasks that need to be performed.

  Remote communication and cooperation can be greatly improved by the ability to share documents. With Web technologies becoming more and more inexpensive and thus popular, new ways of communication are now available that enable close involvement among team members across an intranet or the Internet via videoconferencing and application sharing.
- *Coordination*—Proper coordination of activities among distributed team members requires effective planning. However, making extensive use of different lines of communication can facilitate this. For example, two members in different locations could exchange daily e-mails containing their schedules for the day. They could then assign certain slots within the day for working on a project. In doing so, they would also need to take into account any time differences that may exist.
- *Availability*—The DXP team needs to formulate rules and guidelines to ensure the availability of the team members. The general XP spirit of not denying help to anyone asking for it should extend to being available for remote communication. All team

Part VI

members should be able to easily access a daily or weekly schedule of each team member's availability. Pair programming sessions or testing sessions should then be scheduled based on the availability of the team members, to enable the most knowledge diffusion to take place.

- *Management*—Project leaders and upper management need to learn how to handle distributed teams. In particular, project leaders need to learn how to manage team members who are at different locations. This can include requiring daily or weekly reports from all team members, whether local or remote. It can also include giving regular feedback to team members to give them the feeling that they are connected and thus an integral part of the team. In addition, regular team events can help build trust and motivation among all team members.
- *Infrastructure*—The availability of the necessary infrastructure is critical and not as easy to achieve as it may seem. Important factors in choosing the infrastructure components are ease of use, interoperability with other tools, and availability on different platforms.

Addressing XP Practices and Values in DXP

In addressing the challenges of DXP, we must not violate the practices and values of XP. As identified in Table 44.1, team distribution affects only four XP practices: planning game, pair programming, continuous integration, and on-site customer. This section examines each of these practices in the light of DXP and proposes possible solutions that can be applied to keep DXP within the realm of XP practices.

- *Planning game*—For the planning game with a remotely located customer, support for videoconferencing and application-sharing software is needed. For example, application sharing can be used to write the story cards. Ideally, more than two participants should be supported. Though this is possible with certain solutions, such as CUseeMe, most videoconferencing software supports only one pair of participants.[1]

1. CUseeMe Networks, voice and visual communications over the Internet; see http://www.cuseeme.com.

- *Pair programming*—For pair programming between team members in different locations, Remote Pair Programming (RPP) should be used. This requires videoconferencing and application-sharing support, to share the Integrated Development Environment (IDE).
- *Continuous integration*—Because a remote team member cannot move to a separate integration machine, an alternative must be provided. If one team member is working at the central team site, that team member can invite the other remote team member to do common integration at that machine. If both team members are remote, this is not possible, so integration needs to be done on the development machine.
- *On-site customer*—Videoconferencing should be used to involve remote customers. In DXP, a remote customer is not really an "on-site customer," but a "virtual on-site customer." The big difference is that the customer needs to conform to a certain set of rules, such as coordination and availability.

To ensure that we did not modify XP in general, we would like to revisit the four values of communication, simplicity, feedback, and courage in the context of DXP.

- *Communication*—The use of available tools makes it possible to communicate effectively regardless of physical location. Therefore, the value of communication in DXP is as great as it is in XP, though it may take different forms.
- *Simplicity*—The philosophy "Make it simple" doesn't depend on the physical location of the team members, so DXP does not affect this value.
- *Feedback*—The value of feedback is equally important in DXP as it is in XP. The only difference is that feedback needs to be propagated across distribution boundaries. If there are no hurdles in communication among team members, providing effective feedback should not be an issue in DXP.
- *Courage*—This value is not affected directly by the distribution of the team.

Therefore, DXP does not modify the four XP values.

Experience Report

To put DXP into practice, we set up a distributed team to work on a common project called the *Web-Desktop Project*. The team consisted of:

- Prashant, an Indian, working in Delhi, India
- Michael, a German, working in Munich, Germany
- Angelo, an Italian, traveling between St. Louis, Missouri, USA; Catania, Italy; and Irvine, California, USA
- David, an American, working in Pittsburgh, Pennsylvania, USA

In this section, we describe the project and how the team worked together. We then present our experiences in doing DXP.

Project Description

The goal of our project was to develop software called *Web-Desktop* that would provide the working environment for DXP. The Web-Desktop is a desktop that is accessible via a Web page. All applications launched on this desktop actually run on the machine where the desktop was downloaded. The Web-Desktop provides a set of applications needed for most of the development and management processes. Additional applications are available for on-demand installation.

The Web-Desktop is stateful; the state is maintained in the server that provides the Web-Desktop service and its components. Clients are completely stateless. This makes it possible to have real user mobility. Such software would enable a team member to use any PC connected to the Internet to log on and have the same look and feel and the same working environment. The development team need only provide the URL of the project desktop to the customer to bring the customer "on-site." The solution would give a lot of flexibility to mobile team members working on a project. A mobile team member could go to an Internet cafe and plug in a Web cam and/or microphone and be connected to the rest of the team. There would be no need to download and install software on every machine that the team member uses.

Within the project, we defined roles for each person. David was the customer, and Michael, Angelo, and Prashant were the programmers. Because we had very little time available, only about three weeks, we needed to make sure that we focused on the four XP practices selected in the section DXP (see Table 44.1).

- *Planning game*—We ran several videoconference sessions with David, our customer, discussing user stories. We used a regular editor and shared it via Microsoft NetMeeting application-sharing software.[2] The story cards were then discussed and estimated among the programmers. Finally, David assigned priorities and selected the cards for the first iteration. Similar work was done for further iterations.
- *Pair programming*—We assigned story cards to pairs of programmers and began the development process. We used RPP, as described in the section Addressing XP Practices and Values in DXP, thus making extensive use of videoconferencing and application sharing. We used e-mail to schedule appointments for our RPP sessions.
- *Continuous integration*—We used CVS as our configuration management tool.[3] We integrated our changes directly from our development branch into the main branch, without changing computers because no integration computer was available.
- *On-site customer*—We used videoconferencing to effectively involve our customer throughout the project lifetime. We used e-mail to communicate the time and channel for upcoming videoconference sessions.

Resources Used

We used tools that were well supported and easy to use and integrate in our working environment. Whenever possible, we picked tools that were either supported on multiple platforms or could interoperate with analogous software on other platforms or followed some standard. As an example, both NetMeeting and CUseeMe support the ITU conferencing standard and thus can interoperate.

2. See http://www.microsoft.com/windows/netmeeting/.
3. Concurrent Versions System, GNU Project, Free Software Foundation; see http://www.gnu.org/software/cvs/.

Every computer (desktop or notebook) had a microphone, speakers, and a Web cam installed. We used NetMeeting as the videoconferencing and application-sharing software. For connectivity, we used a variety of links, ranging from 33Kbps modems and 64Kbps ISDN to 100Mbps LAN connections.

Hurdles Encountered

During the project, we experienced several hurdles.

- Our videoconferencing software, NetMeeting, did not allow more than two participants in a session. An additional conference server would have been needed to enable conferences with more than two participants.
- It was cumbersome to capture story cards in a text file. A better solution might have been to use a custom WikiWikiWeb.[4]
- Sharing applications across operating system platforms was not possible using the NetMeeting application-sharing functionality. Virtual Network Computing might be a solution to this.[5]
- We used a simple text editor for brainstorming, making the process quite cumbersome. A tool like MindMapper could have made discussions about new ideas easier.[6]
- Narrow-bandwidth connections (for example, dial-up) hindered the use of video because of jitter introduced in audio, along with reduced responsiveness of application sharing. Our fallback strategy was to use only audio conferencing or to switch to a chat channel.
- Power outage is, at least in India, still a problem. A notebook computer with its own battery can be a valuable help, at least for short outages.
- Lack of uniform access to the source code repository is not a major hindrance but results in inconveniences that can have larger effects in the long run. Because Prashant had to work most of the time from behind a firewall, he was not able to connect directly to

4. See Ward Cunningham's Portland Pattern Repository at http://www.c2.com/cgi/wiki?WikiWikiWeb.

5. AT&T Laboratories, Cambridge; see http://www.uk.research.att.com/vnc/.

6. Mind-mapping software from the Bosley Group; see http://www.mindmapper.com.

the team repository. Other team members had to send him snapshots of the code via e-mail. This process was tedious and could introduce faults.

- Some of the keyboard settings were different among the team members. For example, some characters, such as braces, seemed to work only if the parties involved in the conference used the same keyboard—that is, both American or both German.

Lessons Learned

Our project was quite successful in using DXP, and in the process we gained some valuable experience.

- We found that using a combination of synchronous communication, such as videoconferencing, and asynchronous communication, such as e-mail, was the most effective. Even though we used videoconferencing along with application sharing, it could not completely substitute for the physical closeness and effectiveness offered by XP. A video picture of the partner was sufficient to tell what he was thinking or how he reacted to a comment. However, what was missing was the physical presence of the partner, which usually provides company and can therefore never be completely substituted with any kind of videoconferencing tool.
- Parallel development raises the issue of source code integrity. Tools such as CVS and Rational ClearCase address the issue.[7] Even though these tools support distributed development, we have found that making mutually exclusive changes helps reduce merge conflicts. Therefore, we used an e-mail token to serialize change access when teams were working on common code sections.

Conclusion

DXP can efficiently integrate remote and mobile team members into the development process and is thus a valuable extension to traditional XP. In addition, it enables much more effective involvement of the cus-

7. See http://www.rational.com/products/clearcase/index.jsp.

tomer compared with XP, especially in situations where it seems impossible to have an on-site customer.

DXP can therefore actively broaden the acceptance of XP as a lightweight though effective software development process. We are aware that a virtual meeting through computer-supported interaction can never replace direct human interaction. However, there are situations where such interaction is not feasible and where a form of XP can still be successfully employed.

At the time of writing, we realized that we heavily touched the field of Computer Supported Cooperative Work (CSCW).[8] How DXP relates to this needs further investigation. We have found, not surprisingly, that for computer-supported interaction to be successful, live pictures and tone (video and audio) are elementary.

We plan to document guidelines on how to implement DXP in a project in future papers.

The solutions proposed in this chapter might just be the first steps to a general revolution in human interaction—the long-missed multimedia revolution, which is yet to happen.

References

[Beck2000] K. Beck. *Extreme Programming Explained*. Addison-Wesley, 2000.

[Cowan2001] G. Cowan. "What Kinds of Tasks Are Best Performed Alone?" In *Pair Programming*. Portland Pattern Repository. http://www.c2.com/cgi/wiki?PairProgamming. November 10, 2001.

[Kircher+2001] M. Kircher, D. Levine. "The XP of TAO—Extreme Programming of Large, Open-Source Frameworks." In *Extreme Programming Examined*. G. Succi, M. Marchesi, eds. Addison-Wesley, 2001.

[Schuemmer+2001] T. Schuemmer, J. Schuemmer. "Support for Distributed Remote Pair Programming." In *Extreme Programming Examined*. G. Succi, M. Marchesi, eds. Addison-Wesley, 2001.

8. See http://www.telekooperation.de/cscw/, maintained by Applied Informatics and Distributed Systems Group, Technical University Munich.

[Steinmetz+1996] R. Steinmetz, K. Nahrstedt. *Multimedia Computing, Communication and Applications*. Prentice Hall, 1996.

[Williams+2000] L. Williams, R. Kessler. "All I Really Need to Know about Pair Programming I Learned in Kindergarten." *Communications of the ACM*, 2000.

About the Authors

Michael Kircher works as a senior software engineer at Siemens AG Corporate Technology in Munich, Germany. His main fields of interest include distributed object computing, software architectures, design patterns, XP, and management of knowledge workers in innovative environments. In recent years, he has published at numerous conferences, such as OOPSLA, EuroPLoP, PLoP, Middleware, and XP, on topics such as patterns, open source, software architectures for distributed systems, and XP. Further, he jointly organized several workshops at conferences such as OOPSLA and EuroPLoP. When away from his notebook, he loves to enjoy nature, on foot, by bike, or hunting accompanied by his dog. On nice summer evenings, he enjoys tasty Italian food on the patio of his favorite restaurant. Michael can be reached at Michael.Kircher@siemens.com.

Prashant Jain is a principal software engineer in the Corporate Research division of Siemens AG in Delhi, India. He holds a master's degree in computer science from Washington University. His main fields of interest include distributed systems, design patterns, and XP. His professional experience includes working as a software engineer for companies including Fujitsu Network Communications, Inc., and Kodak Health Imaging Systems, Inc. Prashant can be reached at Prashant.Jain@mchp.siemens.de.

Angelo Corsaro is currently a Ph.D. student at the University of California, Irvine. He holds an M.S. in computer science from Washington University and a Laurea in computer engineering from the University of Catania, Italy. His main research interests are related to real-time embedded systems, scheduling, resource management, software patterns, Meta-Object Protocols, Aspect-Oriented Programming, and lightweight development methodologies. Angelo can be reached at corsaro@ece.uci.edu.

David L. Levine is the director of engineering at CombineNet, Pittsburgh, Pennsylvania. He received a Ph.D. in computer science from the University of California, Irvine, an MSEE/CS from George Washington University, and a BSME from Cornell University. His research interests include development, testing, and performance analysis of efficient object-oriented real-time systems, and XP. Dr. Levine has extensive industry experience in developing software for solving combinatorial exchange problems, broadband telecommunications, high-fidelity electro-optic sensor system simulation, and electric/hybrid and internal combustion engine vehicle applications. David can be reached at levinedl@acm.org.

Chapter 45

The Five Reasons XP Can't Scale and What to Do about Them

—*Ron Crocker*

XP seems to be a good method for small teams to develop high-power software systems. There are concerns about the ability of the method to scale to scopes any larger than 12 developers. It takes only a few changes in the set of practices composing XP to make it a method scalable to quite large scope. Indeed, modifying five practices and adding a few new ones resolves the issues.

Introduction

I have this belief about why XP (and perhaps other "agile" development processes) can't scale up. It's similar to why I had problems with heavyweight development processes (think CMM) scaling down. In both cases, the approaches focus on a set of problems that exist in the target environment (small-scale development for XP) that don't exist in the other environment, and they miss important problems that don't exist in the intended environment but do exist in the other environment. In either case, you can't take the process and simply add more people (or in CMM, take people away) and expect it to work.

Hypothesis: The current set of 12 practices commonly referred to as Extreme Programming, as defined in [Beck2000] and [Jeffries+2000], does not scale.

To prove a negative is difficult, often approaching impossible. We are left, therefore, with a proof by contradiction—we assume the hypothesis and show that it can't be achieved. Such is the case with this hypothesis. In this chapter, I argue that XP as the four values is inherently scalable, but these 12 particular practices prevent the values from scaling. I then propose some new practices that alleviate the failings of the existing practices in the particular case of large projects. No comments are made relative to these approaches for small projects.

The Five Reasons

In particular, these are the five reasons XP can't scale.

- Pair programming expands quadratically.
- Planning game is too introspective.
- Collective ownership leads to chaos.
- Metaphor is too weak.
- No means to effectively coordinate multiple teams exists in the other practices.

When I use the term "scale" here, I mean for teams and problems of a size larger than XP was intended. I don't know what this number is, but let's say it's somewhere between 10 and 20 team members and some number of function points (or other metric) in a period of time that is beyond the capacity of a given team. There is likely a bias in this discussion toward a model of scaling XP that implies multiple (roughly) coequal teams. I recommend against scaling XP into one large team, because it seems to magnify the issues without providing a means of mitigating them. Indeed, Brooks [Brooks1995] notes the issues associated with building teams that are too large.

Pair Programming Expands Quadratically

Pair programming (PP) is too broad a term for anyone to claim that it doesn't scale. In fact, there's likely nothing about PP alone that doesn't scale, as long as it focuses only on the programming task itself—the arrangement of two programmers collaborating in real time to solve a problem. The part of PP that doesn't scale is its use in XP beyond the programming task itself. PP in XP is used to provide a medium to communicate design [Williams+2000] and familiarize developers with the code base. The communication paths of pairs in a team grow as the square of the number of members in the team; double the team size, quadruple the communication paths.

As the team grows in size, it may become distributed to other buildings, other cities, or even other countries. Complexity is added to the pairing process—we have to coordinate across sites, time zones, and languages. Local cliques creep in; teams focus on parts of the system and avoid others. A partitioning of system knowledge has occurred, but not a rational one. The system has now become *N* interacting systems and *N* interacting teams, yet there is no reasoned approach to this interaction, and there is no mechanism for coordination.

Planning Game Is Too Introspective

The planning game is a means to ensure that the team works on the most important tasks at any time. As the team grows, the number of tasks grows as well. As the project grows in scope, the amount of important work grows correspondingly. As both grow, their effects multiply. Combine this with distributed teams and we have a problem: There is no means to ensure that each team is working on the right things relative to the other teams. You can use the cop-out answer that "The customer coordinates this by picking what's important for each iteration," but would you want the customer to be exposed to this degree of your development process? Is it really the customer's responsibility to help you resolve your development difficulties? I don't think so—go back to one of the tenets of the approach: Customers make business decisions; engineers make technical decisions.

It is likely (and has occurred several times in my experience) that a team needs to work on a less important (from the business perspective) task to ensure that an important systemwide behavior is available. Alas, there is no XP means to do this, because there is no overall coordination role defined in XP.

Collective Ownership Leads to Chaos

Collective ownership is a good thing in XP. It enables work to proceed without depending on a particular individual to do the work. That individual may know the area better than others, but the risk of that individual becoming a bottleneck is reduced through collective ownership. Unfortunately, as the scale grows, collective ownership changes from a benefit to a potential source of churn and complexity. The churn comes from two developers (or two pairs) adding conflicting features to the code base. The complexity comes from resolving the interactions of these new features, even when they're not directly conflicting but only cohabiting. Add to this the requirements on tools to support this type of problem resolution, and a huge potential risk has been added to the technical side of the project. Bring on the bonus of no overall coordination and it's game over.

Metaphor Is Too Weak

Metaphor is the least well defined of the XP practices. My reading of metaphor indicates its use as a general compass for understanding the solution space. This use of metaphor is sufficient because PP continually reinforces the metaphor.

Metaphor is insufficient as design, though, because its relationship to the solution is often rather loose. Indeed, as the team size grows, the ability for the metaphor to be sufficient decreases. Combining this with the decreasing ability of PP to meet the communication needs of the team leads to a team that can quickly diverge instead of converge.

No Means to Effectively Coordinate Multiple Teams Exists in the Other Practices

As noted earlier, there is no notion of coordination across teams in XP, because XP is oriented at a single team. This is one of those items left out of XP because it was not an issue in the target environment of XP. However, this leaves a dilemma for scaling XP: Either scale XP by making a single large team, risking collapse under the communication burden; or scale XP by growing several collaborating teams and risk collapse because of lack of coordination.

Solutions

I've heard it stated that "[to] point out issues without providing solutions is whining," and because I don't want to whine, here are some recommendations for new practices to add to XP (replacing existing practices) that enable XP to scale successfully.

Based on my experiences, the following new practices are required to support a multiteam XP environment:

- Loosely coupled teams
- Team coordination layer

Loosely Coupled Teams

It seems clear to me that to effectively scale XP requires choosing the latter of those two options for scaling XP—specifically, to create a collection of loosely coupled collaborating teams. This is both a practice and a philosophical position. The practice part comes from breaking the project into these teams; the philosophical part is to keep these teams focused and functioning in the loosely coupled way. It could be argued that this practice replaces many of the XP practices, including PP, collective ownership, and coding standards, in the highest level of the project and imposes requirements for a new practice.

My experiences in multiple-team development lead me to a strong recommendation: The "prime" team should not dictate or impose a process on the "subcontracting" teams.[1] However the prime team should indeed impose the feature rollout plan (the equivalent of the XP "release plan") on the teams. Our approach imposed the order of deliverables, used a consensus of the development teams to decide the dates, and adjusted the dates as necessary to meet the business objectives.

1. This recommendation is counter to that proposed by Carmel [Carmel1999], but this type of dictation is almost a guarantee for failure; see [Battin+2001] for further explanation.

This position leads to a collection of subcontractors, each with their own development process but with shared dates and deliverables. Because the teams have their own development processes, there's no effective way to coordinate any of the rules of the game—specifically, rules that could be used to share development across the teams, such as the coding or change management rules. Because there's no effective means to ensure the same rules across the teams, it is unlikely that any coding can occur across teams, obviating the need for PP or collective ownership at the "across the teams" level.

Team Coordination Layer

To resolve the issue with coordination, a coordination layer is added (arguably outside the scope of XP) to the project to support the team interactions. This can be viewed as layering the project structure, where at the highest level in the hierarchy there is a collection of teams being coordinated. At the bottom are the individual teams that are doing the work. This type of structure can go on as necessary, enabling the projects to scale to enormous scope.

The team coordination layer replaces the metaphor, PP, collective code ownership, and on-site customer practices with an "Architecture Lite," adds a role ("liaison"), and augments planning game to work with multiple teams, keeping the project needs in full focus at all times.

Up-front Architecture Lite

The division of tasks among the various teams must be rational—a team should work a problem for a reason. That reason can be based on the availability of workers, but that should be the last reason on the list. Indeed, the tasks should be allocated to teams in a way that minimizes the required day-to-day communication among the teams to get their job done. This, in turn, requires that some structure be provided to the solution space to direct this allocation. Traditionally, this would be the role of the "architect" and architecture in the project.

To meet the needs of an agile project, though, often a full "architecture" is not required. Instead, an "Architecture Lite" is more appropriate [Coleman2000; Toft+2000]. An Architecture Lite fully describes the system architecture but at a high level of abstraction. The description includes both structural and behavioral aspects of the system. In our use of this approach, we used the Architecture Lite to define and use a few strongly held key principles. Abstractly, these are:

- Low coupling among the elements
- Well-defined interfaces
- Concise semantics for the element behaviors

This Architecture Lite replaces metaphor and PP, the latter from the perspective of its use to share system design information. One of the keys in my experiences was to provide a stronger metaphor than the metaphor practice typically provides. Indeed, we defined a partitioning of functionality and behavior into "boxes" that formed the architecture. This enabled us to then carve up the work and assign it to the teams in a way that maximally leveraged their particular strengths (which include not only their capabilities but any conveniences caused by their location).

The intent is to enable agility in the large projects; agility implies emergent behavior. We rely on these principles to guide us when a behavior emerges. Because the elements' behavior and interfaces were well defined, they could be developed in a context that was shared among the teams. Because the network elements had low coupling, each team could run independently of both any other team and the architect. The net result of managing complexity at this level is that we are free to distribute the development of any element to any team.

Note also that one of the roles of the PP practice was to ensure that design knowledge permeated the team. The Architecture Lite replaces this role at the highest level in the project, explicitly acknowledging the loss in fidelity of the information.

Liaison

The role of liaison was one we stumbled on but is critical to success in a multiteam environment [Battin+2001]. Liaisons are members of the various teams that join forces to develop the Architecture Lite. By collaborating on the foundation of the system, each liaison has intimate knowledge of the rules of the system—the principles of the system. Because each team has a liaison, this person can act as the conscience of the Architecture Lite, to ensure that the principles are kept. The liaisons enable the teams to work independently by filtering the required communication among the teams, because they understand intimately the roles of the other teams. As the project evolves and emergent behaviors cause the Architecture Lite to become invalid, the liaisons initiate changes to the Architecture Lite so that it can continue to be a useful tool.

The liaisons also fulfill an important role abdicated by the Architecture Lite—they are the keepers of the high-fidelity knowledge of the code that implements the Architecture Lite. In XP subteams, any member should be able to fill this role, reducing overall project risk (by reducing the team's "Bus Number").

Team-wise Planning Game

The Architecture Lite enables a rational distribution of work across the teams, and the liaisons enable each team to proceed without much interaction, but neither of these resolves the issue of coordinating when such work is completed. Planning across teams is a difficult problem; each team can have its own set of issues. A team-wise planning game (TPG) is similar in many ways to the existing planning game practice, so it is more correctly viewed as an enhancement to that practice rather than a new practice.

The key aspect of this approach is to agree to participate in the approach throughout the project; the TPG coordinates the development of those features across the teams. Each team is represented in the TPG—much as the individual developer is represented in the planning game. However, instead of representing an individual, they represent the team. They sign up for the work associated with their team, based on the structure provided under the Architecture Lite. If the new work breaks the architecture, the architecture is reworked for the next iteration (as the liaison role notes).

In the project discussed in [Battin+2001], we had a team of drivers of this coordination. In a certain sense, this team interacted with the customer to determine what the important business feature was and then interacted with the multiple development teams (as proxy customer?) to coordinate their activities. In the role of proxy customer, the coordination team could ensure that the teams worked on what was important from the global perspective.

We had weekly teleconferences among the teams to ensure that information about progress was being shared and to understand the impacts of any late team on any other team's progress. Often, the tasks were interdependent at the system level, in the sense that some portion of the system required both teams to complete their work to support some systemwide behavior. We used the weekly meetings to remind the teams of these dependencies.

This approach works best with subteams using agile development methods, because they are best able to respond to changes in requirements from iteration to iteration.

Conclusion

This chapter has presented the five reasons that projects of sufficiently large scope, larger than that of a single team, will not be successful with XP. It also presented the ways to improve large projects' chances of being successful. These ways include adding some up-front coordination work and actively managing multiteam issues, both of which are beyond the scope of the currently defined XP. Therefore, it is my conclusion that for XP to be successfully scaled, these practices must be included in the method. It is possible (even likely) that other changes are required. In that sense, these changes are only necessary but not sufficient to guarantee success.

References

[Battin+2001] R. Battin, R. Crocker, J. Kreidler, K. Subramanian. "Leveraging Resources in Global Software Development." *IEEE Software*, March 2001.

[Beck2000] K. Beck. *Extreme Programming Explained*. Addison-Wesley, 2000.

[Brooks1995] F. Brooks. *The Mythical Man-Month, Anniversary Edition*. Addison-Wesley, 1995.

[Carmel1999] E. Carmel. *Global Software Teams: Collaborating Across Borders and Time Zones*. Prentice Hall PTR, 1999.

[Coleman2000] D. Coleman. Architecture for Planning Software Product Platforms. Tutorial presented at the First Software Product Line Conference. Denver, Colorado. August 28–September 1, 2000.

Part VI

[Jeffries+2000] R. Jeffries, A. Anderson, C. Hendrickson. *Extreme Programming Installed*. Addison-Wesley, 2000.

[Toft+2000] P. Toft, D. Coleman, J. Ohta. "A Cooperative Model for Cross-Divisional Product Development for a Software Product Line." In *Proceedings, First Software Product Line Conference (SPLC1)*. Denver, Colorado. August 28–September 1, 2000.

[Williams+2000] L. Williams, R. Kessler, W. Cunningham, R. Jeffries. "Strengthening the Case for Pair Programming." *IEEE Software*, July 2000.

Chapter 46

XP in Complex Project Settings: Some Extensions

—*Martin Lippert, Stefan Roock, Henning Wolf, and Heinz Züllighoven*

XP has one weakness when it comes to complex application domains or difficult situations in the customer's organization: The customer role does not reflect the different interests, skills, and forces with which we are confronted in development projects. We propose splitting the customer role into a user role and a client role. The user role is concerned with domain knowledge; the client role defines the strategic or business goals of a development project and controls its financial resources. It is the developers' task to integrate users and clients into a project that builds a system according to the users' requirements while at the same time attaining the goals set by the client. In addition, we present document types from the tools-and-materials approach [Lilienthal+1997]) that help developers integrate users and clients into a software project. All document types have been used successfully in a number of industrial projects together with the well-known XP practices.

Context and Motivation

It was reported that one of the major problems of the C3 project was the mismatch between the *goal donor* and the *gold owner* [Jeffries2000;

Fowler2000]. Although the goal donor—the customer in the XP team—was satisfied with the project's results, the gold owner—the management of the customer's organization—was not. It is our thesis that XP, in its current form, fails to address the actual situation at the client's organization in a suitable way. The main stakeholder—the users and their management—are merged into a single role: the customer. This one role cannot address the different forces in a development project. The users of the future system know their application domain in terms of tasks and concepts, but they rarely have an idea of what can be implemented using current technologies. Moreover, it is often misleading to view the users of the future system as the goal donor. They are unfamiliar with the strategic and business goals related to a project and, more important, they do not control the money.

Therefore, we make a distinction between the role of the user and the role of the client. The users have all the domain knowledge and therefore are the primary source for the application requirements. The client sets the goals of the development project from a business point of view. The client will pay for a development project only if these goals are met to a certain degree.

We begin with a discussion of the roles in an XP project as defined by Kent Beck. We then split the customer role into the user role and the client role. These two roles change the situation of XP projects. Although the user can be seen in a similar way to the XP customer, the client role requires more attention. We address the new project situation by using two document types geared to the client role: baselines and projects stages. We show when and how to use these document types and discuss their relation to story cards and the Unified Process (UP).

Roles in XP

XP defines the following roles for a software development process [Beck2000].

- *Programmer*—The programmer writes source code for the software system under development. This role is at the technical heart of every XP project because it is responsible for the main outcome of the project: the application system.

- *Customer*—The customer writes user stories, which tell the programmer what to program. "The programmer knows how to program. The customer knows what to program" [Beck2000].
- *Tester*—The tester is responsible for helping customers select and write functional tests. On the other side, the tester runs all the tests again and again to create an updated picture of the project state.
- *Tracker*—The tracker keeps track of all the numbers in a project. This role is familiar with the estimation reliability of the team. Whoever plays this role knows the facts and records of the project and should be able to tell the team whether they will finish the next iteration as planned.
- *Coach*—The coach is responsible for the development process as a whole. The coach notices when the team is getting "off track" and puts it "back on track." To do this, the coach must have a profound knowledge of and experience with XP.
- *Consultant*—Whenever the XP team needs additional special knowledge, they "hire" a consultant who possesses this knowledge. The consultant transfers this knowledge to the team members, enabling the team to solve the problem on their own.
- *Big boss*—The big boss is the manager of the XP project and provides the resources for it. The big boss needs to have the general picture of the project, be familiar with the current project state, and know whether any interventions are needed to ensure the project's success.

Although XP addresses management of the software development aspects with the big boss role, it neglects the equivalent of this role on the customer side. XP merges all customer roles into the customer role. We suggest splitting the customer role into two roles: *user* and *client*.

The New User and Client Roles

The *user* is the domain expert that the XP team has to support with the software system under development. The user is therefore the first source of information when it comes to functional requirements.

The *client* role is not concerned with detailed domain knowledge or functional requirements. The client focuses on business needs, such as reducing the organizational overhead of a department by $100,000 U.S. a year. Given this strategic background, the client defines the goals of the software development project ("Reduce the organizational overhead of the loan department by $100,000 U.S. per year") and supplies the money for the project. The client is thus the so-called *goal donor and* the *gold owner.*

It is often not easy to reconcile the needs of users and clients at the same time. What the users want may not be compatible with the goals of the client. What we need, then, are dedicated instruments to deal with both roles.

Story Cards and the Planning Game

We use story cards for the planning game, but we use them in a different way than in the "original" XP, and our planning game differs in some aspects, too. In our projects, users or clients rarely write story cards themselves. They do not normally have the skills or the required "process knowledge" to do so. Typically, we, as developers, write story cards based on interviews with users and observations of their actual work situation. These story cards are reviewed by the *users* and the *client.* The users must assess whether the implementation of the story cards will support them. They thus review the developers' understanding of the application domain. The client decides which story cards to implement in the next development iteration and with which priority. To avoid severe mismatches between the interests of the users and the client, both parties are involved in the planning game. This means that users can articulate their interests and discuss with the client the priorities of the story cards.

Our experience here is clear: Users and client will normally reach a compromise on their mutual interests. But whatever the outcome of the planning game is, the decision about what is to be implemented next is made not by developers but by the client.

If a project is complex, there will be an abundance of story cards. In this case it is difficult for users, clients, and developers to get the overall picture from the story cards. For this type of project, we use two additional document types: *project stages* and *baselines.* These are described in the next section.

Project Stages and Baselines

In projects with complex domains or large application systems, story cards may not be sufficient as a discussion basis for the planning game. In such cases, we need additional techniques to get the overall picture—especially for the contingencies between the story cards. If one story cannot be developed in the estimated period of time, it may be necessary to reschedule dependent stories. We may also need to divide the bulk of story cards in handy portions and make our planning more transparent to the users and the client. We have therefore enhanced the planning game by selected document types of the tools-and-materials approach [Roock+1998]): baselines and project stages.

We use project stages and baselines for project management and scheduling. A project stage defines which consistent and comprehensive components of the system should be available at what time, covering which subgoal of the overall project. Project stages are an important document type for communicating with users and clients. We use them to make development progress more transparent by discussing the development plan and rescheduling it to meet users' and client's needs.

Table 46.1 shows an example of three project stages (taken from the JWAM framework development project).[1] We specify at what time we wish to reach which goal and what we have to do to attain this goal. Typically, the project stages are scheduled backward from the estimated project end to its beginning, with most important external events and

TABLE 46.1 Example of Project Stages

Subgoal	Realization	When
Prototype with Web front end is running.	Presentation of prototype for users	3/31/00
Prototype supports both Web and GUI front end.	Presentation of extended prototype for users and client	5/16/00
First running system is installed.	Use of Web front end by pilot Web users	8/30/00
. . .	. . .	. . .

1. See http://www.jwam.org.

deadlines (vacations, training programs, exhibitions, project reviews, and marketing presentations) being fixed when projects are established.

Unlike the increments produced during an XP iteration, the result of a project stage is not necessarily an installed system. We always try to develop a system that can be installed and used as the result of every project stage, but we know that this is not always feasible. In large projects or complex application domains, developers need time to understand the application domain. During this period, developers may implement prototypes but rarely operative systems. We thus often have prototypes as the result of early project stages. Another example here is the stepwise replacement of legacy systems. It is often appropriate to integrate the new solution with the legacy system to manage risk. Project stages then produce systems that can and will be used by users. But the project team may also decide not to integrate the new solution with the legacy system, perhaps because of the considerable effort required for legacy integration. In such cases, the project team will also produce installable increments, but it is clear that the increments will not be used in practice. Users are often reluctant to use new systems until they offer at least the functionality of the old system.

Baselines are used to plan one project stage in detail. They do not focus on dates but define what has to be done, who will do it, and who will control the outcome in what way. Unlike project stages, baselines are scheduled from the beginning to the end of the stage.

In the baselines table (as shown in Table 46.2), we specify who is responsible for what baseline and what it is good for. The last column contains a remark on how to check the result of the baseline. The baselines table helps us identify dependencies between different steps of the framework development (see the What For column). The last three columns are the most important ones for us. The first column is not that important, because everybody can, in principle, do everything (as with story cards). However, it is important for us to know how to check the results to get a good impression of the project's progress. The second and third columns contain indicators for potential reschedulings between the baselines and help us sort the story cards that are on a finer-grained level.

The rows of the baselines table are often similar to story cards, but baselines also include tasks to be done without story cards. Examples are "Organize a meeting," "Interview a user," and so on.

The way project stages and baselines are actually used depends on the type of development project in hand. For small to medium-sized

TABLE 46.2 Example of Baselines

Who	Does What with Whom/What	What For	How to Check
Roock	Prepare interview guidelines.	Interviews	E-mail interview guidelines to team.
Wolf, Lippert	Interview users at pilot customer.	First understanding of application domain	Interview protocols are on the project server.
...	...	...	...
Roock	Implement GUI prototype.	Getting feedback on the general handling from the users	Prototype acceptance tests are OK; executable prototype is on the project server.
...	...	...	...

projects, we often use project stages but no explicit baselines. In these cases, we simply use the story cards of the current project stage, complementing them with additional task cards. If the project is more complex (more developers, developers at different sites, and so on), we use explicit baselines in addition to story cards. If the project is long-term, we do not define baselines for all project stages up front but identify baselines for the current and the next project stage. Because a project stage should not be longer than three months, we work on a detailed planning horizon of three to six months.

It is often a good idea to sketch the entire system as a guideline for the project stages. We describe the concepts of core system and specialized systems in the next section, to provide an application-oriented view of the system architecture.

System Architecture

In line with the project stages, we divide the software system into a *core system* with *extension levels* [Krabbel+1996]. The core system is an operative part of the overall software system that addresses important

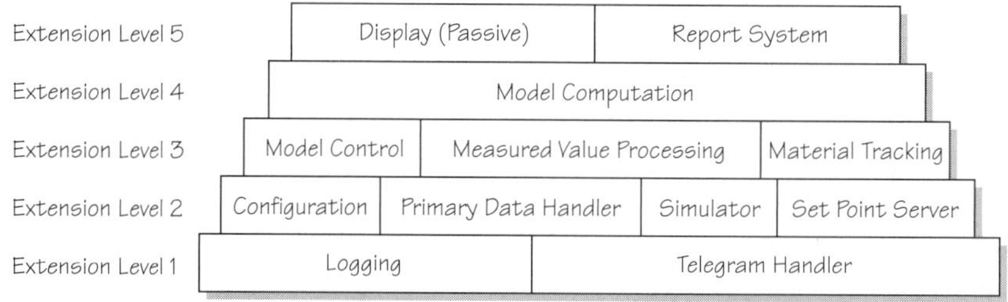

FIGURE 46.1 Example of a core system with extension levels

domain-related needs. It is developed first and put into operation. Because the core system is usually still quite complex, it is subdivided into extension levels that are built successively. An example of a core system with extension levels is shown in Figure 46.1 (taken from the domain of hot rolling mills). The upper extension levels use the functionality of the lower extension levels. This way, we get an application-oriented structure that is useful for planning and scheduling. It is obvious that the lowest extension level must be created first, followed by the next-higher one, and so on.

Specialized systems are separated from the core system. They add well-defined functionality. An example of a core system with specialized systems is shown in Figure 46.2 (again taken from the domain of hot rolling mills). The specialized systems are drawn as circles.

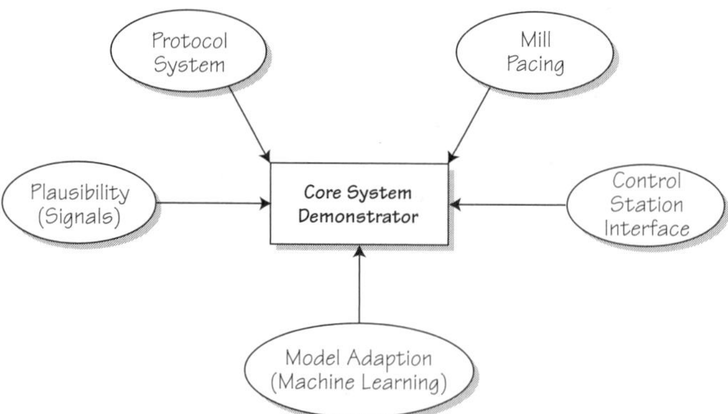

FIGURE 46.2 Example of a core system with specialized systems

Because specialized systems depend only on the core and not vice versa, we can deliver an operative and useful core system very early on and get feedback from the users. In parallel, different software teams can build specialized systems. Adhering to the one-way dependency of specialized systems, we achieve maximum independence among the special systems. They can be created in any order or even in parallel. Obviously, the core system has to provide the basic functionality for the whole system because it is the only way for the specialized systems to exchange information. The core system usually provides a set of basic communication mechanisms enabling information transfer between different parts of the overall system.

The concept of a core system and specialized systems can easily be used in the planning game. Users and client get an impression of the whole system and can negotiate on the different values and priorities (users' needs, client's goals, technical constraints) to reach a compromise on the project's development schedule.

In addition, project stages are used to control the project's progress and timelines for the overall plan.

Conclusion

We have discussed the roles in an XP project as defined by Kent Beck. Based on our experience, we split the XP customer role into two roles: user and client. The user is the source of application knowledge, while the client defines the project goals and supplies the money for the project. Both parties must be integrated into the development project. We have shown how this can be done with the help of modified story cards, projects stages, baselines, and an adapted planning game.

We do not suggest using all the new instruments presented here for every project. They should be used as part of an inventory or a toolbox, together with the familiar techniques defined by XP. The instruments should be used as required for the project in hand. If the project is not complex, there is no need to burden the project with the additional roles and document types. But if the application domain or the project is highly complex, the sketched extensions to XP are worthwhile.

Selection of the proper instruments from the toolbox may be difficult for the project team because we are not yet able to provide detailed guidelines. Evaluating project experience to provide such guidelines for tool selection will be one of our future tasks.

References

[Beck2000] K. Beck. *Extreme Programming Explained.* Addison-Wesley, 2000.

[Fowler2000] M. Fowler. *The XP2000 Conference.* http://www.martinfowler.com/articles/xp2000.html. 2000.

[Jeffries2000] R. Jeffries. *Extreme Programming: An Open Approach to Enterprise Development.* http://www.xprogramming.com/xpmag. 2000.

[Krabbel+1996] A. Krabbel, S. Ratuski, I. Wetzel. "Requirements Analysis of Joint Tasks in Hospitals." *Proceedings of the 19th Information Systems Research Seminar In Scandinavia: IRIS 19.* Lökeberg, Sweden. August 10–13, 1996.

[Lilienthal+1997] C. Lilienthal, H. Züllighoven. "Application-Oriented Usage Quality: The Tools and Materials Approach." *Interactions Magazine,* October 1997.

[Roock+1998] S. Roock, H. Wolf, H. Züllighoven. "Frameworking." *Proceedings of the 21st Information Systems Research Seminar in Scandinavia: IRIS 21.* Saeby Soebad, Denmark. August 8–11, 1998.

About the Authors

Martin Lippert, Stefan Roock, and Henning Wolf are research assistants at the University of Hamburg and professional software architects and consultants at IT Workplace Solutions. Among their current research interests are framework design and implementation, refactoring, Java, and Extreme Programming. They are senior architects of the JWAM framework and have gathered experience with Extreme Programming techniques over the past three years. They are project coaches for Extreme Programming and software architectures, and have given a number of talks, tutorials, and demonstrations on various topics of software engineering and XP at international conferences, including XP2000 and XP2001, ECOOP, ICSTest, and OOP.

Heinz Züllighoven is a professor in the computer science department, Software Engineering Group, University of Hamburg, and is CEO of IT

Workplace Solutions. His research interests are principles of software architecture for large interactive systems and lightweight software development strategies. He has written many books and articles on software engineering topics.

The authors can be reached at lippert@jwam.org, roock@jwam.org, wolf@jwam.org, and zuellighoven@jwam.org.

Chapter 47

Building Complex Object-Oriented Systems with Patterns and XP

—*Eduardo B. Fernandez*

Many important systems are complex. These systems have a large number of interacting entities and complex constraints, and need to satisfy nonfunctional requirements. We use Semantic Analysis Patterns (SAPs), a type of analysis pattern in which each pattern corresponds to a basic set of use cases, to build a global conceptual model in an incremental way. This global model provides XP with a structure in which global aspects such as distribution, security, and testability can be considered. SAPs can also be used at each incremental stage in XP to guarantee the application of good software development principles.

Introduction

XP has been used mostly to build systems of medium or small complexity. Because of its fine-grained increments (one or a few classes each time [Beck2000; Martin+2001]), it is difficult to consider global aspects such as distribution, authorization, and concurrency. However, many important systems—for example, manufacturing, vehicle navigation, and business planning—are quite complex. Their complexity comes from a large number of interacting entities, many relationships between their units, complex constraints on the values of their variables, and the need to satisfy nonfunctional requirements, which normally implies dealing with concurrency and distribution aspects.

The lack of a global view in XP comes from its emphasis on immediate implementation, without explicit analysis and design stages. Although modeling is not explicitly excluded, there is little incentive for it; typically, partial models are used and then discarded [Fowler2001]. This precludes finding commonalities and optimizations in the global conceptual model. Refactoring cannot correct some conceptual problems or consider nonfunctional aspects.

Patterns let us start a conceptual model in the right direction and use the knowledge of others. If the patterns used are carefully selected, they embody good design principles, and a designer can apply these principles transparently [Fernandez2000A], which results in high-quality models. After this, a variety of architectural patterns can be used to deal with design aspects.

We propose building first the conceptual model and the tests for the complete system (or close to it) and postponing the start of implementation until this model is relatively complete. This enables the designers to consider global aspects and build more complex applications. Classes can still be built and tested incrementally, but now we have the guidance of a global model. We have presented the concept of Semantic Analysis Patterns (SAPs) [Fernandez+2000D], miniapplications corresponding to a basic set of use cases or user stories; they can be used to build the global model incrementally. They can also be used at each XP stage to guarantee the application of good software development principles.

Semantic Analysis Patterns

An analysis pattern is a set of classes and associations that have some meaning in the context of an application; that is, it is a conceptual model of a part of the application. However, the same structure may be valid for other applications, and this aspect makes analysis patterns very valuable for reuse and composition.

Analysis patterns can be atomic or composite [Riehle1997]. Analysis patterns have been studied in [Cook+1994] and [Fowler1997], inspired by the work of Hay [Hay1996]. In particular, the analysis patterns discussed in these references are atomic patterns, composed of a few classes; our interest is in larger patterns. Larger patterns can be more effective with respect to reusability and can be used as building blocks for conceptual models.

We have proposed a type of composite pattern that we call Semantic Analysis Patterns. An SAP is a minimal application that corresponds to a few basic use cases and defines a semantic unit that can be combined with other SAPs to build complex systems. The use cases are selected in such a way that the pattern can be applied to a variety of applications. We have developed several SAPs, including patterns for inventories [Fernandez2000B], for reservation and use of reusable entities [Fernandez+1999], for order processing [Fernandez+2000A], and others.

Development of SAPs

SAPs are based on well-known principles such as abstraction, composition, minimal coupling, and regularity. They also incorporate other principles not usually included in most methods, such as authorization, precision, and testability [Fernandez2000C]. We illustrate here the use of some of these principles in the development of an SAP for inventories.

Abstraction

Abstraction is the most fundamental principle of the object-oriented approach. It implies including only the essential aspects of a model, leaving out details that are not relevant or needed. We illustrate this concept with a basic model for an inventory system for discrete items. Its basic functions can be summarized as follows.

1. *Keep track of different varieties of stock.* Keep track of the quantities of each item in stock. Several kinds of quantities may be needed—for example, `onHand` and `Available`.
2. *Keep track of the locations of items.* The inventory should record the distribution of items in specific locations. Locations could be subdivided for easier location of items. Each flow of stock material between locations should be reflected in the inventory distribution.

The most basic inventory model just keeps track of the quantities of some type of item in stock (see Figure 47.1). The items in this inventory can be finished products, components used in manufacturing,

Part VI

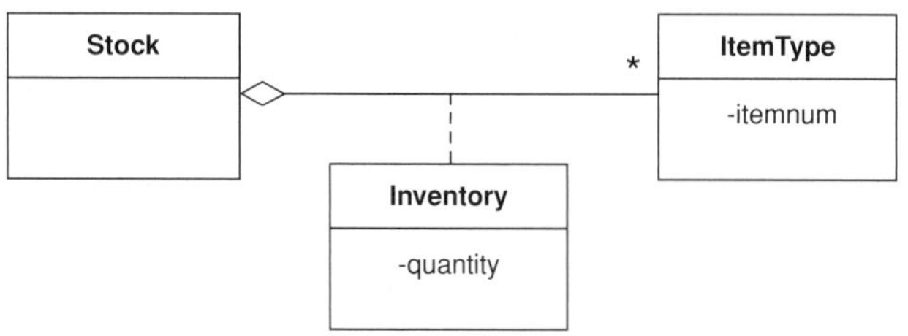

FIGURE 47.1 A basic inventory system

machinery, and so on; in other words, anything of whose existence and quantity we want to be aware. Each item belongs to a unique type, `ItemType`. This is a fundamental abstraction that corresponds to requirement 1. Any inventory system model must have this model as a component. Similarly, we can make abstractions of any other requirements. To realize requirement 2, we need to break down the inventory quantity into location quantities (usually there exist several locations where an inventory item can be stored). This model is shown in Figure 47.2.

We can consider the diagrams shown in Figures 47.1 and 47.2 to be atomic analysis patterns. They describe two abstractions that correspond to the following two fundamental use cases:

- Keeping track of quantities of discrete items (Figure 47.1).
- Keeping track of the locations of those items (Figure 47.2).

Each stage of XP typically implements one or two of these use cases or stories.

Decomposition

To be able to model a complex system, we need to apply decomposition, the divide-and-conquer principle. For example, a manufacturing system is far too complex to handle as a single unit. A decomposition for this system would consist of a set of UML packages such as Inventory Control, Shop Orders, Customer Orders, Shipping, and Money. The interactions between packages are important to define the needed operations in the classes of each package. Decomposition is very impor-

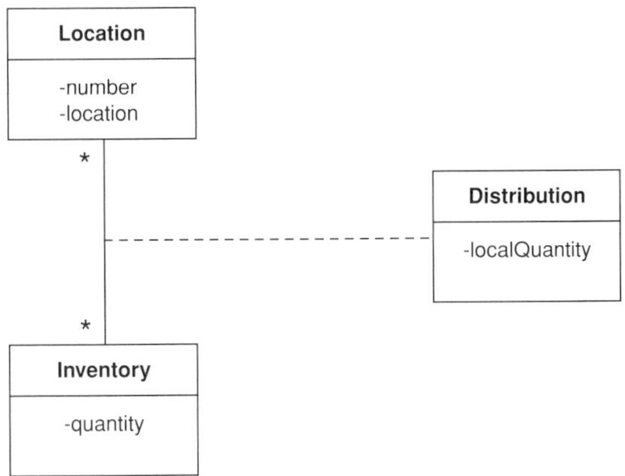

FIGURE 47.2 Distribution of items

tant for XP; each stage implies an explicit or implicit decomposition of the requirements.

Composition

Patterns can be composed to build larger models [Fernandez2000A]. For example, we can compose the patterns of Figures 47.1 and 47.2 to form a larger pattern that keeps track of stock quantities and their distribution. Figure 47.3 shows the composite pattern (this includes authorization, discussed later). Clearly, this principle is also basic for XP, to put together the results of each stage.

Projection

Projection is the combination of different diagrams or views of the system to provide a more complete picture. It can be likened to the need to describe a mechanical piece using different views, or projections; a single view would give a distorted and incomplete picture of its three-dimensional properties. This is a principle not emphasized XP. In particular, complex applications need several diagrams to be fully understood.

Minimal Coupling

This principle is frequently used in design patterns, in which a main objective is flexibility [Gamma+1995]. It is also heavily used in Fowler's

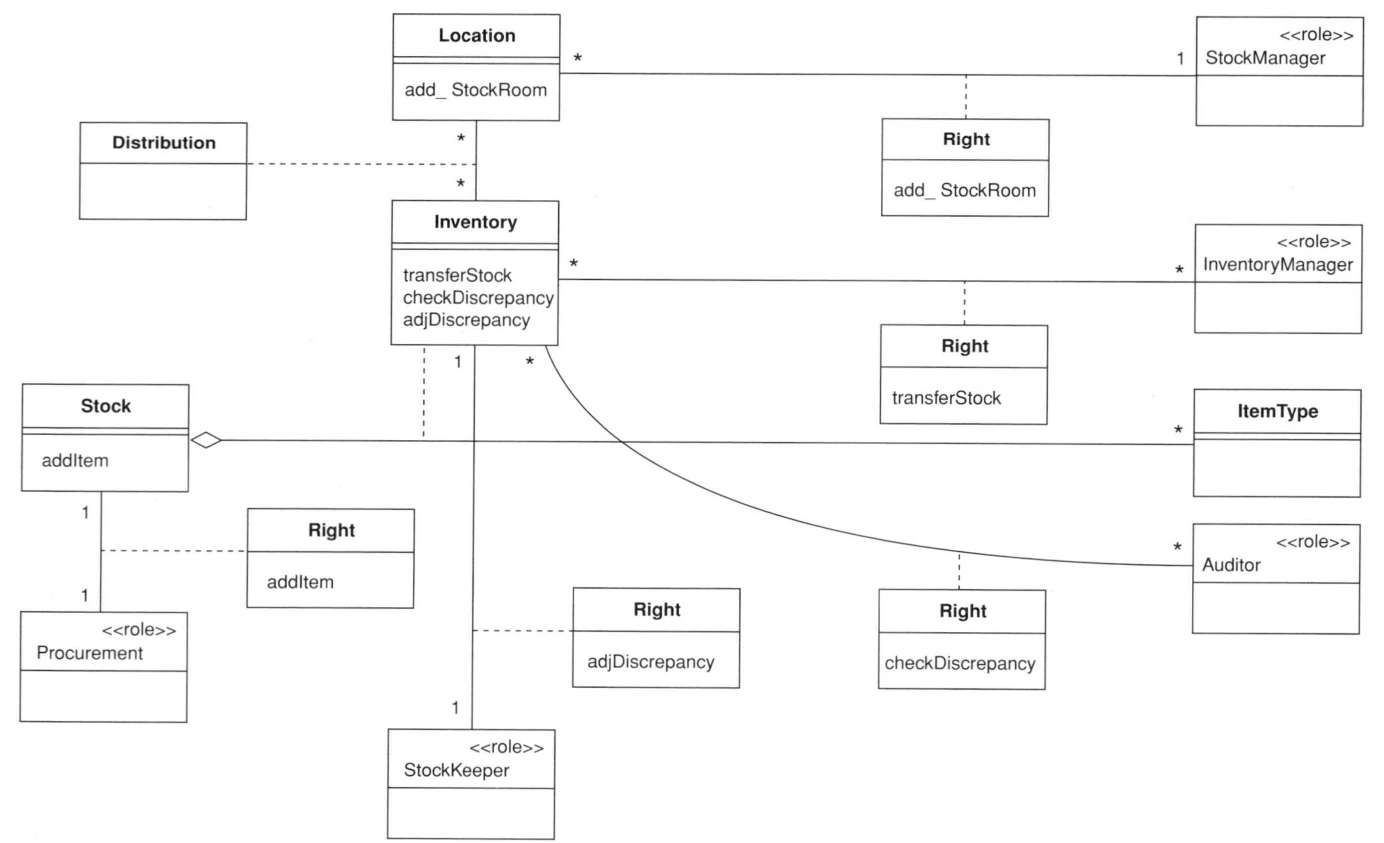

FIGURE 47.3 Authorized inventory

analysis patterns [Fowler1997]. The idea is to separate some aspects to enable them to evolve independently.

In the example, if we had a detailed description of the structure of items, we could use the Composite pattern [Gamma+1995] to describe this structure recursively. This would decouple the structural aspects of a component or product from more basic aspects. We could also decouple other aspects of the item description.

Precision

A model such as the one shown in Figure 47.1 may not be precise enough to represent some of the constraints in the requirements. For example, to indicate that the sum of inventory quantities must be constant in inventory transfers between locations, we need to add a UML constraint. This can be added to the class `Inventory` as follows:

```
{sum of quantities must be constant}
```

However, this is not precise enough for many cases. If we had more complex constraints, statements of this form may be ambiguous. This ambiguity cannot be tolerated in safety-critical applications, for example. Both Z [Cook+1994] and OCL [Wanner+1998] have been used to add precision to UML constraints. A comparison of Z and OCL as constraint languages is given in [Jiang+1999].

Authorization

When we build systems using atomic patterns or SAPs, we know the actor roles in the use cases that correspond to these units. These actors need specific rights to perform the functions defined in the use case. We can then define authorization rules according to the principles of Role-Based Access Control (RBAC) [Fernandez+1997]. For example, in the inventory, we could include the authorizations shown in Figure 47.3, where classes such as `StockManager` indicate roles (denoted by the UML stereotype `<<role>>`). For example, in Figure 47.3 the `InventoryManager` is authorized to transfer stock between locations.

Testability

Use cases (or user stories) correspond to the necessary interactions with the system and define sequences of actions that can be used to test the system [Jacobson+1998]. A system defined following use cases is then implicitly highly testable. For example, for the inventory, we could build test cases to follow the actions of the sequence diagrams of this application [Fernandez2000B] and check whether a Shop Order changes state and the inventory quantities are updated when specific events occur.

SAPs and XP

The explicit use of good software development principles requires considerable experience and is prone to error. For most users, a better way to apply the principles is implicitly, by building a conceptual model through the application of SAPs or another appropriate methodology. As indicated in [Fernandez+2000D], a procedure to build a conceptual model would be as follows. We assume we have a catalog of atomic patterns and SAPs. We examine the use cases and any other requirements and then do the following:

- Look for SAPs. We look first for patterns that exactly or closely match the requirements. Then we try to find analogous patterns that may apply.
- Look for atomic patterns.

This procedure results in a skeleton, where some parts of the model are fairly complete, while other portions are partially covered or not covered at all. We still need to cover the rest of the model in an ad hoc way, but we already have a starting model. Naturally, we can still add design patterns in the design stage.

The point here is that a user applying SAPs is implicitly applying the principles if the patterns have been built by careful application of these principles. This should result in a good-quality conceptual model. This model can be used to guide an XP design by relating each new class to be built to its place in the global order. Individual SAPs can be used at each stage in XP. A well-built conceptual model is easy to change and is well suited to changing requirements. It is also highly reusable. Some nonfunctional aspects should be defined or specified in the global conceptual model—for example, security, as shown earlier. Patterns for distribution, concurrency, real time, and fault tolerance can also be used at this level. Of course, the lower architectural levels must implement and enforce the nonfunctional constraints defined in the conceptual model. This can be done by using more specialized patterns [Fernandez+2001].

Conclusion

We have developed several atomic patterns and SAPs that incorporate principles of good design, and we are producing a catalog of analysis patterns that can be used to produce good-quality conceptual models even by inexperienced designers. All this can be used as a basis for XP development, where the SAPs can guide each stage by relating the partial implementations to the complete system model. This global model can be used as a reference to decide about aspects such as distribution, security, and other nonfunctional aspects. The incremental nature of XP is likely to produce redundancies, and a global model can prevent many of them. SAPs are being tested with students at two universities, but industrial tests are necessary. Initial results have shown that students learning object-oriented concepts can develop rather complex models using SAPs. What we need to verify next is that having these conceptual models helps XP build more complex systems.

References

[Beck2000] K. Beck. *Extreme Programming Explained*. Addison-Wesley, 2000.

[Coad1997] P. Coad. *Object Models: Strategies, Patterns, and Applications, Second Edition*. Yourdon Press, 1997.

[Cook+1994] S. Cook, J. Daniels. "Let's Get Formal." *JOOP*, July/August 1994.

[Fernandez+1997] E. Fernandez, J. Hawkins. "Determining Role Rights from Use Cases." *Proceedings of the Second ACM Workshop on Role-Based Access Control*, November 1997.

[Fernandez+1999] E. Fernandez, X. Yuan. "An Analysis Pattern for Reservation and Use of Entities." *Proceedings of PLoP99*. http://jerry.cs.uiuc.edu/~plop/plop99. 1999.

[Fernandez2000A] E. Fernandez. "Principles for Building Complex Object-Oriented Conceptual Models." *Technical Report TR-CSE-00-24*, Dept. of CSE, Florida Atlantic University, August 2000.

[Fernandez2000B] E. Fernandez. "Stock Manager: An Analysis Pattern for Inventories." *Proceedings of PLoP 2000*. http://jerry.cs.uiuc.edu/~plop/plop2k. 2000.

[Fernandez+2000C] E. Fernandez, X. Yuan, S. Brey. "An Analysis Pattern for the Order and Shipment of a Product." *Proceedings of PLoP 2000.* http://jerry.cs.uiuc.edu/~plop/plop2k. 2000.

[Fernandez+2000D] E. Fernandez, X. Yuan. "Semantic Analysis Patterns." *Proceedings of 19th International Conference on Conceptual Modeling*, 2000.

[Fernandez+2001] E. Fernandez, R. Pan. "A Pattern Language for Security Models." *Proceedings of PloP 2001.* http://jerry.cs.uiuc.edu/~plop/plop2001/accepted_submissions/accepted-papers.html. 2001.

[Fowler1997] M. Fowler. *Analysis Patterns: Reusable Object Models.* Addison-Wesley, 1997.

[Fowler2001] M. Fowler. "Is Design Dead?" *Software Development*, April 2001.

[Gamma+1995] E. Gamma, R. Helm, R. Johnson, J. Vlissides. *Design Patterns: Elements of Reusable Object-Oriented Software*. Addison-Wesley, 1995.

[Hay1996] D. Hay. *Data Model Patterns: Conventions of Thought*. Dorset House, 1996.

[Jacobson+1998] I. Jacobson, G. Booch, J.Rumbaugh. *The Unified Software Development Process.* Addison-Wesley, 1998.

[Jiang+1999] Z. Jiang, E. Fernandez, J. Wu. "Comparing OCL and Z as Constraint Language for UML." *Technical Report TR-CSE-99-28*, Dept. of CSE, Florida Atlantic University, May 1999.

[Martin+2001] R. Martin, R. Koss. *The Bowling Game: An Example of Test-First Pair Programming*. http://www.objectmentor.com/publications/articlesByDate.html. 2001.

[Riehle1997] D. Riehle. "Composite Design Patterns." *Proceedings of OOPSLA'97*, 1997.

[Wanner+1998] J. Wanner, A. Kloppe. *The Object Constraint Language: Precise Modeling with UML*. Addison-Wesley, 1998.

Index

D

Q

R

U

The XP Series

Kent Beck, Series Advisor

The XP manifesto

0201616416

Planning projects with XP

0201710919

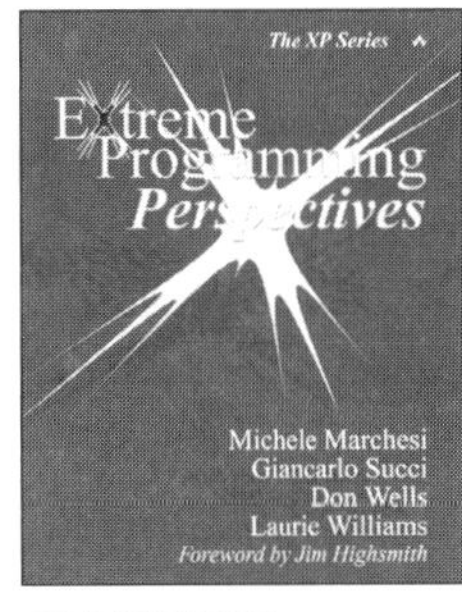

Insights and practical wisdom from leaders in the XP community

0201770059

Get XP up and running in your organization

0201708426

Best XP practices

0201710404

Is XP right for your organization?

0201844575

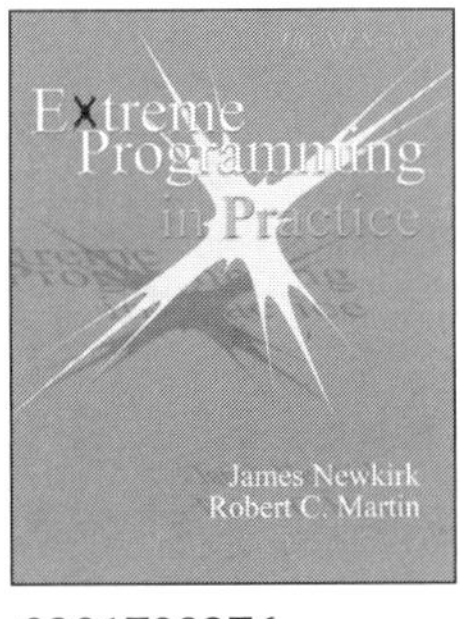

Learn from the chronicle of an XP project

0201709376

Best XP practices for developers

0201733978

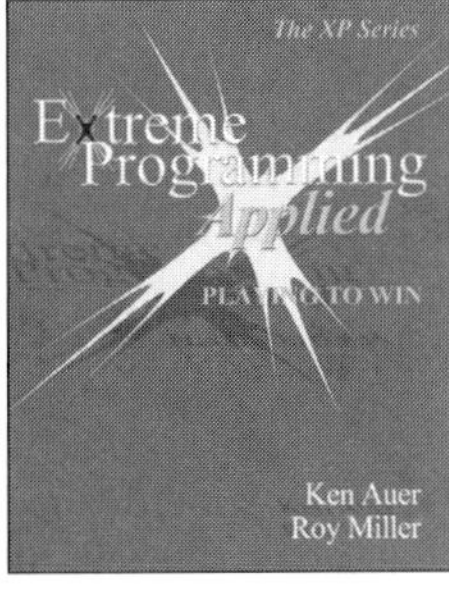

Practical advice from experienced practitioners on how to get started with XP

0201616408

Apply XP to web projects

0201794276

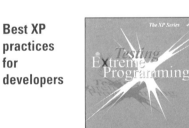

Master the intricacies of XP testing

0321113551